Object Relations
Family Therapy

Object Relations Family Therapy

David E. Scharff, M.D.

Jill Savege Scharff, M.B., Ch.B.

Jason Aronson Inc.

Northvale, New Jersey
London

Copyright © 1987 by David E. Scharff and Jill Savege Scharff

10 9 8 7 6 5 4 3 2

New Printing 1989

The opinions expressed in this book are those of the authors and do not necessarily reflect the views of the Department of Defense or of the Uniformed Services University School of Medicine.

Library of Congress Cataloging-in-Publication Data

Scharff, David E., 1941–
   Object relations family therapy.

   Bibliography: p. 479
   Includes index.
   1. Family psychotherapy.   2. Object relations
(Psychoanalysis) I. Scharff, Jill Savege.   II. Title.
[DNLM: 1. Family Therapy.   2. Object Attachment.
WM 460.5.02 S3llo]
RC488.5.S365   1987   616.89'14   87-1755
ISBN 0-87668-938-1

Manufactured in the United States of America. Jason Aronson Inc. offers books and cassettes. For information and catalog write to Jason Aronson Inc., 230 Livingston Street, Northvale, New Jersey 07647.

For Zoe, Xanthe, and Daniel

Contents

Part III: Technique and Transference

Part IV: Life Phases in Family Therapy

Preface and Acknowledgments

We had been working separately toward this book for about fifteen years. Quite suddenly, each of us simultaneously felt that it was time to write. It made sense to combine our chapters to create a more comprehensive book than either of us could write alone. There was already a substrate for our working together. We had each had a year of object relations theory and family therapy training at the Tavistock Clinic in London, although not at the same time, and we had been teaching together since 1977 with the faculty of the Psychoanalytic Family Therapy Training Program of the Washington School of Psychiatry.

Contributing to curriculum development and selection of reading material for that program, we were frustrated by the relative lack of psychoanalytically based articles on family therapy. As coordinators of the section of the course on the child-rearing phase of family development, we had to put together readings from the psychoanalytic, child development, group process, and organizational systems literature as well as from the family process and research literature. Then we worked to integrate the points of view to support and develop a psychoanalytic object relations approach to families. Thus, this teaching effort generated the concepts on which this book is based, and we have written the book in order to improve our teaching resources. We also want to contribute to the family therapy literature a book that represents the psychoanalytic method of family therapy.

We arrived at our view of object relations family therapy from different backgrounds: David Scharff as a resident and fellow in Boston, London, and Washington, D.C.; Jill Savege Scharff as a trainee in National Health Service hospitals and clinics in Scotland and England and then in Washington, D.C. We part company here to describe our formative professional years so that we each can acknowledge with gratitude outstanding teachers whose influence shaped our lines of development as psychoanalytic family therapists.

David E. Scharff

My interest in family therapy began to germinate in my senior year at college, when an innovative interdisciplinary behavioral science program at Yale, run by Ralph Haber, linked the concepts of John Bowlby and of James and Joyce Robertson on human attachment and maternal deprivation, with anthropological and ethnological studies of infant and family development. A seminar on family therapy taught by Leston Havens and Nancy Waxler at Harvard Medical School began an interest I pursued during residency at Massachusetts Mental Health Center, where Elvin Semrad took the lead in teaching the understanding of the patient through a committed therapeutic relationship. Henry Grunebaum and Nicholas Avery led a workshop where we learned to detect crucial clues to families' functioning from brief family histories.

When I moved to the Beth Israel Hospital for child psychiatry training in 1969, Silvio Onesti, a broad-minded child analyst and pediatrician, encouraged the development of a family therapy program under the tutelege of Richard Chasin, and I had the good fortune to have Carol Nadelson and Richard Brody as family therapy supervisors. That year Leonard Friedman gave a seminar on the British school of object relations. His energetic teaching of Klein, Fairbairn, Balint, Winnicott, Guntrip, Masud Khan, and others was eye-opening, resonating with Semrad's compelling interpersonal clinical approach and the newer family therapy approaches. John Frank, a fellow resident, and I even dictated the beginnings of a paper applying object relations theory to family therapy.

During the next two years, while on the faculty of the NIMH Residency Program at St. Elizabeths Hospital, I worked with Marvin Skolnick, who shared my interest in family therapy, and John Boriello, who introduced me to Bion's fascinating work on groups. My new interest in group process blossomed when I went to an A. K. Rice group relations conference directed by Margaret Rioch—an engrossing experience in applying psychoanalysis to group dynamics. The late Kenn Rogers helped me to understand the relevance of the A. K. Rice group experience to institutions such as schools and hospital wards. It was through his introduction the following year that I met the late Henry Dicks, who was of invaluable help to me personally and professionally.

In my year at the Tavistock Clinic in London in 1972–1973, there were many superb teachers of Kleinian and object relations theory, including Isca Wittenberg, Dugmore Hunter, Fred Balfour, and Robert Gosling. I received a different but equally interesting perspective on children at Anna Freud's weekly conferences at the Hampstead Clinic. Arthur Hyatt Williams, then chairman of the Tavistock Clinic's Adolescent Department, taught me about the reciprocity of projective identification in the family context, and has become a dear friend and colleague. John Bowlby led an invaluable seminar that promoted scientific exploration, and I was able to hear James and Joyce Robertson present in detail their landmark work on brief separation in infancy. My peers that year were among those who furthered my learning most, including Anton Obholzer, now director of the Tavistock, John Byng-Hall, with whom I shared family therapy interests, and Justin Frank. John Hill fostered my research interests, leading to our shared publication in 1975 of *Between Two Worlds: Aspects of the Transition from School to Work*.

During that year I attended the Tavistock group relations conference at Leicester, directed by Pierre Turquet. The consultant staff included Eric Miller, Isabel Menzies, Paddy Daniels, and Roger Shapiro, with Sally Box, Hyatt Williams, and Jill Savege among the membership. That two-week conference has ranked as one of the points of deepest learning and synthesis in my professional and personal growth.

On my return to Washington, D.C., in 1973, I had advanced child psychiatry training with Reginald Lourie and William Stark and was exposed to nonanalytic family therapy by Chloe Madanes and E. James Lieberman. From 1973 until 1981, as director of the Sex and Marital Therapy Program at Preterm, a women's medical clinic in Washington, I worked with Elise de Vries, Sally Bowie, and Ben Ellis to develop a psychoanalytic treatment approach to sexual disorders and development, described in my 1982 book, *The Sexual Relationship: An Object Relations View of Sex and the Family*. During my training at the Washington Psychoanalytic Institute, James Hatleberg, Antoine Hani, Sydney Salus, and Jean Yacoubian increased my understanding of children and their families, and Roger Shapiro spurred my continuing learning about object relations. At the American Academy of Child Psychiatry, Kent Ravenscroft encouraged me to join him in presenting psychodynamic family therapy.

In my present position as Associate Professor of Psychiatry and Family Practice at the F. Edward Hébert School of Medicine of the Uniformed Services University of the Health Sciences, I have worked as a family psychiatrist for the medical students and their young families. I am grateful to them for teaching me about the young adult phase of the family life cycle. Finally, I want to thank Drs. Larry Ehemann, Chairman of Family Practice, Harry Holloway, Chairman of Psychiatry, and Charles Privitera and Richard MacDonald, past and present Assistant Deans for Student Affairs, for their direction and collaboration in the clinical setting and for their support of my family therapy teaching and writing.

Jill Savege Scharff

Throughout my psychiatric training, I have had the conflictual experience of learning from excellent teachers with opposing viewpoints, such as analyst Bill Ogston and social psychiatrist Ken Morrice at the Ross Clinic, Aberdeen, Scotland. My interest in intrapsychic depth and social process coexisted as parallel currents in a state of uneasy truce. Psychoanalytically oriented individual and group therapies sounded equally interesting but poles apart, a conclusion confirmed after a year at Dingleton Hospital, the therapeutic community designed by Maxwell Jones.

At Dingleton, I stumbled upon the importance of the family. Newly referred and discharged patients were seen in their homes by the team of hospital psychiatrist and social worker or nurse traveling to the various border towns, farms, and fishing villages in the counties that Dingleton served. During our visits, family members were often present, expressing opinions and feelings or simply being there in their usual roles. It gave a very different picture of the signs and syndromes of psychiatric illness. The agitation of the elderly man with involutional melancholia that called for electroconvulsive therapy or antidepressant medications in the hospital setting took on meaning back at the farm when I saw him get the shakes every time he thought of driving a tractor. When his elderly wife angrily got on it and drove it herself, he became even more depressed.

From Dingleton, I moved to the Royal Edinburgh Hospital to take the experimental post of Community Psychiatrist, supervised by Jock Sutherland, an analyst and object relations theorist who practiced individual and group analysis, marital therapy, and community development consultation. He was the most important person in my professional development. I continued training in individual and group psychotherapy on the one hand, and on the other I was consulting to groups of social service staff, physicians, and neighborhood workers dealing with a socially disadvantaged population with high rates of physical morbidity and psychiatric illness. Again the currents of individual psychotherapy and social process. But this time they were not kept separate in my mind.

Object relations theory provided an integrating framework. I did not learn it as a theory from Sutherland but, rather, as a way of working, with a language that applied equally well in individual or group situations. I liked it that the view of the personality was no longer linear, or hydraulic, but cybernetic. Suddenly, understanding from individual psychoanalysis could illuminate my understanding of group process in the community, and I could also see how groups shape the development of individual roles and identity. I learned from Sutherland to work with couples using the method developed by Dicks at the Tavistock Institute for Marital Studies. But family therapy was not being done. Minuchin visited the University and impressed me with his personal enthusiasm, skill, and commitment to family therapy, but his methods pulled against the integration I was beginning to feel possible. At the same time, I was realizing the extent to which the community social workers were involved, not just with individuals but with families. It seems now like reinventing the wheel, but I suddenly realized that the family was the crucial link between individual and group process.

With object relations theory as the theoretical underpinning and family therapy as the bridge, I set out to get further training in family work—I moved to the Tavistock Clinic, where I trained in the Adolescent Department. There, I was most influenced by my supervisor, Arthur Hyatt Williams (then chairman of the department), my fellow senior registrar Anton Obholzer (now chairman of the Tavistock Clinic), and my colleagues Sally Box, Jean Thompson, and the late Shiona Williams in the department's family therapy workshop. I also learned a family therapy approach to hospitalization from Peter Bruggen and Zelda Ravid.

To extend my range with families, I took child psychiatry training at Children's Hospital, Washington, D.C., where Jean Yacoubian taught me to understand and enjoy play. When I was a special research fellow at George Washington University, Roger Shapiro and John Zinner contributed generously to my further development as a family therapist and program director. I have extended my interest in group process through association with A. K. Rice group relations conference work directed by Margaret Rioch.

Since leaving George Washington for private practice, I have deepened my understanding of child development and individual psychodynamics during psychoanalytic training at the Washington Psychoanalytic Institute, where I have had many excellent teachers, among them Dexter Bullard and Harold Searles, whose approaches to individual dynamics included an awareness of the influence of family dynamics on the growth of the individual, and Antoine Hani, who allowed me space in his seminar to explore the possible integration of individual analysis with family therapy.

From this point, we are together in our acknowledgments, since our lines of development as family therapists have converged. We are grateful to Irving Ryckoff and to Robert Winer, who, respectively, invited Jill in 1976 and David in 1977 to join the faculty of the Washington School of Psychiatry's Family Therapy Training Program. This has given us a valued group of colleagues including Justin Frank, Charles Privitera, Roger Shapiro, and John Zinner, as well as Ryckoff and Winer. We appreciate their collaboration, friendship, steady support, and inspiration over the years. We also value the chance to work with the family therapy program students who generously gave their responses to our teaching and to early drafts of chapters.

With that faculty under Winer's chairmanship, we have developed a two-year postgraduate course with an in-depth individual and group perspective that is now called the Psychoanalytic Family Therapy Training Program. Designing the curricula, creating reading lists to provide a foundation for our teaching, and refining our interpretation of child development, individual psychopathology, group therapy, and family process research have generated the concepts that we teach and that we present in annual symposia.

The faculty group collaboration has provided the operational base and the enlarging pool of ideas from which we draw and to which we add. This book that two of us have written is not wholly representative of the varying views that others of the faculty hold. We take full responsibility for the views expressed. Nonetheless, we hope our colleagues feel that we have written on their behalf about a shared psychoanalytic way of working and thinking.

We thank all our teachers whom we have separately mentioned as well as those whom we have not singled out as relevant to family therapy. Those who read first draft chapters—Sally Box, Paula Cohen, Justin Frank, Michael Kahn, David Levi, Charles Privitera, Sarah Schott, Charles Schwarzbeck, Roger Shapiro, Robert Winer, and John Zinner—were especially helpful. Additionally, Charles Schwarzbeck provided most of the psychological testing referred to in the text. We are most grateful to Alan Gurman, editor of the *Journal of Marital and Family Therapy* and coeditor of *Handbook of Family Therapy*, for his encouraging response to the first draft and for his suggestions based on a thorough reading of the book and extensive knowledge of the family therapy literature. In addition, we thank him and Michael Nichols, Margaret Rioch, Fred Sander, and Sam Slipp for kind comments in response to the final version of the book.

At Jason Aronson Inc., Lori Williams, our attentive production editor, was always available during the rigors of copyediting, while Joyce Fine dealt ably with book club promotion. We thank Jason Aronson himself for his immediate enthusiastic response to our manuscript and for his continuing encouragement. Tricia Tomsko supplied secretarial and administrative expertise in shepherding the various drafts to conclusion, working at the keyboard with speed and patience. Jessica Cohen also typed parts of the first draft. Our faithful housekeeper, Pearl Green, took loving care of our house and children when both of us were writing.

There were many cotherapists with whom we worked and many families from whom we have learned. We can describe only those cases of family therapy where our learning is relevant to what we are trying to teach. Even then, we have changed identifying details about the family members and have not always specified which one of us was the therapist, so that perhaps even the family will not recognize itself—not to diminish the importance to us of each family's uniqueness, but to allow us to present our work for scientific purposes without burdening any family. We are grateful to the Scottish, English, and American families in hospitals, clinics, and private practice who have been willing to work with each of us. Finally, we want to acknowledge our gratitude to each other for collaboration, encouragement, and patience.

Object Relations
Family Therapy

PART I

Object Relations Family Therapy: An Overview

CHAPTER 1

Object Relations Family Therapy in Context

Its Differentiation within the Field of Family Therapy

Object relations family therapy derives from psychoanalytic principles of listening, responding to unconscious material, interpreting, developing insight, and working in the transference and countertransference toward understanding and growth. The family, however, is not related to as a set of individuals. It is viewed as a system comprising sets of relationships that function in ways unique to that family. These ways may support or obstruct the progress of the family or any of its individual members as they go through the developmental phases of family life. It is to the family system that we listen and address our major interpretations, although we are equally interested in each of its individual members and their experience with each other and us. Insight occurs when we can see together that the way the family relates to the therapist reflects the transference of repressed feelings and behavior rooted in earlier experiences with the families of origin. Repetition of these phenomena in the therapeutic setting allows these feelings and the defenses against them to become conscious.

The therapeutic relationship offers an environment similar enough to stimulate this emergence but different enough to allow reworking. The difference emerges because the therapist, from training, experience, and personal growth, brings to the relationship a well-developed capacity for bearing pain, anxiety, and loss that enables the family members to confront their defenses (which often include focusing on a problematic individual family member) and to face their anxieties as a group. The group then has a chance to work together on the factors that are blocking the family's functioning and to build together for the future. The immediate goal is not symptom resolution but progression through the current developmental phase of family life, with improved ability to work as a group and to differentiate among and meet the individual needs of its members.

Individually trained therapists and analysts will recognize the historical, reflective, insight-oriented process of individual psychoanalytic psychotherapy but may wonder how this can apply to a family group, or why it should, when problems are intrapsychic. Strategic family therapists will recognize the view of the family as a system but may be puzzled as to how insight is used when their interventions require no insight. The structural family therapist will be familiar with using the family's reaction to the therapist to decipher the structures that govern its system and to design the restructuring intervention but would not bring that to the conscious awareness of the family. Both the individually trained therapist and the family therapist of either strategic or structural approaches may be suspicious of an approach that seems to put together disparate views. Kerr (1981), discussing the concepts of Bowen, a major theorist who became a family therapist after some years as an analyst, wrote, "Individual and systems thinking are two distinctly different ways of conceptualizing human behavior and attempts to mix them reflect a failure to appreciate their difference" (p. 234).

In the United States, their difference has been overemphasized, in our opinion, for reasons that are understandable. But the polarization has meant that therapists of one group were unable to learn from those of the other. Excellent research by Bateson and the Palo Alto group (1956) led to the double-bind hypothesis and communications theory, from which are derived the interactional method of family therapy of the Mental Research Institute (MRI) that Jackson set up. Haley (1971), who was with the Palo Alto group, further developed the strategic approach to engineer change in the family system, without which he believed the individual could not change. Meanwhile, psychoanalysis held that although problems develop in the family setting in the formative years, the problems in the here and now have become internalized in the individual personality. Analysts treat an individual without ever meeting the family. Even child analysts may prefer such a purely intrapsychic approach. Minuchin (1974) is a family therapist who values the individual, yet analysts perceive his work as manipulative and therefore alien. In general, analysts view family therapy as dealing only with the superficial and the externals, while family therapists view analysts as having a long-term short-sightedness. Attitudes of suspicion and contempt abound.

Yet analytic influence can be detected in family therapy. Founders of the field included analysts Ackerman, Wynne, and Lidz. Wynne's collaborator in the fifties, Ryckoff, is an analyst. Paul and Framo have been influenced by analytic object relations theory, as were Shapiro and Zinner, both also practicing analysts. Others, identified with systems and structural approaches that do not appear to use or actually reject psychoanalytic principles, had significant exposure to psychoanalysis in their formative professional years. According to Bodin (1981), the influence of the Chicago Institute of Psychoanalysis, especially its association with self psychology, bears upon the work of Satir and by association may have influenced Bateson and Haley, while the interpersonal theory of Sullivan influenced Jackson. Bowen and Minuchin qualified as analysts, although they no longer practice psychoanalysis. In Europe, Selvini Palazzoli practiced as an individual analyst before developing the Milan method of strategic family therapy, Stierlin is presently an analyst, and Andolfi had four years of analytic training and practices analysis at present. In Great Britain, Laing and Cooklin are analysts, Byng-Hall had analytic training, and Skynner, although not an individual analyst, is knowledgeable about analysis and is a group analyst trained by Foulkes.*

It seems that family therapy in the United States turned away from mainstream psychoanalysis because of the dominance of classical Freudian theory, which does not easily lend itself to interpersonal phenomena (Zawada 1981). It holds an intensely intrapsychic focus, viewing the personality as a series of structures, conscious and unconscious, that seek to mediate among unacceptable, instinctually derived impulses toward the objects of their gratification. Reading Freud's case histories, we have always felt that he had a clear sense of what his patients' parents were like, but he did not deal with that reality, only with his patients' perceptions and distortions of reality. That makes some sense when the parents are not part of the treatment, but it leaves us with a theory focused on individual conflict that does not easily transfer to interpersonal situations. Hence, communications and systems theory seemed much more relevant to family work.

Some analysts in the United States have moved away from a

---

*References to the writings of these therapists and their colleagues appear in the bibliography, although not all are quoted.

strictly Freudian approach. Sullivan (1953) developed an interpersonal process theory that did not gain widespread acceptance. We think his ideas, although clinically influential, did not gain widespread acceptance as theory perhaps because, as Guntrip (1961) suggests, Sullivan focused on interpersonal processes to the exclusion of the person. More recently, Kernberg (1975), following Jacobsen's early efforts (1954), has developed a personality theory that derives from object relations theory. His theory is tightly argued, as he carefully outlines crucial points of similarity and difference from traditional theory. Because of that strength it has achieved credibility, if not acceptance, for object relations theory in neo-Freudian analytic circles, but for our purpose that strength leads it to seem mechanistic, reified, and difficult to apply to the interpersonal arena. Kohut (1977) brought attention back to the earliest mother–infant interactions as he explored the deficits in the formation of the self. We have found his concept of mirroring useful in analytic family therapy, while Kahn (1986) has shown how Kohut's concept of the self can be integrated with the Milan systems approach to family therapy.

The goals of analytic family therapy are as open-ended as the treatment itself, because we have found that goals change as growth occurs, leading to an expanded vision of future possibilities. Naturally, this takes time. Family treatment tends to take about two years, with weekly meetings of forty-five minutes to an hour. A family may settle for limited gains and terminate within a year. But a ten-session treatment, described as sufficient by Stierlin (1985), would be reserved in our practices for the treatment of developmental and externally imposed crises. Except in these cases, we would not expect such a treatment to be complete. Length of treatment is a major difference between analytic family therapy and systems therapy. Obviously, longer treatment is more expensive, which is a disadvantage for families that cannot or will not afford it, or for clinics that have limited funding. In private practice we deal with families that can usually pay something, and if we have no low-fee time ourselves, we can match families with advanced student therapists who can offer reduced fees. In clinics, one can argue that the family therapist's time is being used efficiently to reach all the members of the family for the same cost as seeing an individual. In community psychiatry clinics, one can argue that clinical time spent in family therapy is doubling as a preventive mental health effort on behalf of those not presenting as the index patient. These arguments speak in favor of funding family therapy but do not address the funding of longer versus shorter treatments. We do not measure success in terms of symptom relief, and so we would not terminate at that early point. We measure success in terms of capacity to master developmental stress. Clinics decide whether to offer that to their populations or not.

Sometimes we hear such clinic staff say that analytic family therapy would not appeal to their populations. Certainly, clients with overwhelming poverty and social problems want help that is more immediate and less abstract. It was to meet such families' needs that Minuchin and his colleagues (1967) developed structural family therapy for problem resolution. Our method alone does not help in such cases. But our students who work with disadvantaged clients and use a problem-solving focus report that the psychoanalytic method that they practice with families who can accept it helps them to be more fully responsive in their shorter-term, non-analytic family therapy. It should not be assumed, however, that the poor, or the culturally or intellectually disadvantaged, cannot benefit from psychoanalytic family therapy. Some will fit cultural stereotypes of concrete thinking and dependency on directives and gratification, but others, when offered an approach that is more reflective, will take to it. Culture and cognitive style need not preclude psychological-mindedness, given opportunity and modeling. So we agree with Box et al. (1981) that psychoanalytic family therapy is not for all but is for those families that demonstrate in the consultation an interest in understanding, not just in symptom relief. Similarly, not all students would want to work this way, but those who work with a systems approach can use training in psychoanalytic family therapy to prepare the therapist psyche as a plate upon which to receive an imprint of the family system.

Of course, there are similarities as well as differences between methods. Satir is interested in family chronology as we are, yet she and others of the MRI approach use a structured family interview to get the information, whereas we would wait for such material to emerge in association to the here and now. Then again, she would deviate from the standard interview depending on the family's response, which is similar to our preference for following the family's line of thought. The MRI group makes interventions designed to reframe the problems; it uses tactics and prescriptions to effect change. That is totally different from our approach. We rarely assign homework. We never give prescriptions, although we may explore a range of suggestions for alternative behaviors and occasionally give advice.

Like Haley and the strategic therapists, we see symptoms as misguided attempts at changing family difficulty. Haley (1971) views the family in developmental terms as do we, rather than trying to develop a family typology or symptomatology. We, too, view the family as an interpersonal, cybernetic system that has not been able to adjust to a transition. We agree that an individual's problems are manifestations of disturbances in the family system, and we accept the problem as defined by the family (Madanes and Haley 1977). But we do not insist on objectively defined goals; we do not restrict our interest to the problem; we do not strive for the rapid engagement and disengagement recommended to strategic therapists (Haley 1980). We do not agree that the individual cannot change unless the family changes. We have seen individuals change in individual psychotherapy, sometimes inducing change in the family and sometimes not. But our major point of disagreement with strategic family therapy is on the matter of insight. Stanton (1981) asserts that "Being thoughtful, reflective and sitting back and making interpretations merely allows the family to repeat the patterns . . . [it] does not help to bring about change" (p. 370). We believe that interpretation is essential. However, interpreting that fails to lead to insight, or sitting back when interpretation is needed, certainly will not help families. This book demonstrates our use of interpretation and insight, and we hope it establishes the case for their effectiveness in producing lasting change and growth through psychoanalytic family therapy.

Haley's and other strategic approaches emphasize directives. Psychoanalytic family therapy is nondirective. We do not interrupt or silence people, ask them to change seats, or give prescriptions, paradoxical or otherwise. Yet paradox may be operating in that, while appearing to listen and talk about what is being said, we are attending to the links between what is said and not said and to nonverbal communications, so that our interpretations are aimed at elucidating unconscious relationships rather than at solving the problems we appear to be discussing. Psychoanalytic family therapists may at times, however, be more directive, especially around the boundaries of the therapeutic space—for instance, telling a child not to draw with markers on the wall when the parents fail to. We certainly direct attention to overlooked functions or material, but always with the aim of facilitating maximum expression of all levels of family experience from all the generations.

Our approach is more similar to the structural approach described by Minuchin (1974). His approach is not symptom-oriented but includes a search for structures underlying the presenting problems. Aponte and VanDeusen (1981) emphasize the importance of increasing the structural therapist's self-awareness, responsiveness, and accessibility to his or her private reactions. These "become the plate upon which the family leaves its imprint for him/her to read and decipher. Moreover, the availability of his/her own personal reactions allows the therapist the means through which to reach and touch the family in natural responses" (p. 328). This sounds to us like our use of transference and countertransference, and we think the analytic experience has something to teach here, although Minuchin has told us that he does not use psychoanalytic concepts in his family therapy teaching. We suspect that the brilliant clinical interventions we have seen done by Minuchin, Andolfi, Haley, Whitaker, Ackerman, and others, and perhaps even the quality of charisma itself, derive from an exceptional ability to manage and use transference and countertransference experiences. Unless these experiences are made conscious, it is not possible to teach the skill to others who do not have such gifts. We think that our focus on transference and countertransference, the hallmark of a psychoanalytic method, could be found useful by teachers of strategic and structural family therapy.

Minuchin and his colleagues (1967) describe the role of the therapist in facilitating engagement between family members and centralizing engagement between family and therapist. We do not actively structure this development in the same way, but we do focus on both those areas simultaneously. Similarly, we do not structure our position in relation to a family member to procure a predetermined shift, but we do structure our position to be neutral. By "neutral" we mean that we are open to being used in the way family members are used, and yet we remain able to move outside of that to comment upon what is happening to us and thus to allow the family a new experience of such phenomena. We do not think of specific ways to restructure the family, and we do not set tasks. But as in structural family therapy, we do enter into the transaction, relating personally for professional purposes. Unlike some Freudian analysts, we do not behave as a blank screen, although we do offer ourselves as a blank screen upon which the family relationships can be projected. Just as Minuchin (1974) describes "tracking," we, too, use the family's symbols and language to communicate. Not only does this foster communication, but it allows us to take in and relate to the family's experience. We then work to separate ourselves in order to point out what has happened to us and what it means for the family.

An important point of contrast with other family therapy

techniques is our use of a historical approach to understand the early relationships in the current family and in both families of origin. Stanton (1981) characterizes the systems approach as antithetical to the historical-reflective, insight-oriented perspective. He states, "There is no emphasis on the past because it is irrelevant to change. . . . We cannot change the past because it no longer exists" (p. 390). He points out that systems therapists do not deny unconscious process and indeed use it to design interventions, but they do not bring it to the awareness of the client. They do not make the unconscious conscious. They believe change occurs from the interpersonal impact of the therapist but only as it occurs outside the client's awareness. They do not encourage transference; they steer it away. In our view, the past does still exist and is constantly re-enacted in the present relationships. Every family system, healthy and unhealthy, is imbued with or invaded by the past that is woven into its fabric. We feel it is only fair to share our knowledge of the unconscious with the family so that they can make their own interpretations in the future. Like systems therapists, we use the unconscious to inform our intervention, which in our case is usually a verbal interpretation. It may on occasion be a behavioral interpretation—for instance, when we respond with behavior that gets a message across when words have failed, or intervene through joining the children's play. There may be action, but action does not characterize the psychoanalytic approach.

We have no interest in keeping our impact outside the family's awareness. We would rather it be recognized and examined as a prototype for processing past and future events at the family boundary. To the same end, we do not steer away from transference but use it for interpretation. We aim for derepression, for the emergence of unconscious motivating forces and the elucidation of repressed relationships.

We also work with affects. Stanton declares that systems theorists do not encourage emotional catharsis. Andolfi, a systems therapist who integrates structural and experiential modes of therapy (Andolfi et al. 1983), demonstrated, on videotape, interventions that aimed to extinguish affective responses that he viewed as manipulative attempts to control the therapy (Andolfi 1985). We had the impression that this denial of affective communication encouraged affect storms, from which the family also learned. Be that as it may, we value the emergence of affects as signals of unconscious distress or excitement. Behaviorists point out that learning takes place during states of arousal, and we find that families learn and change when interpretation is linked to material expressed with affect.

Selvini Palazzoli, using the Milan method that she developed with colleagues (Selvini Palazzoli et al. 1975), gives positive connotation to the family's adaptive homeostatic mechanism. In our work, we might point out the benefits of a defensive position, but we would not suggest that the position should be retained because it is a good thing. We would more likely ask about the severity of the family's losses, if such small gains seemed so valuable despite their cost. Paradox and counterparadox are the hallmarks of the Milan prescriptions. Selvini Palazzoli (1985) reported an astonishing case where the use of a universally applicable prescription reversed chronic psychosis. A universal interpretation would be impossible in the psychoanalytic method. Her interpretation focused on the right and responsibility of the parents for a private life. We agree that differentiation of the marital couple from the children in the family is a universally applicable concept, but we have to use many slower ways to work with the forces operative against the marital sexual relationship.

Van Trommel (1984), a strategic family therapist in the Milan tradition, focuses particularly on the relationship between the therapist system and the client system. His thesis is that to understand the family he has to understand himself, otherwise he cannot work. When describing his understanding of the Milan model, he outlined the therapist's assessment tasks of eliciting the complaint, understanding the function of the complaint, searching for a pattern to that function in the family system, and then finding that pattern recreated between the family and himself (Van Trommel 1985). This approach of history taking, pattern recognition, and working with the mutual impact of the family and therapist systems is quite similar to our approach. Van Trommel made an interesting point that, although we think we work with composites of parts of one system in relation to parts of another system, in fact we deal with individuals. It seems absurdly simple, yet we find it a crucial point. In our view, the systems that we deal with are systems of human relationships between individuals and groups. We address those relationships among individuals of the family within the context of a healing relationship between the family and the therapist, all of us with humanity that can transcend the mechanics of systems. To us, paradox and counterparadox defy the system without engaging the conscious effort of the individuals. This is where we part company with strategizing.

Bowen (1978) is a family therapist who appreciates the individual, to the point of finding family work often more effective when done with one individual than with the family or couple. The therapist "coaches" the individual to intervene in various parts of his extended family system to produce change. We do not work that way. But as analysts working with individual patients, we are aware that our view of the intrapsychic dimension is influenced by our family therapy experience and by object relations theory as a frame of reference that applies to both individual and family therapy (Winer 1985). We are interested in Bowen's description of "the family projection process," which refers to the way the undifferentiation of the parents is transmitted to one of their children in order to stabilize a precarious marital fusion between partners of equivalent levels of undifferentiation of self. This is compatible with our theory. Following Zinner (1976) and Shapiro (1979), who applied Klein's concept of projective identification (1946) to marital and family work, we aim to develop specificity about what is projected into which children, and to understand with which projections they identify and which they repudiate.

Our work is closer to that of the "reactor-analysts" described by Beels and Ferber (1969), among whom were included Boszormenyi-Nagy and Framo (1965) and Paul (1967). Framo (1970, 1976, 1981) now works on family problems by attending to the parental marital relationship. We may focus for a time on couples sessions only (or individual therapy, for that matter) as indicated by the overall family treatment, but we do not exclude young family members from most of the treatment as Framo does. We include grandparents, as many family therapists do, but we have not used marathon sessions with grandparents as Framo (1981) describes. Nagy speaks more to individuals within the family context, organizing his work around the issues of loyalties and ethics (Boszormenyi-Nagy and Framo 1965, Boszormenyi-Nagy and Spark 1973). Our approach is less abstract, more of a joining with the rough-and-tumble of family life. Of course, we include children as do Minuchin and Haley, but our view of their play is closer to Zilbach's (1986). Within the reactor-analyst group, our approach is closest to that of Box and her colleagues (1981), with whom we both worked at the Tavistock Clinic, and to that of Shapiro (1979), Zinner (1976), and Zinner and Shapiro (1972, 1974), inasmuch as one of us was trained by them and both of us collaborate with them. The similarity to Shapiro's and Zinner's work lies in the use of group-interpretive method and the reliance on the group therapy of Bion (1961). We recognize family group patterns as defenses that can be named. Then their functions in protecting against as yet unnameable group anxieties are pointed out until the anxieties can be revealed and worked through. We are like Box in our emphasis on counter-transference, which we and she learned in Kleinian supervision at the Tavistock Clinic. Although there are similarities in technique, our approach differs from those of Shapiro, Zinner, and Box in relying most heavily on the object relations theory of Fairbairn. In practice, too, we are different in that we seek to include young children and babies in our family work. As child analysts, we tend to assess families in developmental terms, like Skynner (1976), a child psychiatrist who also uses a group-interpretive approach based on object relations theory. Stylistically, he is more authoritative and directive than we are, and he spaces his sessions a month apart to minimize dependency on the therapist. He also believes in limiting the length of treatment and thus de-emphasizes working through with the therapist.

Some of the distinctions we have described between ourselves and other family therapists may seem arbitrary. They are based upon reading, occasional viewing of videotaped interviews, and personal discussion. We recognize that there is often a difference between what people do and what they say they do. There is no way to do justice to the complexities of other approaches when we have not studied them by doing them. Our intention is to show how our approach fits into the family therapy field. We view that field as a system of parts defined by the theories that characterize them all in relation to each other, some fitting smoothly together, others grating. Each part has a contribution to make to the whole. Similarly, we feel that therapy can intervene at any part of the psychosocial system, including both the intrapsychic level of the individual and the interpersonal level in family or group therapy. In our roles as psychoanalytic family therapists, we intervene at the microlevel of the interior of the family and its relation to the developing interiors of its individual members.

B. and F. Duhl (1981) have said that individual persons are subsystems of the family, and these subsystems themselves contain subsystems such as levels of awareness and conscious and unconscious experience. To this we add that within the individual are subsystems of relationships that reflect the experience of relationships at different developmental levels in the family of origin. Then we notice that these internalized relationships seek expression in relationship to the members of the present family. Thus, in the family group we have interdigitating systems of relationships, all affecting each other for better or worse. Psychoanalytic family therapy recognizes these complexities along the intrapsychic–interpersonal continuum. Object relations theory provides the theoretical framework for understanding, and the language for working with, the dynamics of both the individual self and the family system.

Its Roots in Psychoanalysis

Object relations family therapy derives from the application of object relations theory to family development. It uses psychoanalytic techniques of listening and following associations, making the unconscious conscious through interpretation of resistance and defense, developing insight, and working through toward change (Freud 1917c), but it does not draw from the structural theory that Freud (1923) later developed, although his interest in structures in dynamic relation within the individual psyche is akin to our interest in structures operating in a dynamic system within the family. We do not find classical psychoanalytic theory helpful in understanding families because the theory is intensely intrapsychic. Human personality is described as resulting from the necessary compromise between the urge toward expression of sexual and death instincts and the demand for their suppression to accommodate social reality. Ego psychology, which stresses the organism's adaptation to the given environment, emphasizes the internal conflict resulting from and promoting mastery of the drives to meet the conditions of reality (Hartmann 1939). Although fully aware of the sexual and deathly feelings, fears, and fantasies in individuals and families, we cannot see these as primary in determining family life but rather as arising within relationships.

Instead, we are influenced by the ethological research of Bowlby (1969, 1973a, 1980), who described the fundamental human need for attachment and the destructive effects of early separation from caring figures. Early research by Mahler and colleagues (1975) explored the development of the child in relationship to its mother through the stages of separation and individuation. More recent infant observation research (Brazelton et al. 1976, Schwarzbeck 1978) focused not only on the quality of relationship to the mother but, following the early work of Benedek (1960, 1970a), also to the father—but not to a couple. Fraiberg and colleagues (1975) reported treating the mother–infant dyad. There is as yet not much psychoanalytic research on the quality of family interaction as a determinant of individual growth in the early years, although its effect at later stages in individual pathology has been described (Shapiro 1966, Shapiro and Zinner 1979, Shapiro et al. 1975, Zinner and Shapiro 1972). It is difficult to integrate these observations, which are interpersonal, with mainstream Freudian and neo-Freudian psychoanalytic theory, which is fundamentally intrapsychic, although useful attempts have been made (Grunebaum and Chasin 1982, Kahn 1986, Sander 1979). Analyst and family therapist Fred Sander wrote to tell us that he still hopes to meet the challenge of integrating structural theory (emphasizing its adaptive aspects) with other family systems and object relations ideas. We, however, think that the need for such efforts at integration calls attention to the lack of an interpersonal theory of development. This theoretical desert has contributed to the polarization between traditional individual psychoanalytic theory and family systems theory.

Flügel (1921), an early Freudian analyst, produced a scholarly compilation of analytic theory and showed how it applied to the growth of the human personality in the family context. He ventured to make some observations on love and hate in sibling relations and in parent–child relations. From the historical point of view, it is not surprising that the family he described comes across as a series of dyads, each negotiating the forces of infantile sexuality and oedipal striving. Although Flügel was restricted by the limitations of his theory and the psychoanalytic context within which he wrote, he could nevertheless make important observations that presaged the object relations point of view, as when he wrote: ". . . in adopting his attitude towards the members of his family circle, a child is at the same time determining to a large extent some of the principal aspects of his relations to his fellow men in general" (p. 4). He noted, with regret, that so little was then known about the marital relationship that he had to omit discussion of it rather than do it injustice.

Writing in the United States in 1960, another Freudian analyst, Grotjahn, saw a connection between the unconscious processes of the individual, the family, and the group. He had treated family members in analytic group therapy, had done parallel interviewing and sometimes treatment of analysands' family members, and used family conferences to support analysis or relieve resistance, especially when it took the form of intellectualization. He concluded, "Families which lack structure, or whose members do not have clearly defined roles will produce children with unclear or vague ego identities" (p. 88). He also wrote, "The neurotic family, like the neurotic individual, has lost the ability to communicate easily and freely with the unconsciouses of its different members. The growth and motivation of the entire family is endangered because such a family is cut off from learning by experience" (p. 123). Searching for theoretical insights to bear upon his observations, he quoted Freud's paper (1921) on group psychology and papers from the 1936 Psychoanalytic Congress on the theme of family neurosis. Although Grotjahn was personally freethinking, his loyalty to individual analysis may account for his not taking the step of treating whole families by 1960; nor did he develop his observations into a theory of family dynamics. We think that Freudian theory cannot support such a development.

Object relations theory does provide the possibility of an analytic family systems approach, because it is an intrapsychic psychoanalytic theory that derives from an interpersonal view of development. At first, it was an individual psychology, but because of its interpersonal derivation, it has been successfully extended to the psychology of couples (Dicks 1967), groups (Bion 1961), and families (Scharff 1982, Shapiro 1979, Shapiro and Zinner 1971, Skynner 1976, Zinner 1976). It was developed by Fairbairn (1952, 1954), working in isolation in Scotland, by Balint (1952) and Winnicott (1965b, 1971b), of the British independent group, and by Guntrip (1969), all influenced by Klein (1932, 1948), as Sutherland (1980) has described. It is to Fairbairn that we turn for a coherent theory into which we will later integrate concepts from the other writers. Fairbairn, following Freud's interest in structural theory, was interested in describing endopsychic structure. Whereas Freud thought the structure evolved from the organism's adaptation between instinctual strivings and reality, Fairbairn hypothesized that structure developed from the organism's adjustment during helpless infantile dependence to the reality of its experience with its first human relationship. For Fairbairn, the fundamental drive was not the gratification of an impulse but the need to be in relationship. The theory is not hampered by being quasi-scientific. Instead it is empirical and practical. In individual analysis, object relations theory has immediate relevance to the therapeutic relationship because it grew out of awareness of the importance of that relationship in clinical work with individual patients.

In giving an introductory summary of object relations theory (Fairbairn 1963), we must remind ourselves that this is only a model of human personality. It is not to be taken as a concrete reality nor as "the truth" but as an imaginative construction that gives us a way of thinking and working (Sutherland 1963). We expand on object relations theory in Chapter 3. Fairbairn viewed the psyche as an ego comprising a system of dynamic structures that arise in and are modified by the course of development in the context of early relationships. The infant at birth seeks attachment to its mother. Because of its helpless dependence, the infant is acutely vulnerable to her responses and to whether its needs for closeness, comfort, and food are gratified or frustrated. Aggression is not instinctual but arises from frustration as an attempt to right the situation between mother and baby. The child's ego deals with its experience by introjecting, or taking in, the frustrating aspects of the relationship to the mother and then repressing them, along with the part of the ego that suffered them and all the intolerable feelings that were evoked. Frustrating experience is described according to whether the infant's needs for attachment were uncomfortably rejected or were overstimulated to the point of distress. These experiences of the other are called the *rejecting object* and the *exciting object*, respectively. The parts of the ego that suffer in relation to these objects are called the *antilibidinal ego* and the *libidinal ego*, respectively.

Thus we see that there are two repressed systems within the ego: the libidinal system, characterized by need, excitement, and longing; and the antilibidinal system, characterized by aggression, rage, hate, and contempt. This leaves the rest of the ego, called the *central ego*, free to deal with future experiences with attachment figures in calmer, more reasonable ways. The central ego maintains its own object, called the *ideal object*, as a relatively desexualized and de-aggressivized object from which the repressed exciting and rejecting objects have been shorn.

The more intolerable the anxiety resulting from experience with the mother, the more intense the repression and the less of the ego left to relate freely. In health, with good-enough mothering, the infant develops a personality that consists mainly of unrepressed central ego in relation to ideal object. This central system is capable of integration and learning, of making transactions with potential objects, and of adapting to its environment. It takes over eventually from the mother as the first organizer. It is an open system, flexible and adaptable, and tends to fashion future relationships in a form reminiscent of the satisfying aspects of early relationships. But it is inevitable that its functioning is colored to some degree by the antilibidinal and libidinal systems that have been repressed to protect the central system and its main relationships.

Sutherland (1963) noted that the repressed systems, being out of contact with the external world, operate as closed systems, very stuck, coercing their objects to fit an image corresponding to the unsatisfying earlier experiences. The repressed object relationships in these systems are unable to learn from new experience and to grow because they are not conscious and because they are gratified within the self. But the repressed object relationships do seek outlets through repetition of their infantile experience in the here and now and in relation to other psyches into which they are projected.

Here Fairbairn acknowledged the influence on his thinking of the Kleinian concept of projection. It is the addition of the concept of projection that makes object relations theory so helpful. It gives us a way of thinking about why people in groups and families treat each other as they do. Fairbairn suggested that the repressed systems attack the central ego, thus reliving the early traumas, partly in secretly horrible confirmation and partly to protest early losses. Also, to protect good memories and the potential for satisfying relationships, the repressed antilibidinal and libidinal systems may be got rid of, expelled outside the ego into the psyche of the attachment figure. There they will be experienced as repetitions of the originally unsatisfying relationships with the attachment figure, either as the victim or the aggressor. As the infant moves through the developmental stages, and as thinking capacity matures, there is less need to resort to splitting off the frustrating experience to preserve the good experience, for by then ambivalence can be tolerated, allowing for a whole object relationship. The healthy, more open, central system can relearn and rework its repressed system colorations in the light of experiences at higher levels of emotional and intellectual development.

Dicks (1967) applied object relations theory to couples' dynamics as he pioneered a psychodynamic method of marital therapy. He studied the way that each individual endopsychic structure interdigitates at conscious and unconscious levels with that of the spouse. During selection of a life partner, the central ego system chooses on the basis of finding an ideal object in the spouse. Because marriage offers a relationship that is similar to the early mothering experience, in that it offers a permanent attachment to a caring figure, it elicits feelings from the infantile experience. Of course, in adulthood the psyche is dealing with dependence that is not one-sided and helpless but a mutual, agreed-upon interdependence. Nonetheless, in the safety of the marriage commitment, the repressed object relationships signifying the original parenting experiences return to seek expression for better or worse. Each spouse now views the other as partly ideal and partly exciting and rejecting of need, as were former objects. In health, this offers an opportunity for reintegration of the repressed systems and expansion of the central ego system. But where the interlocking parts are in a rigid closed system, the repressed relationships are repeated and further repressed to preserve the marriage despite impoverishing it. In this case the central ego, instead of confirming the separate identity of the object found in the person of the spouse, expects it to conform to this inner picture. This mutual collusion to repress troublesome object relationships is a problem for the couple.

When a couple has children, unmetabolized remnants of the repressed object relationships now pose a new threat to the family. The tendency is to preserve the marriage relationship by projecting the libidinal and antilibidinal objects or egos variously onto the psyches of the children. To put it simply, the child is seen as a hated part of the self or the spouse and bears a resemblance to a hated part of the grandparents. Any one child may be more or less predisposed by constitution, physical likeness, birth order, and circumstance to carry any one projection. Then hate or uncomfortable longing is felt inside the parent toward the child or from the child toward the parent, depending on whether it is the repressed ego or object that has been projected.

In this way, we find the object relations theory of Fairbairn particularly applicable to understanding family dynamics, as does Skynner (1976). In the United States, Shapiro and Zinner at the National Institute of Mental Health were the first to refer to Dicks and to Kleinian theories of projection and projective identification (Zinner 1976, Zinner and Shapiro 1972). Paul, Framo, and Boszormenyi-Nagy all record interest in object relations theory (Paul 1967, Paul and Grosser 1965, Framo 1970, 1976, 1982, Boszormenyi-Nagy and Spark 1973). Cooklin (1979) modified Fairbairn's theory to develop a psychoanalytic framework for family therapy consistent with the systemic model. Selvini Palazzoli (1974), thinking about the move from the intrapsychic to the transpersonal approach to anorexia nervosa, wrote: ". . . only a psychodynamic theory based on object relations (particularly on relations with the negative aspects of the introjected object) can make a substantial contribution to the psychopathology of body experience" (p. 84).

But the underlying object relations conceptualization appears not to inform her technique of paradoxical prescription for the family system. Slipp (1984) has promoted object relations theory as a bridge between individual and family therapy.

At this point we need to describe Melanie Klein's contribution. We refer to Klein's writing (1935, 1946, 1948, 1957) and to Segal's introduction to the work of Klein (1964). Although Klein and Fairbairn both departed from Freud's theory, Fairbairn followed his interest in psychic structure while Klein, influenced by Abraham, was more interested in the function of the instincts that Freud always held to be of central, motivating importance. In child analysis, Klein (1961) had the opportunity to discover and describe the primitive phantasies that accompany the infant's attempt to gratify or deflect instinctual urges in relation to the mother. She particularly stressed the operation of the death instinct. In her view, as discussed in 1935, destructiveness is derived from the death instinct, the force of which is constitutionally determined. Klein focused on the individual patient's instinctually derived destructive forces, operating to spoil the early relationships. She wrote that primitive attempts to deflect the power of the death instinct led to processes of splitting of objects into ideally good and bad, and then to projection of parts of objects into other psyches. The projection served either to preserve the self as good or to preserve the object as good.

This hypothesis was applied to the functioning of groups by Bion (1961), Ezriel (1950, 1952), and later Turquet (1975). Bion viewed the work group as a group beset by behaviors that relate not to work but to defenses against anxiety. Certain individuals deal with their confusion and helplessness by projecting parts of themselves into other group members who, for their own reasons, become like the projections. Multiple processes of projective identification cluster around subgroups within the group that express basic defenses against the anxiety of the whole group in relation to the group leader. This theory proved applicable to families, which can be viewed as small groups trying to do their work of raising the next generation, with the parents as leaders of the family group (Shapiro 1979, Shapiro and Zinner 1979).

Object relations family therapy uses the historical-reflective, nondirective analytic approach of Freud, but its theory derives largely from object relations and group relations theory. It is further informed by psychoanalytic theories of child development and mother–baby and father–baby interaction research. And it uses the techniques learned from play therapy to communicate with younger family members. Its mode of operation consists in listening, talking, and playing in the therapeutic space between family and therapist. Within that space occur the processes of transference and countertransference essential for the elucidation of the object relationship system of the family as experienced in relation to the therapist, the crucial place where insight can occur. Psychoanalytic family therapy holds that insight is required for change and for developmental progression to occur, and that working through is needed to consolidate gains.

So far our introduction to object relations family therapy has been condensed. We realize it is only fully comprehensible to one who is already conversant with object relations theory and the family therapy literature. Our intention is to present an overview and indicate the direction of the book. Subsequent chapters offer a fuller discussion of the three major psychoanalytic theoretical influences on the development of an object relations theory of family therapy: object relations, child development, and group relations theory. Then we outline the characteristics of psychoanalytic family therapy: assessment of developmental level, defense and anxiety, group psychoanalytic technique, transference and countertransference, sequencing of individual and couple therapies with family therapy, and the role of play and other techniques with child-rearing families. A section is devoted to work with families in special life situations. Finally, we deal with working through and termination.

As a transition from this introduction to the heart of the book, we next present a clinical illustration and then a chapter on the difficulties of moving into psychoanalytic work with families. The brief clinical vignette was chosen not because it is a perfect example of brilliant clinical work but because it shows ordinary psychoanalytic family therapy in action. We have reconstructed this account from the videotape of the session, observed by D. E. S. (who was the therapist) and J. S. S. (who was acting as his consultant), as together they review his work. D. E. S.'s discussion of his countertransference responses is in italics, while J. S. S.'s commentary on the process is interspersed throughout as part of the text. We realize that you may feel thrown in at the deep end, inasmuch as the concepts have not yet been discussed at length, but we want to let you see right now what we do and how we think about it. Through this illustration, we hope to provide an early shared clinical footing from which to explore the later elaboration of concepts. In the example, characteristics of object relations family therapy are illustrated briefly and referenced to their points of emergence in subsequent chapters. There they will be brought into focus, one by one. You may be interested to read this illustration again after you have finished reading the book.

Putting Theory into Practice: A Clinical Sampler

Martin, age 8, was referred to Dr. S. [D. E. S.] for evaluation because of not doing well in school and feeling unfairly treated by friends. Psychological testing had already demonstrated a developmental language disorder that explained much of his academic difficulty. An individual psychiatric diagnostic study and the psychological testing confirmed that Martin had an overanxious disorder of childhood, with depression and identity concerns. When stressed, he had a tendency to become briefly disorganized, which left him feeling helpless to respond effectively.

The parents welcomed a family meeting as part of the diagnostic process because they felt his sister was aggravating Martin's problems with friends.

The family arrived to meet Dr. S., who welcomed them and was introduced to the siblings, Billy, age 5, and Rachel, age 11. Father, a successful physician, and Martin seemed very masculine, with short-haired, clean-cut looks. Mother, a housewife, wore loose-fitting blouse and pants, her long hair hiding her face, as did Rachel's. Billy had girlishly long, tousled hair. Father and the children sat on the sofa with Rachel at the far end, then Billy, Martin, and Dad. Mother sat alone in a chair between Father and Dr. S. Father had his arm along the sofa, as if sheltering Martin, who, in turn, would put his arm around Billy, while Rachel at the far end of the sofa and Mother in her chair seemed isolated and squared off opposite each other.

Father began by looking at Rachel and saying sarcastically, but fondly, "Rachel is thrilled to be here." Mother explained that Rachel had not wanted to miss school and therefore was reluctant to come.

Here is a hint of the importance to the family of Rachel's school performance, as well as Martin's. The family begins the session with a sarcastic remark that states the opposite of what Rachel is feeling. There is a friendly, physical coalition among the males and isolation of the combative females.

Dr. S., noticing the father's fond sarcasm, smilingly asked if there was a lot of teasing.

To the observer, it almost feels as if Dr. S. is teasing, too, and all are smiling.

Dr. S. reports later how much he liked this nice friendly family, and yet he sensed in the first minute that Rachel was being victimized. He was thinking that the family had put all their resistance to treatment on her and had said she was thrilled when she was not. So he supported Rachel to speak up and chose not to address the group process of collusion at this stage.

The boys said they got teased and tickled. Their giggling suggested they enjoyed it, whereas Rachel said she got picked on.

As they sat, the boys began to play, Martin zooming with an airplane and Billy twirling the propeller of a helicopter.* Meanwhile, the parents began to discuss the essence of the problem, namely that Martin felt kids should play fair and not change the rules. If they cheated, he got angry and expected his mother to make the world right for him, which she could not do. Rachel added that when she and Martin were outside together with friends, Martin himself changed the rules and got mad when confronted. Both parents said at length that they expected Rachel to play fairly and not go along with her girlfriends who would change the rules and take extra turns when playing against younger children. As they talked, Martin began to smile. He put down the airplane and picked up the helicopter-ambulance, which he flew all over.

Dr. S. was working on the notion that the family was concerned about someone being a victim and someone being at fault for that, and that they were anxious to decide whose fault it was because that felt better than feeling like a victim. Billy pointed his finger at Rachel and said it was her fault. Martin hugged him and swooped the rescuing ambulance around until Billy's plane shot it down. Dr. S. said the family was wanting Rachel to be a rescuing ambulance for Martin and that Billy was shooting down that idea. He said that there was a family rule that kept getting broken, namely that Rachel should look after Martin and if she did not, she was not being cooperative. Mother restated that indeed Martin needed to be taken care of (at which Martin smiled more than ever) and that Rachel did

---

*Children's play in family therapy; see Chapters 13 and 14.

not cooperate (at which Rachel began chewing on her lips). She soon became upset, accusing her mother of caring more for Martin than her, and of being a Cub Scout leader for him and not for her. Father and Mother protested and laughed at the outrageousness of the accusation. Dr. S. said he had learned of another family rule, namely that when Rachel was upset, she was to be proved wrong, whereas when Martin was upset, he was in need of care.

We do not want to suggest that we always try to define family "rules." This word is chosen to fit with the index patient's symptom. But we are interested in defining the shared unconscious assumptions by which the family operates.*

Dr. S. reports that he was aware of continuing to support Rachel's speaking up against the family tendency to invalidate her reactions.

The parents responded diversely to his interpretation. Mother, crying, said it had upset her, not that what Dr. S. said was actually true, but that it was truly how Rachel saw things. Father responded by moving next to Rachel to put one arm comfortingly around her and the other around Billy and Martin, quietly listening as Mother spoke: "I don't know how to get through to her that I love her as much as them. I take her to music lessons, wait for her, and I don't mind doing it. But when she says, 'You never do anything for me,' I think, 'What have I been doing, if she can't even remember it?' She says I was a Cub Scout leader for him. But she forgets I was a Brownie leader for her."

Dr. S. said, "Rachel is telling you that you are a bad mother."

Mother said, "No!" Rachel said "No!" and they got stuck, unable to communicate.

As Dr. S. supported Rachel, he seemed to have joined forces against Mother. With hindsight, we can see that Mother could not bear to be thought bad and Rachel could not bear to share such a good mother. There must be something that Dr. S. could not bear either, leading to his rather bald comment that focused prematurely on an anxiety instead of on the family's defense against it. The comment was also difficult for the family because it singled

---

*Shared unconscious family assumptions; see Chapter 7.

out a pair instead of relating their interaction to the group process.*

Dr. S. reports later that he felt as if he had done something wrong and that it might endanger the alliance. He had been hard on the mother, just as he felt the family had been on Rachel. As an oldest child and as a parent, he knows that he is sensitive to issues of a parent being hard on the oldest child. He therefore decided to back off while he reviewed this countertransference.†

The session recovered when Dr. S. asked what they had felt about what he had said and was then able to take a correction from them.

At that moment, Dr. S. says, he was feeling guilty, unable to do the family justice, which is not a usual feeling for him and therefore one that might have been a response to the family's transference to him. From his experience of blaming Mother when feeling guilty himself, he recognized his collusion in a family process. This countertransference analysis enabled him to become more effective in interpreting the family's tendency to assign blame in order to avoid being a victim.

Dr. S. pointed out that when Martin felt like a victim, the parents blamed Rachel, feeling she should do more for him. Then Rachel, in turn, felt like a victim and blamed her mother, who then felt like a victim. Mother accepted this description of the family pattern, saying, "That's a fair statement."

This established some trust, after which Mother felt sufficient promise of understanding to open up on the painful topic of her poor self-esteem as a woman.

Dr. S. asked if it was like this for Mother growing up, and everyone listened intently to her reply.‡

Mother told of being the second youngest of five children. The order was girl, boy, girl, girl, girl. She said, "So you see, I was supposed to be a boy, and I wasn't, and I never could make up for it. I was always trying to do well in school, doing better even than the

---

*Reverting to the dyad as a defense against countertransference; see Chapters 2 and 10.

†Unempathic interpretation as a defense against countertransference; see Chapters 2, 9, and 10.

‡Taking parental histories and generational transmission; see Chapter 8 on assessment and Chapter 9 on technique.

older ones, but I still felt inferior. No matter how much I pleased them, I was disappointing. I realized it by the time I left home. I went to college also to please them, but at least once I got there, I got good grades, not for them, but for *me*."

Her husband said, "Now she hardly does anything for herself. She always puts the children first, shopping for clothes for them, never for her." Dr. S. said he felt the family wanted Rachel to be perfectly good, especially to help her brother be good, because Mother felt so bad about herself not being a boy and not being a good enough girl. "I'm glad *you're* not a boy," said Father, squeezing Rachel, who responded coyly and appreciatively.

Here we have a nice example of a fatherly intervention with his daughter tending to undo generational transmission to her of poor female self-image and envy of the male, possible because Father felt himself to be a successful male who had enough boy children. We wonder why he was more comfortable supporting the feminine image of his daughter than of his wife with whom he had no physical contact in the session, and we note that the father–daughter alliance took place at the expense of the mother. We might hypothesize that he might be putting into his wife a repressed feeling about himself as inadequate, with which she has a valency to identify through the processes of projective and introjective identification.*

Dr. S. asked how Father had been viewed as a boy in his family. Father said that he was the favorite, the oldest and the only boy, and he unabashedly enjoyed it. As he said this, Billy began to play with the cherry-picker truck, unfolding its extending ladder and pointing it at Martin's genitals. They were all enjoying this phallic image of "Dad the greatest." Yet Father added that he had not been ambitious as a child, content just to pass. "Just like me," muttered Martin. Not until he was in junior college did Father realize he had the ability to do university work.

Mother told of how hard it was for Martin to manage small motor tasks, such as musical fingering and handwriting, whereas Rachel shone in these areas. She began to talk admiringly of Rachel, praising her at length. "I'm so proud of her and I don't want her feeling I don't care," she cried.

---

*Projective and introjective identification; see Chapters 3, 5, 6, and 10.

Once Mother's resentment of feeling inferior as a girl had been owned and the family accepted the interpretation about Mother's needing Rachel to be so good because she herself felt bad, Mother was then able to talk of how outstanding Rachel actually was.

Dr. S. said that Rachel nonetheless feels she is not special, just as Mother felt her parents thought she was not special. "That's fair," agreed Mother. Dr. S. continued, "Martin, being a boy, is felt to be just right, as Father was in his family, but the reality is that Martin is not just right because he has some weaknesses that he really does need professional help with, and until now, the family has wanted its well-coordinated girl to cover for him. At the same time, Father is off doing something special at work, while Mother is covering for him, raising the children, often alone."
"That's fair," said Mother again.

Her judging his interpretation as fair or not fair reflects her tendency to judge reality in those terms also. This view of reality has been taken up by the children, too, who experience, in their games, the family conflicts about the privilege and responsibility of being older or younger, male or female, successful or unsuccessful.

Dr. S. recommended family therapy and tutoring for Martin, both of which were agreed to.

This interview presents the family, the therapist's responses, and the observations made by a consultant in order to give a working demonstration of the concepts of object relations family therapy. The session presents a way of working that is the sum of the many aspects to be explored in what follows. Taken together, they represent a method of joining the family that allows the therapist to develop an understanding of the life they share, their relationships with each other, and their inner worlds. We offer a context of tolerance and concern in which family members work to know more about themselves and to improve their relationships. But the prospect of engaging with families in this way does not always seem easy. Accordingly, we begin by examining the issues that surface when an individual analytic therapist or a family systems therapist begins to work with object relations family therapy.

CHAPTER 2

Resistance to Beginning Object Relations Family Therapy

The Individual Therapist Moving to Family Therapy

We have noticed among therapists and clinics devoted to individual psychotherapy an increasing interest in family work. It is, however, a tentative interest, full of hesitation. Individual psychotherapists do not realize that clinical skills can transfer to family work, and they shrink from feeling like novices all over again. But in fact, they have experience that is good preparation for family work. The mature individual therapist is experienced in permitting the expression of drive material and the acting in of the patient's multiple transferences to various objects at different developmental levels. In competent individual therapy, there is recreation of the family of origin and its representation in the recreated family of present life within the transference. Individual therapists have already been trained to experience and work with transference manifestations and countertransference responses, ranging from painful noninvolvement to uncomfortable turmoil, that require serious study and commitment to working through areas of vulnerability. This training is the single greatest asset for family work. Complicated networks of inner object relationships are already being worked with, so therapists need not quail at the thought of dealing with similar complexity in a family therapy setting. Then, why do they?

They know the work is hard with the series of individuals they see in a day of therapeutic hours. They tend to imagine that in one such hour family therapy will multiply the task proportionate to

the number of members. Common sense dictates that there is wisdom in not attempting so much. Those trained in a Freudian drive
theory approach imagine dealing with a multiplication of drive
material and fear that the conglomerate ego will be overwhelmed.
It seems simpler to stay in individual therapy practice with what is
known and keep away from the hurly-burly of trying to treat six
people at once. The intrapsychic arena seems more manageable in
contrast to this fantasy of family therapy, which results from idealization (with the usual mixture of contempt); for family therapy
seems too omnipotent, offering so much to so many compared to
the modest self-image of individual therapy. It is imagined to be so
different that individual clinical skills could not possibly transfer.
We are convinced that they can, particularly when object relations
theory is used as a bridge.

Of course, there is a difference that we do not mean to minimize. Dealing with driven object relations in fantasy in the transference is different from engaging the object relations in the flesh
with all or even some of the bodies present. The noise and activity
level impinge more on one's attempt to be reflective. It can be
distracting. It can feel out of control, very confusing. But psychodynamic training in tolerating ambiguity, dealing with countertransference responses, and reliance on theory will support the
individual therapist willing to take the plunge. The theory that we
have found most useful is object relations theory because it gives us
a conceptual system of multiple transferences that helps us to work
with the real and fantasized relationships in the family and in their
relation to us. The family meeting is not simply a fleshing out of
the individual patient's inner object relations but a living demonstration of a dynamic system of object relations in which the
individual members participate each with his or her unique mental
structure.

Even when there is no interest in becoming a family therapist,
the individual therapist might find a family meeting useful for
learning about the origins of individual psychopathology, for supporting ongoing treatment, and for treating a person who is too
scared to admit to the need for individual treatment. It offers a
chance to *see* the transferences develop out of family experience. It
sets the patient in context. These are some reasons the individual
therapist might find family work useful—but many anxieties
emerge at this point, not just about trying something new but
specifically about working in family settings.

The Family Systems Therapist Moving to Analytic Family Work

Our students include family therapists already trained in structural and strategic family therapy. One of them felt very competent working with and supervising therapists' work with families. She said she "felt like the Wizard of Oz working as a supervisor behind a one-way mirror and making interventions." Her competence transferred to the initial stages of psychoanalytical family therapy. But she lacked the experience in tolerating ambiguity and working with transference. When therapy got under way, her tendency was to revert to giving directives and being active. Learning to be still and receptive, following the family's themes, and holding, rather than managing, the family's anxiety, was the challenge for her. Her resistances were not to dealing with families but to experiencing them in depth and to the painful feeling of waiting and not knowing. These resistances are based in anxieties about the therapist's personal capacity for bearing pain, which can be explored and worked through incrementally as the family work deepens.

Individual therapists have the advantage of exposure to the core of psychoanalytic work, which they do not recognize as an asset, whereas nonanalytic family therapists have the advantage of exposure to the context of family work, which they can value and from which they can benefit. Both types of therapists can use their previous backgrounds as a starting place from which to learn psychoanalytic family therapy, and both must expect to encounter resistance that, as therapy proceeds, will be located more and more at the core.

Conscious and Unconscious Anxieties

Many of the anxieties about beginning to work analytically with families are illustrated in this report of a class discussion in the Psychoanalytic Family Therapy Training Program at the Washington School of Psychiatry.

The first anxiety admitted to was that the father would not attend. Two examples were given of phone calls to wives who said that their husbands were too busy or could come only at night. Others wondered if a single parent or divorced parent or blended family would "count" as a family for fulfilling clinical requirements of our course. [Here was an anxiety about incompleteness, damage, irregularity in the family where the marital couple was not willing to be together. There was some conflict about having to face being unable to make the family perfect or being party to excluding the father.]

The discussion continued, focusing next on the fear of angry scenes, maybe violence, then on discomfort about talking about sexual material with children present. [Working with the whole family can bring up uncomfortable, childish feelings of being in the middle, provoking parental fights, wanting to watch what grown-ups keep private.] Next, the class moved on to discuss the fear of being "sucked into the family system," [a more primitive anxiety about being undifferentiated and helpless]. Someone noted that a cotherapist is helpful in dealing with that anxiety: If one should get "sucked in," the other can perform the rescue. [The worry is that the therapist will be so engaged emotionally by powerful family dynamics that any sense of role and, indeed, all ability to think and talk will be lost as the therapist gives in to a regression to preverbal helplessness.] The question was raised: "Can one remain objective when the family inevitably evokes one's own family position with its inherent vulnerability and automatic defenses?"

We moved on to discuss the problem of taking sides, one person feeling sympathetic to troubled adolescents, another to tired parents, and yet another to abused wives. The group listened as one member illustrated this with a vignette about her identification with a mother she was treating biweekly, on alternate weeks treating her provocative son. She and the mother discussed how to manage the awful boy, and when she met with the boy, she herself felt all of the mother's helplessness about dealing with him. The group could not move past this example, asking for more and more detail about the case. [The group's intense interest in discussing this treatment arrangement of alternating individual therapies revealed the tendency to retreat to the dyad in the face of the anxiety of family work.]

The dyadic treatment format of individual therapy may be chosen to protect against anxieties of family work: competition and sharing, being observed at work, being taken over or excluded. The family is indeed a complex system that magnifies the therapist's experience of anxiety. The transferences are formed and active right at the start of treatment. But the individual therapist already knows how to contain multiple transferences in middle-phase individual therapy. We teach a similar holding function in family therapy, for which individual therapists are better prepared than they realize.

Resistance to Doing Family Work

Resistance to family work is understood as a series of specific defenses against the anxiety of maintaining the holding function of treatment while the family's holding function is painfully stressed. Understanding of these resistances can free individual therapists to expand their range to include the practice of family assessment and therapy. We have found that sharing and discussion of these resistances has been helpful to students in making the transition. Furthermore, it is a way of demonstrating during teaching the careful, empathic analysis of resistance to family therapy that is a necessary part of the initial work with the reluctant family in the establishment of the family's commitment to treatment. Presenting these findings in a paper about resistance proved helpful and encouraged therapists to face their anxieties and become open to learning to do family therapy.

The Interplay of Individual and Institutional Resistances

Resistance against doing family therapy operates not just at the intrapsychic level, consciously and unconsciously. Resistance is affected by the system the therapist is in, while the system's resistance to new modes of treatment reflects the individual anxieties of its staff, particularly the director.

A child analyst, director of a child guidance model clinic, told us that he had read many articles that led him to believe that family therapy could be useful, but he was uncomfortable with insisting that all members attend. So he continued to see the child and parents separately, as before. When he learned from junior colleagues that family therapy could be done with the portion of the family that would attend, he felt that he could now try family therapy. For him, family therapy had implied a directive, authoritarian, and rigid approach to the treatment contract, an approach within which he, with his nondirective style, could not work. His clinic now teaches family therapy.

His resistance was aggravated by the family therapy literature, in which structural and strategic approaches predominate. Much of this literature describes directive, short-term methods, which are alien to the analytically trained therapist, who finds them superficial. Furthermore, traditional analytic drive theory, being intensely intrapsychic, is not easily applicable to group situations. And even ego psychology, which might seem less mechanistic, is still insufficiently interpersonal. Both these analytic theories lack a communication and feedback loop for dealing with interaction. Because of this, analytically trained therapists have either avoided family therapy or have eschewed their analytic backgrounds in favor of developing a systems-based or communication-based approach that fits the family setting better than psychoanalytic drive theory and ego psychology. We view this polarization as a way of avoiding anxiety rather than as an informed choice between mutually exclusive alternatives.

Once therapists actually start with families, there is another wave of resistance that has to be faced and worked through. It takes the form of not finding families or having no-shows or premature terminations of recently begun family therapy.

A group of students was discussing why they had few family cases. The first to speak said that her agency did not do family therapy and therefore "had no families." There was a teenagers' waiting list, but it had not occurred to her that, of course, they might live in families and would do as well in family therapy. Obviously, at least one case could be made from that list but not while the therapist lacked conviction and projected ambivalence onto the agency. Further discussion helped her see this. She was then able to take responsibility for her resistance and decide to go for a case.

One family leads to another, and the therapist who successfully brings in families will influence the agency to welcome rather than ignore families. Like a child growing up in a family, the therapist has attitudes that are influenced by the agency director's policies and work habits but are also influenced by external contacts with peers and teachers. By growing and developing, personally and professionally, the therapist may demonstrate to the agency the possibility of change. The agency has developed its policies in order to carry out its task of providing a service. In any agency, such policies can be viewed as the pooled result of the anxieties and defenses of all the therapists working there (Jacques 1955, Menzies

1960). One major conscious anxiety is the fear that there will be too many clients in need—more than can be coped with. A family represents just that. But the family therapist can show that that fear can be addressed and that all family members can be helped efficiently for the price of helping one.

There followed further discussion of the difficulties. Some students felt uncomfortable about insisting on family attendance. Other students felt anxious about having to have a case for supervision and thought this was provoking a premature interpretation of dynamics in hopes of making a case continue in treatment, with the result that the family was often too frightened to return. I said that their anxiety appeared to be about meeting requirements of the course but really was about meeting with a family. Students admitted believing that if they were well trained for individual work, or for structural or strategic family therapy, they were set in their ways. Couples were not so difficult, but in-depth family work was felt to be harder, as there were more people and dynamics to be aware of. Others confirmed the statement of one who said, "You feel the pain; it's so real, it's not just a report. I feel much more aware of my own unfinished business." The sense of competence in individual work was lacking in the family setting, while the sense of mastery of family systems therapy could no longer be relied upon and a desperate need for more authority was expressed.

When confronted with a family, the individual therapist tends to feel much more exposed, quite vulnerable, and aware of a lack of the usual sense of competence. There are witnesses to the work. The therapist is dealing with a group, to whom he or she is the outsider, if not the enemy. The pain is immediate. The inexperienced therapist is protected in individual therapy by listening to a story about others in the patient's world and has time and privacy in which to learn and work. Not until much later in treatment does the patient reenact in the transference with full affective involvement, and by then, one hopes, the therapist is ready for it. But in family therapy, the interactions are right here, now, ready or not. It can feel overwhelming.

How do therapists get more authority? Some theoretical schools teach a directive style, a deliberate attempt to identify with the father to get control of the family. Battles for control may follow, and the inexperienced therapist can feel exhausted. Of course, the authority needed is the kind that derives from in-depth experience with families and from family therapy training. Until then, the therapist needs help to put up with this insecure feeling. Teachers, or enlightened institutions, can provide a holding environment while the anxiety is faced.

Holding in the mind the total experience of the family is what we try to teach. Tolerating the complexity is quite stressful, both for individually trained therapists and for family systems therapists. It calls for the therapist to maintain a balance between engagement and neutrality that takes time to develop. By engagement, we mean the willingness to be used as an object into which the family projects its anxieties. By neutrality, we mean the ability to be dispassionate in reviewing this experience with the family without retaliation or reenactment. Engagement includes tolerating a state of projective identification when the family invokes in the therapist a state of mind that is experienced by one of its members. Neutrality includes being able to observe what has happened and to use it for therapeutic purpose. Engagement occurs with the family as a group, as well as with each individual, while neutrality permits equally empathic responses to all the individuals, regardless of role, sex, or pathology. Before this balance of engagement and neutrality is achieved, the experience of becoming one with the family threatens the loss of the observing capacity. The therapist feels like a little child confused and molded by the older ones. Tolerating this experience while working with it is stressful, and the therapist may allow the family to absorb and destroy his therapeutic potential.

The therapist's overwhelmed response can be viewed as a countertransference experience that relates to how overwhelmed the family is when facing its developmental tasks, including the monumental task of attempting to right its own course in therapy. We want to teach the management of that countertransference experience without defensive displacement or acting out. But until it can be contained, a number of defenses may be in use, among them unempathic interpretation of dynamics, the overuse of distancing, taking sides and reversal, reverting to the dyad, and simplification. These can be detected during assessment, but they become most troublesome during mid-phase therapy. At that time, the engagement/neutrality balance is put severely to the test, struggling therapists usually experiencing another wave of resistance that has to be worked through by analyzing the defenses against the countertransference.

Defenses Against Overwhelming Countertransference

Defenses against overwhelming countertransference first detected during assessment become more obstructive as family therapy moves into the mid-phase.

Distancing. The therapist may choose to remain distant to avoid various imagined traps. Then the therapist may be painfully locked into an outsider position from which he or she sees more but feels less and learns less about the experience of being in the family—unless, of course, the family has an unconscious need for the therapist to be kept out, and the therapist can detect this, and examine and learn from the experience. This excluded position brings to mind the pain of many personal family experiences of being excluded as a child from the parental bedroom, from the play of siblings, or from important family events or discussions. More than in individual therapy, the therapist with unresolved difficulties in these areas will be forcibly confronted by his distress. More than in systems therapy, where the therapist becomes active in altering the situation, the analytic family therapist will feel pain and confusion. At this point, some therapists quit rather than face the need for personal exploration, for process and review with peers or supervisor, or if necessary, a therapist.

Unempathic Interpretation. Another defense against the anxiety of analytic family work is the unempathic use of interpretation, which can scare the already overwhelmed and overwhelming family away. Being rid of them, the therapist feels relieved but also guilty, and with the next case is compelled by guilt to repeat the process. This resistance to working with families ensures that there will be no ongoing family therapy case. Some of the families are culturally disadvantaged, with poor object constancy and little appreciation of commitment, and might have quit anyway. So working with the student on the destructive force operating to get rid of the family is a tricky matter. The supervisor does not want to confront the student too early because this increases the defensiveness and guilt and compounds the problem, yet a way to intervene must be found. We want to encourage the student's appreciation of the dynamics while restraining the defensive use of such knowledge, either in the actively aggressive form of premature interpretation or in the passively aggressive form of withholding interpretation. Underinterpretation is just as frightening to the family, particularly if material of an aggressive or shocking sort has been revealed. Unless this is actively responded to, the family members may fear that they have killed off the therapist and prefer not to return to the scene of their crime. Although we agree that the helpful, nonjudgmental acceptance of the family as a client (with the attitude of joining in the task of understanding) is an important part of beginning family work, it is appropriate early interpretation that really hooks the family, that reaches into the family unconscious and offers the members a way of looking at their past and finding their future. Therapeutic tact and timing are needed in family work just as in work with individuals.

Taking Sides and Reversal. Others defend against the anxiety by siding with a family member, an attempt to avoid loneliness in the family by cutting down on the size of the group, as if size were the cause of the anomie. A therapist who prefers not to feel excluded will project that feeling into the family and will have to defend against preferring to exclude a family member. This then presents as a conscious worry that a certain person will not attend, for instance, that the father will be too busy or that the parents will not include the preverbal children. This expresses a difficulty in relating to and including that role in the work—for instance, a fear of confronting the uninvolved father or of including the little children who make messes.

Reverting to the Dyad. Here is a further example of defending against the anxiety of family work by constricting the size of the group, in this case by returning to the dyad.

A supervisee presented a complex family with a history of violence, sexual abuse, and much yelling and crying. Mom and Dad always sat together, two teenage girls sat together, and two latency children did not attend the sessions. There was so much of interest to discuss, yet the first thing the supervisor focused on was the nonattendance of the pair of latency-age children. The therapist said that she did not think of including them, since they were too young and seemed to be a separate group not involved in the acting out. Later, she was able to realize that she excluded them because she did not know how to work with them. [Here is a resistance not just to dealing with children's communication and play but to being open to learning from the family by experiencing.] Within this family, various pairs expressed a resistance to group functioning, and in agreeing to exclude the younger two, the therapist was colluding with this defensive pairing against some imagined and already enacted calamity. In supervisory meetings, the supervisee sat very close to the supervisor while reporting multiple interactions she had had with individual family members. Together, in close friendship, they could have re-enacted the family's wish for a dyad. Instead, they examined this phenomenon and agreed to make more distance between them in order to make room for presentation of the whole family. This was an important step in helping the supervisee not to relate solely to individuals but to keep enough distance so as to be able to contain the family experience, with its magnification of anxiety.

Simplification. If more complex defenses fail, then the final resort is simplification.* Simplification is an invidious defense because it allows the therapist to continue working with the family while murdering in-depth understanding. In this category falls the premature use of directives, according to the notion that telling people what to do will result in their doing it. Of course, directives can be useful when accompanied by analysis of the resistance to accepting them; in which case we would not find their use unhelpfully defensive. The tendency to simplification is often not recognized. It may be blamed upon the family's resistance to psychological-mindedness or may be seen only as characterizing other therapists' work.

Overcoming the Anxieties

There are two practical ways of reducing anxiety, which can ease the process of acquiring family therapy skill. It has been our experience that the move from individual to family therapy is made easier by working with couples first, because the two-person system is not quite so confusing. We have also found that entry to family therapy is made much less stressful if there is a cotherapist. Like a couple of parents gradually learning to create and manage a family, the cotherapists can support each other through their developmental transition from individual to family therapy. Both of us had the benefit of this form of peer-teaching in our early training

---

*We are grateful to Fred Sander, M. D., for his critical discussion of an early draft of this chapter, which led to the addition of simplification as a defense.

and while in supervision at the Tavistock Clinic, as did family therapists who trained at NIMH in the 1960s and early 1970s with Shapiro, who notes with regret that it is difficult to justify the expense in the present financial climate.

The most crucial asset for work with families is the ability to tolerate personal discomfort and disarray among one's own object relations until this can be used to therapeutic advantage. Individual therapists already have training in tolerating ambiguity, in not knowing, in dealing with transference, and in waiting for resolution. What turns this training into clinical skill with families is practice, which cannot be had until the resistances we have described have been confronted.

It makes sense to analyze these resistances prior to seeing families and again as they resurface during family therapy practice and training. The therapist who takes responsibility in this way is creating a personal flexibility for doing the work and is providing for the family a model of recognizing resistance and working on the individual contribution to the dynamics. Work done at this stage prepares the therapist to work with countertransference, which is the central part of psychoanalytic family therapy. At this stage, the therapist will benefit from further exposure to family and group process, child development, and object relations theory.

Awareness of these defenses against overwhelming countertransference can alert the therapist to areas of functioning that require process and review, and perhaps consultation. Only when the therapist can face the anxiety being defended against will the family be able to.

PART II

Theory and Development

CHAPTER 3

Object Relations Theory and Family Therapy

Object relations theory refers to a psychoanalytic theory of human personality that holds that the human infant is capable of relating actively from birth. Freud's concept of the baby as a narcissistic creature governed by instinctual impulses has been rejected. Instead, the baby, from birth, is seen as an active partner seeking to develop relationship with its mother, responding to and modifying her ways of relating, in the course of which needs for food, warmth, entertainment, and rest are met. This view was not developed from infant observation research, although recent findings confirm the intellectual and psychological competence of the baby as an initiator and partner in the human relationship (Tronick et al. 1978). Instead, the idea was deduced from clinical experience with regressed states in treatment, which yielded a retrospective view of infancy through its reliving in the relationship between patient and analyst. Object relations theory refers to various theories that rely upon this central concept that the "ego" (that part of self that copes with reality) is capable of relating to an "external object" (the object of attachment, namely the person that cares for the infant) from birth. The experience with the object is internalized within the psyche as an "inner object" in close connection to a corresponding part of the ego, both partly in consciousness and partly repressed into unconsciousness. And subsequent progress in the two-person situation of pre-oedipal development and the three-person situation of oedipal development rests on this foundation, be it shaky or secure, and is colored by its specific configuration.

The word *object* in the term *object relations* does not refer simply to another person, nor to a memory of a person or experience. It stands for "internal object," which is a mental structure inside the ego, which is a composite of introjected experiences with the significant others over the course of development. When *object* is used alone it may refer to either the "external object" (the object of attachment, namely the mother at first and the father very soon after) or the "internal object" (the intrapsychic structure). If the context does not make it clear which type of object we are talking about, we will specify whether the object is internal or external.

The various theories comprising object relations theory were developed independently, mainly by Balint, Winnicott, Fairbairn, and Guntrip, each theorist known for his emphasis on a certain aspect. But because of their shared basic premise, they have been grouped together retrospectively as the British object relations theorists (Sutherland 1980). American readers may point out that Klein is also an object relations theorist. But Klein focused on the reconstruction of the infant's effect upon its internal objects under the influence of the instincts, rather than on the structuring of internal object relations as a result of the need for human attachment. Within the British Psycho-analytical Society, the Kleinian group, sometimes called "The English school," is quite separate from the "Independent" group to which Balint, Winnicott, and Fairbairn belonged (Guntrip was not a member of the Society). And so we consider Klein's contribution separately. The theoretical difference matters when analysts must choose a group to belong to or require consistency of theoretical approach. We are not in that situation here and cheerfully use from either group concepts that make sense in the clinical setting with families. The distinctions deserve to be made, however, as we trace in brief the contributions on which our point of view depends.

The British School

MICHAEL BALINT

Balint (1968) noted that not all patients conformed to the neurotic picture of a person whose drives had to be inhibited by actual or imagined forces of reality. There were some who, far from needing to discover something that was repressed, had to face the awfulness of there being nothing but an emptiness, something missing in their personality. Balint realized that this was an early, fundamental flaw that influenced the way the ego related to objects thereafter. He called it "the basic fault" and suggested that it arose from a failure of fit between mother and baby. He described how the basic fault led to insecurity in future object relations, so that the ego might cling to objects for support or might become so afraid of new object relations that it would overvalue its existing inner objects or, more creatively, dwell on artistically producing from within itself, instead of through relationships, objects more satisfying than the original ones. For Balint, the basis of personality development rested upon satisfactory object relations, and so the therapist would have to offer himself as an object with whom the patient would dare to relate again in order to repair the fault and recover human relatedness.

DONALD WINNICOTT

Winnicott (1965a) also became aware of a split in the personality resulting from difficulties in early mother–baby interactions. Unempathic mothering can cause the baby to try to mold itself to its mother's needs, when its mother cannot respond flexibly to her baby. This leads to the infant's suppression of its "true self" in favor of the development of a "false self" that is apparently compliant, while the true self dwindles or is nourished secretly inside the self. Thus, like Balint, Winnicott (1956) describes the condition of good fit between the needs of mother and baby as essential to healthy development. This condition is met in health by the mother's natural state of "primary maternal preoccupation." She feels taken over by and devoted to her infant, closely identified with the baby's inner state and ready to respond to both physical and emotional needs. The mother is prepared for this by the close physical and psychological connection to her baby in the months of pregnancy. Of course, her state of preoccupation cannot be total when she has worries, other children to feed, money to earn, and so on. Her mothering need not be perfect, only "good enough" (1960a) that the infant can feel loved and cared for by her and valued for him or herself. In this situation of trust, the infant's true self will develop without distortion.

The baby's internal world is organized by the presence of its mother, specifically through her holding, handling, and picking up, through her voice and her gaze as her baby prompts her to respond to its physical and psychological needs. Winnicott (1971b) called this relationship between the mother and baby the "psychosomatic partnership." The infant's ego finds a trustworthy object in its experience of its mother. Sometimes the use of the word "object" suggests that there is something objective about the whole process. Not so. At this stage, the infant and mother are as one; the object is just there, experienced as part of the self until the infant's cognition develops to the point of recognition of otherness.

This takes us to Winnicott's major contribution to understanding self and otherness. He described a continuum from the baby's sensory experience of his own thumb in his mouth and of finding his fist to the woolly familiarity of stuffed animals presented by the mother. Winnicott (1951) called these "transitional objects," perceived as presenting themselves in the "transitional space" between mother and baby. To the baby there is ambiguity as to whether these objects are "me or not me," "mother or not mother." The baby's exploration of this question at the boundary of the self promotes further definition of self and other. The transitional space is one that both partners contribute to as a place in which to relate creatively and playfully with each other quite intimately without invading each other's boundaries or regressing to earlier stages of physical fusion.

RONALD FAIRBAIRN

Neither Balint nor Winnicott developed their contributions into a systematic theory of the structure of personality. Thus, neither formally challenged Freud's structural theory, which derived from his views of the infant as organized primarily to seek gratification of instinctual impulses. Fairbairn, using his philosophical background, did not shirk the theoretical implications of his discoveries. He found that schizoid states result from the infant's feeling unloved, and he, too, concluded that the primary human need is to be loved and validated rather than to be instinctually gratified. Instinctual impulses are not free-floating energies but are aspects of ego functioning, arising within developmental phases in the context of the primary relationship. So for Fairbairn there is no id, no seething cauldron of forbidden libido (sexual and life instinct) or destrudo (death instinct). There is no destrudo at all, because aggression is not instinctual but arises in response to frustration. There is libido, which resides in the ego, driving it to seek objects, seen when the human infant naturally seeks attachment to its mother (Bowlby 1969).

Prior to birth, the infant is in a state of totally reliable dependence on its ever-present mother. At birth its relationship to its mother changes. Even though she is more or less able to meet her infant's needs, the experience of being mothered after birth is comparatively less satisfying than being in the womb. Because of the infant's dependence on the adult and its helplessness to alter this, the relatively unsatisfying situation cannot be changed but has to be dealt with. Fairbairn proposed a model of how the infant psyche copes.

The infant psyche at birth is a unitary pristine undifferentiated ego (the part of the self that deals with reality) in relation to its object (its experience of its mother). This object is inevitably relatively unsatisfying in comparison to uterine bliss. To defend against the anxiety of the new uncertainty and the pain of frustration, the ego introjects the unsatisfying object. "Introjection is the process whereby a *mental structure* representing the external object becomes established within the psyche" (Fairbairn 1954, p. 107). Thus the internal object so formed is not a memory but a defensive constellation signifying a painful relationship. The ego further defends itself against the now internal object by splitting it into its relatively satisfying aspect, called the *ideal object,* and into its intolerably frustrating aspect, called the *rejected object* (so called because it is rejected into an unconscious area of the ego). The rejected object is further split by the cognitively limited primitive ego into two aspects, the need-denying aspect called the *rejecting object* and the need-exciting aspect called the *exciting object.* The ego splits off and represses two aspects of itself that invest in these rejecting and exciting aspects of the rejected object, namely the *antilibidinal ego* and the *libidinal ego,* along with their relevant affects of rage and intolerable longing, respectively. This leaves the remaining part of the ego, called the *central ego,* in relationship to the ideal object in the more conscious, more rational area of the ego (Fairbairn 1952).

Otto Kernberg (1975) has interpreted Fairbairn's views to indicate that splitting is the more primitive defense mechanism and is associated with borderline and narcissistic character outcomes, whereas repression is the higher-level function, associated with neurotic and normal functioning. We must be clear that Fairbairn's view was that splitting and repression are part of the same mechanism and always exist together. The issue for the infant's mental development is not whether there is splitting or not but how higher-level experiences with the original and other objects which are also split modify the original splits. Rather than discussing *whether* there is splitting, we have to consider in each case the level and degree to which splitting persists instead of giving way to tolerance of ambivalence about an object (Fairbairn 1952). The object relations theoretical term "split-off" implies that both splitting and repression have occurred, and that the object and its corresponding part of the ego are sequestered in a repressed, closed-off part of the ego. In summary, according to Fairbairn (1963), the ego thus comprises (1) a conscious core of central ego in relation to its ideal object, (2) an unconscious antilibidinal ego in relation to the rejecting object, and (3) an unconscious libidinal ego in relation to the exciting object.

The conscious central ego system is an open, adaptable system that deals with reality and learns to integrate new experiences with its objects. It maintains its freedom by repressing the libidinal and antilibidinal systems. But the unconscious antilibidinal system, characterized by repressed affects of rage and contempt, and the unconscious libidinal system, characterized by repressed affects of longing and uncomfortable excitement, constantly threaten to reinvade the central ego functioning unless repression is severely maintained. The central ego has a secondary agent of repression in that the unconscious antilibidinal system represses the libidinal system to an even deeper layer of unconsciousness in the ego. This occurs because the affect of longing for the need-exciting object is more painful than the experience of rage toward the rejecting object.

Because of their repression, the rejecting and exciting objects remain unmodified by further experience, and the libidinal and antilibidinal egos do not develop more mature ways of relating to such objects. With good mothering, the relatively unsatisfying situation of dependency on another to divine and meet one's needs can be adjusted to. Then the repression need not be so massive, and less of the ego is sequestered in unconscious relationship to internal objects. Fairbairn recognized that the quality of mothering is a large determinant of the nature of the internal objects and the severity of the splitting. Of course, the infant's flexibility and adaptability influence the outcome, but unlike Klein, Fairbairn did not view the infant as the sole determinant of how the mother is perceived. Nor did he think of internalization of the object as a fantasy of oral incorporation of the breast, as she does, but as a process of mental structure formation. Unlike Klein, he thought that aggression is not a product of the death instinct but is a result of frustration in being mothered.

HARRY GUNTRIP

Like Fairbairn, Guntrip regarded instinctual activity as part of the functioning of the mental structures derived from the object relationship. He added to Fairbairn's view of endopsychic structure a further hypothesis. He suggested that in severely regressed schizoid states the libidinal system is further subdivided when part of it is split off as a withdrawn, regressed unconscious self that has no object to relate to. (Guntrip preferred the more personal term *self* to the more scientific term *ego*.) This withdrawal from reality into the self may become the major part of the psyche in severely pathological states, or it may be a heavily defended, secret part of the self that is not readily discovered. The need for such withdrawal is proof of terrifying anxiety about losing the self and disappearing into the void.

The Contributions of Melanie Klein

Guntrip emphasized that Klein (1928, 1932, 1948) was the first to challenge Freud's theory of the structure of personality when she noted that infants were capable of object relations much earlier than he had thought (Sutherland 1980). Her work heavily influenced the development of Fairbairn's theory, but unlike Fairbairn, she retained Freud's emphasis on the instinctual basis of development. For her, object relations derive from fantasies. The fantasies occur in relationship to the mother, or more specifically her breast, and arise from the force of the instincts upon the situation. Klein's work (1948) emphasized the infant's primitive perceptions and mental mechanisms rather than the actual quality of mothering.

THE PARANOID-SCHIZOID POSITION

Klein hypothesized that in the first half year of life, the infant organizes experience by primitive mental processes of splitting, projection, and introjection. The infant is made anxious by the force of the death instinct, which it seeks to deflect by projecting the resulting aggression into the image of parts of its mother, such as the breast or her imagined penis. The breast is now felt to be attacking, and when it is reintrojected it forms an inner "persecutory object." Under the sway of the life instinct, the breast is experienced as loving and comforting, and the infant projects its good feelings into it and then reintrojects the good feelings and good experience as the "ideal object." (Klein's use of the term *ideal object* does not correspond to that of Fairbairn but is closer to his "libidinal object." For her, "ideal" means ideally good, while "bad" means ideally bad. For Klein, the "good object" is a more mature whole object, not a part object, and is thus a later phenomenon.) The infant, imagining the ideal object to be the source of all goodness, may greedily devour it or envy its power, either case leading to destruction of the desired object, with a confused sense of disintegration inside the self. The infant projects aggressive and loving feelings out into the external object to protect the good experience from destruction within its chaotic, destructive self. It reintrojects the aggressive feelings to protect the object from destruction. The good feelings are reintrojected to counter the bad feelings inside and to give a sense of possessing the ideal object inside (Segal 1973). The reintrojection occurs as a fantasy fueled by the oral incorporative drive, its sucking being an expression of the life instinct and its biting a derivative of the death instinct. Both the ideal and persecutory objects are part-objects, because the very young infant is not capable of ambivalent awareness of the mother as a whole person. The paranoid-schizoid position remains as a primitive constellation even when normal development allows the personality to attain the next position.

THE DEPRESSIVE POSITION

At about 8 months, the infant begins to recognize its mother as a whole person about whom ambivalence is felt. As an object, she need no longer be split into part-objects that are kept separate. Experiences with her cannot be idealized because the persecutory aspects are not split off. Instead she provides a whole "good object" whose ideal parts are mourned and whose persecutory aspects are tolerated. The good object is found to be vulnerable to envious, greedy, and aggressive attacks, and its temporary loss is mourned. The infant develops guilt about its destructiveness. The infant now has a capacity for concern for its object and learns to make reparation. In the face of such guilt over its own destructiveness, the infant may become so despairing that there is regression to earlier paranoid-schizoid mechanisms. Or there may be manic flight from, or control of, the object. But in the normal situation, the depression is tolerated, and the gains of the depressive position can be maintained. Once the mother can be recognized as a whole person, the infant constructs a fantasy of mother and father united in intercourse. The fantasy at this time is based on the instinctually derived oral incorporative wishes; thus the parents may be imagined to be feeding each other, eating each other, or generally engaged in ultimate gratification from which the infant is excluded and therefore feels deprived and envious.

INTROJECTIVE AND PROJECTIVE IDENTIFICATION

Two other Kleinian mechanisms that we find useful in understanding marital and family interaction are introjective and projective identification. These are described succinctly by Segal (1973). *Introjective identification* "is the result when the object is introjected into the ego which then identifies with some or all of its characteristics" (p. 126). Conversely, *projective identification* "is the result of the projection of parts of the self into an object. It may result in the object being perceived as having acquired the characteristics of the projected part of the self, but it can also result in the self becoming identified with the object of its projection" (p. 126). *Pathological projective identification* "is a result of minute disintegration of the self or parts of the self which are then projected into the object and disintegrated" (p. 127). Projective identification has varying aims: to avoid separation from the ideal object; to gain control of the source of danger in the bad object; to get rid of bad parts of the self by putting them into the object and then attacking it; to put the good parts of the self outside to protect them from the badness in the self; or "to improve the external object through a kind of primitive projective reparation" (pp. 27–28).

Object Relations Theory and the Family

Object relations theorists assert that the establishment of secure object relations during the first year of life is the necessary foundation for the infant's movement to two- and three- (or more) person relationships within his family. By analogy, we state that a thorough understanding of the individual personality developing within the matrix of the early dyad is essential to building a theory that encompasses marital and family relations. At the beginning, the configuration of object relations that develop between individual family members is largely determined by the nature of the marital relationship, the excitements and frustrations of which echo the earlier dyads of each parent during his or her childhood.

It is mainly from Fairbairn's study of the early dyad that we draw our theoretical premises and our language. We use his model of psychic organization because it works so well for understanding the interaction between one psyche and another in family life. It gives us the beginning of a view of the mental structure of the individual fundamentally shaped by experience and by the child's immature understanding of those experiences at the time they were going on. It lets us conceptualize the way the baby understands and records the experience with mother that provides the blueprint for future psychological experience. And in turn, it lets us see how this actually affects the real relationship with the real mother. This gives us, in short, a bridge between the internal world of the child and the reality of life within the family, a way of moving back and forth between internal reality and external reality. The link is provided by the Kleinian concepts of introjective and projective identification.

Although we disagree with the instinctual basis proposed by Klein, we find many of her observations helpful. Thus, although we cannot accept that projection derives from the need to deflect the death instinct, we recognize that it occurs in situations of anxiety, rage, and envy. We find her concepts of introjective and projective identification useful for understanding and treating relationships. But mostly what we have taken from Klein is her language. Because it describes psychological processes as instinctual, it is graphic, immediate, and physical. We use Kleinian language because it is close to the body.

Unlike Klein, we do not focus on introjective and projective identification as deriving only from the infant. We see them as mutual processes going on between spouses, mother and baby, parent and child, siblings, and also between the family group and the therapist. We see them as processes that arise from the drive to foster vital relationships, not merely from the force of instincts seeking gratification. Although we agree with Fairbairn that within relationships aggression arises in response to frustration, we also agree with Bowlby (1969, 1973a) that aggression is a fundamental quality, intrinsic to all species. As Klein recognized, some infants at birth are temperamentally more liable to frustration than others, and some are constitutionally more active and aggressive then others. We attribute this not to instinct but to their genetic inheritance.

Development after birth is a result of the combination of constitution and shaping by the environment through the mother, father, and other caretaking figures. We are in debate with Fairbairn, who said that the inevitable dissatisfaction with the object (compared to uterine bliss) was the only motive for defensive introjection of the object. Although we agree it explained introjection as a defense, we suggest that pleasure in the object relation is also a motive for taking in, and that simply having any experience might be motive enough. Taking in is not just a defense but is an operation which allows mental sorting. It is the infant's primitive way of thinking and organizing experience. This is closer to the Kleinian view of fantasy incorporation.

Fairbairn describes the repressive action of the antilibidinal ego against the libidinal object within the psyche. When two people enter into close relationship, as in marriage, the shared antilibidinal system often attacks the need-exciting object and its libidinal ego, effectively furthering their repression so that eventually the person is unaware of his longing. We see this clinically as a couple fighting and complaining about each other but unable to speak of the underlying hurt and longing. However, we have also seen couples whose overconcern and constant sexual or affectionate gestures masked their basic contempt for each other. Thus we add to Fairbairn's view the possibility that the libidinal system may also repress the antilibidinal system.

Fairbairn further realized that the quality of mothering affected the basic situation of unsatisfaction. The normal mother is inevitably rejecting at times by ignoring or pushing the baby away, by being sick or in a bad mood, or by not responding accurately to her baby's signals. Obviously, there is a continuum of rejection from occasional and mild to frequent and severe. Most infants do not have intentionally neglectful or abusive parents, yet all will have some experience of intolerable rejection of their needs. Furthermore, as they get older, they may experience appropriate, growth-promoting limit setting as partially rejecting.

On the other hand, the desired mother who cannot be possessed may nonetheless offer herself as if she could, thus tantalizing her infant. She might for instance offer the breast when it is not needed, or at a later age offer candy instead of crackers, or take a bath with her toddler who is overwhelmed by feelings about the sexual characteristics of her body. Again there is a continuum. And as Klein emphasized, the baby's innate aggression colors the fantasies through which the breast or later the mother is perceived. Thus the internal object arises from experience with an external object that may be (1) relatively unsatisfactory compared to the prebirth state, (2) actually rejecting or exciting, or (3) felt to be rejecting or exciting by the infant.

In psychotherapy, the reconstruction of this is hypothetical despite the confidence in the evidence from the transference, but in family therapy, because the history is memorialized in the present relationships, we can often be clearer as to what we are dealing with. The range in severity of need-exciting and need-rejecting situations and the variations in the lines along which they variously appear (e.g., feeding, elimination, respecting bodily privacy, and so on) account for the wide variety of normal personality traits, for the form of pathological outcome in mental structure, and for their distribution as differing traits among family members.

We do not rely as directly on the work of Balint and Guntrip for the elaboration of analytic family theory, although we do find their work illuminating in clinical situations. For instance, family therapists are familiar with the situation of discovering a family secret, the revelation of which is often important in leading to improvement, although not magically so. We liken the keeping of the secret to Guntrip's idea of the harboring of a withdrawn, secret part of the self and learn from him that this happens because of the terrifying anxiety of falling into the void. Similarly, the family may harbor a secret part of itself, the revelation of which is resisted because of the family's dread of it. The family fears that if this part of its experience is exposed it will annihilate the family. Not until this fear has been interpreted (or in nonanalytic family treatment, surmounted by therapeutic paradox or behaviorally unlearned) can the secret be shared. Balint comes to mind when we see families that convey a feeling of emptiness, of there being nothing there for the members. Just as Balint described the individual's reaction to "the basic fault" as a clinging to objects or inventing of objects, family members may cling to relationships with each other rather than risk relating to peers, or may invent objects or ways of relating within the family. Both these solutions operate simultaneously in the incestuous family. There is something missing in the sexual relationship between father and mother; yet father clings to objects within the family, and so he and his wife invent a more gratifying object for him in the form of his daughter.

It is to Winnicott's description of the mother–infant relationship and the transitional space that we now turn as we try to conceptualize the basis of family functioning and the therapeutic task.

An Object Relations Model of Family Functioning

THE MOTHER–INFANT INTERFACE

In the beginning, the baby dwells inside the mother. Even as the blood that flows across the uterine interface with the placenta comes into an intimately structured interaction with the internal environment of the baby, so the baby has intimate contact with every aspect of the internal environment of the mother. Even as the baby occupies a space that is physically inside the mother's own space, it also creates access to her psychological space. Much has now been written about the psychological fluidity of the pregnant mother, her liability to "primary process" or irrational thinking, and her openness to psychological reorganization (Bibring et al. 1961, Jessner 1966, Wenner 1966). There is more emotional lability, more emotional in-touchness, and a preoccupation with herself and the growing fetus whom she identifies as a potential baby. This means that the baby has dramatically enlarged the mother's channels of communication with her internal object life, including the split-off repressed areas. The interlocking influence of self and object is such that her preoccupation with the growing object means a substantial reorganization of her self.

For its part, the baby before birth has no internal mental organization in the sense of containing images of experience with the external world, but it does have some sort of organized apparatus, an increasingly complex "wiring," which forms the undifferentiated ego at birth. And it contains the history of the intrauterine experience in some way that we do not yet know how to talk about, although some evidence is being gathered (Liley 1972).

THE PSYCHOSOMATIC PARTNERSHIP

The next phase, beginning with the delivery of the living baby, introduces a time when the mother gives up this internal experience of being in touch, usually with a combined sense of relief and of loss. What replaces the intensity of this internal connectedness is a relationship that occurs through extensive and highly structured physical contact. Winnicott's term for this, *the psychosomatic partnership* (1971b), evokes the richness of an intense relationship that is at once extremely physical and fundamentally psychological. The baby's internal world is organized completely through the care of its mother, specifically through her holding and handling. She stimulates the senses of vibration and proprioception as she moves her child (Freud 1905a) and engages, visually and vocally, gazing, cooing, and adoring. These vehicles communicate her feelings and fantasies about her infant, and the organization of the infant's responses form the basis of his or her personality.

The psychiatric literature has tended to present the mother as the active agent for the first weeks during the so-called "autistic" phase (Mahler, Pine, and Bergman 1975). But mothers have always known that their babies appeal to them quite powerfully by their reaching, molding, and sucking, long before a true smile appears. Infant research now presents the infant true to the mother's experience, as a capable, active partner from the start, provided he or she is not suffering from neonatal distress or disability. Compelling research documents the infant's capacity for reciprocal interaction with the mother in vocal conversation, visual gaze, and affective expression (Brazelton et al. 1974, Stern 1977, 1985). These reciprocal physiological patterns of the various systems are co-coordinated according to certain rhythmically occurring sequences, which lead to a sense of organization (Call 1984). The speed with which the infant's rudimentary equipment becomes organized is such that by the age of 3 months the infant can communicate mood and can engage in purposeful play with its parents.

This means that a great deal of the organizing of the interior of the infant is going on in the "sleepy" first few weeks—through the holding and handling, the early attuning of the mother to the rhythms of the baby and of the baby to the rhythms of the mother, and through the patterns of feeding and changing, waking and sleeping, and the more microscopic patterns of the momentary exchanges that form the building blocks of mood and interpersonal meaning (Brazelton, Koslowski, and Main 1974). In the beginning, the visual and vocal exchanges are an integral part of the early physical matrix of interaction, and are only later teased out from it and progressively differentiated. The physical relationship is more important in the earliest mother–child relationship than it is in any later human relationship, although the closest adult echoes to it are heard in the adult sexual relationship, in which similarly physical aspects of a psychosomatic partnership carry a major part of the adult couple's relationship (Scharff 1982).

Over the months of pregnancy, delivery, and early infancy there is a progression in which the partnership is at first mainly physical. The pregnancy relationship is biologically symbiotic and goes on without the need for willing participation of mother or baby. This ends with the dramatically physical event of birth. But it has formed the biological precursor out of which the psychosomatic partnership is delivered, and that new partnership begins at the moment of birth. It then continues over months and years, only gradually transforming into a partnership that is primarily psychological, even though it continues to contain a large somatic component. The sequence can be outlined as follows:

Physical Symbiosis

(with large psychological effects)

↓

Psychosomatic Partnership

(balance of physical and psychological components)

↓

Psychological Partnership

(with large physical component)

The psychosomatic partnership can be thought of as one in which the physical interface between the mother and baby is like a semipermeable membrane providing a structured but highly porous surface over which exchanges occur, influencing the internal world of each partner. The literal presence of a highly physical interface begins to give way to the symbolic inheritor of this physical partnership, a space between the mother and baby, named by Winnicott the "transitional space." This gap between mother and infant is an external reality that is matched by an expanding internal space inside the infant in which he or she begins to grow and to think, really to become a person (Winnicott 1951). It is the space across which the psychological aspects of the partnership now occur, the vocal and gaze conversations and the games between mother and baby. It is the space that inherits the intensity of physical provision for the baby during the pregnancy and the first few months of the mother–infant relationship. It is in this space that the infant growing to adulthood will develop the capacity for sexual intimacy.

Centered Relating

Exchanges between mother and baby occur in and define the transitional space between them. We observe mother and baby relating intently, gazing at each other during arousal cycles, or we may find the baby, with eyes closed, tucked into a nook on its sleepy mother's body. When the baby cries, the mother experiences a tingling or let-down sensation inside the breast. As the nipple enters the vigorously sucking mouth, the mother feels her milk being pulled out of her and may also experience a drained feeling throughout her body after such concentrated giving to her infant. We imagine a parallel mental process of relating to and taking in each other's experience, of mutual identification. We hypothesize that mother and baby are each relating intently at the boundary of the bodily self, while also reaching into the center of the body and of the mental self to communicate intimately there, each validating the identity of the other. We call this *centered relating*. Centered relating is facilitated by a mirroring function in which mother reflects back to the baby its moods and its effects on her, while baby reflects back to mother its experience of her mothering. Through the experience of relating to each other centrally, at the very core of their selves, the nucleus of the infant's internal object relations is built and the mother's internal object relations are fundamentally modified as the baby contributes the experience which gives her identity as a mother.

Centered Holding

The creation of the transitional space and the establishment of centered relating are contributed to actively by both mother and baby. However, it is the mother who bears the responsibility for enabling their development. The success of this venture depends on the mother's ability to relate to her baby empathically, during nursing or feeding, molding to its body, lifting and settling, interacting through gaze and voice, responding to cues of alertness or fatigue. We might summarize these actions as the mother's *handling* of the baby. And as we have shown, this physical interchange is the medium for demonstrating emotion and appreciation of the other. In other words, handling conveys the devoted, focused attention to the baby's needs and anxieties that leads to a feeling of being loved and valued and understood. We give the term *centered holding* to the mother's ability to provide the space and material for centered relating through her physical handling of and mental preoccupation with her baby.

Contextual Holding

The space in which this centered relating takes place is in communication with the space around the mother and baby. By her absorption with her baby, the mother narrows down this space to a comfortable boundary around herself and her child. Just as the infant is born with a stimulus barrier against external pain and noise, so the mother develops a "primary maternal preoccupation" that excludes irrelevant interruption to the nursing couple (Winnicott 1956). There is a physical correlate to this psychological envelope in which the mother holds and protects herself and her baby, although there is a wide range of normal variation. The physical space around them can extend to the infant's carriage, crib, and bedroom or beyond. The mother marks out the distance at which she can still feel in communication with her baby. For some working mothers this may extend to her office downtown and require that she hand over the handling or "centered holding" to a trusted substitute for a period of time that she and her baby can tolerate. But it is still the mother who provides the envelope. We call this the *mother's contextual holding.*

Here we need to consider the father's role in provision of holding for the baby. Of course he, too, has direct exchanges with his infant. These are of a different character, more excited, more centered on the father as an object the infant has to be drawn to than one with whom the infant enjoys a symbiosis. Thus, the father's direct or centered holding is not usually central in the ongoing way it is with mother and baby. In fact, his exchanges with the baby have the purpose of pulling the infant out of mother's orbit for gradually increasing lengths of time. His needs for sexual relationship with the mother reclaim her body from the infant and help her to separate from time to time from her symbiosis with the infant. This paves the way for the later separation and individuation of the infant from the mother. Part of the father's role, therefore, is to interrupt the mother's centered and contextual holding. But mainly he supports the holding, by protecting his wife from the demands of family or other children, by supporting her financially when she cannot or chooses not to work, and by meeting her needs during the postpartum, which may be a regressed experience for her. In other words, he holds her as she holds the baby. We call this the *father's contextual holding*. By not making demands on her time, he supports the attachment of mother and baby, feeling content that she is biologically equipped to do the mothering on his behalf. In modern marriages, some fathers share equally in the tasks of caring for the baby, and in others the father becomes the primary caretaker. In our view, the baby relates at first to one mothering object, even if the external source of that object is the father or a composite of experience with one or more caretakers. Although the infant differentiates experiences with different external objects from the beginning, it centers on the mothering object.

Contextual holding provides an environmental extension of the mother's presence. It offers the infant a gradually dawning sense of its otherness, but only centered relating gives it its sense of individual uniqueness. As the infant matures to about 7 or 8 months, relating with the father becomes as important as relating with the mother in establishing the core sense of self. The infant can now experience itself as mattering to two people. Beyond this age, the contextual holding expands for the infant to include more significant others. Of course, long before that, the love and interest of fond grandparents and kind neighbors have supported the parents in their attempt to provide contextual holding.

In summary, contextual holding occurs at a number of levels. At the outermost circle, we have neighbors. Next in, we have grandparents and family. Then, we have the contextual holding provided by the father for the mother and baby. Last, we have the envelope that the mother provides for herself and her baby. The parents provide a further important aspect of contextual holding in their commitment to each other as loving, sexual marriage partners, which provides a context of safety in which the child can feel secure despite its destructive, jealous wishes. Of course, the contextual holding is also subject to attack, especially by envious siblings, by illness, or by marital strain.

At the center of these circles of support is the centered holding in which mother and baby communicate and interact, sharing, building, and modifying their internal worlds through their centered relationship. We note that contextual holding and centered holding exist on a continuum—they are interdigitating parts of parenting and relating. While recognizing their coexistence, we want to differentiate between them in order to locate points of difficulty in family functioning.

Centered and Contextual Holding in Family Therapy

These distinctions in centered holding and contextual holding also apply in object relations family therapy. They delineate two necessary aspects of the therapeutic relationship. They inform the modifications of technique necessary between individual therapy and couple and family therapy, as we discuss in Chapter 4. They clarify the concepts of transference and countertransference as described in Chapter 10. To put it briefly and simply for now, we might say that the family therapist needs to offer both aspects of centered and contextual holding in the therapeutic engagement with a family.

The therapist's contextual holding is mediated through the handling of the arrangements, the competence in interviewing, the conveying of concern for the family's safety, and, at the most basic level, simply by seeing the whole family. Having established this contextual holding as we work with, listen to, and exchange views with the family, we provide centered holding in which the therapist engages with the heart of the family matters, and the family encounters the therapist as centrally caring, interactive, and understanding. It is here we must "hook" the family, just as the mother "hooks" the baby by her capacity for in-depth understanding.

This prepares the way for us to use our interpretive skills to reach to the center of the family's experience. We reveal at our own center a willingness to experience the core experience of the family, and through this centered relating we can arrive at a central understanding. As the family receives our understanding of its experience, each member can hope to be able to understand more about the other, that is, to become more capable of centered relating, and the family can become a better holding context for its members.

Although we understand the need to provide both these types of holding with families, we are experienced by them as if failures to understand represent failures in contextual holding only. This happens because families deal with the situation by responding with a regressive shift in the transference toward the contextual end of the spectrum. At this point, the perceived failure of context is taken to represent and obscure the failure of the more complex network of combined centered and contextual holding. We will discuss the vicissitudes of this transference expectation of failure in Chapters 4 and 10.

Improving the Family Holding Capacity and Centered Relating

The foregoing discussion of the forms of holding allows us now to make a statement of the aim of family therapy based on an object relations approach: It is to expand the family's capacity to perform the holding functions for its members and their capacities to offer holding of each other. Thus, the pairing of the process of providing understanding of their overall situation with the process of helping each of them to have more understanding and compassion for each other forms the essentials of the task, which is analogous to, and derives from, the mother's paired tasks of creating the mothering environment while communicating with the baby's internal world. In the contextual holding relationship, she provides the context for the construction of the infant's world of internal objects. In the centered relationship, she gives the building blocks for the construction of inner objects. In family therapy, we provide the expectation of understanding. That is, we provide a holding function that allows the family to move toward truly understanding each other at the core. We are providing the holding around them, and then interpretation helps them to modify their internal object relations system.

The object relations approach, like the process of raising children, is a matter of being with our patients. Our attempts to share our understanding are more than language. They are our ways of both holding the whole family and getting in touch with the family's core. Our interpretations are intended to let the family see what we are doing to understand them and to bear their anxieties. At the same time, the interpretations offer the family and its members the opportunity to respond to us, to look us back in the eye, and to set us straight. They need to be able to do this with us if they are to manage to do it with each other.

The object relations approach is, fundamentally, a way of working and understanding. It holds that family members need to relate to each other, and the difficulties in the way of that need are the difficulties that constitute their troubles. When we join them, trying to offer a better way of relating, we bring a way of working with them and of understanding the unconscious object relations that are interfering with further development of more mature object relations in the family. The theory is useful only to the extent that it helps us along the way (Sutherland 1985).

In Chapter 4 we turn to a model of family and couples therapy based on the developmental considerations we have been discussing. In proposing this model, we compare and contrast it to a model of individual therapy, and in so doing, we show that individual and family therapy should be entirely consistent with each other, both theoretically and practically. When they are thus fundamentally related to each other in the clinical setting, individual and family therapy should be compatible, complementary, and mutually catalytic.

CHAPTER 4

Models of Therapy

We can use the elements of the early relations between mother and child to build a model of the relationship between the actions of individual therapy and those of the conjoint therapies (family therapy and couple therapy). As each derives from aspects of the early parent–child relationship, these forms of therapy have their influence through the particular echoes of it that they recall.

In the last chapter we explored the origins of contextual holding and centered relating and holding. In the beginning these grew out of the psychosomatic partnership between mother and baby. Each of the early holding situations corresponds to a later level of interaction between adults, or between an adult and an older child. We will make a more detailed exploration of the development of the child within the family in the next two chapters, but let us first locate the experience and function of the therapist with the individual patient, and with families and couples.

A Model of Individual Therapy

The internal object life of the patient is communicated to the therapist through conscious communications and through the medium of direct communication by the central ego. What is communicated overtly contains all the material needed for the understanding of the unconscious, split-off and repressed, internal object life. In this unconscious realm, the relationship between parts of the self and the object are out of awareness but are communicated indirectly along with what is intended to be consciously communicated. This is familiar to psychoanalytic psychotherapists as lying squarely in the realm of transference. To family therapists it is the realm of metacommunication: those things that are relatively clear to the trained therapist as part of the message but that are outside of awareness or avowed intent of the patient, to one degree or another. The communication that we care about in any therapy that goes beyond being purely supportive and problem-solving in the most limited sense, involves the patient's capacity to communicate with the interior of the therapist. The therapist has an internal object system whose organization corresponds to that of the patient, although we rely on its being less split, less rigid, and less thoroughly repressed.

Therapists should have better access to these repressed areas that consist (just as the patients' do) of repressed objects and repressed parts of themselves. We rely on the relative maturity of the therapist, and on his or her more flexible self-understanding, to have these internal object relationships more available. Being more comfortable with them, the therapist can feel their activation when something happens with the patient, and being able to work with them, he or she can begin by first appreciating the patient's experience. That is, the therapist can empathize and then can feed back a digested or metabolized internal experience to the patient. In accepting the "projection" of the patient's internal objects and acknowledging it, the therapist is performing the eye-to-eye function, like the mother who validates the baby's experience. This has been broadly discussed as "mirroring" by several writers (Kohut 1977, Pines 1982, 1985, Scharff 1982, Winnicott 1971b). In the words we are using to describe these interactions, this goes on in the zone of centered or core relating. It is in this zone that communication between aspects of repressed inner object relations of therapist and patient can occur. It is in this zone that internal object relations can be modified by direct influence.

The fundamental building blocks of these crucial communications are projective and introjective identifications, for it is through these that each partner is able to allow the other into his or her interior space. As these accumulate over time, they constitute the transference/countertransference interaction that is the heart of psychoanalytic psychotherapy. We can note, therefore, that the kind of transference we are highlighting is the focused transference between the interior of each person, and that there is another transference we have not yet discussed. It is the transference of the patient to the therapist's ability to provide a holding environment, the contextual holding that is analogous both to the mother's holding and protecting of the baby and to the father's holding of the nursing couple.

In the discussion of individual therapy or psychoanalysis, differentiating between these aspects of transference has great potential. We do not yet have a language for the difference in the use of the transference of psychoanalytic psychotherapy and that of psychoanalysis proper. In the absence of such a language, the difference may be felt to be distinct, but it cannot always be described. This is especially true at the blurred edges of the boundary between the two, when psychotherapy becomes quite intense, or when psychoanalysis has not yet produced a transference neurosis or is making progress by using supposedly "nonanalytic" techniques that Eissler (1953) has called "parameters." The differentiation of transference into two distinct types deriving from these separate parts of primary relationships allows us to call the transference to the mother's and father's holding capacity the *contextual transference*, and the transference to the mother's centered relating the *focused transference*.

THE CONTEXTUAL TRANSFERENCE

The contextual transference is directed at the therapist as the provider of a holding environment that contains the patient's anxiety. The therapist creates the space in which the patient can mature and develop new psychological strength, where formerly the patient would have been blocked or incapacitated. When we discuss the way the therapist provides a holding context, we are discussing one function that is included in Bion's larger concept of "containment" (1967). This concept of containment is one of the most helpful of Bion's contributions. Sally Box (1984) has explored containment as one of the fundamental growth-promoting processes in families of adolescents. As Box shows, the whole process of containment includes both the provision of a container to the infant's or patient's anxiety, and the capacity for reverie—the absorption of the anxiety and fantasy that are unmanageable for the baby or patient. Thus, the concept of containment includes contextual holding, centered holding, and centered relating. The contextual transference is the transference only to the contextual holding aspect of containment. It can be differentiated from the focused transference, which emanates from the patient's early experience of both centered holding and centered relating. Elements of transference to the therapist's holding function that contribute to the contextual transference are:

1. To mother's holding of the baby
2. To father's holding of the baby
3. To father's holding of mother
4. To father's holding of mother and baby
5. To father and mother's sexual holding of each other
6. To father and mother's united holding of the family, including siblings
7. To the family's holding of father, mother, and the children
8. To the previous generation and its holding of the current family

In the early part of a psychotherapy or an analysis, it is the contextual transference that is activated, as the patient tells the therapist or analyst about his life and travails. Failures of understanding are due not to therapist inadequacy in internally processing the received experience of the patient's inner world but, rather, to the failure of the therapist to provide the holding context, which the patient relies on but is unsure of at the beginning. In this phase, the therapist has not become an internal object for the patient but is more like a fond relative with whom the internal objects can be discussed, just as the patient might tell a relative about his or her nuclear family. In the therapist's understanding presence the patient can explore his or her internal objects. The therapist's role is crucial, and it can catalyze internal reorganization, even including the remodeling of internal objects and self. But the therapist is not yet installed as a major internal figure.

THE FOCUSED TRANSFERENCE

The moment that the therapist does become a permanent internal figure, the patient is hit with the realization that a major shift has occurred in the therapeutic relationship. In a therapeutic setting, the impact of this shift is analogous to falling in love. This shift does not ordinarily occur in psychotherapy, but in analytic work this is the moment of the crystallization of the transference neurosis. And once this unique kind of attachment to the analyst has cemented, a new kind of work is possible because the therapist, previously only an external object, has now become a fully formed, new internal object for the patient. It is now possible for the therapist to become the internal object that reorganizes the whole history of internal objects. The principal components of the focused transference are:

1. To the centered relationship with mother
2. To the centered relationship with father
3. To the relationship with mother and father as a couple
4. To the centered relationships with siblings
5. To the relationships with extended family members, grandparents, and to any other primary caretakers

A brief example will illustrate the two kinds of transference in operation.

AN EXAMPLE OF FOCUSED AND CONTEXTUAL TRANSFERENCE FROM INDIVIDUAL ANALYSIS

Miss Harvey came into her analytic session in her third year of analysis, lay down, and began to argue with the analyst. "Say something to me. Don't you know this is no way to do this with me? You're so stubborn." On this occasion, the analyst tried to ask her a question, but she burst out, "No, that's not it. You just interrupted me again. You never ask at the right time." The analyst said he felt silenced. He asked what this reminded her of from her early life. Although Miss Harvey could not always answer such questions, on this day she said, "You know goddamned well it's my mother. So what else?" He said he had not thought she yelled like this when she was little. "No, I never yelled. I couldn't speak. But she yelled at me, and I just felt worse and worse." Now the analyst could say that he felt she was acting like her mother and treating him the way she felt treated then, and that their job was to understand the reason she had to act this way now.

In this example, the patient complains about the contextual transference, but in fact she works openly and trustingly within it. It is actually part of her trust in what has been called "the therapeutic alliance" that lets her go on to enact the transference (Greenson 1965, Zetzel 1958). This is in marked contrast to the early part of the analysis, when she was too fearful of the treatment relationship to allow this kind of material to emerge. At that point, she hid the most painful parts of her internal world because her contextual transference to the contextual holding provided by the analyst was pervaded by distrust derived from her early experience. Now that she can convey the substance of her internal world, she reenacts an edition of the core relationship, and the therapist becomes the recipient of the transference from the internal representation of a part of herself while she acts like the internal part-object based on her experience of her mother.

The study of which kind of transference is the predominant one operating at a given time in individual therapy can extend our understanding of the differential actions of psychotherapy and psychoanalysis. An examination of the contextual transference will do much to clarify the progress of a patient in psychotherapy.

However, the use we wish to make here of the focused and contextual transferences is in family therapy. Individual psychotherapy cannot ordinarily take full advantage of the focused transference, and psychoanalysis must wait for a long time (at least a year) before the focused transference becomes crystallized into the transference neurosis. But the family brings the entire set of already installed transferences into the therapist's office, and these focused transferences to each other are available for study and modification. This does not mean that family members each develop a focused transference to the therapist, but it does mean that the focused transferences already active in the family are in the room with the therapist, rather than being only reported on as in individual psychotherapy.

A Model of Family Therapy

When the family comes to the family therapist, it brings its contextual transference, just as individual patients do. The family is concerned about the therapist's capacity to listen, observe, understand, and provide for their emotional safety. The family therapist works with this contextual transference, and it is here that the work primarily stays. Although the individual therapist also has the contextual transference to frame the work, interest is focused on the patient's internal object world, even though its contents are not yet matters of the individual patient's transference to the individual therapist.

Not so for the family therapist whose view is primarily on the family as a group and on its capacity to offer holding to the family members. The transference that corresponds to this perspective is the family's shared transference to the therapist's holding capacity for the family members as a group. This constitutes the family's shared contextual transference.

Shared Family Holding

The family's overall shared holding corresponds most simply to the combination of the mother's arms-around holding of her baby, the father's support of that, and the parental marital relationship. Within this envelope, mother and baby have their eye-to-eye centered relationship, out of which the baby first builds internal objects. In the more complex situation of the family, the family-as-a-whole provides the envelope within which to foster the growth of multiple centered relationships—between all the children, parents, and any close grandparents or babysitters. Within this space, the family members provide the material and experience for each others' internal objects. What makes the family a unique group is this ongoing process of both contributing to each other's internal objects and living in intimate relation to them. This means that in treatment the family always brings these internal object relationship sets as many focused transferences.

Individual therapy works early on with individual transference manifestations that, in analysis, crystallize later into the transference neurosis, which is a re edition of the original object relationships. In the family, however, we find various multiple re-editions of the original object relationships transferred onto the others—parents, siblings, or even pets. While the family therapist understands the vitality and importance of the multiple focused transferences, they are too complex to be clear as clinical transferences that can be used in the early stages of family therapy.

The attitude the family shares toward the therapist is pooled in the contextual transference to the therapist and to the therapeutic situation. As family therapists, we should primarily consider the transference from the family-as-a-whole because this is the most powerful way of organizing our understanding and intervention.

When we examine in detail the family's holding capacity for its members, we find that it is more complex than we have so far described, since it also includes the sum of the several dyads' holding of each other and of the ways the dyads support or undermine each other's holding. Clinically we will eventually be interested in this complex tapestry of transferences, but we begin with the family group's shared contextual holding capacity. This shared envelope provides a boundary within which the members maintain the private space in which to be a family and across which they transact business with other groups, including ourselves. The combined holding capacity can be sensed through the countertransference as we encounter the family at this boundary.

The way the therapist relates to the family in psychoanalytic family therapy is derived just as much from understanding of transference as it is in individual psychotherapy or analysis. This will be made clearer in Chapter 10, devoted to transference and countertransference because these are the cornerstones of psychoanalytic family therapy, as in any psychoanalytic approach. But as we have seen, the source of the transference is different here. While the individual therapist gets information from the internal object world of the patient, the family therapist gets transference information from the interactions in the shared holding space of the family. Family members in therapy interact mainly with each other, and their difficulties are understood as difficulties in the function they all contribute to, providing the holding for each other. We can recall here that it quickly becomes baby's job to provide holding to mother in her job as mother, just as she has from the beginning provided holding for her baby. In just the same way, the children provide their share of the holding for their parents, and although we could say that the child's is the minor share, this is not a useful way of approaching the situation. The children, and all family members, provide their own contributions to the shared holding function in the manner appropriate to their ages and development. And anyone's incapacity to do so becomes a deficit for the family as a whole and must be compensated for.

The source of the transference that is the business part of family therapy is, therefore, the contextual holding transference. It is here that we become affectively aware of the family's difficulty in providing holding for its members, and it is this failure that we consult to in doing family therapy. At a practical level, this means that we should begin by being emotionally equidistant from each of the family members, with an overall notion that we are really on the side of the family as a unit in its job of helping each of the members to grow, to love, and to work. Helm Stierlin (1977) stated this nicely when he said that when the family therapist finds himself on the side of or against one of the members, it is a countertransference signal that there is something wrong. Of course, this happens constantly in the family therapy setting, but on each occasion, it is a sign of a strain in the family's shared holding, and that is the useful point for our attention.

In organizing our understanding of the family at this level, we in turn provide an envelope around the family and around its presumably flawed holding capacity. Within the safety of the holding we provide, the family can begin to risk relaxing its own holding function in order to attempt new holding patterns.

The building blocks for these new holding patterns are the daily minute transactions that occur among the individuals and influence the whole group. In our therapeutic setting, we see samples of these within the container we provide. When we do so, we absorb and try to understand the anxieties the family shares, and to feed back our understanding of these. While we may do so by speaking to one individual, our primary focus is on the way that one individual speaks for the shared anxieties of the whole family group. Our ability to help them with the shared difficulty will help them to hold each other and help each other.

The interactions in family therapy come in many forms, however. At any one time the therapist and the family may be focusing on one person, or on a subgroup of two or three people. This means that the individual and the subgroups, not simply some theoretical action of the family group as a whole, form the sources of information. But in each of these transactions between subgroups, the family as a whole is affected and reacts or fails to react in some way. Some of these family-wide reactions are helpful for the overall holding function, and some are not. The most useful transference is the one at this level, and it is this level of organization that helps us determine where to intervene. When we do so, it is with an awareness that even if we speak momentarily to an individual family member or to a subgroup, any effect will immediately have consequences for the whole family.

AN EXAMPLE OF TRANSFERENCE IN A FAMILY SESSION

The Jansen family had three boys, but at the time of this session, the older two were at camp, and only Tom, age 11, was at home. As the family came in, Mr. Jansen said they would like five minutes at the end to discuss the payment of the bill. I had confronted them about this two weeks earlier with good results toward the resolution of a chronic problem of late payment.

Tom now opened the session with unusual exuberance. On the

way to the session, Mrs. Jansen had said to her husband that she was not going to ride in the car with him if he did not get it fixed. Tom looked hangdog, demonstrating the way his father had looked, and said, "Yes, yes, I meant to do it" in a way that sounded like a good imitation of his father feeling pushed around. I saw a bit of a glint in Tom's eyes as he closed with Mother to take on Father. He went on, "It's one thing to just let something go, but when you might be risking my life or Mom's, or if the steering goes and you kill someone in another car, that could be serious." Both parents laughed gently at Tom's supercilious caricature of Father. Mr. Jansen acknowledged that he was supposed to have taken up the matter, and Mrs. Jansen showed mercy in not driving home her point. She did say, "The procrastination sounds familiar, doesn't it?" But here she was referring to my frequent confronting of the two of them over the repeatedly late payment of my bill, and to previous discussion of her inveterate procrastination. It appeared now that Mr. Jansen shares more of the pattern than he had previously acknowledged.

Now that Tom had had his innings, but without much disruption of the parental pair, there was a lapse in what to discuss. Mr. Jansen introduced the topic of Tom's difficulty with friends. "Why don't you tell the Doctor how your difficulty with the boys has been going?" This was usually a sure bet to rankle Tom, and he said, "Dad, I told you on the way here I didn't want to talk about it!" Mr. Jansen persisted, so Tom got up, crossed to the couch, and whispered firmly in his ear something which I took to be a reminder of Tom's getting them to agree to avoid the topic. Mr. Jansen seemed to be on the way to demurring, and I felt, as usual, disappointed. Mr. Jansen tried to say, "How about on the bus? That kid punched you and what did you do?" "I hit him back," said Tom. And as he said this he grinned at Mr. Jansen in a way that reminded me of his gloating in the beginning of the hour as he was taking Father on directly. But the grin was shared by the two of them this time.

Mr. Jansen returned to the offensive again and said, "Really, we ought to talk about this because it's a problem for you and it's what we came about." Tom put his feet up and swiveled the chair so his back was to us. He pulled his head down.

I felt an ill-defined uneasiness about the persistent attempt Father was making, violating a promise not to insist that Tom talk. At the same time I, too, was feeling stymied if he would not; so I found myself siding with Mr. Jansen momentarily in "wanting to make Tom talk." I even felt like pressing him, for instance, by saying, "Come on now, Tom, this is important. How do you expect to get anywhere if you won't discuss your problem?" But I knew that then he would withdraw and feel attacked, probably much the way he did at school. Finding myself wanting to say this, I was checked by the sense it would be picking on him.

I was caught up in Mr. Jansen's attempt to make it Tom's problem, which seemed to come from his feeling picked on by Tom (with Mrs. Jansen's backing) and by Mrs. Jansen herself. This meant to me that the session had begun with a reenactment of the family's struggle to make it the problem of one family member as a scapegoat. But I was not yet aware of this, only that I was uncomfortable joining in the "picking on Tom" even though I also wanted to. I was joining Mr. Jansen countertransferentially in a feeling that was mildly sadistic and counterproductive. What I did instead was respond to another feeling that I shared with Mr. Jansen: the wish to know about Tom's difficulty. I felt this was a good and operational part of his wanting to be a good parent, just as I wanted to know because I wanted to help and felt blocked as a helping person if I could not.

I turned to Mr. Jansen and asked, "Why are you so much wanting Tom to talk about all this in view of his feeling so attacked by it? You must have some important reason. Maybe it would help if you could tell us how you feel when you're wanting Tom to talk about it and he won't."

Mr. Jansen took this question seriously and began to tell Tom. As he began, I remembered that a large part of our difficulty in therapy had been Mr. Jansen's not wanting to be there or to talk. He now said that he felt stymied when he didn't know how to help Tom. He and Mommy were supposed to be able to help him, and they didn't always know how. Mrs. Jansen joined in, looking a bit tearful already, agreeing that it made her very unhappy for Tom, so that when they were questioning him or wanting him to talk about it, it was not to hurt or criticize him, or to make him feel bad. It was to try to help.

I now asked if it was also true that Tom's difficulty made Mr. Jansen feel like a failure as a father when he didn't know how to help. Mr. Jansen said that was indeed true. Now Mrs. Jansen began to weep, partly for Tom and partly for herself feeling so bad about not knowing what to do. No mention was made at the moment of her own extreme feeling that her mother didn't care at all about being a mother. But it was part of the moment.

Tom now began to talk, quite openly. "Well," he said, "I think the problem is going to go better. I just didn't know the rules, that's all. And now I do."

"What sort of rules, Tom?" I asked.

"Oh, its hard to say, but, you know, like not overreacting when they say things. Or how to push back without its being a big thing. Like they all tease each other and I didn't know that, so there's no point in overreacting and making it a big deal."

Mr. and Mrs. Jansen looked at each other with relief. "So you just punched that kid back, right!" said Mr. Jansen.

"That's right!" said Tom, and they grinned at each other. "You just have to know the rules of how to get along with kids. There are others, but I'm not sure of them right now," Mrs. Jansen now said that there were still concerns. Tom would be starting camp in a week, and he had trouble last year there as well as in school. "That's true," Tom admitted. "I did, but I think I'm going to be OK!"

Mr. Jansen said to me, "It's true, too, that Tom is much better with kids. In fact, he gets along extremely well with small groups of kids and now only has trouble with big groups."

At this point, I said that as we had only five minutes, if they wanted Tom to leave, we could work on the finances.

"It's not about you, Tom, don't worry," Mr. Jansen said.

"He knows all about it, dear," Mrs. Jansen said to her husband.

"I'll be in the car," chirped Tom, and out he ran.

I now met with Mr. and Mrs. Jansen over getting the bill back on track, which they finally seemed to be doing.

As we talked, I chuckled to myself because of the parallel of this process to the session: we, too, finally seemed to be getting the rules straight. But I did not say it aloud this time. I had confronted them separately two weeks ago, and since it seemed to be taking, I did not want to rub it in.

This session illustrates the importance of the transference which stems from the holding function of the family, and the role of working with individuals and subgroups as it relates to the holding function of the family-as-a-whole. The therapist sensed a persistent family pattern that represented the family's difficulty in providing holding for a child, which stemmed from the quandary experienced by all three members of the family. The therapist directed a question to one member, the father. When the father answered the therapist, he spoke to his son at the same time. The son was then able to speak about his own difficulty in the wider world because he felt "held." At the same time the parents felt stronger both in their capacity as parents and in their relationship to each other. As they did this, the son relaxed his concern about the shakiness of their marital relationship, and the family became an incrementally better container for all of them.

A Model for Couple Therapy

Therapy with couples is of particular theoretical interest in the model we are developing. It has an intermediate standing between the family therapy work with the contextual transference and the work with the focused transference with individuals. For some people, work with couples seems to be the most difficult of the therapeutic modalities. This reflects the way a couple can set up a mutually reinforcing system that exerts strong pressure to exclude an outsider, even if it is the presumably trusted therapist.

In a couple, each partner has his and her world of internal objects. As they relate to each other through central ego functioning, their split-off internal objects "recruit" these conscious aspects of communication in order to establish unconscious communication at the same time. This establishes the same projective and introjective identification which we have discussed in families, and which also offers the basis of the transference in psychotherapy. However, here the mutual projections and introjections may assume a rigidity that comes from the relatively closed feedback loop of a two-person system. This may be especially true in couples whose core relationship is colored by entrenched and time-tempered pathology.

The couple also has a holding capacity for each other that derives from the mother's holding of the infant. When we first explored the holding situation, we noted that the infant has in turn a contextual holding function for the mother. In the beginning, in this reciprocal process, the infant is the minor partner, whose part quickly becomes a major one. So when the courting partners begin to test out their capacity to perform this function for each other, there is a history to it from early childhood. And again here, we differentiate the contextual holding from the core or centered holding, which is the holding aspect of their centered relationship.

To sum up, the couple has a centered relationship that involves the direct communication of their internal worlds, central and repressed, and a contextual holding relationship that provides the envelope for this. This means that the contextual holding relationship, as long as it derives from the two of them alone and not from the wider family, is by definition and by limitation a two-person holding. This is then, by definition, a more limited situation than exists in family therapy. When the holding involves three or more persons, it becomes a situation of infinitely greater complexity—and family therapy, therefore, often offers more leverage or points of entry to the therapist who wishes to intervene in the couple's interlocking relationship.

THE OSCILLATING TRANSFERENCE IN COUPLE THERAPY

The therapist's approach in work with couples employs the transferences from both individual and family work, and ends up being in the middle. Our attention is divided between the interior life of each member of the couple, which is closely connected to their core relationship, and their mutual holding situation. We receive transference signals in a fairly equal mix from the interior worlds of the two and from their shared difficulties in the holding situation. When we feel stuck with the rigidity of the shared contextual holding situation, we can refer to the interior of either or both partners in order to get information about the difficulty which sets up an impasse. In turn, when their holding situation is going well, we can see much more of their interiors because they are providing the interpersonal confidence to each other so that the exploration of internal blocks and difficulties can go on. In this sense, we sometimes work with the contextual holding difficulties because the sense of trust in each other is so impaired that nothing from inside can be shared until we do.

On the other hand, we may need to shift to the internal world of one partner because the holding situation cannot improve until we learn more about the sources of the shared difficulty in contributing to a safe and secure holding. If we are lucky or skillful, we may be able to turn first to one member of the couple for some internal exploration and then to the other. The fact that they have shared constitutes a moment of core relating, and this moment of their history is memorialized in the growth of their shared contextual holding capacity. The following example illustrates the shifting focus of attention in work with a couple.

AN EXAMPLE OF CONTEXTUAL AND FOCUSED TRANSFERENCE IN A COUPLE

Pete and Sarah Masters, both in their fifties, have been married fifteen years and have no children of their own, although he has two girls by a former marriage, to whom they are quite close. Sarah also helped to raise her younger brother, and his child is like a grandchild to her. They came in originally because they felt their marriage was falling apart with the onset of an autoimmune disease, systemic lupus erythematosus, in Pete. However, he responded well to initial treatment, and it was not until he had a relapse two years later that he became obsessively careful about his health, controlling of his medications, his diet, and his environment. Sarah felt dispossessed of the marriage over the next year as Pete countered his anxiety by becoming more controlling. They could not make excursions that took them in the sun lest it aggravate his condition, and he invested heavily in his diet, meaning they could no longer enjoy going out to restaurants easily and frequently. But what bothered her most was his taking over the house in a similarly controlling way. Because he was an engineer who worked at home, he said he could not have things moved around and changes made in his environment. And he needed his books available just where he left them.

This session occurred after Sarah had been able to confront him about the enormous anxiety he had for his health, the way their life had changed since his relapse, and the failure of his denial of death. He was able to admit that it was not just Sarah who was worried, and that he had tried to handle his enormous concern by becoming terribly controlling. Following this breakthrough they relaxed, began to discuss issues, and seemed much closer. They said that they felt they were getting back to the loving kind of relationship they had before the illness, although Sarah said she now realized there were discontents that remained. Most of these dated from the time before the illness.

We can note that the Masters' holding situation had been fractured by the event of the illness and its relapse, and that their difficulty in accepting and sharing the anxiety about the threat to Pete's health was the stress that created the disintegration from their previous holding situation. However, this had been largely restored by the time of the session that follows, and the process of restoring it had actually made the overall holding capacity greater—although the presence of the therapist was still required to make the holding adequate.

In this session, Sarah reported that things had gone well for the last five days, after they had had a big fight the previous weekend. Pete was in Europe selling his latest invention, and while he was gone, Sarah moved his books to another room onto temporary shelves and had the floors and walls of the house redone. Pete now accused her of redecorating the house completely while he was gone and, specifically, without telling him a word about it. She denied it: "I only rearranged things and just did the maintenance that needs doing. He will never let me do it when he's here. He insists the house has to be a place he can work in peace." But she admitted that she got a fabric cover for the sofa and a new rug "on spec" and brought home a framed magazine cover showing one of his inventions, beautifully done, and hung it on the wall.

Pete got home and, after recovering from jet lag, told her he was very angry. When he did, she had a temper tantrum, grabbed the fabric off the couch, and "I just lost it, Dr. Scharff! I just went and had a temper tantrum myself. But I went and watched TV to calm down. But Pete had an even bigger one. He turned over the dining room table with food on it." She stayed in the TV room while he cleaned it up, although she said she could not remember the TV show she watched.

All this time, I was feeling shut out and distant. Her description of the house and the redecoration was endless and tedious. Pete was silent and yet she kept saying "I wish you could come and see our house. We talk so much about it. I wonder if you ever do that?" It was as if then I could really understand something about her and about them which she was feeling completely unable to get across. Her idea that I might see them at home did not seem to constitute so much an actual request as an urgent wish that I could understand her and the "house inside her" and know how she was in her inner space. Sarah now described the house in such a lively way that it began to live for me, and I began to feel more included. So the "distance" yielded and I began to feel more "included" not only in the house but in their fight as well.

Pete now said that he never agreed to the moving of the bookcases which was part of her rearrangement. Sarah said that he did. I now felt caught between them, unsure whom to believe, as though I was supposed to believe one of them against the other. Pete said that if he did agree, it was only to get her off his back, and he did not mean it. He also said that he had not felt very involved recounting the argument in the beginning, because they have been getting along well, but he'd started to get more back into it now. Now he was feeling controlled and that nothing in the house was his.

As I moved from feeling shut out and detached to feeling included in their bind, I was beginning to get a sense that the problem they have with each other is the same as what I was struggling with: they each feel shut out and excluded and feel hopeless to change the situation.

I now turned to Pete and asked, "How does this relate to the recurrent feeling you have about being controlled by your mother?"

"My father left when I was 8," he said. "My mother was very controlling, as you know—and she was very attached to me. Well, it's like this. On my fiftieth birthday I gave a speech, and she corrected my grammar! Recently, I've been feeling furious about her being so controlling. It's true that Sarah doesn't do what my mother does, but I find myself reacting as though she does. And I would say that today I've been feeling she was *just* like my mother."

I now turned to Sarah and said, "Did you *really* do all that redecorating without telling Pete?" I said it in a way that reflected the fact that I was feeling incredulous.

"I have to say I did," she admitted. "It's because he would *never* let me do it if I told him. He really wants to keep everything as it is. His work needs are just an excuse for that. He'll never change or allow me to change anything about the house." She started to cry.

I turned to Pete: "So that fits with her as your controlling mother?" Pete agreed that it does. I continued, "But why is it so crucial to you, Sarah, to be able to redecorate—really to be able to 'control' the house? Does it have something to do with your experience growing up?"

"I haven't really told you about my family," she said. "You know that my mother was sick. I was sent away when I was 6 because my mother was always sick—hypochondriacal, probably. My father was a doctor from Chile who was devoted to her, and he would take jobs in hospitals so that she could stay in them. So he couldn't take care of me, either.

"When I was 9, I was sent to a tuberculosis sanatorium for a year, although I never had TB. The next year, I went to live with an aunt. My cousin and I had to share a room. I drew a line down the middle of the room and wouldn't let her cross it. So I never had a home of my own, or a place with my parents. I always thought my mother was dying, and that was why Daddy had to take care of her. But then she recovered miraculously when I was 10, and she got pregnant with my brother. Then they got a new home, and I got to live with them."

"What about your father?" I asked.

"I thought he was so special. But my mother kept me from him with her illnesses—and later she got depressed. Now he's half senile and it's different. But then, I loved him and I missed him terribly."

She was still crying. I felt suddenly relieved, in touch with her and them, and as if I had really been let into the house. As the session drew to a close, I said the following things over a few minutes.

"Sarah, you felt shut out of the house and out of your family. There was no house and no room for you. It was out of your control because of your sick mother. And you, Pete, had just been on a trip when Sarah was missing you—really yearning for you and still worried about your illness while you were away. That has echoes of her mother's illness and the real fear she might die, but also the feeling illness is used to control her and rob her of love.

"Pete, you feel she is controlling you as if she were your mother, and then you feel the absence of your father and you long for him. When you feel she is trying to get something out of you, you feel something will be taken from you, and I think that relates to your own sense of lost love, and your loss of control of yourself, which is embodied in the sense that your mother controlled you once your father died.

"It all comes together for the two of you around the house. It is the place where you desperately want to feel cared about, a place with the caring parents you both wish you had. Then if you don't feel that way, it's bitterly disappointing."

A few sessions later, Sarah said she felt they had become much closer, and perhaps she did not have to insist that Pete keep coming much longer. He said that if they could hope to have more of the kind of help they had been getting, he was more than willing to keep coming to therapy.

In this session, the holding and containing transference was nicely symbolized by the house. In the countertransference I felt shut out, as both of them had been feeling both acutely and chronically. As they described their house, I felt more included and more able to provide a holding context for them. The battle over the house became the transference to me: I felt caught in the cross fire and unable to help or even to know who was right or unreasonable. This was a battle over more discrete internal objects and their failures as reexperienced in the present. My feeling in the countertransference led me to ask questions about the internal object relations impasses for each of them. Their work in this area provided immediate associations that clarified what was operating to undermine their shared holding capacity. As they shared this, they made steps to rehabilitate those internal objects—really to share in the process of redecorating the "home" inside their shared holding space.

Thus the work of this session included the reception of transferential clues both from the failure in the contextual holding capacity of this couple for each other and from their own internal worlds in direct communication with me and with each other. My comments were initially directed at the influence of their internal world on the holding experience at the moment, and then expanded to talk about their shared experience of its failure and their sense of taking back rejection when this happened. The focus with marital partners is more fluid in moving back and forth between the core of their internal objects and the difficulties in their shared holding capacity.

In the next two chapters we will turn to some aspects of the growth of the family and the child, which will add to our ability to understand the vicissitudes of these problems.

CHAPTER 5

The Couple's Invention of the Family

The Formation of the Couple

FALLING IN LOVE

Falling in love is an experience of being taken over by a feeling of love and wonder that happens only in relation to the loved one. There is a preoccupation, a quality of withdrawal of energy from outside investments in order to allow dedication of the self to the other. People in love describe adoring their loved ones and enjoying being found so lovable themselves. There is a boundlessness that is matched by a personal feeling of being in flux, where internal attitudes, feelings, and impulses express themselves quite differently or more fully than before. Falling in love describes two personalities entering into a loving space in which they fall into each other and emerge altered by the experience and by their continuing relation to each other. There is a loss of boundaries, distortion of the sense of time, a feeling of the irrelevance of the surroundings and the company. All this suggests a merging of one unconscious with another. Of course, there are also conscious aspects to the choice and to subsequent commitment.

THE MARITAL BOND

A number of forces are operating prior to and after the marriage to destroy or cement the match. These function at three main levels, described by Henry Dicks in his classic book *Marital Tensions* (1967, pp. 129–131).

1. The subsystem of social norms and values
2. The subsystem of personal values
3. The subsystem of unconscious forces

We have found this a useful categorization, but we have added an unconscious dimension to Dick's first subsystem, and then we have renamed and renumbered the subsystems for our purposes.

Subsystem 1: The Public Reality—Conscious Level. Partners are attracted by similarity in religious, social, racial, or cultural background. Sometimes it seems that the attraction has been to the opposite in background, but usually it will be found that this applies to some but not all aspects of background. The match may be expected to thrive when supported by parental and community expectations. Sometimes, however, it flourishes in spite of public dismay, sometimes even finding a purpose in refuting public expectations.

Subsystem 2: The Public Reality—Unconscious Level. There are also unconscious community expectations of the couple. The older generation invests the young with vigor and sexuality, hoping for a coupling that will bear the projection of fantasies of togetherness, sexual fulfillment, and communication on behalf of the wider community. There is a longing to see a relationship proceed to marriage in order to give a reborn image of the couple's parents as youthful, immortal, loving providers. There is a need to identify with the loved one. Our point is that the couple is a focus for the unconscious projections of their own parents and relatives and of the wider community, just as their baby will be for them.

Subsystem 3: The Personal Reality—Conscious Level. What drives the coupling is the conscious need for a sanctioned relationship. This includes needs for fulfillment and validation, for giving and receiving love and admiration, for secure attachment, and for recreating and raising the next generation. Dicks noted that this level corresponds to Fairbairn's concept of "mature dependence," which characterizes a healthy couple where the individuals are quite differentiated and so are capable of cooperative relationships with differentiated objects.

Subsystem 4: Personal Reality—Unconscious Level. Here the split-off and repressed exciting (libidinal) and rejecting (antilibidinal) object relations are active in forming an unconscious bond. The excited or libidinal system is less repressed during the personality fluidity of being in love and functions to support the commitment made at the executive level of the central egos. It does so by investing the ideal object of love with excitement, sexual attractiveness, and romance. Thus, the loved one comprises an exciting and ideal object for the lover. The antilibidinal or rejecting system is more often ignored because it is particularly heavily repressed under the force of loving idealization. This seems to be necessary to permit marriage to triumph over ambivalence. The present phenomenon of living together before marriage appears to be an attempt to face the unconscious antilibidinal system without idealization, but in fact we find that the moment of marriage is nevertheless experienced as the crucial step of commitment that permits the inevitable return of the repressed. We agree with Dicks that the mix of the unconscious interactions in this subsystem determines the longer-term quality of the marriage.

In summary, coupling occurs by conscious and unconscious processes operating at societal and personal levels. There is some conscious assessment of suitability and compatibility, but mainly the relationship is formed by intuition based on a feeling of fit. This fit occurs at all levels of the personality, and so it is no surprise to find, as Bowen (1978) did, that individuals in a marriage tend to be at a similar developmental level of maturity.

In the healthy marriage, the two individuals have personalities largely formed of central ego, where much of the personality is available to interact in consciousness and without undue conflict or difficulty. The lover perceives the loved one realistically, fondly, and consistently. The libidinal system is helpfully activated to produce sexual excitement, romance, and adventure. In general, the central ego perceives the ideal object as just right and copes with flaws and anxiety about rejection because these are not of intolerable degree. This being the case, there is a feeling of commitment and acceptance of the self that is liberating to the personality, so that in a marriage of trust, there will be a return of the repressed aspects of the personalities without undue threat to the overall bond.

Repressed parts of the self to be projected into the other include feminine and masculine aspects. Grotjahn (1960) elaborates on this: "Falling in love, the man projects his own femininity upon the girl and loves it there." If he cannot, "but must keep it introjected within himself, he will not be able to love a woman with all his heart." Similarly, woman's "masculine ambition and needs are lived out in this projection onto her husband" (p. 93). If, let's say, the wife has to split her masculinity and project only a part of it because of envy or contempt of her husband, she will not be able to "fully become a woman," according to Grotjahn. Although we agree with the basic point of projection of male and female elements, we disagree with the conclusion of the necessity of total projection for self-fulfillment. Instead, the healthy relationship allows for projection and reintrojection so as to secure the establishment of a mutual projection equilibrium that promotes sexual identity, empathic identification with the spouse, self-fulfillment, and partnership in reproductive and other life goals.

The healthy marriage is able to contain the projections of unwanted aspects of the self that the lover attempts to put on the loved. In the atmosphere of love and trust, these can be accepted, worked with, modified, and returned. Each partner can thus discover the hidden aspects of the personality, experience them as they control, upset, or manipulate the partner, and take responsibility for them. Thus, the partners develop and the marriage matures through its life stages.

In health, the central ego remains in close contact with the libidinal ego and is not diminished by constant attack from the antilibidinal system but is vigorous in seeking relationships, creative work, and pleasure. This is the healthy state of mind, which less-than-healthy personalities approximate when in love. After a period of marriage, however, they revert to more usual levels of functioning. This occurs when these elevated levels of functioning are invaded by the return of the repressed exciting and rejecting systems. In the best circumstances, the marriage will tolerate and may even benefit from this. As the individuals work through the conflicts, the marriage reaches a new level of maturity, with a capacity for bearing infantile and even primitive processes.

It is best for their future offspring if this can be done before the couple has children. It develops the partnership and solidifies it against threat from conflicts, and it stabilizes the object relations "set" of the marriage, prior to its further disruption by new arrivals. It gives the couple preparation for dealing together with child-rearing problems, and it gives them experience with their own infantile emotions, which will enable them to deal with the demands, frustrations, and helplessness of an infant. This is an essential preliminary to preparing for parenthood and establishing the family as a healthy "psychologic field" (Benedek 1970a, 1970b).

The Couple's Invention of the Family

The environment of the marriage and its level of development affect the couple's relatedness to the infant. Where there has been enough time to allow the working through of the emerging repressed object relations systems, the field will be clearer for starting the enterprise of the family. We cannot overemphasize the importance of the quality of the marital relationship. It holds the family at the center just as the mother and baby hold each other centrally by looking into each other's eyes. The object relations system of the parents' relationship operates as a genetic pool of personality from which various aspects are expected to be selected in the formation of each child. At the psychological level, there is the establishment of a prebirth personality potential based on the projection into the fetus of parts of the parents' personalities. This is just as important as the genetically inherited physiological bases of constitution and temperament. Further variables occur in the physical and emotional environment of the pregnancy, the circumstances of the delivery and the opportunities for parental bonding with the infant, the nursing situation, the child rearing practices, and the management of the expansion of the family to include siblings.

The couple cannot wait forever to have a child, however. Pursuit of perfection in the object relations system of the couple is a denial of the reproductive span and, ultimately, of death. There will always be projection of unconscious fantasy into the unborn child, preshaping its personality. It is only a matter of how well metabolized this process is by the couple. Obviously, the level of the development of the couple will change from one birth to the next, giving each child a unique object relations environment. This has as much influence as have the formal effects of birth order on personality development. When the couple gets pregnant before the work is done, there is the likelihood that unresolved processes involving unconscious repressed object relations of the couple will lead to an exaggeration of splitting off and projecting onto the baby. A well-supported couple or a sturdy baby may survive this, but it can be tough going when the couple has to weather its own object relations storms as well as adjusting to an infant.

Conception: Physical and Mental

Once the couple is ready for pregnancy, there is then a delay of the three to six months usually needed for conception. This offers an extension of the time to work on the return of repressed object relations. Excited ways of relating may derepress with the thrill of purposeful sexual activity, fondly referred to as "saturation bombing" by one couple. Or antilibidinal forces may emerge forbidding sexual activity until "the right moment" as calculated by the basal thermometer for a perfect result. Already, the approach to conception affects the couple's view of the resulting infant. Either way, the fetus is related to as an ideal object, since it is just what the couple wanted. There is also activation of the unconscious longings that are part of the couple's libidinal systems, as the fetus is also related to as the exciting object for which, however, they have to wait. The worry and frustration associated with antilibidinal systems tend not to emerge until late in a planned pregnancy, by which time there is sufficient interference with the couple's sexual activity and life-style to cause resentment.

In the unwanted pregnancy these surface earlier, as the fetus is viewed as a persecutory object that has trapped the mother and father into a long-term relationship or has deflected them from other life goals. These frustrations may be worked through with adjustment to reality and acceptance of the pregnancy, or they may continue to afflict the couple and affect their view of the fetus. If all goes well, they will accept each other as reproductive partners. Pregnancy as the proof of their creative union confirms them in their view of each other as ideal, a view that then extends to their perception of their fetus.

Painful unconscious object relations are particularly stimulated when there is a failure to conceive. Conception becomes a higher priority than spontaneous sexual intercourse. Not yet conceived, the child is dominating the couple, as they feel longing to have the child yet feel spurned by it. The elusive fetus becomes the exciting and rejecting object. If conception occurs, the couple tends to relate to the fetus as very special. If they cannot conceive, they face an immense challenge to cope with the loss, with the blow to self-image, and with the disappointment in each other and in their union. They have to give up the projection of the ideal object into the potential fetus and return it to their relationship. Then, each member of the couple reexamines the ideal object as found in the loved one. If the new reality cannot be found ideal, then the couple will become bitter and may split up. But if the ideal object is resurrected in the loved one, the couple then adjusts to childlessness or decides to adopt.

Infertility and Adoption

Tom and Alexis had been married for five years. Although no contraception was used, Alexis had not become pregnant. She said that they had not yet worked on becoming pregnant because she was not sure she wanted children. Tom longed to have children naturally or by adoption, for he wanted very much to be a father. Alexis felt his drive to be so strong that she was afraid that he wanted to be a father more than to be her husband; so she felt compelled to test him on this point by refusing fertility studies. In couple therapy, Alexis explored her reluctance. She had been adopted into a loving family and she carried the sense that she had not been loved for herself by her biological mother while being told she had been "chosen for herself" by her adoptive mother. Consciously, she felt it was more natural for her to not have a child or else to adopt, like her adoptive mother. Unconsciously, she was afraid that only her child would be loved by Tom, while she would be rejected as she had been by her biological mother. Tom's wish to be a father was driven by an unconscious need to replace his own father, who had deserted him. He wanted to give to a child all that he had missed, but in his haste to do this, he was not giving enough to Alexis. Alexis talked of an experience as a child when she did not get enough support to cope with a terrifying appendectomy. Tom was so helpful to her in reworking this memory that she decided to undergo laparoscopy after all, if he would be there. Tom was very supportive during the procedure, so that they were able to go ahead with corrective surgery. Because he was appropriately attentive to Alexis in general, they were able to consider adoption, should surgery fail to correct the sterility.

Many marriages flounder under the stress of infertility. But, if not, the couple will be strengthened by mastering their loss, and if they should decide to adopt, they will be able to relate to their to-be-adopted infant as an ideal object, provided they have completed their mourning. As they wait, the couple will be preparing to become parents of a child that they cannot imagine as embodying their own qualities. They face the task of commitment to a stranger, a totally unknown quantity. The central ego has to find its ideal object quite suddenly. An easy baby facilitates this, but a difficult baby can make it very hard. More likely, its arrival will activate unconscious rejecting objects. Because of the adoption, the couple finds it difficult to express rage and disappointment about the baby, but the adoption social worker can facilitate full negative expression between the couple so as to protect the baby from being drawn into a guilty, rejecting pattern or into a reaction formation of overindulgence. Expression of aggression also allows the discovery of loving feelings that otherwise get repressed along with aggressive ones. Then the baby need not be confirmed in a rejecting object position but can be once again the ideal object for the couple.

Pregnancy

The gestational period offers the couple a further nine months of readjustment, growth, and development in their relationship, as they cope with the stress of pregnancy (Brenner and Greenberg 1977, Greenberg and Brenner 1977, Jessner 1966, Jessner et al. 1964, Jessner et al. 1970). The changes are gradual, allowing time for response and adaptation. The woman adjusts to bodily, hormonal, and emotional changes, while the husband adjusts his view of his wife. A man may become rejecting of his pregnant wife's body because of guilty reaction to his sexual desire for her in her maternal form, or because of a reactivation of rage against his own mother who became pregnant with a sibling. The couple may fear that the baby will take them over or that it will take one of them over in an intense pairing that excludes the other parent. The baby may thus be perceived as a rival, an interloper, and a spoiler of the idealized twosome.

Pregnancy gives the mother a period of physical adaptation to her infant. As her body expands and its boundaries change, so her emotional boundaries go into a state of flux. This accounts for the unexpected emotionality of the pregnant woman. Her object relations are incorporating and developing a subset, just as her body is accommodating to and nourishing her fetus. As she regresses, she relives an experience of being mothered, this time by her husband as he supports or pampers her through pregnancy and coaches her through delivery. In turn, she supports the fetus, later the infant. Pregnancy may be easy and she may not need much support, but some women need help to get through nausea, breast tenderness, and the discomfort of weight gain. If the pregnancy is very difficult and the husband is insufficiently supportive, the couple may equate the tiresome quality of the pregnancy with the personality of the fetus. They relate to the fetus as a rejecting, persecutory object that is dreaded. Once born, if the baby is colicky or has sleeping difficulties and anxieties that are aggravated by anxious parents, the punishing object relations persist. But a well-regulated baby or a satisfying experience of being able to soothe the baby may turn the situation around, particularly if the mother feels better after delivery.

During the first trimester, the woman becomes aware of being pregnant, but the fetus itself does not have much reality to her until the heartbeat is heard. Even then, it still feels like an additional part of herself. Once the movements are felt, the fetus becomes a separate person. Soon, the husband can feel the movements, too, and now the couple has proof of the baby's existence. As the baby kicks or hiccoughs, they can get used to its buffeting the mother's abdomen. These fetal actions, which may be variously interpreted as antics or distress, confirm the baby's reality and separateness and form a basis for speculation about its identity. The parents imagine that it will be an active baby, quite a handful, or that it will be lazy and passive. When it is not doing anything, they may worry that they may have harmed it, or that it has died. In the third trimester, fantasies of damage become more pronounced when fears of having a handicapped child threaten even the normal couple or plague the guilty couple who expect punishment for aggressive thoughts or deeds.

Projective Identification

THE DEVELOPMENT OF EMPATHY

Fantasies about the fetus are responses partly to the signals from the baby and partly to the couple's wishes and fears about what kind of baby they have made. Husband and wife can enjoy fantasies about the baby, using them to develop a way of understanding their child, of building a basis for communicating together in later child rearing, and of developing parental values. These fantasies, based on their experience of the growing fetus, are the earliest examples of projection. The mother, who is in constant physical relationship to the fetus inside her, learns about the fetus's rhythms of stillness and movement, fantasizes about who it will look like and whose qualities it will have, and, while physically meeting its needs, automatically prepares for responding to its needs after birth. In attending closely to her inner experience, she picks up physical clues and, putting herself in the baby's place, imagines its feeling state. Thus, she develops empathy which paves the way for sensitive mothering after birth. If the mother denies or rejects the pregnancy, or is too sick to think beyond her own feeling state, this process of the development of empathy is interfered with. After birth, the infant's experience may then include nonempathic mothering.

THE ESTABLISHMENT OF PERSONALITY AND PATHOLOGY

Unconscious fantasies may not promote empathic understanding of the baby. Instead, the baby may be used as a repository of unwanted or secret parts of the selves of the parents. Then the couple does battle with what it finds in fantasy in its child, rather than struggling within the couple relationship.

Simon and Renee's fetus carried a projection of a secret, libidinal part of them. Simon and Renee married when he was 56 and she was 32, the same age as his only daughter. Simon had been divorced after twenty-five years of unhappy marriage to a cold, antisexual woman. He was delighted to discover a warm and loving partner in Renee and even more pleased when she wanted to marry him and have his child. He protested that he was too old for her and might not live to support her and the child. No matter. Renee wanted to spend her life with him, whether it would be one year or twenty, and if he should die, then at least she would have his child.

Renee soon got pregnant and miscarried, then immediately got pregnant again. She said she was thrilled, but she seemed more invested in talking about the miscarriage than the pregnancy. So I asked if the miscarriage had been hard for her. She smiled and said, "You know how it is. There's no baby like the first one. It will always be most special to me."

Renee had been the only child of older parents. After her mother died and before her father died, Renee accompanied him on business trips and was an accomplished hostess at the age of 18. So for Renee, the dead fetus had the significance of an oedipal baby from her father, the more so because, like him, it had died. I was concerned that Renee's investment in this fantasy would interfere with her maternal preoccupation with her soon-to-be-born baby. But, in fact, the circumstance of the miscarriage allowed her to bury this unconscious fantasy and spared the live baby the burden of incestuous fantasy that might otherwise have been projected into it.

Simon had been ambivalent about raising another child at his age. Having lost the first fetus, he realized how much he wanted a child with Renee but had had to suppress this wish because of his fear of dying and because of his incestuous fantasy about Renee being like a daughter to him. The miscarriage propelled Simon and Renee to integrate the denied incestuous aspects of their relationship, to the benefit of their live baby.

Child-Rearing Practices

The child needs empathic parenting, but it also needs clear limits and consequences from two parents who work together to implement shared policy with the child. Conflict between the parents, or pathology in one parent that is not confronted by the other parent, can get acted out in relation to the child. This can be seen at birth with the development of the nursing situation. For instance, the mother who gives her baby the breast at every cry is not thinking of differentiating among and responding to its needs. She is meeting her own need to have a quiet, attached baby and to be gratified in physical relationship with her baby.

If her husband objects, but she persists, then their conflict is not addressed while she substitutes allegiance to the baby for cooperation with her husband. If he does not object, then the mother is acting on behalf of the father, too, in ensuring that the infant does not experience any rejecting aspects of the nursing situation. This could only occur when a couple is repressing the negative object relations at the oral level because of discomfort with rage and greed. Their infant would never seem angry or greedy, and indeed its aggression would be actively repressed. At the same time, however, the breast that is sucked on a little at a time and is not given the chance to deliver a stomachful of milk is not satisfying but, rather, quells the vigorous experience of hunger, sucking, and relief. It becomes a smothering, exciting object, which by being overexciting stimulates aggression and greed and may soon be perceived as rejecting and even persecutory, invading the child's right to experience frustration. So the cycle is perpetuated. One also sees negative object relations operate when there is strict adherence to a four-hour schedule, with emphasis on making the child "learn to wait." Here there is anxiety about "spoiling" the child, which is based on a fantasy that the child will greedily exploit the mother. Infants vary one from another, and an infant's feeding needs vary from day to day. Either demand-feeding or schedule-feeding can be too literally interpreted under the influence of the unconscious exciting or rejecting object relations, resulting in unempathic mothering for an infant.

In this situation, the infant is helpless to effect its own satisfaction and cannot make the mothering feel good enough. To the extent that this is intolerable, the experience of relating to the exciting and rejecting objects will have to be repressed. The more intolerable it is (which depends both on the actual mothering and on the infant's constitutional temperament and adaptability), the more severe will be the repression. The impoverished central ego will have a more diminished ideal object to identify with, leading to poor self-esteem and unsatisfactory relationships. The specific ways of dealing with repressed aspects of objects determine the nuances of character traits and pathology.

This is not to blame the mother but to show how what actually happens in the early experience shapes the personality. The mother acts as she does because of her own personality, and her experience with her own mother and with her husband. The couple's relationship is critical. The mother can be helped to bear an appropriate amount of crying and can work with the baby to find out what is needed, if supported by her husband. Some husbands put wives under pressure to keep the baby quiet so that they do not have to be disturbed, literally and figuratively, by the enormous responsibility of care.

Bob and Mamie married when he graduated from technical college. Mamie was 24 when their first son was born. She had had an easy pregnancy with a normal delivery, and nursing was well established by the fourth day, when she returned from the hospital. She was relaxing, glad to be home, when the baby started to cry. His diaper was dry. She tried holding, rocking, walking—but he still cried. When she tried to nurse him, the baby kept arching away and refused the nipple. She became panicky and could not think of what to do. Her husband came downstairs and took over. He said he thought the baby might be exhausted from leaving the hospital, and he put him down in a quiet room. The baby continued to cry; Mamie was terribly anxious, and her breasts hurt. Her husband put his arm around her and said, "Let's wait and see." In five minutes, the baby was asleep, and the new parents took a nap, too. An hour and a half later, they awoke to renewed crying, and this time, the baby was eager to be fed.

Mamie learned to recognize a tired cry and to put her baby down at those times. When her mother saw this during a visit, she

hovered near the baby's door, anxiously grabbing her chest, worrying and almost in tears. She berated Mamie, saying she had never
done such a thing to Mamie but had been devoted to comforting
her in every way. Mamie then was able to reassure her mother as her
husband had done for her.

We can see how Mamie's relationship of trust in Bob enabled
them as parents to develop a policy of dealing with their baby, so
that they averted a repetition of Mamie's experience with her
mother. Mamie's mother's husband had been a prisoner of war
when Mamie was born, and being a single parent colored her
response to Mamie and led to the shaping of Mamie's personality
as anxious, dependent, and prone to depression.

Further experience at the anal stage, phallic-narcissistic stage,
or genital-oedipal stage confirms, intensifies, or modifies the object
relations of the infant. In health, later interactions allow for new
experience at progressively higher levels of development, when the
infant has progressively more advanced cognitive powers, becomes
able to think in whole-object terms, and is no longer dominated by
primitive unconscious fantasy and mechanisms of splitting and
projection for dealing with anxiety. Physically, the toddler is less
helpless and therefore less dependent on its caretakers, and so can
afford to function more autonomously. Thus, at each level the
rejecting and exciting aspects of the object can be integrated with
the ideal object, with corresponding gains in integration of the ego.
But parental difficulties with relating to the growing child at
different phases will skew this development, as will unexpected
loss such as death or divorce, or relative loss of the mother such as
that due to the birth of a sibling or to maternal depression.

The Caseys came for help with the relationship between Mrs. Casey and her daughter, Sandra, age 7. She felt exhausted by Sandra's
needs for attention and demands for favors and treats such as watching late television and sleeping with her mother when she was
frightened. Sandra was whining, controlling, and provocative, and
seemed happy only when playing with friends or when buying and
eating candy. Mr. Casey was oblivious to the conflict until it was
quite out of control, because it reminded him of unpleasant scenes
between his mother and sister. In his father's absence on military
service, he, as the only male, had felt called upon to stop these but
could not. The Caseys had two older boys who were also messy and
rude at times, but Mrs. Casey had no trouble with them.

In a family meeting, Mrs. Casey talked earnestly about Sandra, while Sandra played with her little sister, Miriam, age 3, and the two older boys, Adam and Bob, drew a fleet of airplanes. Sandra was exceptionally sweet and tolerant of Miriam. Mrs. Casey explained that Sandra had been adorable as a baby and never went through the terrible twos as Miriam had. She said that she and Sandra had gotten along beautifully until Sandra was 4. I asked what happened then (silently noting that Miriam must have been born). Bob replied that Sandra's favorite cat had died and Mrs. Casey said that her aunt had died. I heard about these losses and their meaning for all of them. Then, I asked whether Miriam's birth had been hard for Sandra. "Not at all," they replied. "She got difficult after the deaths, which were before that." Later, it became clear that the difficulty first emerged when Mrs. Casey's pregnancy must have been beginning to show. Mrs. Casey had left Sandra for a week to be executor of her aunt's estate. Since then, Mrs. Casey and Sandra were locked into a mutually frustrating relationship. As Mrs. Casey talked, Mr. Casey strolled around my office, looking at paintings and diplomas. He was not exerting sufficient fatherly authority to help pull them apart. Meanwhile, Mrs. Casey found Miriam to be just marvelous, and she continued to admire and dote on her very prominent husband.

The Casey's relationship was organized to forbid any echo of painful internal objects. Mr. Casey did not want to find in Mrs. Casey a new edition of his aggressive, scolding mother, and she wanted to keep him as a serene replacement for her mother, who had died just as she left for college. The importance of her mother's death was denied by Mrs. Casey, who never mourned and instead glorified her memory of her mother.

With the birth of Sandra, and again with the new baby, Mrs. Casey had recreated the marvelous relationship she had with her mother. Then Sandra's withdrawal and negativity over the next pregnancy was experienced as a total loss of the dear Sandra. It was as if she had died, like Mrs. Casey's mother did, leaving Mrs. Casey bereft, unsupported by her husband, just as she was by her father. Her own repressed rage at her mother for abandoning her was now expressed along with her rage at Sandra for abandoning her. She felt desperately that she must squash Sandra's rage and depression because she could not bear to discover her own. It seems likely that much of the rage came from a denied and repressed painful relationship Mrs. Casey must have had with her mother, whose ideal object quality had been retrospectively falsified, and from a repressed resentment Mr. Casey had with his mother but which he projected onto his sister, who fought on his behalf just as Sandra was doing now. Without intervention, these repressed aspects of the parents' relationships to their mothers would be replayed in relation to Sandra, who had identified with the projection and was indeed developing into a critical, controlling girl.

The couple may love a child for itself and respond empathically to its needs at many levels but be blocked in a limited segment.

Stuart and Maria Blackie had just had a girl called Teresa, who was a delightful, easy baby, but Maria was depressed. Stuart already had three grown-up girls from a former marriage and was happy with another, but Maria had wanted a boy and was depressed at not getting what she wanted. As treatment progressed, she explained the basis for this wish and her depression turned to anger. When she was 13, her menopausal mother had unexpectedly had a late baby, a boy, whom Maria cared for as a second mother. When she left home to go to college, he had been so hurt at the loss of her that he gave her the cold shoulder every time she returned home on vacation, a source of great pain for her. Having a baby boy would have offered her the opportunity to replace that loss, to be the number one mother, and to produce a male child as her mother had done. Stuart had been abandoned by his father when he was 2, and was then raised by his mother and sisters, so he was more comfortable with female children. He admitted that he was afraid he might not have known how to deal with a boy, but he did not realize how much he longed for a boy. That had to be repressed along with his longing for a father. At this point, they had adjusted to their situation, both loved the baby without reservation, Maria was no longer depressed, and they terminated treatment.

I saw them again when Teresa was 5. She had become very rebellious, fighting with her mother over what to wear, insisting on wearing an inappropriate party dress to school every day. I discovered as we talked that this was Teresa's only dress. Maria had bought her mainly unisex clothes. As a baby, she wore play suits and as a toddler overalls, and now, as a 5-year-old, she was supposed to wear dungarees and blue jeans to nursery school. Her clothes were quite feminine in style and color, but Teresa wanted dresses. Maria gave in, with Stuart's approval, and let Teresa pick out five dresses—all of them party dresses. It was an uneasy truce.

The next year, when Teresa was 6, Maria delivered a second child, after an anxious few years of secondary infertility. This one was a boy, and Maria was thrilled to get what she wanted. Stuart discovered that he was delighted to have a boy and suddenly remembered he had been depressed when his oldest girl, now 26, had been born. He helped Maria more with the baby's care than he had done with Teresa. Maria noticed that she was now more thrilled with Teresa, too, and was glad that she was a girl. Teresa and Maria got along much better, and Teresa became interested in wearing shorts and jeans as well as dresses.

The Blackies loved Teresa as a child but not specifically as a girl. They did not deny her femaleness, but unisex clothing kept alive the possibility of her being both boy and girl, just as the name Teresa had been chosen because it was the same in English (Stuart's family had been from England) or Spanish (Maria's family was from Nicaragua). Teresa had enough ego strength from positive interactions with her loving parents to enable her to fight for validation of her femininity and to force her parents to confront their unconscious suppression of it.

This final example shows how the parents' unconscious projective identification, together with the child-rearing practice, can determine the child's personality and identity. It also demonstrates the effect of the birth of a sibling, in this case experienced not as a trauma but as a relief. The repressed object relations return through the child where they may rest uneasily or be trapped to the detriment of the child. In health, however, the system will be open enough (or will be breached by therapy) so that through the child, the repressed may first be expressed and then reworked. Multiple future interactions at progressively higher levels of development modify the child's expectations of relationship, so that a more mature perception of the exciting and rejecting aspects of the ideal object can be held in consciousness without needing to be split off, projected, or identified with.

Lichtenstein (1961) has noted that the mother not only conveys to the child its identity but that the child is "the organ, the instrument for the fulfillment of the mother's unconscious needs" (p. 208). But we would say that the child serves this purpose for the couple, not just for its mother. The child becomes the organ and the fruit of their relationship. The child, in doing this, gives identity to its parents and receives identity as their child. However, the child's reaction to the couple's invention of their family shows that the infant, and later the child, does not accept this role passively. Children fully contribute personally and developmentally to their own identities and to the invention of the family in which they grow.

CHAPTER 6

The Infant's Reinvention of the Family

This chapter takes as its starting point an observation made by Fairbairn (1944). He noted that the oedipal situation is constructed around the two early split images of mother as an exciting figure and as a rejecting figure. When the child later tries to adjust at the same time to two ambivalent relationships (namely with mother and father) he or she seeks to simplify what seems to be an impossibly complex situation by assigning the exciting aspects of both mother and father onto one parent, and the rejecting aspects of both onto the other. In this way, the nature of each of the internal exciting and rejecting objects and the potential for relating to each parent are modified. Fairbairn notes, ". . . by so doing *the child constitutes the Oedipus situation for himself*" (p. 124). In this chapter we will reexamine these observations in light of both modern observational research on infant and child development and clinical experience.

The internal need to distort reality according to developmental demands causes the child to "invent" the family in a series of forms. We also use the word *invent* partly in the way Winnicott (1971b) used it to describe the way the child "invents" the transitional object and even the breast. While it is necessary that the mother put her breast there to be found, it is also necessary that the infant who finds it be left with the illusion of having created it. The invention of the family as the child grows is not, of course, a new, patentable invention. The family was there before, but it is a *reinvention* in which the infant does several new things that reshape the family so fundamentally that it becomes a new family, not only for the newcomer but for the other members as well. In fact, the failure of a family to reshape with the arrival of each child is a serious indicator of pathology.

Four Forms of Inventiveness

There are four ways in which infants invent their families:

1. Infants have to discover the already existing aspects of their families for themselves, as though they had invented them.
2. The presence and growth of its infant change the family so fundamentally that the infant can be said to invent the new form of the family.
3. Infants invent the family out of their limited ability to understand what they see. Their early ways of interpreting the family invoke splitting, employ the limited logic of infancy, are concrete, and tend to be rooted in bodily thinking and experiencing.
4. Infants reread their previous experience and history as they go, influenced by the mode and developments of their current stages. At each stage, they reinvent history retrospectively.

We will briefly describe the first two forms and elaborate at length on the third and fourth, which form the main argument of this chapter.

First, the infant has to discover already-existing aspects of family life by suddenly noticing, at certain developmentally determined moments, details that were there all along. The parents' relationship is one of these matters.

Second, the infant's presence and growth alter the family, and this reshaping creates new forms for them all. The family's newfound instability during the baby's growth creates a shared illusion that the baby is almost intentionally causing them all to change.

Third, and central to our discussion, the infant sees the family in ways invented as he or she grows. These serial views of the family are idiosyncratic because they are based on the infant's limited ability to think and formulate, as determined by chronological age and stage of development at the time of each new observation. They are also influenced by the issues that energize the infant at the time of each observation—for instance, on the heightening of separation and autonomy at age 2, and on the heightening of genital sexuality at 3 and 4.

There is something notable about this idiosyncratic skewing of the way a child sees things. Despite maturing cognitive capacities, in each new phase, the child still partly sees new issues in terms of the previous developmental mode of thinking and object relating. It is like trying to understand calculus by going back to algebra, or even by returning to geometry or simple arithmetic. Although these earlier mathematical disciplines may give a vocabulary, the new concepts have to be distorted to fit the old system. The growing child does just that. In attempting to understand growth in these archaic terms, children distort each new step, and this constitutes the first way in which they actively "invent" the meaning of events. Actually, they reinvent them regressively and explain new events to themselves as though they were variations of old situations. So an infant's explanations are inventions, although ones based on familiar principles. He or she seriously distorts things in the process, but this distortion tends to get split off, repressed, and remain unmodified within the personality. It continues to exert itself, first because it is repressed, and also because it came first and has the tenaciousness of early models. The early thinking is close to "bodily" thinking (i.e., to the bodily ways of organizing that precede thinking). These early explanations are shot through with the young child's bodily experience, which is immediate and unrefined by complex thought and verbalization.

As we have seen, the earliest of the infant's relationships are highly physical, consisting of holding and being held, molding to mother's body, and vocal and gaze interaction. They have all the primacy of physical bodily experience. Therefore, the bedrock to which the infant can revert is the physical aspect of relating. We know that these relationships with mother and father get inside the infant. In the beginning, the physical exchange organizes the child's biorhythms—the capacity to sustain alertness and to achieve some order in sleep/wake and hunger/satiation cycles. In addition, the emphasis on physical exchange remains relatively prominent through pre-oedipal development. So the regression to early forms of explanation means that the child's thinking reverts to being more based in the body.

In illustration, we quote a normal 3-year-old girl who said to her mother, "Mommy, my bottom is like an alligator." She had organized her new awareness of her vulva as being like her mouth and as related to oral aggression, which had been heightened by the birth of a brother when she was 2. An example of skewed development illustrating this point is given by a woman patient who was able to examine her confusion of sexual identity in analysis. She finally realized that it was based on early cloacal confusion that originated between the ages of 2½ and 4 when she experienced genital arousal in confusion with anal interactions with her mother, who gave her suppositories, and with her father, who beat her on the buttocks.

It is this regressive quality of the child's thinking to which we are referring in saying that it is in a sense the infant who invents the family, because there is a way in which the most interesting and important distortions that the child introduces into the family by the age of 3 or 4 derive from the thinking and sorting process carried forward from infancy. It is the child's infantile thought processes, dominated by body experience and by early splitting mechanisms, that most fundamentally distort oedipal reality and introduce the most inventiveness. We can partly agree with Fairbairn that the perceptions of both the exciting or "libidinal" parent and the frustrating, rejecting or "antilibidinal" parent are ultimately based on the relationship to mother. But we also have to modify this statement, based on what we are learning about fathers and babies.

The idea, however, that oedipal splitting occurs along sexual lines is introduced by yet another factor. This fourth kind of inventiveness comes from the genital sexualization of experience that occurs during phallic and oedipal development and constitutes a confusing distortion, stemming from the child's new growth, which supplements and modifies the retrospective invention. Melanie Klein (1935) held that the earliest oedipal phase occurs between 6 and 12 months, when the infant has an image of the parents together locked in intercourse, which he or she envies and attacks. Klein's description of the infant's image of the mother as having the father's penis inside her poses difficulties for many people. Observations of children in the first year do not lead us to think that the genitalia have such a special meaning for the child, neither its own genitalia nor those of the parents. Knowing that Melanie Klein took her observations from analytic work with children between 2½ and 5 years of age leads us to propose that what she observed is the sexualization of early experience by the phallic- and oedipal-aged child. In this stage, earlier experience is rewritten retrospectively. Thus, the advancing edge of the child's growth introduces the fourth inventive force influencing understanding of events and relationships. We suggest that it is these inventions that Klein reported, and that the children led her to report a sexualized version of early development.

Contributions from Infant Observation

We turn now to the findings of infant observation since the early 1970s. First, there is the finding from split-screen research and observation that the infant enters into mutually cued vocal and gaze interactions with its mother or primary caregiver from very early on, at least from 3 or 4 weeks. Very quickly, these develop a specificity to the mother, so that by the age of 3 months, the mother and infant's pattern can be distinctively differentiated from that of the infant with a stranger. Incidentally, these patterns can also be differentiated from the mother's earlier interactions with siblings when they were infants. Yogman (1982) compared infant–mother, infant–stranger, and infant–father interactions filmed with split-screen techniques that allowed for assessment of the pattern of interaction. He found infants' interactions with fathers have different characteristic patterns than those with mothers and perhaps, therefore, they indicate differentiated developmental functions.

Characteristically, the father–infant pattern was one of quicker arousal, a shorter plateau of intense arousal, and sometimes a briefer deceleration phase. This was somewhat similar to the infant's pattern with a stranger, and this similarity lends support to speculation that one function of the father is to be a partial outsider.* Up until this time, the father's role had been seen as partly similar to the mother's, as a secondary attachment figure. He was seen as serving primarily to secure or contain the whole process of making the attachment, to be a container for mother and infant, protecting them from the wider world. At the same time, he acted like a friendly fifth columnist, drawing the baby out of the protective symbiosis from the beginning. Yogman's findings that the baby is more excitable in interaction with father, with more sudden stimulation and more large-muscle motor games, suggest more specifically that the father is, from early on, less a part of the background or context of the baby's growth and existence, and more a special focus, a newfound object that the infant must continue to examine, while the mother provides the contextual background of the baby's existence. It is not only in the oedipal period, as was formerly thought, nor even in separation–individuation that the father gains special focus. From the beginning, he has a special role, even though it is not in genital terms. The father is more of an exciting object, the mother more of an object providing

---

*We are grateful to Dr. Charles Schwarzbeck for contributing to the development of our understanding about the differences in response to mother and father.

safety and offering limits—and therefore also a potentially rejecting or neglectful object. Let us examine this thesis further.

We have seen that with father, the infant invents a pattern of
achieving a high-intensity arousal cluster, then shifting away
quickly, averting gaze and withdrawing attention. This gives the
infant the experience, in object relation terms, of practicing a
relationship with the earliest libidinal, exciting object. The father
offers an experience of moving between the "ideal" (or good-
enough) object and the exciting object, while the mother forms
more of the model for the infant's modulation of the frustrating
object in juxtaposition with the aspect of the ideal that is more
quietly reassuring and limit-setting. We have in mind the frequent
observation that a father is usually greeted with excitement after an
absence, whereas the infant is rejecting and angry toward a mother
who returns from an absence. Thus, the difference we discern in the
two early cue-and-response patterns forms the basis for these two
polarities of interaction with objects, while the different use of the
two parents also promotes the development of the earliest interpersonal splitting mechanisms. From the earliest weeks, the infant
thus uses each parent a bit differently, but between the two of them
the infant can have the experience of moving between exciting and
frustrating objects while not losing or killing the relatively bad
object. We must now modify Fairbairn's statement that it is the
early mother who forms the base for oedipal splitting. The father
also plays a discrete role in the infant's earliest relationships, and
this influence on subsequent oedipal development must be given
equal consideration.

The Infant and the Parental Couple

We have looked at the differing functions of mother and father. But
from almost as early on, the infant has a relationship to the parents
as a pair. We know of no comparably extensive research that has
looked at the infant's reaction to both parents together and in
relation to each other. Mahler and colleagues (1975) note that the
infant "probably very early perceives a special relationship of the
father to the mother, the significance of which, during the separation–individuation phase and in the later preoedipal phase, we are
barely beginning to understand" (p. 91).

Melanie Klein's notion of an infantile oedipal configuration
reappeared in child observation literature in Ernest Abelin's papers

(1971, 1975). In his 1975 paper, "Some Further Observations and Comments on the Earliest Role of the Father," Abelin documented the pains of a boy, Michael, at 7½ months and 11 months of age, over seeing his parents hugging and of wanting to be in their bed. It was clear to Abelin that before 1 year of age Michael had begun to vie for the attention of more than one person. If Michael actually resented anyone as a rival, it was his mother. By 18 months, Michael was insistent on putting his parents together. When he was about to go for a walk with one parent, he would say "Daddy, too!" or "Mommy, too!" Abelin writes, "For him, there appeared to be no substitute for the parental couple" (p. 300). By 2 years he was playing at alternating triangular arrangements between himself and his parents.

In discussing this, Abelin focused on the child's wish both to put the parents together and to put himself together with them. He thought that the play was perhaps a defense against the anxiety concerning earlier triangulation. The play is described as having the quality of excitement that we would associate at a later age with sexual arousal. What seems important here, however, is the anti-anxiety effect of the use of the play with his parent's relationship as a way for this child to explore all the possibilities of being included and excluded, and to master all the permutations and feelings of the shifting situations in between. Abelin concludes:

Very early Michael began to acknowledge the *relationship with his parents as a couple.* After a fleeting indication of rivalry (with mother) a ritual game of "getting his parents together" developed at the onset of the rapprochment subphase. This is one of the many possible compromise solutions to avoid the full achievement of the anxiety-provoking "early triangulation" process. This process, if completed, would involve "identification with the rival parent," formation of a mental image of the self, and the positive cathexis of a neutralized intragroup relationship [p. 30].

In American psychoanalysis, these observations represent a new view. Even if we do not wish to interpret the early involvement of the infant with its parents as a pair—or of them simply as a group of three—as an oedipal event, the early triangulation hypothesis leads to the notion that the infant brings a prehistory of experience and involvement with triangles to the oedipal period. There is, then, a developmental line or history of the child's relating to triangular situations that comes to a focused point in the third or fourth years but that has an important prehistory beginning in early infancy. Because of the infant's need for splitting and joining of the pair, two parents are needed from then on.

During this period that predates an emphasis on triangular situations, it is dyadic relationships that occupy center stage. We might say that the main plot in the early acts consists of two dyadic relationships—one to mother and one to father—but that there is an important subplot. It is only in the oedipal phase that the triadic subplot suddenly comes to center stage. But until then, the early dyadic relationship gives the infant at least one and often two attachment figures. While sitting on mother, the child looks over to father, or sitting on father, looks at mother. The same occurs when the child uses mother or father as a perch from which to observe strangers. The situation is actually more complex because many infants have more than two attachment figures: mother, father, perhaps a grandparent, sibling, or housekeeper. At first, the infant seems to move between attachment figures or uses one to view the other from a distance. But late in the first year, at about 8 months, there is a cognitive shift, and the relationship between the attachment figures becomes important precisely because the infant understands more. In Piagetian terms, the infant has a sensorimotor substructure for the schema of the permanent object and of relationships between objects (Piaget 1962). This is also the period of Klein's "depressive position" (1935). The growth of the infant's new concern with the relationship to two figures corresponds chronologically and cognitively to the infant's primitive attempt to mend its splits and to hold in mind a single object that is both giving and depriving.

The Parental Couple and the Separation-Aged Child

We have seen that as the infant continues to mature, he or she attempts to deal with two individual, asymmetrical relationships. There are differentiated responses to each parent. There is, in addition, a wholly different response to the two of them together, and a set of anxieties about the meaning of their pairing. This offers additional exciting possibilities, and also offers additional possibilities for rejection and exclusion. We must include gender differentiation as one of the developmental issues that skews matters at this early stage. We are moving, at 18 months, well into the period in which boys have become boys, and girls are girls. By the age of 2, this should be solidified. An illustration of gender identity on its way to formation is provided by a vignette of a 15-month-old boy who touched his penis in what could not yet be called masturbation, and as he did so, said, "Daddy"—to the delight of his older sisters. Gender differentiation is supported or undermined by each parent and, as well, by the overall family constellation and by aspects of family sexualization of relationships as the child moves back and forth between two exciting objects. This should be both permitted and enjoyed with a view of the baby as a boy or as a girl. But some families may err and support femininity only, feminizing all boys, or perhaps only one particular boy because the niche for a masculine boy is already taken. In a well-differentiated family, the biological and psychological identities have a congruence, but the relationship to father for a boy is different from that to mother. The boy is valued for being "like me" by the father and for being "like your father whom I love" by mother. The situation should be reversed for the girl. When one parent has difficulty with this, the effects of the two parents may correct for each other or may add to each other.

For example, if a boy's father has a shaky sense of himself as a man and is anxious or threatened by his son's arrival, this may be compensated for by a wife who has a healthy regard for boys and men, and who can therefore support her son's masculinity. But, on the other hand, if the wife also has a fear of masculine identification—which is the reason she picked a shaky man to begin with—the boy's assumption of masculinity is in doubt. We can add to this a reminder that the couple's relationship to each other around these issues is also internalized by the growing boy or girl. It constitutes a separate and independently contributing factor. To caricature one such situation, if the mother is threatening and "castrating" to the father, cutting him down to size at every opportunity, the boy internalizes that both as a feature of relationships and as a significant factor having to do with his being a boy. If the mother is gentler, even though not very supportive of masculinity, that feature is taken inside differently from the situation with a castrating mother. All of this happens long before the oedipal era but is revived then as an important influence.

During the separation–individuation phase, the infant's perception of the parental relationship changes. Abelin (1971) noted that children in the second year invoke father when disappointed with mother, for instance, by calling him on the play telephone. Father is also used to buttress the child's efforts to become separate from mother, to support against the anxiety and loss involved (Greenspan 1982). But the child frequently must also differentiate from the two parents united as a couple. It is now, as words begin to develop, that the child begins to have an image of the specificity of the parents' shared relationship and how it is different, for example, from the one between parent and housekeeper, or parent and sibling. This awareness forms another precursor for the Oedipus situation, although again it is not specifically sexualized at this stage unless the parents contribute a climate of early sexualization that leaves its imprint on the child's development.

This is another invention of the child—the urge to leave the parental pair. It is both painful and necessary, and it is particularly important in setting the stage to eventually allow the child to take the loss of both objects when the same-sex, antilibidinal object can be allowed to win the opposite sex parent.

The Parental Couple and the Phallic-Narcissistic Child

Now we turn to the last pre-oedipal stage. Nagera (1975) has talked about first- and second-stage oedipal development for girls. In his view, in the first stage the little girl acts out her fantasy that she is a little boy and takes mother for her positive choice. Later, in the second stage, she reverts to acting like a girl, with father as her choice. Although this scenario gives credit to the girl's bisexuality, which we must consider, it is almost certainly wrong about the ordinary girl.

Edgcumbe and Burgner (1975) have taken issue with Nagera, giving research evidence to support their contention that the girl knows that she is a girl all along, and raising considerable doubt that a girl's fantasy of being a boy is a major factor in normal development or even in the development of most neurotic girls. They suggest that "the phallic-narcissistic phase" is a precursor to oedipal development proper. This phase is the last one in which dyadic relationships predominate and the first one in which the genitalia are the leading bodily edge of relationships. It is not that little girls act like boys but that girls and boys are not yet genitally differentiated. Both use their bodies, and now, for the first time, both use energized genitalia as the leading body part when they attempt to relate to both parents. Children do this in ways that are determined both by their own history and the history of the relationship to each parent up to that point. So the boys and girls both leap exhibitionistically, using the whole body to exhibit prowess to either parent. Both boys and girls exhibit their genitalia to mother and father, expecting admiration, and they look with a new interest at the genitalia of both sexes. When castration anxiety now suddenly drives both boy and girl, it is not yet centered on the hope the penis or vagina provides for being able to replace mother or father in the triangle. The child is still concerned mainly with self and object, with one-to-one relationships. The sexualized urge of the boy for his father, and of the girl for her mother, undoubtedly forms the substrate for later negative oedipal issues, that is, for the sexualized object that soon becomes a countercurrent to positive oedipal development. But in this earlier dyadic, phallic-narcissistic phase—in the normal child with a family that allows it—we usually see two strong and relatively unrelated positive urges. The phallic child is sexually driven toward each parent without a clear sense yet that these two longings are in any logical competition with each other.

At the same time, splitting is still going on, so that while the dual tracks of phallic appeal to each parent are gathering steam, the child is an experienced splitter, albeit one who has learned to split background safety and calm regulation onto mother, and excitement and locomotor stimulation onto father. We have seen that father has a long history by now as the exciting object. This means that when the cognitive leap occurs, the excitement is seen as vesting in "father-the-object" for the girl and in "being-like-daddy-the-exciting-object" for the boy. This goes along with the boy's investment of himself as being exciting and more active, for which he is biologically prepared, compared to the girl's movement into becoming more alluring to the exciting object.

In summary, the transition between these developmental stages—in which boys and girls are relatively alike and undifferentiated—is triggered by a new cognitive awareness in which three main currents now converge: First, the child has just become sexually energized; second, he or she becomes cognitively aware of genital differences and anxious about them when showing them off in order to woo the two parental external objects; third, the child now reinvokes splitting.

Splitting and the Reinvention of the Triangular Relationship

Splitting is an old mechanism for the child, as we have seen. Originally, he or she divides aspects of each relationship but invokes splitting to divide the parents from each other. The child has used splitting to do things like providing a new base for recovery when hurt by one primary object, moving back and forth between parents. And there has been the analogous but not identical process of dividing the parents from each other and putting them back together again. Now the child has new reason to split along sexual lines, because of genitally sexualized interest in the two objects that differentiates them and gives an entirely new impact to the old interest in pairing. The child develops a new investment in splitting all aspects of the exciting object onto the opposite-sex parent and then forming a pair with him or her until the threatened loss of the parental pair and of the same-sex parent becomes obvious. This loss, which the child actually engineers, slowly brings its own sadness and anxiety. If the parents resist being broken apart, the child feels confronted, and though perhaps angry or frustrated, less guilty. If the parents collude with the split for their own reasons, the child takes even more of a loss, bearing the guilt or dread of retaliation inherent in the secret knowledge of being responsible for the relationship and initiating this stage while they merely reacted. Therapeutically, it is a long task to uncover the defenses that cover this knowledge, but the introjection of the angry, retaliatory bad object that results from this outcome is no stranger to our therapeutic work.

In such a complex field, then, it is no wonder that the child moves to simplify the situation by marshaling good and bad, desired and feared objects, along sexual lines. The child has invented a complex situation. Although vastly more competent cognitively than a few months previously, the child, who has invented a complex situation, cannot resolve it readily and so once again settles the new world of understanding by reverting to the old way of understanding: splitting is reinvoked and used to settle the matter, but now it is sexualized splitting. That is the new invention of this developmental period. We can now see that it is not a question of whether splitting or repression is used that determines the level of development and, later, of pathology. It is the developmental level of the splitting, its extent, and the fate of the object that is treated by splitting that determines character and pathology.

A word about children's development in two very common situations that theory does not usually address. The oedipal situation is almost always discussed as though it is about first children with two parents. When there are already siblings in the family, the current theory would imply a disadvantage. In fact, younger children have a different experience that includes the presence of one or more brothers or sisters, who may sometimes compete for care but who also may act as caretakers. These form the basis for the early presence of one or more secondary "primary objects." We might say, for instance, that the child who is a younger sibling would have a less centered attachment with more early incursions into the exclusive relationship with mother but would also have more early experience with being drawn out, and with competition and cooperation. There seems to be less exclusive specialness of attention and admiration and, therefore, less fear of rejection by the bad object. Although oldest children may value a more exclusive focus, this is a mixed blessing with its own narcissistic issues and complications. There is often benefit from a modified field.

The other situation that must be mentioned is that of single-parent families, whether headed by mother or father. We will look at some of the clinical issues for these families in Chapter 16, but we need to consider the developmental issues here. We have reviewed the way fathers and mothers partly fulfill similar roles and partly have complementary roles. Of course, a single parent can fill a multiplicity of roles, but it is not easy. It may be that the absence of the father (or mother) makes the initial symbiosis tighter and the separation harder. It is likely that splitting of the single object into good and bad will be overworked, with a diminished opportunity to split and form two whole figures. In addition, there is the outright absence of the image of the parents as a pair. This represents a handicapping developmental deprivation in that a major way of perceiving and testing relationships is missing for the child. This deprivation can presumably be overcome through the use of compensatory pathways, as can physical handicaps. But alternate pathways are always harder to employ. A single parent is likely to have other relationships, which may fill in many of the missing functions. But relationships between parent and grandparent, lover, or siblings are different. We all know of the many children who long for their absent parents, who make up fantasies about them, who cling to shreds of evidence that they exist or care, or who invest heavily and promiscuously in substitutes, sometimes seemingly without loyalty for the parent who is there. There is both a fantasy accentuation of the exciting internal object and a heightened sense of the rejecting object. But it is the image of the parents together, in a relationship with its vicissitudes, strengths, and capacity to support the child's attachment and attacks, which is most complex. It is hardest for the single parent to represent the parental pair to the child before and during oedipal development.

The Genital Sexualization of Triangular Relationships

We will now try to integrate some of these currents. Let us start with Klein's graphic, and perhaps alarming, notion of the child's fantasy of the parents locked in intercourse, with a multiplicity of reactions to this fantasy. We have been discussing the experience the child has from very early on, at least from 7 to 8 months, of two parents together, sharing a great deal. Although we cannot confirm Klein's explanation that this experience is genital in the beginning, we can imagine where she got the idea and why it appears this way in the analysis of 3- or 4-year-olds. Psychological experience, and the relationship to mother and father, are, in the beginning, intensely physical experiences—what we have been characterizing as the psychosomatic partnership. So the oldest aspects of the relationship with the parent would tend to be couched by the child in physicalized terms, because this is the primary "language" of relationship for the child. It would be a kind of "physical intercourse," even if not specifically genital. By the time the child enters the phallic and oedipal phases, he or she constructs the genital issues in terms of the earlier experience of relationships, and at the same time, reconstructs the earlier experience in terms of the current interest in genital sexuality. There is, then, distortion of the past and the present as the past is reinvented in the new language of genital concern, and at the same time, the present is understood with the old way of thinking and organizing. Furthermore, the child's first way of understanding sexual matters, such as anatomy and intercourse, will tend to be remembered and stored away, drawn on, and relived because it is the first model, and has the particular power of models that are first laid down (Bowlby 1973b).

We can define oedipal development, then, as the genital sexualization of triangular relationships by the child. This occurs because of the concurrence of a new cognitive step in understanding genital differences in the phallic stage, a new sexualization of the genitals, and a shift of interest to triads and their vicissitudes. Suddenly, the child can no longer ignore the triangular implication of his or her wishes, feelings, and actions, because cognitive advancement makes this recognition inevitable. Both relationships are valued, as were both kinds of arousal clusters early on, and the child who has been having it both ways can suddenly no longer deny what he or she has been up to. Then, there are two separate issues of loss. To use the example of the girl, her threatened loss of her mother and concern for the aggression aimed at mother is one thing to deal with. But soon, the additional implication of the loss of the parental couple has to be dealt with. At this point, the defensive use of splitting becomes useful—as the bad object can be attacked and disposed of with considerably less concern, and the dyadic relationship between the girl and her father can be over-valued to make up for the loss of mother and for the loss of the parental pair as well.

The sexual energizing makes the child's splitting of the paren-tal pair occur, if at all possible, along sexual lines, but this does not produce pure gain for the child, even in fantasy. Not only is there the threatened retaliation and loss of the good parts of the rejected parent but there is the threat of the loss of the combined protecting and containing parental image—essentially, the loss of the inter-nalized family unit. The whole family is seen as intertwined, and the child is most safe and loved, inside that unit. Thus, the loss of the opposite-sex parent presents the child with the threat of the loss of the couple as a container, and therefore of the keystone of the family's holding capacity. This becomes an amplified threat in families in which oedipal splitting is strongly supported by the parents. Some examples will illustrate these developments.

A 4-year-old girl said to her mother, "I'm sorry, Mommy, I love Daddy more than you, but I love you as much as I can. When I am six, I will love you as much as Daddy."

This girl was struggling with the simple ambivalence about the fate of this dyadic relationship and, while acknowledging the sway of the situation, trying to make up for it and doing her best to shore up the family's holding capacity. A bit later she drew a picture of a banana and a feminine tree with a hole in it, labeled "Family Memos," indicating some work on the family unit (Fig. 6.1).

Another 4-year-old girl asked her mother to get a divorce and leave her with her father. Her 8-year-old sister intervened, saying, "Don't say that to Mommy. It's all right to think it, but don't say it."

By then, of course, the concern for the mother and for the couple had surfaced for the 8-year-old sister. But we also have the repeated experience of children of divorce from 4 or so through adolescence who respond to the divorce by trying to get their parents

Fig. 6.1 "Family Memos."

reunited, and who mourn the loss of the united parents as much as the loss of either of them individually. Frequently, siblings attempt to substitute their relationship to each other for the lost parental relationship, often saying out loud, "We are the only ones who share the particular experience of moving between the two parents."

Reactions to the Parental Pairing

TWO EXAMPLES FROM INDIVIDUAL PSYCHOANALYSIS

For many analytic patients, missing the parental pair constituted a point of real difficulty in their development.

In the first year of the analysis of one young woman, the only primal-scene episode recounted was as follows. When she was 13, her mother left her and her 16-year-old sister in the care of the sister's older boyfriend. During the weekend, the naive 13-year-old stumbled upon their so-called caretaker having intercourse with her sister. The patient associated the memory with her profound sense of an absence of parenting. After her parents' divorce, she rarely saw her father and experienced her mother as neglectful. Although she missed Mother and longed for Father, there was a more poignant sense of missing a sexual pair that could have cared for her. The sister and boyfriend were really an empty caricature of the lost parental pair. This patient's subsequent difficulty could be seen to stem in part from having to pair with her mother to provide not just a father but a pair for the family. For instance, she and Mother often together took care of this older sister. Later, the patient had difficulty both with confusion of sexual identity and in maintaining intimate relationships.

Another example comes from the analysis of a young man. Behind his long-standing feeling of being mistreated by his father stood a memory of father barring him from the room while mother nursed one of his many younger siblings. The patient was probably 3 or 4 in the memory, but the original displacements were from age 1 and 2. Although this seemed a typical oedipal scene in which father barred him from mother, the oedipal rendition represented a serious skewing of events. The patient felt deprived by both parents. He began analysis by blaming father for all of it. With increased tolerance for ambivalence, he could begin to be angry with mother as a "baby machine." Later in the analysis he presented primal-scene memories not just as a picture of his father barring him from Mother but of his own injured retreat from the exclusion by his parents as a pair. He had solved this by blaming Father, by narcissistically exhibiting himself, and by homosexual submission. With the progress of analysis, he became aware of a discrete sense of exclusion by his parents as a pair.

A FAMILY EXAMPLE

A final example comes from 7-year-old Laura whose parents, Mr. and Mrs. Wheeler, asked me to see her because of her poor school performance and her fear of monsters and of being kidnapped. Her fears became particularly acute if her parents were going out at bedtime. I knew Laura's family well, because I had seen the parents for sex therapy, couple therapy, and individual psychotherapy over the previous three years.

In the waiting room, Laura greeted me warmly, left her mother without hesitation, and skipped beside me to the playroom. She chatted easily and asked to play with some clay. When she had been molding it in her palms for a minute, she touched my hand to show how warm hers was and then immediately looked to the door and asked anxiously if anyone could come in—a clear reference to fearing her mother's possible intrusion on us. When I asked her to draw her family, she drew a line of smoke that connected a phallic house to a buxom sky (Fig. 6.2). This I took to say that the house and world were constituted by a sexualized relationship. She then added two families: one of three birds on one side of the house, and another of four octopuses on the other. She had a sister two years younger than herself, and she seemed to be struggling with her own place in the family.

This picture of her family turned out to be the invention of an

Fig. 6.2 Laura's house, family, and sky.

overexcited happiness—a defensive attempt of an early-latency child attempting to cover oedipal fears—for when we had a family meeting, she drew a quite different picture (Fig. 6.3). Here she drew a picture that she said was herself and her parents around a swimming pool. The likeness to a bed, her care to maintain equidistance between her parents, and the slip in drawing that turned one of her arms into a phallic protrusion made it clear that she saw herself coming between them in a sexual way. When we see these two pictures together, we can see that she viewed the world in a sexualized way and her relationship to her parents in sexual terms.

Her fears represented partly the repercussions of her sexualized wish to intrude on her parents. In the family, Father sexualized relationships overtly, while Mother, who feared sex, had withdrawn from it during Laura's early years.

In the family session the next week, Father drew the family, portraying himself as an exciting Indian with his three women in their teepees (Fig. 6.4). The glint in his Indian's eye leaves little doubt about his role as an exciting object. Laura's mother's family picture

Fig. 6.3 Laura and her parents at the pool.

Fig. 6.4 Father's Indian and teepees.

portrayed the angry, rejecting relationship between Mother and Laura. She put a fight between them at the center of a family break- fast scene (Fig. 6.5). This fight was also a displacement of similar struggles Mother had with Father. Thus, Laura's two sexualized pic- tures of family issues can be seen as sexualized versions of her own attempt to relate to her parents in the middle of their struggles. The intercourse between the house and sky in the first picture is one version. In the second picture, the way she comes between them with her prominent phallic arm tells us a good deal about current internal struggles that led to her fear of retaliation.

Earlier fears were soon revealed, however, and these make the point that the Wheeler family attempted to use sexualized relation- ships to overcome real fears about aggression and about threats that the family would split up. The actual rejection by the mother soon became clear, driven partly by Mother's fear of being replaced by Laura with Father. Laura soon drew a picture of a "witch mother," whom she paired with the monster who would come to harm her when her parents were not there for protection (Fig. 6.6). This mon- ster and witch are her internal "bad couple" and at the same time are a feared version of her parents' relationship.

Fig. 6.5 Mother's family fight.

Laura's negative view of herself is shown in a picture with the message, "I made a mess-up" (Fig. 6.7). For purposes of our discussion, this view of herself can be understood to mean that she is bad because she "messed up" her parents' sexual relationship. But these pictures also reveal that the sexualized versions of the phallic family, and later of the oedipal family when she was drawn to father in an excited way, are new editions of earlier rejecting and persecuting relationships to both parents, now split onto an exciting relationship to father and a frightening one with mother. And this earlier view of the rejecting and persecuting relationships had both a reality basis in the overall family's difficulty with fears of abandonment, and a fantasy basis in Laura's developmental contribution to these. Shortly after revealing these versions of the family, Laura and the family as a whole began to do much better.

A good deal of Laura's fear stemmed from the quite realistic fear that the parental relationship would fail, depriving her of the pairing of her parents. But Laura's fear that she would be left *entirely* alone was emphasized beyond reality, because she understood the par-

Fig. 6.6 Laura's "witch-mother and monster."

Fig. 6.7 Laura's "I made a mess-up."

ents' difficulty to be a result of her own oedipal intrusiveness. It was also built on the earlier experience of hostile mothering and inconsistent fathering, now understood by her as a genital oedipal crisis. Laura and both her parents all needed help with several levels of object-related difficulty that impinged on the oedipal difficulty. But for each of the three, this involved splitting all the fear and rejection onto maternal objects, handling pre-oedipal fears of abandonment and inadequate attachment through an oedipal disguise, and splitting positive and negative elements of the maternal object along sexual lines. All three shared a concern about the adequacy of the self when deprived of the parental pair, which was understood to be a result of their attacks as children on the pairing of their own parents. Early in Laura's growth, these fears had blocked oedipal development. Later, the fears became an organizer of the "invented" experience, a focus of the harm Laura feared her new sexual interest would do to her parents in destroying them as a couple. The clinical histories of the parents suggest that each of them had gone through a simliar process many years earlier.

Family therapy does not illustrate the individual developmental aspects of these distortions as well as analytic work. But we do get to see the sexualization of the early issues in the symptomatic picture of both parents and child, and we are able to see the *in vivo* interaction of child distortion and parental influence. Here, sexual symptoms were built out of pre-oedipal issues for Laura and for each of her parents. The culmination of therapy with this family was a well-constructed internalization of a family unit within each of the three symptomatic family members, and considerable resolution of both oedipal splitting and oedipal sexual distortion.

Another point is made in this example that we, as family therapists, cannot ignore. Although we have been emphasizing what the infant and child contributes to his or her own developmental story, external reality obviously shapes the situation. The way the infant shapes and distorts history by the "invention" and "reinvention" of it provides many possible explanations, but the family reality and the conscious and unconscious responses and directions from the parents and significant others provide an equal influence both on the child and on the unconscious character of the family.

Incest

In the terms in which we have been talking, incest would be the ultimate outcome of the child's invention. In reality, of course, it is not. The universal presence of these phenomena in the child's internal life make it clear that the parents' responsibility to shape reality is crucial. It is their obligation to provide safety from these fantasies. The child contributes a constant longing for both parents, with a sexualization predominantly of one of them after the fourth year. If the parents collude, for instance by inviting daughter to take mother's place with father, or if both parents encourage brother and sister to act out sexually in their place, the fate of the fantasy is severely altered. There are serious implications for mental structure and for internal object relations, especially for girls. The more the child grows up feeling the incestuous acting out has been all right, the more she will be sexually functional and the poorer her object relations will be. If the child is healthier and has a yearning for a higher level of object relations, growth will put her into increasing conflict about "oedipal" acting out, and, at least in our experience, the less sexually functional she is apt to be. This fundamental violation of oedipal development is a topic that can shed a great deal of light on the limits of the child's own contribution to his or her growth.

The Meeting of Reality and Fantasy

The early fears of the mother and father, as in the case of Laura's family, have everything to do with actualizing the child's way of seeing reality, and it is these realities we first try to understand in family therapy. In individual psychotherapy, we emphasize the patient's fantasy contribution as a way of interpreting reality, which causes things to keep happening. That is to say, we emphasize the way the patient keeps reinventing the family. But in family therapy, we also look for the ways the family keeps patterns going, which make the child's inventions inevitable. The two ways of viewing history are both true. They are mutually compatible and complementary. Although we have been emphasizing the child's inventiveness, we are also well aware that the invention finds what is actually there. In part, the most inventive aspect is the child's idea that he or she made it happen. This point recalls an adult man who had come to feel he wanted to split his parents apart and was himself responsible for their divorce. Years later his aging father admitted hating him as a 3-year-old for binding father and mother together by his existence.

What have we meant, then, in saying that the infant invents the oedipal situation, even though it does not predominate until the fourth year? We mean that there are three full previous years during which the infant and toddler has full experience, including bodily internalization, of the relationship each of the parents has to each other. In the early years, the child's overriding interest in that relationship runs throughout development, normally without any special conflict. To be sure, there are fits of splitting, of envy and jealousy, but while the child is becoming a boy or girl during those years, he or she does not see this as a conflict in the relationship with each parent or with the two of them combined unless the parents' own issues make it so prematurely.

Then comes the moment when dyadic development becomes sexualized and genital differences suddenly compel new awareness. These events summate, and the child suddenly sees other differences and is faced with having to solve the situation both of suffering when shut out of the relationship and of wishing to shut out. Earlier primal-scene episodes are now revived, or earlier feelings about the parents' relationship are reinterpreted in sexualized terms, splitting is reinvoked, and a bodily-sexual interpretation of things is imposed. The whole experience of three or more years of having two parents in a relationship is revived and reinterpreted. That is to say, it is reinvented. On the one hand, the information the 4-year-old uses has been stored in a language heavily invested with bodily experience. On the other hand, the new genital sexualization of relationships now causes the child to understand history as though it had always been one of genital bodily events. So the attempt to split good and bad along sexual lines happens, first, because splitting is revived. Second, the genital power of the 3- or 4-year-old makes gender identity and sexual relating especially significant. Third, it happens because the cognitive capacity of the child, although advancing rapidly, is still limited. Finally, the child now focuses on the parental pair as a competitor against his or her wish to pair with each parent. The exciting aspects of relationships to fathers as the secondary figures are now employed differently by boys than by girls. But both reach back to draw on the bodily interactions that the father introduced to the child from the earliest months. Now that we know the two different parent–infant kinds of relationships are stored in two different modes of relating, we can see further why the child values both parents and both modes of relating and is loathe to lose either relationship.

So the child makes it up, "eliminating" one parent, perhaps offering the mother or father a distant seat in a different generation, as Little Hans offered his father the chance to be a grandfather (Freud 1909). The child's invention relies on infantile experience of the physical relationship to the mother, which is already, at the advanced age of 4, the most significant experience of physical interpenetration with objects—the envied state that the child now tries to reinvent along sexual lines.

CHAPTER 7

Relevance of Group Relations Theory and Experience

The family therapy we practice is based on psychoanalysis, particularly on object relations. But psychoanalytic family theory should not be regarded as deriving solely from individual work. If anything, group analytic theory has been more influential in developing our approach. We rely especially on the formulations of Bion, a Kleinian analyst, who described group process in object relations terms, and of Ezriel, a group analyst at the Tavistock Clinic. But we have also been influenced by the work of Foulkes, a Freudian group analyst, as taught to us by our colleagues at the Group Analytic Institute in London, England. Group psychotherapy is a useful skill that transfers well to family therapy. Particularly, the experience of being a member in a process group is most useful in developing a sense of how one tends to deal with group situations and, by analogy, with one's family group. We have found this so useful that we seek experience in Tavistock or A. K. Rice group relations conferences as members, staff, or (in the case of D. E. S.) Director, to continually develop the group process expertise of our own work, and we recommend that our students do likewise (Rice 1965, Rioch 1970a). In this chapter, we will use such conference experience to illustrate the mutual relevance of group process understanding and family therapy.

Group Analysis: S. H. Foulkes

Foulkes (1948, 1964, Foulkes and Anthony 1965), a Freudian analyst, was a pioneer of group therapy. His main idea was that the individuals comprising the group can be spoken to as individuals with their own histories and uniqueness but can also be addressed as to their parts in the group. They can be viewed as nodes on a system of connections at which certain group stresses may emerge. In other words, the individual may thus express something for the group. "The group conductor," as he called the therapist, attempts to bear in mind each individual, including himself, as well as the group of which they are a part.

Group Analytic Approach to Families: Robin Skynner

Skynner (1976, 1981) applied Foulkes's ideas to work with families. He describes the group analytic features of his family work succinctly:

1. A simultaneous study of the part and the whole are not seen in any way as incompatible, nor is one seen as a denial or rejection of the other. . . . The therapist therefore has to listen to and observe both the individual contributions (which will all have their separate meanings, when taken together in relation to the individual concerned) and the communications of the group-as-a-whole (disregarding who says what, and taking it all together), constantly attempting to relate them and understand one in terms of the other.

2. The family, like the small group of strangers, is seen as possessing inherent potentials for constructive understanding and for facilitating growth and positive change, as well as for creating confusion and blocking development. The main task of the therapist is therefore seen, as in the artificial small group, as the facilitation of these inherent growth-enhancing factors, and the creation of circumstances in which they can emerge and operate most effectively.

3. Though the therapist has a responsibility for leading the individuals composing the group, and so must accept a position of responsibility and authority in relation to them, the wisdom and understanding potentially inherent in the group-as-a-whole will exceed his own; he must therefore be attentive to, and respect, what it is telling him about himself, and be willing to be corrected in the course of his work with it [1976, p. 192].

We find these premises to be fully compatible with our views, which, however, arise not from Foulkes but from Bion. Pines (1982), who also trained with Foulkes, has been interested in the role of mirroring in therapy and human development. He makes the point that the group functions as a mirror of its individual members, often detoxifying some of the more difficult aspects of interactions by spreading out the reflection among several other members. He likens this to the Medusa myth, in which a shield could absorb the toxic view of the Medusa in order that she could be attacked indirectly. We have been interested in applying this concept to family therapy. The developing child grows not only in relation to a mother, as traditional psychoanalytic theory often seems to suggest, but in a group, each member of which reflects back a different aspect of the child, who thus builds up a multi-faceted view of himself or herself from relations of different ages, sexes, roles, and responsibilities. The child has a view of the family group as a reflecting background in which to see the conglomerate significant other, the past, the present, and the future, while the family members, in turn, will look into the baby's eyes, searching the face for an image of their own heritage and destiny.

Group Relations Theory: Wilfred Bion

Bion (1961) developed group relations theory from his study of small work groups in a military setting (Rioch 1970b). As the group attempts to get on with its task, whether the task is the selection of a military officer, fighting in battle, or examining its own process, he noted that it tends to show not only work behavior but also dependent, aggressive, and sexual behavior that may support the work but that often disrupts it. He felt these other behaviors expressed unconscious needs for gratification and relief that were so strong and occurred with such visibility and predictability that they could be seen as the expression of subgroups coexisting with the work group. These subgroups are constituted not on the assumption that the task must be done but on the assumption that unconscious needs must be satisfied. Bion named these "basic assumption groups," and classified them as follows:

1. Dependency
2. Fight/flight
3. Pairing

Bion (1961) recognized that basic assumption groups could support or subvert the task; for instance, dependent behavior would be appropriate to a military setting where orders had to be accepted but inappropriate when the orders had to be carried out without supervision. Fighting would be called for during battle and flight would be appropriate to defeat, whereas fighting among themselves or going AWOL would disrupt the work group. Pairing could be helpful to the group when two were sent on a mission that required their paired skill, or where two created a strategy better than either could alone. But when two members paired to exclude and deskill the others, that would not promote the task. The group members would collude with such pairing in hopes that the pair would produce something to save the group from its difficulties, just as a couple may become pregnant hoping that the baby will be the savior of the marriage.

From studies of the large group, Turquet (1975) described merging or fusion as a defense against threatened personal identity, dislocation, alienation, and annihilation in the anxious situation of the anonymous large group. One type of fusion he described involved homogenization to remove differences so as to avoid envy.

In his study of the large group, Springmann (1976) was struck by the process of *fragmentation*. He noted that inconsistency and incoherence were major obstacles to understanding and suggested that this type of basic assumption functioning was more fundamental than the three Bion had outlined from the study of the small group. He proposed that fragmentation was an attempt to fractionate the potentiated aggression of the horde and to defend the leader against destructive attack so as to maintain the hope of dependency upon him. Hopper (1977), in response to Springmann, agreed that social fragmentation occurred as "a way of protecting the conductor from the colossal rage of a collection of people" (p. 10). He felt that the rage developed when wishes for dependency were not met. In recent conversation with Hopper, we learned that he has further studied the coherence/incoherence dimension. Drawing from the concepts of fusion described by Turquet and of bizarre objects introduced by Bion (1967), Hopper now hypothesizes that merging phenomena occur as a defense against separation and individuation to avoid the envy that comes with recognition of differences in endowment. Individual group members fear that the resulting envy will be so malignant and of such magnitude that it could fragment the object or the self. When it is projected into the group to keep the individual sane, the projections are fragmenting to the group experience and wreak havoc with coherence and consistency. They are then experienced as bizarre, meaningless attacks on meaning.

Group Transference: Henry Ezriel

Like Bion, a Kleinian analyst, Ezriel (1950) also viewed the group situation in object relations terms. He described how each member projects his "unconscious phantasy-objects" upon various other group members—each of whom will stay in the assigned role only if it coincides with his own unconscious fantasy and "will try to twist the discussion *until the real group does correspond to his phantasy group*" (p. 68). Ezriel restricted his interventions to here-and-now transference interpretation that focused on how the group was behaving toward him. He tried to figure out what the group wanted from him (which he called "the required object relationship"), what the group could not bear to want from him ("the avoided object relationship," which the required relationship obscured), and the disastrous consequences that the group feared would occur if the required relationship needs were not satisfied ("the calamitous object relationship") (1952). Every interpretation included his estimate of the feared calamity, which he called the "because clause," showing the group why it had to adopt one course of behavior and avoid another (1952). Ezriel felt that the sharing of this hypothesis allowed reality testing to begin and found that thereafter the avoided object relationship could emerge in less disguised form. Integrating this in our work with Fairbairn's theory, we have noticed that the required relationship could be either a libidinal object relationship being used to avoid an antilibidinal object relationship or vice versa, and that the calamity can be viewed as some version of the intolerable state of infant helplessness with organismic panic and threat to survival. We have been impressed with the usefulness of the "because clause" in allowing the work group to grapple with its present reality and to rework the influence of past experience in the light of more mature thinking and relating.

The Group Interpretive Approach to Families: Roger Shapiro and John Zinner

Roger Shapiro and John Zinner, now colleagues at the Washington School of Psychiatry, applied Bion's theory to their study of the families of adolescent inpatients in a clinical research project directed by Shapiro (1979) at the National Institute of Mental Health in the 1960s and early 1970s. They described the family as a work

group facing a lifelong series of developmental tasks that are interfered with by basic assumption group functioning, which they
called shared family unconscious assumptions, generated by in-
stinctive needs and defensive requirements.

Zinner and R. Shapiro (1974) also developed the concept of the
family group as a single psychic entity in which characteristics of
the group may be denied but then emerge in one of its individuals
through the process of projective identification. This is the basis
for the familiar process of scapegoating, particularly obvious when
the scapegoat carries all the confusion and becomes the index
patient. Shapiro (1979) and his group also applied Kernberg's theory
of borderline personality (1975) to their experience with the families of borderline adolescents. Zinner and E. Shapiro (1975) reported that the families, too, are characterized by splitting of those
self and object representations that are libidinal from those that are
aggressive. They wrote, "Within the family group, attributes of
'goodness' (providing, gratifying, loving) and 'badness' (depriving,
punishing, hating) are separated one from the other and parcelled
out to different members so that each family member appears
relatively pre-ambivalent and single-minded in his relation to the
troubled adolescent" (p. 104). Splitting arises as a defense against
the shared family unconscious assumption that hating destroys the
loved object.

The Development of Unconscious Assumptions

Bion (1961) suggested that each individual personality contributed
unconsciously to the group process by expressing its characteristic
"valency" for certain types of involvement. Valency is "the individual's readiness to enter into combination with the group in making
and acting on the basic assumptions" (p. 116). It is "a spontaneous
unconscious function of the gregarious quality in the personality
of man" (p. 136). An individual's valency in one direction is aug-
mented by association with similar or complementary valencies in
other personalities. Drawn together by their similar and complementary valencies, they then function as a group, seeking the
satisfaction of their shared unconscious needs. Our experience with
families throws light on these processes.

These valencies developed in the individual in the first place
during growth in the family group, a group that is beset by anxiety,
competing needs, and jobs to be done like any other. Thus, the

family group process contributed to and was influenced by the developing personalities within it. The valencies or, in family analytic language, transferences to each other within the group and to other groups outside are formed and are continuously being reinforced or modified as the individuals experience each other at progressively higher levels of development. Often, however, this reworking is blocked because of anxiety and the shared defenses against it. Thus, in protecting itself against perceived threat, the family perpetuates fixed unconscious object relations systems that prevent further growth.

The family that comes for treatment is a small group with a task. It has to support its members through interrelated developmental phases from birth to maturity and from generativity to death. It also aims to ensure reproduction. Thus, it functions on behalf of both the individual and the society whose culture it carries and whose aims for perpetuity it expresses biologically. Like any work group described by Bion, the family finds some way to get on with this task. It also, however, has the same tendency for group action to occur not only in relation to the task but also in response to the shared unconscious needs of its members for dependency, aggressive outlet (or escape from it), and sexual pairing (in rivalry with, or in default by, the parents as the marital, reproductive couple). These needs give rise to the three types of group process described by Bion as the dependency, fight/flight, and pairing basic assumption groups, and to the fusion basic assumption described by Turquet and amplified by Springmann and Hopper to include fragmentation. In the family, the basic assumption group processes sometimes support the work group but at other times interfere when they are not appropriate to the current developmental phase.

For instance, dependency assumption behavior is consonant with the task of supporting the family members through crises of life and death, whereas fight/flight phenomena are appropriate to states of separation and individuation and to the defense of the family against attack from other groups or even from illness or stress. Pairing assumptions support the unity of the marital couple, and pairing of a parent and child can support the child's learning or can help the child to recover from an injury. But pairing of a parent and a child at bedtime, where the parent is continually drawn to the sleepless child during the night, clearly attacks the parents' pairing. The parents are separated and cannot do their work of maintaining their marital relationship through private talking, relaxing alone, and enjoying sexual intercourse. Here one kind of pairing that is based in a dependency family assumption precludes the genital parental pairing that is part of the family's work.

Fusion basic assumption group functioning in families supports harmony, empathic identifications, and togetherness, appropriate to the early infant–mother bonding. When dominated by this principle at later stages, the family uses fusion to deny difference, conflict, and loss. Others have described this as *enmeshment* (Bowen, 1977). Fission basic assumption group functioning promotes conflict, differences of opinion, and divergent goals, but in the process, as Hopper suggests, object relations are so attacked that they are split up into many bizarre object bits. The threatened family regresses to primitive merging (fusion) or splintering (fission) in order to remain safe. In either case, understanding and progress are blocked. In fusion, merging substitutes for understanding and conflict resolution, whereas in fission, conflict attacks linking and murders understanding. These processes predominate, sometimes in alternation, in psychotic families in response to fear that an integrated experience will lead to annihilation of the self, of the other, and of the family.

In family work, we usually deal with a nuclear family—a small group that represents a much larger extended family group of which it is a part. Furthermore, the inner object relations set of the family has many layers corresponding not only to earlier developmental levels but also to the transgenerational projection of object relations derived from relationships to grandparents, parents, aunts, uncles, cousins, and so on. We do not find it odd that we might experience phenomena more typical of the large group in the small family group setting. In the family, the small group contains the large group. All families struggle with these phenomena and find ways to defend against their breakthrough most of the time. But with families that demonstrate psychotic functioning, we frequently see processes of both fusion and fragmentation.

This leads us to postulate another mode of basic assumption functioning more primitive than those Bion described. We call this the *fusion-fission basic assumption.* For purposes of application to family therapy, we propose a hierarchy of basic assumption group functioning as follows:

1. Fusion/fission
2. Dependency

3. Fight/flight
4. Pairing

As D. E. S. (1982) has pointed out, these follow the traditional psychosocial steps of development, from an early fused stage (fusion) with paranoid-schizoid anxiety (fission) through oral (dependent), anal (fight/flight), and genital (pairing) to oedipal (cooperative work) stages.

Family therapy, using a group interpretive approach (Shapiro 1979, Skynner 1976), can enable the family that is stuck to learn to detect the basic assumption group interference and to attend to their underlying unconscious needs and fears, so that they no longer interfere with the family's ability to carry on with its task.

Group Relations Experience and Family Therapy

It seems to us, reading group theory and working with families (or even just living in them) that the parallels fit. Further evidence comes from an innovative technique for studying family dynamics using group therapy: Kraft and Marcus and colleagues (1959) referred family members each to different therapeutic groups. When the therapists compared notes, they found that each family member reenacted within the therapeutic group the behavior habitually displayed within the family group.

This congruence is not fully convincing, however, until we have been powerfully affected by experiencing the theory in action. When we are caught up in a basic assumption group process with others who are willing to recognize their part, too, we experience a state of arousal, due, we think, to the mobilization of unconscious fantasy, that facilitates active personal learning about valencies, group process, and attention to task. The laboratory in which to have this learning experience is at one of the A. K. Rice group relations conferences (Rice 1965), based on the Tavistock model and introduced in the United States by Margaret Rioch (1970a), or the Tavistock conferences in Great Britain. The conferences are designed to enable members to examine how they exercise authority in the pursuit of the task of understanding self and group functioning as the conference proceeds through a series of different group events. These include a series of small group meetings of stable membership with a consultant to their group process, a series of more confusing large group meetings, and an intergroup event in which the membership decides for itself whether or how to form groups and how to study the relationship between groups, including the problem of how to relate to the group of consultants who are managing the event and available for consultation. Thus, the conference is a laboratory for the examination of processes that are representative of those that occur in the world of work, neighborhood, society, and nations. We have also viewed it as a recreation of the family, with its interrelated subgroups and extended family groups.

The conference is based not only on Bion's group relations theory but on systems theory as well, which we also find helpful for family work. Miller and Rice (1967) described an enterprise as a complex, well-regulated system of interrelated, clearly defined activities that had to do with taking in raw material from the environment, processing it in various ways, and returning it as a finished product. "Like a system of activities, the individual or a group may be seen as an open system, which exists and can exist only through processes of exchange with the environment" (p. 14). We see the family as an enterprise taking in the raw material of the genetic and social pools as the self-selected couple engage in the conception and bearing of children, then move into the maintenance and processing phase while the children are in the latency and preteen years and, after a finishing-off phase during adolescence, deliver the autonomous adult to the world of work or further education and peer and sexual relationships. Simultaneously, the family enterprise is promoting the development of mature parents who are able to let their children go and to accept the next stage of their own life cycle, with greater emphasis on the couple's relationship, work, and leisure.

The family is an open system in communication with other groups in the extended family, as well as with other families and with work, school, and community groups in its environment. The family makes transactions with these other groups across its boundary. Within the family, boundaries delineate various activities and subgroups or task forces. A generational boundary separates the children and parents. In systems theory, because the enterprise has to relate to its environment to survive and yet must attend to itself to remain safe, the tensions of transactions at this boundary are particularly emphasized. Features of the boundary tend to reflect the interior of the group that it bounds. Behavior between groups reflects not only their own characteristics but also their fantasies about the other groups.

Like the small group at the A. K. Rice or Tavistock conferences, the family is a group of individuals relating to each other
intensively, sharing a history, and existing in relation to other
small groups with similar and different histories. Like the elec-
tively formed group in the intergroup event, the family must deal
with other groups: its extended family, social agencies, commercial
enterprises, government, schools, and the like. Tavistock conference experience can enhance the therapist's ability to help the
family set itself in its historical and sociocultural context.

Although, in one sense, "family" may refer to quite a large
group, the family that presents itself for treatment is usually of
small group size. Its membership is relatively stable over long
periods of time, with individual members interdependent as they
move together through interrelated developmental phases from
birth to maturity and from generativity to death. Unlike the newly
formed conference small group, the individual members of the
family group already have the others there with whom to engage in
their characteristic ways. In the small group of the conference, each
of us with our individual tendencies for characteristic interactions,
or "valencies" as Bion called them, find new people with complementary valencies with whom to engage in behavior typical of such
groups, and of us in our family groups.

Growing up in a family provides the individual with a set of
changing but constant personal relationships with which he or she
lives in the everyday sense and that form the basis for an intrapsychic structure of expected relationships between self and others.
These relationships become more or less modified by reality, but
their earlier versions are still there to be reinvoked under stress.
Each person arriving at a Tavistock or A. K. Rice conference develops such unconscious relationships within the group. It is the mix
of personal valencies of the members for such relationships that
determines the predominant assumptions of the group unconscious.

We had the opportunity to learn very specifically about this
during an innovative group relations conference we have designed,
which is modified from the Tavistock model to focus not on authority but on teaching and learning (Scharff and Scharff 1979).
The design includes small groups, large groups, and some new
events, among them one called "The Inner Group in the Small
Group," in which the task is to recall memories of teaching and
learning experiences from early childhood and to examine ways in
which these influence present teaching and learning. An example

from one of these conferences shows how the conference group experiences derive from early group experience in the family of origin.

In an opening small group I [J. S. S.] consulted to, an older white man was directing and teaching the group very actively, which younger members encouraged because they invested him with knowledge and saw themselves as receptacles. A young black man became very persistent in denouncing the group as a waste of time; he felt he would rather be learning from black political figures at a rally. It was interpreted to the group that while part of the group was rejecting the assumption that all knowledge was invested in the teacher, it was at the same time invoking other, better teachers to depend on, because of its fear of black and white, man and woman working creatively to teach and learn from each other. The black man pounced verbally on a silent white woman and tried to get some words out of her. It seemed to me the group was afraid that I, as a woman consultant, could not or would not offer a learning experience and so turned to feeding on an older man "teacher" or to raping with questions the silence of the woman member.

Let us leave the small group event there and move on to the next day's event, "The Inner Group in the Small Group," one of our modifications of the basic Tavistock model.

The older white man talked proudly of his memories of his father, who was still alive and whom he felt he had still so little to teach. The black man, who had no father, talked of his mother, who never seemed to listen to him. He got into fights with her because he complained she didn't do things as well as his grandmother, who was the one *he* wanted to be like. The group learned to make the link between these memories and the previous day's group and to see how the older white man had been unconsciously fit to be chosen as a leader by the group because of his wish to be in his father's position. The black man had expressed the group's disappointment in the group as a frustrating mother (the group being an extension of the ungratifying consultant, too), and his preference for effective political activists was motivated by his love for his grandmother. He was the one to reject the notion of the all-giving father as a group dependency assumption alternative and to introduce the fight/flight imagery of the political rally.

Further illustration of the shaping of group experience by early life can be seen by focusing on the silent woman mentioned earlier. She was viewed by the group as the surrogate consultant, always outside the membership.

During the inner group event, she recalled being excluded by her mother after her baby brother was born. Another group member said he learned from that memory that she must feel removed from the group in the same way. In striking contrast to her withdrawn silence, she then talked about her nonparticipation at such length that another relatively quiet woman angrily burst out that she felt very excluded, as if the one talking now was the loved baby brother in the center of attention.

These two women shared a tendency to withdraw from competition. On behalf of the group, they expressed flight into silence, which quickly changed to fight for recognition. Because men were seen as the ones with words and wisdom, this group dynamic was a basic assumption process to defend against anxieties about male-female cooperation leading not to work but to babies. This issue was heightened by the design of the event, and by the two consultants being married.

Our next example is taken from a small group experience in a standard Tavistock-model group relations conference, focused on issues of authority and leadership, which J. S. S. attended. It illustrates how major trauma of a personal or sociocultural nature can invade the boundary of the here and now of the group and can threaten the clarity of the task.

Our small group worked as one might expect, feeling angry at the consultant for criticizing our efforts to stay on task, trying to integrate learning from the small group with other events, yet flying off the point and pairing instead of working, and so on. We would examine all this and get back on task until Rosh Hashanah, when an undercurrent of tension between a German and an Israeli became full-blown. The Israeli was deeply depressed. He had seen his family killed by Nazis, and as he held his father dying in his arms, he promised him that he would never speak to a German in his entire life. For twenty years he had lived in Israel and kept his promise, but in the group, he was now confronted with a dilemma. In telling this to the group, he was speaking to a German. The frozen-faced, bull-necked German showed less sympathy than did the others in the group and adamantly maintained that he was not responsible for the acts of his forefathers. The group continued to work, but we were always aware of this unresolved problem. It invoked in the group feelings of horror, rage, and guilt of such intensity that it seemed we could never overcome it. The German maintained the group was using the difficulty of the pair as a defense against further work and refused to collude by getting involved in discussion. We got away from the problem during intergroup events, and occasionally we got on to other issues, but they were overshadowed: the work on them, although quite substantial, felt hollow.

On Yom Kippur, which the Israeli noted was the Day of Atonement, he said he had seen the German working like the others in the group and realized he could work with him, too, if he forgave himself, his father for inhibiting his learning, and the present-day Germans for the sins of their fathers. The German had done little to earn such forgiveness, yet his uncompromising attitude may have been crucial. To my surprise, he shed a tear and became a much more flexible member of the group. We were then able to turn with relief to the conference issues in general, which seemed necessary but somewhat mundane.

I, as a Scot, shared in a persisting national attitude of fierce independence to threats of English oppression in earlier centuries. Through songs and family stories, I also shared in the British World War II spirit of determined opposition to Hitler, and I had to admit painfully to some lingering anti-German feeling. Thus I felt deeply for the Israeli, and yet I had to agree with the German that the perpetuation of the trauma by allowing it to invade the work of the group was a defense. Certainly it was defending against other anxieties of religious and racial difference among other group members that could not then be faced. But until it was accepted by the group and dealt with, nothing could change and no other work felt real. This inhibition of work can occur in families, too, where interpretation and working through of resistance to dealing with trauma and pain is needed before reality can be faced.

EXPERIENCE AT THE BOUNDARY

In group relations conferences, we learn to examine processes at the boundary. We see how the surface of the group reflects its inner structure and dynamics. In family therapy, we can apply this sensitivity to boundary issues in many areas of family interaction with institutions in the outside world. Two of the most interesting areas for study are the boundary between family and therapist in the first visit, and the boundary between the presenting nuclear family and extended family groups.

Mr. and Mrs. Aspen were concerned about their prepubescent 12-year-old girl, Jane, who although a "neat kid" who had friends and did well at school was troubled by outbursts of panic and rage when she came home. She could not be comforted or calmed down until the attack ran its course or her father came home. Her 17-year-old brother, Malcolm, was an apparently successful, self-reliant adolescent, who was rather rejecting of his kid sister's childishness because he had suddenly had a late growth spurt and was now more interested in sports and dating. The parents were very articulate in describing their much-loved but worrisome child, and at the same time were deciding whether to bring her to see me at all. They described her as wonderful, sensitive, so wise, yet troubled. In later sessions, I [J. S. S.] would hear them describe me as wonderful and intuitive, and yet they were crippled by anxiety that I would "screw them" by missing sessions or charging higher fees than was customary. I recognized this as a transference to the previous generation but could not yet make sense of it.

The session continued, and I learned that Jane's talent was writing poetry. Samples of her written work proved her ability to be expressive, yet she could not talk about what was bothering her to her parents. In her individual diagnostic session she could not talk to me at all and experienced me as seductive, tempting her to say things she didn't want to. I was affected by the family's distrust of me, and at the same time, Jane reminded me of two sexually abused girls I had treated.

In a family diagnostic meeting, Jane was much more relaxed and contributed freely to family discussion and drawing. I could see that this was a family with a great deal of affection for each other, an optimistic view of life and its possibilities, intellectual strength, and a great deal of difficulty being in conflict with each other. There was also a view of Jane as being different from the others, and a mild squabble developed over who she was like, with Mother denying that she was anything like Father's side of the family. She did look very much like her dark-skinned Mexican mother, whereas Malcolm was fair like his father. Mother kept the child very close to her, sheltering and protecting her and speaking for her. Occasionally, she would get frustrated by her wordlessness but felt guilty about her anger.

I wondered aloud with the family about there being a family fantasy that this child, Jane, was not her father's child, that she was only her mother's child. I was silently speculating about the origin of this fantasy in, say, an affair Mother may have had or an unresolved oedipal attachment between Mother and her father. Mother and Father later told me privately that there had been an affair during their marriage and that there had been not just an oedipal fantasy but an incestuous reality between Mother and her father.

Now the family transference first expressed at the boundary between family and therapist in the diagnostic phase could be explored. The hypothesis that this was a transference to authority and the previous generation could be confirmed and clarified. On Mother's side, her brilliant father had seduced her; on Father's side, his powerful, rich parents kept him controlled by gifts of money he could not touch. The parents could follow how this had affected their relationship with me and could see how it might be similarly affecting their children, but they could not and would not share the information with the children.

Mother had begun to admit to herself only recently in therapy that she had had intercourse with her father and was still ashamed and upset by it. Her mother had ignored hints about it and suppressed knowledge of it. Mrs. Aspen could not tell this to her children; she had only just begun to tell it to herself, her husband, and me. In subsequent family therapy, I continued to work with them, knowing of this history but respecting her need for secrecy at the present time. Just as in the small group with the Israeli and the German, I found that work of a useful sort could be done, but we could not address the underlying issue directly. Somewhat later in therapy the following event brought the problem of nonrevelation to a head.

One weekend, relatives were driving in from all over to celebrate the son's graduation, but Mother's parents did not come, as usual. Malcolm persisted in asking his mother why they never came. Normally very articulate, the mother said, "I don't know, they don't want to see me." (Mother had been forced to promise her father she would never tell their secret.) Malcolm asked again, "Why don't they?" "I don't know. I don't know," said Mother in a way that was strikingly like Jane's way of not answering questions, both of them curled up and hugging themselves, shaking their heads and seeming confused.

I pointed out that Mrs. Aspen and Jane shared a way of not knowing, when knowledge would be painful to them. Mrs. Aspen said, "But I think of myself as someone my children can tell anything, anything." Jane, normally very quiet, shouted in tears to her mother, "You would never understand!" Mother tried to persuade her she could tell her anything, but spoke for so long as to defuse the moment and prevent her child from saying more. It seemed possible to me that Jane, too, may have been sexually abused by her grandfather, yet her parents never thought of this, much as Mrs. Aspen's mother had ignored hints from her. It is equally possible that Jane had not been sexually abused by him but had taken on a nameless, wordless anxiety by identifying with projected anxious, shameful, excited, and guilty parts of her mother with whom she was at some level still fused.

The family kept it this way because to separate from Jane would cause Mother to relive the unbearable pain of the loss of the fantasied oedipal baby she might have borne from union with her father. With this fantasy baby she had identified her look-alike Jane. Whether sexual trauma had been repeated in this generation or not, the invasion of the boundary of family safety was such that the family task could not get done. The 12-year-old could not be helped to move into puberty without pathological anxiety, and the parents could not be productive in the independent areas of their careers.

As family therapists, we are aware of the significance of family secrets (Pincus and Dare 1978). Telling the family secret does not magically restore the family to health. But we notice that unless it is dealt with, nothing else seems real. In Tavistock conferences, we have often seen that secret relationships disturb the task: problems among staff tend to reappear in the membership in fantasy or reenactment. In this family, the dreaded secret had been kept until sexual development was at the leading edge of the children's growth in adolescence. Then it was shared among parents and therapist, but it's still being kept secret from the children blocked our further understanding. It was not possible to say whether the family was dealing with a reenactment or a fantasy. All that could be said was that knowledge of certain matters was expected to be devastating, a derivative of the family assumption that sexual knowledge would be destructively incestuous.

Dependency assumptive group functioning was well illustrated in the family. Mr. Aspen's family had excited a dependency conflict in him by giving large gifts of money that he was not, however, allowed to control. Mrs. Aspen had never been able to depend on her parents for a safe environment. Together, they valued family closeness and harmony and generosity to each other. They put a high priority on building their family as a safe place in which to recover from the world. During the early child-rearing years, the dependency assumptive group life fostered the task of holding, feeding, and providing for helpless children. When the children became adolescent, this aspect of family functioning moved toward meeting age-appropriate dependency needs for being driven around, for organizing activities, and for having homework checked. The homework checking was useful in promoting excellent grades, but it became apparent that what was lacking was the parents' ability to advance *themselves* at work, and to allow the children to have confidence in their *own* ability. There was a retreat from the successful use of aggression.

Fight/flight mechanisms were rarely seen in the family as a group but were expressed on their behalf by Jane's tantrums. Neither parent wanted to deal with the children's expected rage at their possibly frustrating the children's dependency, nor at their own rage about their dependency needs not having been met in their own families. If rage should be expressed, they feared that it would kill, and so it was suppressed and projected. Jane was the one to express rage, panic, and thoughts of dying in the isolated panic attacks no one understood. To relieve Jane of her symptoms, the family would have to own these destructive feelings.

Despite the mother's negative experience of pairing, the parents were able to maintain their marital and sexual relationship. Pairing of an unhelpful sort could be seen when Mother was too protective of Jane, holding her and speaking for her. It did not have a sexual aspect to it, as if to say that such an incestuous pairing would never occur, but dependent needs for pairing of child and parent had now to be recognized and satisfied without accompanying sexual exploitation. The sibling pairing that had been pleasurable for brother and sister before he became a sexually mature young man was sadly interrupted. They could no longer support and enjoy each other because of the family unconscious assumption that pairing between child and male adult would be disastrously sexual.

It seemed that that assumption also accounted for Mother's closeness to Jane, ensuring that she did not get too close to her father. Incidentally, the reason that Mother did not become overattached to and identified with Malcolm as a baby was not only because he was a boy but also because he felt so separate from her, unlike Jane. He had his father's coloring and looked even more like Father's father. He was also a self-contained, nonanxious baby who simply did not seem vulnerable to his mother's states of mind, whereas Jane was much more cuddly and needy of her mother, and more sensitive to her mood.

GENERATIONAL TRANSMISSION ACROSS THE FAMILY BOUNDARY

Jane's panic attacks began at the age of 15 months after a visit with her mother to her family home. No incidents of sexual abuse were suspected, but the infant's personal boundary was nonetheless invaded so that anxiety could no longer be managed. This occurred at an age when she would have been developmentally practicing for separation and individuation from her mother, and therefore would be vulnerable to picking up anxiety about autonomy. Her anxiety was amplified rather than modified by her mother, who was finding the visit stressful as the old themes of guilt, sexual excitement, and exclusion of her mother revisited Mrs. Aspen. Themes from that branch of the family were permanently highlighted in the mother-child relationship from then on but did not come up for review until adolescence brought to urgent attention issues of separation and sexual relatedness.

The Aspen family case illustrates the process of transmission of past experience. We have tried to show how this happens, not in any magical or mystical way but through the functioning of the inner object relationships. These inner object relationships are built up as an inner working model of how the self can expect to engage in relationships. The model includes the history of the way the self actually did relate to the parents, the way the parents expect the child to be able to relate to others, and the way the family group relates to the previous generation and the community. This model expands our concept of transference from the narrow definition, referring to the patient's distorted perception of the analyst, to the broader definition of transference as a reciprocal interaction among parts of the self, with parts of another self in multiple combinations, some more and some less conducive to creative, cooperative work. Object relations theory, group theory, and systems theory come together to provide a model of the family as a group that is part of a wider system. Within the group are subsystems, not just of activities or task-oriented groupings, but of interconnected object relationships. As the family conducts transactions at its boundary, it projects out its unconscious object relationship system. Thus, when the family comes for treatment, it displays its unconscious object relations system in its transactions with the therapist, who can then experience it and help the family to understand and modify it. This provides the substrate for psychoanalytic family therapy.

PART III

Technique and Transference

CHAPTER 8

Assessment

The Rationale for Meeting with the Family

A family does not usually present itself for evaluation. More commonly, a parent calls about a child, hoping that you will talk to the child and find out what is wrong. A case has to be made for including the whole family, and there are plenty of superficial reasons to justify doing so. A young person can use the support of the family when entering the unfamiliar situation of the psychiatrist's office; parents can be reassured by being there as part of the process. The child's problem developed in the family setting, so it makes sense to view it in that setting. It is a good idea to hear what everyone who lives with the problem wants to say or do about it so as to learn as much as possible about the problem and to mobilize the family's resources for dealing with it. Individual therapy can deal with the child's internal conflict, but the dependent child can't always progress without help in ameliorating the environment.

Beyond these reasons lie theoretical considerations that compel us toward family work. It is interesting to examine the total picture of the family in which the index patient is growing. From there, it is a short step to becoming interested in how the family enables or blocks the growth of all its members. We now know that the index patient is usually not alone in feeling pain but may be bearing symptoms on behalf of others. Thus, the symptomatic individual is a signal of distress in the family system, just as the symptom is a sign of disequilibrium in the personality of the individual. Psychotherapeutic intervention can be focused effectively on the figure of the individual, or on the ground of the family, or on both.

What we try to teach is a wide-angled focus on the family interaction but with a lens that also has excellent resolution at the

center of the field. It is not so much that attention oscillates between individual and family as that it hovers evenly at the levels
of the family group dynamic, the intrapsychic, and the interpersonal process between individual and family group and therapist.
Process and content, verbal and nonverbal behavior all are given
equal weight. There is a similarity between this and Freud's recommended techniques (1912a) of "not directing one's notice to
anything in particular," and of "maintaining the same 'evenly-
suspended attention' . . . in the face of all that one hears"
(pp. 111–112).

In psychoanalytic family therapy we teach the development of
that receptive, open-form type of listening. We have also found
useful Boszormenyi-Nagy's concept of multidirectional partiality
(1972) and Stierlin's rephrasing of it (1977) as "involved impartiality." That is, we intend to be equally empathic to the experience of
parent, child, adolescent, or grandparent. We say "intend" ad-
visedly, because it often happens that we will get pulled toward one
side or another in response to family dynamics in the patient
family or our own. Any deviation from the model of unencumbered
empathic listening is then a subject for the therapist to examine
with the family. This willingness to work with one's experiences
offers the family a model for self-examination and personal sharing
and an attitude of valuing process and review of experience. It also
reduces family anxiety about being in a fishbowl.

Having taken in the verbal and nonverbal information, the
content and the process of the interview as we see it from our
vantage point, equidistant from the generations in the family, what
do we do with it? And how do we use it to relate therapeutically to
the family? Here again, we are advised by Freud's description of the
analytic method (1912a). He recommended that the analyst "must
turn his own unconscious like a receptive organ towards the trans-
mitting unconscious of the patient" (p. 115). From the way the
signals resonate in his unconscious, he then reconstructs the patient's unconscious. At the time of writing, Freud was referring to
the origin of the patient's drives and the conflict with their expression in relation to the objects at whom they were aimed.

Using object relations theory, we think of the unconscious not
so much as the origin of the sexual and aggressive drives but as the
repository of the repressed object relations that derived from family
experience in the pursuit of the fundamental drive for attachment
to significant others. Applying object relations theory and analytic
method to family work, we tune into the unconscious processes

that have formed within, between, and among family members and their extended family. We allow these processes to resonate in our own unconscious. Then from this experience we work toward reconstructing the family unconscious. In order to be free of interference in the psychic receiving and resonating apparatus, psychoanalytic family therapists will ultimately find personal therapy a centrally important part of training, as it is for any therapist. We want to eliminate censorship of information, to recognize bias in interpreting its meaning, and to develop an awareness of the therapist's own internal family with its strengths and weaknesses.

We have to describe the analytic family assessment method at the beginning, because it applies from the first interview. Thus, from the first moment of the evaluation, the family will experience in the therapist an attitude of personal openness to the data and a willingness for self-examination. That is the crux of developing with the family a collaborative group approach to understanding and facilitating desired change.

Arrangements

There is no need to explain any of this when a potential patient calls but simply to have it in mind. This is what imparts conviction in our approach as we describe our consultation process. We have a flexible four-to-six-session assessment that allows for at least one meeting with the child alone, with the parents alone, and with the family as a group, as well as psychological testing by a colleague for the child if indicated. Finally, in an interpretive and planning session, we give our impressions and recommendations and then work with the family to plan the treatment. We prefer to do this in a family meeting because we want everyone who has contributed to get the feedback and because we want to elicit the family's reaction to the evaluation itself and to our recommendations. This allows us to work with resistance in the family and paves the way for the acceptance of a recommendation for family therapy.

We would not try to describe family therapy on the telephone but would say that the consultation process is a mutual process of assessment in which the family members can evaluate their responses to different therapy settings and to the personal style of the therapist before making any decision about therapy or commitment to a particular therapeutic mode. During the phone call, we usually describe the assessment format, explain the fee structure, and set up the first appointment, which may or may not be the family meeting. We let the person who is calling decide how to begin, because that person has already begun negotiating possible entry to treatment on behalf of the family. Not all families seen will agree to or would benefit from family treatment, but most families will agree to a family evaluation session.

We charge a higher fee for the four-to-six evaluation sessions. This allows for a lengthier session if necessary, for telephone work to pediatrician or school teacher, for collaboration with psychologist, and for cancellations. We do not charge for missed sessions because there is no commitment to work together over time. The higher evaluation fee protects against therapist anxiety about being paid when the family is ambivalent about attending. In family work, there is more possibility of cancellations because of the complexity of arranging for a number of people to be physically healthy and present at the same time, which is almost always inconvenient for someone. We offer to be quite flexible about time, reserving late afternoon time, one evening a week, or Saturday mornings for family work.

Exclusion or Inclusion of Subgroups

A word about exclusions. Some therapists prefer to exclude children who cannot talk. We feel this is a mistake. Only if all are present will we know how the family functions. If the baby is left at home, we will miss the nature of the family's adjustment to the new arrival in the everyday sense. If the toddler is left behind, we will miss the reaction to chaos and mess. In the course of treatment, a family may elect to delegate its work to a subgroup that does not include its baby and toddler, for instance. But that would be a family decision, not something imposed on the family by a therapist who, by excluding certain children, reinforces their fears of bringing their mess and needs to the therapist.

Some families may want to exclude younger children so that they will not be contaminated by the adolescents' acting out. Others will want to exclude the perfect child who gets straight A's and should not be upset by having to come to therapy. We say it is important that the siblings all come to support the index patient and to learn for their own sakes. We expect both parents to attend. We think that fathers are absolutely crucial to the therapy and give it an authority it would otherwise lack. It seems that in the child-guidance clinic setting where other children may be seen alone, brought to sessions by their mothers, fathers may be more reluctant to attend. The therapist who values the father should not have trouble getting him to attend.

One family therapist who demonstrated enormous commitment to having the father present was Peter Bruggen, who set up an adolescent unit at Hillend Hospital, St. Albans, England. The unit was for young people who could go nowhere else. He insisted that those with legal authority for the child—that is, both parents or the social service worker who had custody—must attend any admissions meeting, and review meetings thereafter. That was the only condition under which the child would be admitted (Bruggen, Byng-Hall, and Pitt-Aitkens 1973). Such a clear expectation was immensely useful, but its successful implementation probably depended on having the hospital bed as a lever.

In outpatient treatment, we can communicate the value we put on parents' authority, and hope through this and the usefulness of the first assessment interview to warrant a commitment from the whole family. If, however, a family resists coming in its totality, we begin with whichever subgroup will attend. Then we work with the meaning of the absence of the other members and hope to analyze the resistance to their being present. This is not always possible. Insisting that they meet us "where *we* are at" drives many families away from needed treatment; so we always start with families "where *they* are at."

Mrs. Sanders called about her 18-year-old daughter Elizabeth. She was depressed, on drugs, and out of control. I was able to arrange a family meeting in which I became aware of a powerful destructive force between the parents. Mr. Sanders was contemptuous and belittling of Mrs. Sanders's tendency to fall apart. Under his attack she did indeed crumple, which annoyed him so much that he refused to attend further therapy. The son, Stewart, was clearly siding with his father, displaying a cruelly nonchalant attitude and claiming that he was fine. Mrs. Sanders was making frantic facial gestures to indicate to me not to press them and to implore me not to send them away. I said I could see this going on, the men preferring to see all the weakness in the women in the family. I said I thought it was a loss for the family not to use the opportunity for treatment but that I would agree to work with those interested, not because they were sick and weak but because they were ready for treatment. I worked with Elizabeth individually until she went to college that summer and with Mother individually for about two years. The first part of the work with both women was to focus on what their attendance for therapy represented for the family and to mourn the loss of the family therapy opportunity and the lack of family commitment. Both were able to confront their feeling of being let down and unsupported, and both were able to improve their self-esteem.

So far, we have mentioned the child as index patient. When an adult calls for treatment, the idea of a couple or family meeting should also be kept in mind.

Mrs. O'Leary, age 45, called for help with increasing anxiety, recent aggravation of lifelong asthma, and feeling exhausted by coping with her family and her husband, who had been less available recently, and with her job. I asked if it might be helpful to meet as a family, and she readily accepted. In the family meeting, it soon became apparent that she was anxious about the potential loss of her family. Her husband was drinking heavily every evening at home, and the children were disgusted with him. He never drank on the job and so denied that he had any need of treatment. During an extended family evaluation, both parents' family backgrounds were explored. He came from a drinking family and culture, from which he had emigrated to the United States. But his mother came, too. He drank to avoid his wife's bossiness and her similarity to his mother. Of course, his drinking evoked the very behavior he dreaded and unconsciously found exciting. All this was pointed out, but he did not choose to stop drinking. The wife became only more "bossy," except that she now directed her assertiveness at herself, making plans for a separate vacation and, ultimately, a separate house. The O'Learys separated.

One could say that Mrs. O'Leary could have reached her decision just as well with individual intervention, but an important impetus came from the children, who were helpful in confronting the drinking problem that Mrs. O'Leary tended to downplay. The family work gave Mr. O'Leary a therapeutic opportunity, and his turning it down gave a clear signal to the rest of the family that he intended to drink as before. The threat of separation did not make for temporary improvement. So the family work demonstrated clearly to all present that there was no hope for the marriage continuing. As she faced reality, Mrs. O'Leary became calm and able to breathe again.

Six Tasks of Family Assessment

The following list outlines the six major tasks of a psychoanalytic family therapy assessment:

1. Provision of therapeutic space
2. Assessment of developmental phase and level
3. Demonstration of defensive functioning
4. Exploration of unconscious assumptions and underlying anxiety
5. Testing of response to interpretation and assessment format
6. Making of formulation, recommendation, and treatment plan

Provision of Space in the First Interview

Patients may expect a psychoanalytic family therapist to be remote and noncommunicative, a cartoon of a blank-screen analyst. Although we teach a method that is receptive, free-form, and nondirective at the unconscious level, we do not behave that way at the conscious level. We greet the family in a welcoming, friendly way, and introduce ourselves to each family member as they come in. We do not sit in silence waiting for anxiety to build. Instead, we say what we know (about the phone call, the referral, the fact but not the content of other meetings) and indicate our readiness to learn more. Here we have communicated an expectation that the family members will also say what they know, and together we will learn and work.

SETTING UP THE ROOM AND USING PLAY MATERIALS

The room is set with chairs around its perimeter in a vaguely square or circular setup, with a table for drawing on or displaying art media or toys. We have found that it is best to have the play material in the center of the family so that everyone, including parents and adolescents, sees that they are intended for use and are part of the work. Young children use play to defend against anxiety and also to communicate their conflicts; for both reasons, we want them to play freely. Furthermore, adults find that whether or not they use them, play materials evoke useful memories of childhood that help in relating their own experience to that of their children.

We aim to establish the office and the relationship to us as a safe space in which we can learn. Because of our psychotherapeutic training, we bring to the situation an experience of dealing with transference phenomena, primitive anxiety, and regression. Although we can never be sure we will be fit for the task with any particular family, we can reasonably expect to be able to manage our reaction to whatever affective storms and dynamic processes occur. We are ready to deal with issues of life and death. This willingness communicates itself to the family so that members can risk revealing themselves. We are actively concerned to enable this, by listening, following the family's thread, responding, and working internally to cope with our own defensiveness in areas they address and to face anxiety that is stirred in us. We refer to this process as *providing a holding environment*, which is similar to the process of *containment*, a term borrowed from Bion (1967) and described in family therapy by Box (1981b).

We contain the emerging family anxiety so that the family has a place to hold it while they look at it and learn about it. Without this, they would be condemned to suppressing it as before. The anxiety stems from the fear that the repressed relationships will return and destroy the goodness and generativity of the family. We offer not to be destroyed by this anxiety and yet not to reject or control it. We accept the anxiety as it is and work with our experience of it. This is the fundamental point about using the object relations approach: It permits enough distance in time and space from the anxiety so that the family can find space within itself for containing and metabolizing it.

The holding environment we provide is not to be viewed only as a peripheral boundary or holding function around the outside; there is a quality of holding from the inside, too. This is communicated through interpretations based on our analysis of our experience of the family's inner object relations system. This gives an immediacy to the communication about the family's experience because it has been felt and responded to at the therapist's deepest personal level. Accurate, sensitive interpretation is what "hooks" the family and interests them in further work. We have thought of interpretation not as a simple hook that catches a fish but as a grab hook with a number of prongs that reaches around and into the material and through to the core of the family's experience. It is important during the evaluation process to assess the effect of interpretation, to test the family's capacity for change, and to let the family see the possibilities of growth through understanding so that an informed choice about commitment to long-term psycho-analytical family therapy can be made by both family and therapist. This approach will not appeal to all families, only to those that are looking for growth beyond symptom removal.

A family therapy student at the Washington School asked me to come and interview a family she had been seeing, consisting of mother and three daughters, ages, 10, 8, and 5. I asked what toys I should bring for the interview. She replied that she did not know because the children had not played, and it didn't matter because they were very verbal. I took along a few toys anyway. The children played eagerly with art materials and puppets while talking about the loss of their father and their home and of their anger at Mother for not playing with them and not comforting them at bedtime. The student was surprised and felt encouraged to make her toys more obviously available in future sessions at her office. A month later she reported that the children had begun to use dolls to enact situations of competition and blame. This play was an indirect expression of the girls' conflict over being sexually abused by their father. This was a topic that they could not address directly, yet through the medium of the doll play they could reveal the problems and develop a vehicle for the working through. Much later in treatment, the mother became able to play in the sessions, too—an important prelude to better communication with her children at home.

By attending to play and to words we indicate our interest in the grown-up's and the child's expression of experience. Furthermore, we try to speak simply and without jargon, using words like *love, hate, wish, mad, sad, scary, good,* and *bad,* so that the youngest child can understand as much as possible. Through the arrangement of the office and the underlying attitude, we establish a cooperative working together between adults and children and family and therapist as partners in understanding.

An opening question may be needed: "What can you tell me about the problem?" We begin with the presenting problem and unhurriedly explore its nature. "How do the others react to this?" Then we begin to hear the interactions around the problem, which are representative of the family's style of relating. And the family creates an interaction in the here and now of the evaluation with each other and with the therapist, the outsider. Although one may be perceived as a potentially helpful expert, one may be related to as a good parent, a bad parent, a grandparent, a precocious child, or a pet, to name a few possibilities. We do not behave in a silent, neutral, withholding manner to elicit family transference to us. We behave in a normal, socially appropriate manner that tends to focus more on the transference between family members in present and past.

But inevitably, in the course of therapy and even during assessment, transference to us occurs and must be understood. At the assessment stage, the transference is usually to the contextual holding situation. If there is a rush of focused transferences that represent a first approach from disparate individual transferences, that is a sign of more severe pathology stemming from a deficient capacity for contextual holding in the family. This deficit may be so intense that it invades the family's capacity to work in family therapy until the family's shared capacity for holding is reinforced, perhaps by some individual or couple's work that attends to centered holding.

Our hypothesis is that during the first evaluation session the family's anxiety about meeting a therapist at the family's boundary will propel the expression of the pathological dynamics in relation to that task, just as they are expressed under the pressure of dealing with its developmental tasks. The family will project into the therapeutic holding situation its own holding, and then the gap between what the family expects and what we can really offer can be demonstrated right away. Addressing this contextual transference manifestation at the beginning modifies the resistance to treatment and is a basis for securing the alliance, just as early transference interpretation of resistance and anxiety is important in psychotherapy and psychoanalysis (Gill and Muslin 1976). It also paves the way for further contextual and core transference work later in therapy.

We learn about the family's cultural and religious background, their attitudes about themselves and their community, and their values. We do not want to summarize these varieties here, as this sort of information should not be used to stereotype the family interaction, but we refer to the comprehensive textbook *Ethnicity and Family Therapy* (McGoldrick, Pearce, and Giordano 1982) for background knowledge that prepares us for the practicalities of dealing with a range of families. We are aiming not at an attitude of categorizing the families but, rather, one of openness to understanding and respecting their unique cultures and values.

Assessment of Developmental Phase and Level

We try to get a sense of each family's developmental life phase. As we become familiar with their interactions, we can define an underlying mode that characterizes their interactions but may not be appropriate to the current developmental phase. The following example illustrates this.

The Browns consulted me because of their unhappy family life, much of it centering on arguments about how much freedom their 16-year-old daughter, Ashley, should have. In the first family meeting, Mr. and Mrs. Brown complained that neither of their children would do as they were told. Their younger daughter, Deirdre, age 11, would not take a bath without a huge fight, and Ashley left messes all over the elegantly decorated house. The children agreed that they were generally unpleasant and rebellious at home but said they performed very well at school and that they were good about doing their scheduled chores once a week. Mrs. Brown wanted her husband to control the children, but, as he hated her yelling, he did not want to back her attempts at getting order. He also did not like her attempts to control him, interrupt him, and criticize things he said to the point that what he wanted to say never got said. He gave up in a silent, defeated, passive way, while Mrs. Brown was further enraged by his passivity, and the children were made anxious by his withdrawal into self-centeredness.

In the second couple's meeting, Mrs. Brown gave an example of how Mr. Brown would take twenty minutes to pass a bowel movement, happily reading and stinking up the bathroom, right before bedtime. Why could he not use the children's bathroom or use deodorant spray? He felt she was jealous of his pleasure because she had problems with constipation, and he was as offended by the smell of deodorizing spray as she was by the smell of his bowel movement.

Another area of difficulty was money. In the second family meeting, the parents described how they both worked and contributed to a joint account, but they did not earn enough to cover their expenses and were constantly in debt to credit card companies, the bank (and inevitably, me). Apart from therapy, the main additional expenses that threw them over the edge were redecorating and refurnishing their house and refashioning jewelry. Ashley said that she was particularly angry that a ring she had loved just as it was had been altered for her as a surprise to show off the somewhat sunken stone to a more brilliant advantage. To her, the ring had been taken and ruined and was now "a piece of shit." The parents were horrified at her ungratefulness and at her foul mouth and were sad that this wonderful little girl had turned out so badly.

This example illustrates the predominance of a way of relating that derives from the anal psychosexual level. The family's intrusiveness in matters of elimination, conflict over money, covering over, undoing, and redoing because of a fear that things are unacceptable or "shitty" are all signs of this shared level of psychosocial operation. Students may say, "But this is not the object relations approach; this is classical developmental theory." True, it is based on Freud's classical psychosexual stages of drive theory, but it is amplified by Erikson's contribution. Erikson (1950) pointed out that the developing individual personality negotiates the vicissitudes of each stage in relation to its mother, developing an equilibrium, the nature of which depends on the individual's constitution, mothering, and unique adaptation. Difficulties at the anal stage, for instance, may lead to "disturbance of the anal zone (e.g., constipation), of the muscular system (e.g., flabbiness and rigidity), in obsessional fantasy (e.g., paranoid fear of inimical substances within one's body), and in the social spheres (e.g., attempts at controlling the environment by compulsive systemization)" (1950 [1963 ed., p. 83]). We apply Erikson's concept of the individual mind and body in interaction with its environment to the social sphere of the family influenced, as it has been, by the individual family members' personalities in developing its unique character.

This use of the family's developmental level is also an extension of Fairbairn's idea that growth occurs from infantile dependency, which is heavily oral, toward the achievement of mature interdependency, which includes the capacity for genital relating. The stages between are marked by the use of "transitional techniques" for relating. These characterize the individual's attempt to deal with the vicissitudes of human dependency (Fairbairn 1941). In the same way that the individual employs these intermediate techniques during growth, so the family develops a shared developmental level that represents the pooled individual efforts of their members. This, then, constitutes the matrix of the family in which development occurs, is facilitated, or is inhibited.

It is uncommon in our experience for a level to be consistently demonstrated over time. One more usually finds a mixture of modes. Students often ask, "Why is it necessary to evaluate this?

How does it help?" It helps to be aware of the level we are dealing with. For instance, an estimation of the level and of its rigidity or fluidity gives an idea how hard the work will be and how long it will take. The Browns, for example, would need to progress from the modes of operating at the anal stage through the phallic and oedipal stages to arrive at a more cooperative way of dealing with each other. The liability for the therapist would be that of getting into control battles, retaliation with sadistic use of words in interpretations, rigid positions, struggles over the fee and the time, taking sides, and trying to clean up the family. The therapeutic attitude helpful to these issues from that anal stage is to value each family member's productions, to be flexible and negotiable, and then to follow through with clear limits and expectations.

Demonstration of Defensive Functioning

The individual therapist who has dealt with a fixation at the anal stage will be familiar with the notion of the boy who holds on to his feces (or such substitutes for them as words or ideas) in order to at least have something of his own and thus keep separate from mother and her demands and intrusions. Also, he defends himself against the fundamental worry about whether there will be any more supplies coming in from her. Consistent with this finding from individual work is the finding from family work that the whole family worries whether there will be enough to go around.

Another area of difficulty for the Browns centered on food. Because both parents worked, it was an effort to shop for, and plan ahead for, meals. When Mother did this, there was a satisfactory meal, but when it was Father's turn, he might make do with canned ravioli. In either case, the parents felt that the children were frequently ungrateful about the cooking effort, whereas the children longed to come home to a Mom who had a snack ready for them. During family outings there were frequent arguments over treats. One parent might buy expensive candy, or someone would eat a box of cookies without owning up. The parents were contemptuous of fast food and preferred to take their children for an occasional meal at a good restaurant so that they would learn to appreciate fine food. Eating out was perhaps their most enjoyable family activity. Despite their limited budget, the parents put a high priority on being fed well occasionally but not on feeding themselves or their children consistently.

From this example we learn of a preoccupation with food. We can now hypothesize that the anal mode of relating was a transitional technique of relating, or a defensive mode of functioning aimed at warding off anxiety about insufficient oral supplies and dependency needs not being met. In talking with the family we would not use those words but would work toward showing them how the struggles over control and perfection happened to help them avoid their dissatisfaction in the basic area of being fed and cared for. In this way we can help the family by both naming these defenses and then demonstrating how they defend against anxiety.

Exploration of Shared Unconscious Assumptions and Underlying Anxiety

We can help the family explore the sources of shared unconscious anxiety with some open-ended questioning about family history. This approach helped Mr. and Mrs. Brown to discover a shared anxiety that had led to their developing a shared unconscious assumption about each other.

In the second family meeting, the Browns talked of their early lives while the children listened. Mr. Brown had been indulged as the only child by father, mother, and aunts who fed and cared for him and picked up after him. He was disappointed that his wife was not more loving in caring for him and the children. Mrs. Brown had had a difficult relationship with her mother and lost her father as a teenager. She longed for Mr. Brown to provide for her, which she felt he failed to do adequately; as a result, she had to work and had no energy for looking after people. Mr. Brown had never learned to take care of himself, and Mrs. Brown wished not to have to. The children perpetuated this unresolved conflict by resenting how much they had to do to keep the house neat, by demanding more chauffeuring, and at the same time, insisting on their rights to be entirely self-regulating as to bedtime, cleanliness, party-going, talking on the telephone, and watching television.

The family shared the unconscious dread of short supplies. Much of their anger and disappointment could be seen to emanate from the shared assumption that there was a constantly inadequate supply of food and care, and that others in the family were likely to

use more than their share. In addition, being controlled by someone else meant unconsciously that one was not free to fend for
oneself in making up for deficits.

The Use of Transference and Countertransference

Further understanding of the family develops from watching the
emergence of transference manifestations toward the therapist.
That is to say, we try to be aware of how we are being treated, of
what is expected of us.

In the second family meeting, I pointed out that the drawing
materials were for their use and suggested that it would be helpful to
the assessment if they would draw a picture of their family life.
Deirdre said she could not draw. Mother said she would not draw;
she had been to a lecture on family art therapy and thought it was
full of "bullshit" inferences. Father said he was "not going to pay
one dollar a minute to paint pictures." Ashley was interested but got
talked out of it. I did not think the drawings were essential to our
task, although I would have liked to have the drawings to work with
and in illustration of my research. Although I did not insist, they
behaved as if they had to thwart a directive. This is the only family I
have ever seen that has refused to draw. Mr. and Mrs. Brown denied
any anxiety about using the paper and crayons. I could guess that
they might be worried about messing and having me criticize and
judge them. Instead, I worked with their need to be in control of the
session and not be dependent on or controlled by me. These parents
had high hopes of me, as they had of their daughters, but they did
not want the family revolving around my whims and needs.

In the countertransference, I felt momentarily angry at being
thwarted. I thought, "If I want to write up this example, I won't
have the illustration. Nothing." Then I thought, "That doesn't
really matter. We can do the work without it," and I gave up my
suggestion. Looking back on this, I would say that I viewed my
needs for research as secondary to theirs for therapy, much as a
good parent has to give up selfish needs in order to promote a
child's development. Still, I heard in my thoughts the refrain: "But
I won't have the illustration. Nothing!" Then I thought, "That is
what their drawing is. It is a drawing of nothing and of the feeling

that they do not have it and will not have it." From this counter-transference experience, I could deduce their avoidance, through angry exchanges and rebutted refusals, of the shared feeling of nothingness at the center of the family. The word *nothing* interested me. I have learned in individual analysis that *nothing* may refer unconsciously to the female genitals. Here was *nothing* describing my experience of the family. I began to wonder about the parents' sexual relationship.

Testing the Response to Interpretation and Assessment Format

In both family meetings Ashley sat in a chair in the corner while the parents sat with Deirdre between them on the couch, Mother and Father alternately cuddling with her, although she seemed too old for that. I said that from their angry exchanges I had learned that the parents and children were disappointed in each other and had spoken as if there were nothing loving or positive going on. From Mother's and Father's cuddling with Deirdre, I could see that each parent was demonstrating a need for affection and closeness between them, whereas Deirdre was representing for herself and Ashley a wish to fill the emptiness. The parents agreed and said that they had used Ashley that way, too. They were already disappointed in each other before she was conceived, and when she was born they turned to her with wonder and delight. As we talked, Ashley reached quietly for the paper and markers she had been talked out of using earlier. She sketched a seductive young woman's face, half seeing, half seen (Fig. 8.1). I said that Ashley became a perfect, doted-on child who fulfilled their need for an ideal object until adolescence.

In subsequent sessions, Deirdre would take her own chair.

To find her own identity and to separate from her parents, Ashley had to rebel against their projection into her. When she did so, it was with the vehemence of the return of the more repressed projection she had also received, that of the disappointing, rejecting object that has been destroyed or made "shitty" by greed and rage.

Following my interpretation, Ashley drew another picture of an attractive young girl's face, which I took to be the need-exciting object on which my comments had focused. No sooner had I

Fig. 8.1 Ashley's first drawing.

thought this than she "spoiled" the beauty of the drawing by writing "Aargh" coming from the mouth (Fig. 8.2). In this way, I thought she had demonstrated and confirmed what I had just said to the family: that she had been a "beautiful," tantalizing object for her parents but had been spoiled by growth and the family situation.

The interpretation in the session focused on the way the rejecting and angry elements operated to secondarily repress unrequited mutual longing in this couple, pointing out that the children were needed to assuage the intolerable pain coming from a sense of

Fig. 8.2 Ashley's "Bad Drawing."

failed love in the parents' relationship. The couple's capacity to accept this statement with little defensiveness and to make use of it to spur further understanding provided positive evidence of their ability to work therapeutically. As they did this, Ashley provided evidence not only of her unconscious agreement with my interpretation but of the family's capacity to work productively and even creatively in the family therapy situation, when she drew her picture illustrating and "fleshing out" what I had been saying.

In a couple's session that followed, I referred back to the family meeting and asked the couple about the emptiness in their relationship. They said they had had no sexual life recently and very little since Ashley's birth. Mrs. Brown felt too angry to want it and often caused a fight before bedtime. She was angry that this was important to Mr. Brown when other things, such as being more ambitious about earning money to provide for them, were not. Mr. Brown was unhappy and felt frustrated, but he did not pursue his sexual aim assertively.

Making a Formulation, Recommendation, and Treatment Plan

Shared difficulty at the anal level rooted in anxiety about dependency precluded further development toward genital sexuality. The family came for treatment when Ashley, at 16, was no longer willing or able to substitute as their idealized exciting object but instead was becoming tentatively interested in her own adolescent sexuality. This is often a point of stress for a couple with an empty relationship, because it brings back longing and hope from earlier years and sometimes an unbearably envious response.

The Browns accepted a recommendation for family therapy in which the couple would meet once a week and the family once a week. Ashley, who had been the index patient, refused individual assessment or therapy because she felt her parents' relationship needed so much work. Although she was resisting the emergence of her unconscious, she was nevertheless handing back to the parents their projection of the good-object-gone-bad. Given the family's financial circumstances and Mrs. Brown's prior commitment to her individual therapy with a psychiatric social worker, we agreed that the couple and the family would come on alternate weeks.

Mrs. Brown asked that I provide medical coverage for her individual therapy for purposes of insurance reimbursement. I felt that in supporting her request, the family was wanting me to take care of them beyond what I could do. Here was an example of projecting their shared family unconscious assumption onto me. I was able to decline and interpret this to them, and they were able to accept my decision not to sign insurance forms. I noticed their ability to respond to the limit and to the interpretation, and I felt reassured about their capacity to work with me and to make a commitment to family therapy.

Sometimes the family process during assessment can go beyond the boundary of the assessment with the therapist.

The Browns were referred by the mother's social worker, a former colleague of mine. I did not seek any information from her, as I prefer to learn from my experience with the family, but I talked with her after the assessment to discuss the treatment plan and my reasons for not providing a medical signature for her work, which seemed agreeable to her. Some months later, she confronted me with my failure to thank her for the referral by phone call or by letter. I protested that I had called her, we had talked, and I thought we *were* working together. I felt accused, like Ashley, of not being polite or grateful, and then I responded defensively, like Mrs. Brown, listing all I had done.

This illustrates another phenomenon of the assessment process, described by Britten (1981): that family dynamics can resonate among referring and treating agencies. Awareness of this helps to contain the destructive potential of this process and to use the information in our work with the family toward establishing a boundary around the assessment task. It also reminds us that relationships with colleagues need continual attention beyond the formalities of courtesy if the referral network is to contain successfully the projected anxieties about starting treatment.

During the assessment process, we try to get a picture of the family's strength and resources, and of their weaknesses. We assess the ability to tolerate frustration, to develop a psychological-mindedness, and to work in therapy. We can see whether they respond to interpretation with insight. We also assess individual members' pathology and need for individual treatment. Based on this, we recommend family therapy, individual therapy, couple therapy, or a combined plan that meets their levels of need and motivation.

CHAPTER 9

The Technique of Object Relations Family Therapy

"The point about an object relations approach is that it is not so much a theory as it is a way of working" (Sutherland 1985). The object relations approach to families provides emotional space for a rediscovery of each other and of the lost parts of the self that have been put into each other. These projected parts of the self may have been put into others for safekeeping, as in the case of a good part of the self that is threatened by one's own hate, or for good riddance, as in the case of a hated and rejected part of oneself. The space we offer provides the basic safety for the family to sort out, modify, and reintroject projections in a metabolized form. Object relations family therapy works to understand these projections and the failures of the family's holding capacity that have resulted from and contributed to them.

The basic "technique" is therefore not a technique at all, as we have said before. The truth of this is such that it is with some hesitation that we write a chapter like this one, lest the details be mistaken for the basic approach or be reified into bylaws. There are techniques, learned from experience, that make the practicalities of the situation flow more smoothly and that can be passed on, and so need not be reinvented by each new therapist. These are the kind of specific methods we discuss when we supervise students. But these technical methods do not in themselves constitute doing an object relations brand of family therapy. They help, but they are not inviolate. Even following them as shortcuts during a therapy hour may trigger us to question why we said a certain thing at a certain point. For instance, although a comment may have seemed technically correct, examination of the transference may later let us know that it represented a misunderstanding of the family situation.

Technique contributes to, but cannot replace, the basic approach of understanding the family's situation as completely as possible in the time and space allowed, and of joining with the family members as a group in making this useful to them. Without that, the lesser matters of technique amount to nothing.

In the rest of this chapter we will discuss some of the procedures for getting started and working with a family. A number of basic issues are dealt with elsewhere, however. We have already discussed assessment in Chapter 8, while the cornerstone of technique, namely, transference and countertransference, will be taken up in Chapter 10. There we will also refute the nonanalytic family therapy idea that transference is irrelevant and to be avoided. In making a decision whether to discuss technique or transference first, we had a chicken-and-egg problem. The discussion of technique is in some ways empty without a prior discussion of transference, whereas the discussion of transference can make sense only after we have discussed some basic techniques. So we will take the course of discussing some practical pointers first, and discussing the heart of our method of understanding afterward. The two chapters should therefore be read together as a section on technique.

Provision of the Frame

Zinner (1985), applying Langs's concept (1976) of the frame of therapy to family therapy, has discussed the manner in which family therapy offers the "provision of a frame" in which work can go on. By providing the time, space, and structure for the therapy, we give form to the provision of the holding space. Thus, if we establish a weekly pattern of family meetings, for instance, the family's treatment of that framework becomes a vehicle through which to take up their issues about the provision of the frame. Although the setup needs to be adequate and appropriate to the job to be done, we are not suggesting any single arrangement here. Working weekly with the whole family is one common arrangement, but we also might work with the family while working with the parental couple and one or more individuals. The format should be the best fit we can arrive at by thoughtfulness and flexible planning. Once we establish a frame, however, we take the view that what the family does to bend the frame constitutes information about their use or difficulty with the holding situation.

Thus, for instance, it makes all the difference whether we plan for one of the parents to have concurrent individual therapy or whether a parent breaks out of the frame we have provided to seek an individual therapist as a way of escaping the family situation. If a patient bolts into individual work without discussion and planning, there is every chance that the family has colluded with this attempt to "bend the frame" rather than to work within it in order to defend against what might otherwise emerge within the treatment situation.

THE FLEXIBLE FRAME, NOT THE BENT FRAME: WORKING WITH SUBGROUPS

There are times when a flexible frame is necessary. We frequently work with the parents as a couple or with one or more individuals concurrently with the family work. This is the subject of Chapter 12, which deals with integration of family and individual therapy and is entirely consistent with our way of working. In addition, however, it may be useful at times to work with a subgroup of the family. When we make such a plan, we do not regard it as bending the frame, as we would when members who agreed to attend have opted not to. The plan to meet with a subgroup to help them develop issues they share is an active part of fashioning a more flexible frame. We will have examples of both alterations in basic format in subsequent chapters.

The Family Enters the Office

First we note how the family assembles in the room with us. Since we are not discussing the initial or assessment session here, let us assume that we are working with a family in the middle of a series of sessions. As they come in we note where they sit, the process of taking seats, and the general mood they bring into the room with them. It is not usually useful to remark on the seating arrangement in the beginning, but it is a good idea to store the information either to help organize our understanding later in the session or to make use of the shifts in physical seating from one session to another. Here, as in many aspects of technique, what matters is not the literal seating pattern but the meaning it has for the family.

There will be different meanings for each member of the family, and a single seating pattern may have different meanings at different times. For this reason, it is impossible to know what an event means right at the beginning, and we are often in the position of having to wait to get it clarified.

In any family with young children or adolescents, the mood around the seating process often yields additional information about the family's feeling about being in the office on that particular day. There may be comments about why they would rather be elsewhere—at a soccer game, doing homework, or anywhere but in our office. Or the competition between two children for a particular chair or spot next to, or at a distance from, parents gives a burst of information that we can note with or without comment. If we need to make a comment at this point, one with a humorous edge is often most useful. It avoids our looking too serious to the children, or so ridiculous as to be concerned with something as banal as seating.

A useful kind of comment is, "It looks like a struggle to give up the math for this evening!" said with a bit of a grin. Or, "How's the soccer team going to do it without you today?" Of course, whatever you say has to come from a comfort with your own style. The comment at this point, as at others in the session, has to aim at the anxieties that often surface right at the beginning of a session about being there. Thus, a balky 12-year-old may be kicking about "having to do this dumb thing." In this case, an assessment has to be made of the family resistance this child is speaking for.

Analysis of Resistance

This brings us to two crucial points that go beyond a narrow conception of technique. The first is that of resistance as a fundamental factor in any psychoanalytic therapy, and the importance of the ways we deal with it. The second is the question of when the individual is speaking for the group, and in what ways he or she is doing so.

We may be in the situation of feeling we have a solid alliance with the parents, who are motivated and willing to do as the therapist requests. Such was the case with the parents who brought their elder daughter for the treatment of obnoxious behavior of the sort that another mother once called "terminal unpleasantness." It became clear that this girl had no individual motivation for psychotherapeutic work but that her parents did want help with the situation and accepted a recommendation for family therapy. Predictably, this girl was reluctant to come to every family session, and the conscious motivation had to be supplied by her parents. She was speaking for their resistance in a deeper sense, however, for after we relied on their willingness to come and to get her to the session, we then found that talking about important matters was something they all resisted. Now her superficial resistance could be thought of as representing something for all of them.

INDIVIDUAL RESISTANCE ON BEHALF OF THE FAMILY

It would be inaccurate to say this family was not motivated, but it was true that all five members of this family had to overcome something within themselves to be able to come to the session. The father clearly had doubts about the value of talking both in treatment and at home. In this doubt, he had been represented by his elder daughter, by her younger sister, who made faces about having to be in the office on a Saturday morning when she (and they) would have preferred to be in bed, and by his son, who remained silent and facially unexpressive. But the children's resistance also represented an internal family battle against the mother, who had been the talker in the family and would always have preferred more communication. In this context, the children's resistance to coming and to talking meant siding with and "speaking for" father against mother. The therapist takes the rap for mother in this situation because of representing the dreaded task of which therapist and mother are now the symbolic leaders.

It is in this light that the technique of making a comment becomes relevant. Once this kind of pattern is known, the therapist can make a decision about the handling of the resistance, which is now present at several levels. The first is at the conscious level of the index patient, who would rather be anywhere else, but preferably home in bed. At the next level, her resistance is supported by her sister, who openly agrees with her. Third, both girls and their impassive brother speak for the unconscious denied reluctance of the father to join in the therapy. And at a fourth level, we note a persistent family response to having to come to treatment, which represents an attack by mother on the reluctance of the whole family to talk with her in the way she would like. Yet another aspect of this resistance is the mother's reluctance to speak for her own wish, which she avoids by assigning the therapist the job of "making everyone talk." In this way, she gets out of her own painful family role at the same time that she feels she gets an ally in that role. Finally, resistance is an aspect of the transference, but we will have to defer this important consideration until the discussion of transference itself in the next chapter.

Opening

So far we have gotten into the opening minutes of the session. This brings us to questions of who is responsible for starting the session and how to organize sessions. Should the parents or the children be the ones to begin to speak?

In a practical sense, the therapist's job in the first few minutes of each session is putting the family enough at ease to be able to bring up what is important to them. At some points in work with families, there is a crisis or topic of enough moment that it will be obvious to everyone that it should be the matter to be discussed. In that case, we would expect that someone will bring that up at the beginning. If no one does but we know of the crisis, perhaps from a phone call or because we work in a milieu setting where the matter is generally known, we might want to intervene quickly to point out that the family is ignoring a topic of importance. We can then wonder out loud why this should be true, or venture a reason if we have one, or we may decide that the pattern of avoidance and its study would constitute a further distraction and that the family needs to get on to the troublesome topic directly.

In most cases, however, after some initial exchange aimed mostly at reestablishing the boundaries of the therapy setting, we will leave it to the family to decide what topic to focus on. As in individual work, it is fine for the family to wander around for a bit, and on occasion even for quite a long time. It is also within the spirit of the work for them to tell the therapist about something that went well inasmuch as we are interested in everything, not only in the problems. Usually, the parents will take the lead in establishing topics in the early stages of the work. This will be more true if the children are openly reluctant or if they are very young. How they choose to get going, as well as what they say, gives us a preliminary context for what we will see and hear later.

Fundamentally, we hope that the introduction of a topic will act as an opener, not as a lecture or a way of closing a topic. It does not matter who brings up the topic, except that as soon as possible in the work we should like to establish the policy that we are interested in each family member's point of view and that each of them has an equal right to introduce agenda items as well as to comment on them. There are a number of examples throughout the book of ways sessions can begin, including some later in this chapter. For the moment, the technical point is that we should do whatever we need to in order to get the flow of information and the interaction going in a helpful way, without compromising our basic position. We are there to understand everyone's aspect of a difficulty and to help them grow or solve their situation, mainly by sharing that understanding.

Enlarging the Field of Participation

In the last example, the mother began by saying that the girl was unpleasant about doing her homework this week and that she managed to drag the whole family into a squabble about it. Having listened to the mother's point of view to get enough of a description to understand the basic situation, we would then try to enlarge the field of participation and the scope of our own and the family's observation.

We might do this by asking for another family member's view of the situation. Logically, we could now turn to the girl and ask for her picture of the events. If this is the first time this situation has been outlined, this is probably the thing to do. What often happens, however, is that the family brings in several problems repetitively, and the therapist may feel like the index patient—he has heard this complaint before. We do not mean the mother is doing something wrong to bring up a recurrent situation. Indeed, she should if it is a persistent problem. But in this case, we begin to need alternative ways of attacking the problem in the family therapy hour. Let us suppose that we have had enough experience to think that the daughter who has just been accused will again be negativistic about answering. We might decide not to ask her directly for her rebuttal but to turn instead to another family member. For instance, we might turn to the younger sister, who we know is identified with the problem but not in the hot seat at this moment, and ask how she saw the situation. Or we might turn to the older brother, who is relatively uninvolved, and ask his point of view. In a way, we are stalling for time, but we have a strategy of trying to enlarge the working space between the mother and the index daughter. At the moment of the mother's introduction of the topic, the daughter is on the spot and will probably react by closing up, getting angry and negativistic, and treating her mother as a persecuting object who is being attacking and rejecting. We want to introduce more space into the defective centered relationship and holding capacity of the mother–daughter pair, and the way to do this is to get the family as a whole to provide more adequate holding to the pair.

This leads to the technique of getting the others to be more active in their participation in this situation. Let us say that the older brother now says that his sister did kick up a fuss, whereas although he was upset, too, he knew enough to go off to his room and read a book, or to go shoot baskets with his friends. Now he has introduced himself as a sympathetic object for her. We would ask what he was upset about and learn that the parents had been fighting that afternoon, or that a grandmother had been visiting and was upsetting everyone. At this point, we might involve the other sister, or we might now turn to Father or back to Mother to ask if they were upset by Grandmother, or were they fighting, and if so, what about?

If they can begin to describe their own upset or marital disagreement—and there is almost always some context within the family for the child's "unexplained behavior"—then we can begin to link the two. This constitutes far more than a behavioral link. To show what we mean, let us say that we turn to Father and say, "Is it so, that you both were upset by your mother's visit?" He replies, "Well, my mother is old and forgetful, and as she's aged, she's gotten bossier. It is hard on my wife, but we actually get in fights because my mother tells her how to cook. I want her to humor my mother, and she wants me to tell Mother that it's our house. But I feel guilty. Often it means we have a fight after she is gone." Now, we might turn to the wife and ask for her side of it, *or* it may now be about time to turn to the index daughter. Notice that we are now distant from the problem the mother originally presented: the daughter's disruptive behavior around homework. This has the effect of letting the girl off the hook. But in another sense, we have spiraled underneath the antilibidinal pairing that tends to keep mother and daughter locked into the repetitive fighting that mars their core relationship. We are not now asking the daughter to suffer the humiliation of denying fact, reporting on herself, or restarting the battle. We are now asking her to do what the others have been doing—to report on the family situation.

Often, the girl can become a useful reporter at this point, if not on the first occasion of such a question, then by the second or third time we circle around. If she is able to feel freed enough from balking, she might sneer slightly and say, "Yeah, they're always uptight when Gramma comes. You should see them. They think I'm bad about my homework, but Mom tells him to cook the f——— food himself if he wants it cooked when Gramma is there." She also might not say this much, and it may be a smaller beginning. But if we got this much, the angry, adolescent, attacking contribution would constitute a great deal. Although she has seemed surly, she has joined in to contribute her view of a parental problem. We could then ask, "How do you feel when they get into this kind of fight?", or we could take a less direct approach and ask, "How do you feel about your grandmother being around?" How direct to make the questions would depend on the therapist's feel for how much the child or any family member can respond to, the only difference being that this child is the one who is guarded at this moment. But we know that in thinking about what kind of questioning the girl can tolerate and still answer, we are modeling a kind of holding the family has been unable to demonstrate.

At this point we might be able to make an interpretive comment. We might say, for instance, "I wonder if the homework difficulty is related to the fight between Mom and Dad during the afternoon?" We might say more, but perhaps we would stop here and see how much they could do in making the link. It is useful for the family to do most of the exploring themselves, but if they cannot, there is no cause to be stingy about contributing to the general understanding. Sparsity is not a mandate for family therapists, although of course there is no need to overwhelm the family by talking all the time.

Accordingly, if the family is unable to extend the exploration or sharing, or if we want to demonstrate the kind of understanding that we are encouraging them to have of the context of the homework spat, we might extend our comments considerably. We might say to the adolescent, "Your upset could be a way of trying to cope with something in the family at large," and to the parents, "She seemed to be upset by the fight between the two of you parents, and went upstairs. But she may have felt someone was right and someone was wrong in the fight. For instance, if she felt Mother was wrong, her own fight with Mother may have been to support Dad without saying so. Or she may have felt that the family treats her just like they seem to feel about Gramma, and this is her way of saying that. Does any of this seem to hit home?" This last question may be an open-ended one for anyone to respond to, or it might be directed to a child or to the parents.

These alternatives present two versions of using an interpretation to create a new kind of thinking and holding in the family. In a way we can think about levels of these interpretations. The first is simply a linking comment followed by a question. The second extends the linking to the offering of a rough hypothesis about motivation and setting. These, so far, are not profound interpretations, but even so they offer a new attempt at a solution. They say to the family, "Instead of joining in with a blaming and angry attempt at solutions, why don't we try to understand what gets people upset and at odds? It may make a difference in the way you see things and in the way you feel like treating each other." If we get our guess reasonably right, and if the family members are able to work with it at that moment, then they may follow our interpretation by doing another small piece of work.

Perhaps at this moment, the index patient may offer a slightly grudging nod and say, "Well, yeah. I did get upset about Gramma, because she's a person, too, and she means well. Sometimes I feel they don't like me any better than they like her. But when Mom and Dad fight, I just get scared. And I was upset. So that might be right." This would be quite a lot for her to give, but it does happen. And if she did, we could comment that the homework trouble, at least on this one occasion, was now more understandable, and that other instances of difficulty might have different but also understandable reasons behind them.

In addition, we could now consider whether to have the family at this point consider possible rivalry between the adolescent girl and Mother for Father, or possible deeper causes of disappointment with Mother that might be working at the next level of explanation. Lest we give the idea that this is about the child rather than the family, let us point out that an equally fruitful avenue of inquiry might involve Mother's disappointment with her daughter, who Mother may feel is not turning out well and is therefore a bad object for Mother, a kind of living accusation. Another might involve an exploration of the scope of marital disagreement, which happens to focus on the maternal grandmother in that instance. Or better yet, all these would be explored over time and slowly linked into a broadening understanding of the family-wide pattern and its multiple sources.

Core Affective Exchange: Here and Now versus There and Then

More important than the choice of topics is the emotional distance between the topic and the family. Some families may need more distance than others, and their need for distancing may vary. This is one of the matters to be considered as each session and each series of sessions unfold. Another aspect of emotional distance is the degree to which the topics are themselves external to the session, as when we are focusing on something that happened outside the room, called in group process language a "there-and-then" event. Essentially, this means we are reviewing something in the past and in another setting. When there is less need for distance, the feelings under discussion come alive in the therapeutic space, and we are then dealing directly with here-and-now events.

If we choose to work in the here and now, we might explore an event in the therapy hour, such as a dirty look, an argument in the room, or the family's difficulty in talking about anything meaningful. This brings the exploration into the transference situation. The family is here to do a job in the here and now of the therapy session, and the exploration of events during the session occurs in the container we provide. Any successes or failures have implications for the family's overall relationship to us as therapists and to our provision of that container. We may choose to highlight that transference implication at a given moment, or we may choose to observe and absorb it without calling it to attention. The choice depends on a number of factors, which will be discussed in Chapter 10.

The advantage of a here-and-now event is that family and therapist share the experience, lending immediacy and credibility to their examination. Although the choice between the options of exploring here-and-now or there-and-then matters may seem difficult, in practice it often is not. The discussion of the back-home situation may be proceeding relatively well until someone gets angry or sends a look of deep misunderstanding. This is the moment to cut to what is happening now in the session, to inquire about the feeling that went with the look, and then to ask the receiver how the look felt—all to enlarge understanding in the here and now.

This is the reason that the trivia of everyday life are informative subjects for exploration. These are, as we noted in Chapter 4, the building blocks of the core holding experience, just as they were in early parent–infant exchanges. Talking in sessions about difficulties in daily ordinary exchanges at home is the most direct route to moments of core affective exchange—the golden moments for understanding and for change. At those moments, the core experience of the family is in the room with us, and we can work more closely with it than at any other time. These therapeutic moments that capture the transference are the essence of our psychoanalytic approach. The following example is a good illustration of this.

The Roberts family consisted of Father, Mother, Debbie, age 12, and Bill, age 10. The parents had originally seen me for sexual and marital difficulty three years earlier, with some improvement in the presenting picture, which was Mr. Roberts's lack of interest in sex with his wife. They had returned a year after the sex therapy to ask for help with Debbie. At this point, Mother said that she had for years felt Debbie to be an intolerable thorn in her side. Debbie was clearly depressed, doing poorly in school and clinging desperately to one friend at a time. Bill was seen by both parents as an easy child who scarcely ever caused trouble, did well in school and sports, and could speak to his parents diplomatically. A good deal of strain remained between the parents. Mrs. Roberts continued to see her husband as rejecting of her sexually, and in a number of ways as an immature nuisance. Mr. Roberts also had difficulty at his work in the city public schools, where he had locked himself into a sinecure without responsibility. He spent his time accusing his superiors of violating his rights. Saying that his responsibilities to the school system meant that he needed to retain the information, he accumulated so many unread documents from work that whole areas of the house were taken up with them.

Today, the family was discussing Mrs. Roberts's version of a time when Debbie had refused to do the dishes. Mrs. Roberts had asked her to clean up the table as she was rushing off to a meeting, while Bill had been sent upstairs to do a report. Debbie turned to Mother and said, "It's not true. You didn't tell me to do the dishes. I offered, and you said to me, 'You never do them anyhow, so it's about time.' And when you said that, I said, 'Well, if that's the way you feel, then I won't.' And you said, 'Well, you see? That proves it!'"

At this point, Debbie was looking staunch in confronting her mother. And her mother did well in replying calmly, "Well, if I said that, then I can see why you might have been upset."

A small increment of positive feeling between them seemed to be in the making. The conversation went on for a moment and then turned to a phone call from Mrs. Roberts's mother. Debbie gets along pretty well with her grandmother, whereas Mrs. Roberts regards her mother as crazy and resents her for emotionally neglecting her in her childhood. Mrs. Roberts resented her mother's enlisting her for compulsive shoplifting when she was small and for overloading her with discussions of her problems, including the fact of her mother's many affairs. The discovery of one of the affairs finally led Mrs. Roberts's father to leave the family. Mrs. Roberts also felt her mother babied her sister, while looking to Mrs. Roberts for parenting.

In the phone call of this week, Mrs. Roberts had been short with her mother and had turned the phone over to Debbie, who had a friendly chat with her grandmother. Afterward, she came downstairs in a good mood and asked if a friend could spend the night.

As this was being discussed in the therapy hour, Mrs. Roberts tucked her legs under herself on the couch, turned to me, and said, "Well, it's the only friend she has, and I suppose she's lucky to have that one."

Debbie now shot her an angry and hurt glance, and her eyes began to tear. I interrupted Mrs. Roberts, who was about to go on, and asked Debbie how she had felt when she had just looked daggers at her mother. Holding back her tears at first, and then sobbing, she said, "It's just like this at home. I don't do anything, and Mother turns on me. It's not fair! Mother doesn't like me very much. Why did she have me if she felt like this?"

I decided at that moment to try to enlarge our understanding of this affective moment. I did this because the question Debbie had for her mother was a repetitive question that had not been answered in several months of work with the parents and had not gotten much further in the family sessions we had been having for the last six months. At that moment, for the first time, I had found an instance of the underlying basis for much of the trouble.

Accordingly, I turned to Mr. Roberts and asked him what he felt about his wife's statement about Debbie.

He said, "Oh, it's true that she says these things. I'm terribly upset about the way she treats Debbie. She never treats Bill this way, and I agree it's not fair."

Having established Father's identification with Debbie, the split in the family, and the splintering in its holding capacity that was represented at this moment, I now turned to Mrs. Roberts and said,

"What were you thinking at the moment you said that she was lucky to have even one friend?"

"I was just mad at her," she said. "I guess if I think about it, I would have to say there was something about that conversation she was having with my mother that got to me. Sometimes I feel Debbie is just concerned about herself, just like my mother. She didn't care at all what happened to me, she was so concerned with herself. I think when Debbie gets along with my mother—well, it's Ok with me that she does—but I think it gets to me, too. So when she came downstairs after that phone call, I was upset but I was sitting on it. When it came up again here, it caught me off guard, and I didn't stop myself. I find it hard that she likes this woman who happens to be my mother and who I think did me in."

"See! It's not fair," said Debbie. "I'm supposed to be able to have a grandmother, but she thinks I do it against her."

Now Mother began to soften and said, "It's not Debbie's fault, really, but I do find I hold it against her, as if she and my mother gang up in not caring about me."

I said, "I think sometimes you feel Debbie and your husband are also together in not caring about you, but some of the anger you feel at him is easier to direct at Debbie."

"It's true," she said. "I find it hard to get mad at him. I'm scared of him. Can you believe that? That pathetic man! And I'm scared of him. But I'm not scared of Debbie."

"Are you aware that Debbie is catching some of the bad feeling your wife has for you?" I asked Mr. Roberts.

"No. I don't think I have been. I know I don't think it's fair, but I've just felt they had something bad going. It's often a reason I'm mad at my wife," he said. "In fact, sometimes I feel it's Debbie and me being rejected by my wife, who seeks out Bill for love."

"I think this moment of bad feeling contains the history of rejection you both feel," I said. "I'm sure it happens all the time at home. Look at all it contains about the family!" I wondered whether I would learn of other contributing object relations.

This extended section of one therapy hour contained many things, including an important reference to the mother's history, and a repeated complaint by both mother and daughter about feeling at odds and disliked by each other. What organized the session, however, was bringing into the present the strength of feeling of the issue, as caught in the exchange of the hurtful comment the mother directed at her daughter, and the dirty look that the daughter directed at her mother. Thus, in the therapy hour, we had an example of a dramatic centered relating experience of mutual rejection that therefore failed to provide centered holding. At the same time, the family's shared holding capacity could also be seen to be inadequate to the task of working things out in any better way, as Father's allegiance to his wife quickly shifted so that he was siding with his daughter in her hurt, and the wife felt alone and responsible just as she did with her mother.

Now it is possible to describe this shift of parental alliance in terms of family triangulation (Bowen 1978). There is no doubt that there is an oedipal triangle that is significantly skewed in the family and especially at this moment. But it is skewed in a highly specific way that can be described in detail. More important, it is skewed for a set of reasons that can be explored and ultimately also described. Conveying specifically how these reasons involve the hurt and longing of the family members enables each of them to feel understood. We have described this as the "because clause," which we will discuss later in this chapter. At first they feel understood by the therapist in each other's presence, and later, in small steps, they can feel more understood by each other, and ultimately become more understanding. The change in the external object modifies the internal object. Shifts in the internal object alter the self, which affects the external object in new ways. The reciprocal sides of the process are interlocking and mutually reinforcing; object and self are tied together in a never-ending cycle.

Kinds of Intervention

In the following comments, we are not trying to discriminate between the various levels of interpretive work as Edward Bibring (1954) has done for work with individuals. Rather, we suggest that there are four areas of intervention to consider: First, there are comments aimed at organizing the session, speaking to the need to give various individuals room to talk, calming chaos, or initiating exploration. Second, some comments are aimed at giving support and advice. The third level is understanding—the comments running on a continuum from superficial comments, which aim only to name or clarify the current situation, to interpretive comments, which attempt progressively deeper levels of explanation. Further, some comments are aimed at invoking or examining the transference. We will elaborate on this aspect in Chapter 10. And finally, all levels of intervention will be evoked over and over during the working through, until the family takes on the task of understanding for itself and approaches the ending phase of treatment.

ORGANIZING THE SESSION

A certain amount of the therapist's activity is aimed at beginning the work, giving family members a way into the conversation if they lack one, asking others to speak less or allow someone to finish, and intervening in repetitive quarrels to request other kinds of input, such as information about a parent's childhood history to illuminate the puzzling repetition. This kind of activity is a derivative of the parental function of organizing the family, showing the way when necessary, and being the more mature and knowledgeable partner in a living environment. Through this facilitation and organization of the therapeutic space, we act as parents do in being responsible for the feeding, training, education, and cleanup of the children. At first we may need to do a larger share, but this is not always so because there is great overlap between these functions and the current similar parental functions in the family. Many families, therefore, will take the responsibility for organizing much of their experience from the beginning, and our work will focus more on understanding what is happening.

Nevertheless, in almost all families, we must do a certain amount of facilitation. There is no reason to avoid it when it is called for. We are responsible for "managing" the space and its use. The complexity of the space calls for more organization than in individual therapy. This is one of the reasons that therapists who conduct both individual and family therapy usually find that they are more active in the family setting and that this increased activity seems to be appropriate. These managerial aspects of family therapy apply in our psychoanalytic approach as well as in other modes of family therapy that we have observed.

The technique of asking questions about the family's history of object relations deserves specific note. We want to encourage older family members to share their experience growing up within their families. Although such information may arise spontaneously from the family, at other times we need to ask specifically about it. This is often best done by asking one family member about associated experience in the family of origin at a moment of impasse in the therapy or at a time when this information would facilitate understanding or empathy. We hope to get at that moment a history of the object relations of the specific situation that has just been outlined in the therapy in front of us.

These questions are posed as being about the memory of interactions with parents and primary figures. In fact what we get is a history of relationships as they have been experienced and internalized. This history of internal objects and experience with them includes the fantasy distortions of experience interwoven with the record of the interactions themselves. This is a more accurate history of internalized objects than it is of facts. This information often leads quite directly to our ability to make a linking or interpretive comment about the meaning of a current set of family interactions.

GIVING SUPPORT AND ADVICE

Support in the family setting can have many roles. It may be that we want to support an individual or the family to tolerate something unbearable. It may be that we are willing to play a supportive parental role to offer the function of holding parents that the family has been missing. Support may be given by actually saying something encouraging or validating or may be implied in the therapeutic process itself. For most families, the most supportive thing we can do is to be interpretive so that the holding capacity improves. The process of continuing the exploration, encouraging them to widen the space for mutual understanding, and expecting that they can and should tolerate more is enormously supportive. This provides a model of the parental function of holding an ideal of future development that encourages growth (Loewald 1960). It is the kind of support that the mother gives to the infant to grow, to risk more, and to become more. She thereby encourages the baby to be a separate individual within her protective sphere. But if the family, like the baby, needs more direct support in a given developmental phase, then we, like parents, should give it. But we should know that we are doing so, and roughly speaking at least, why we think it is appropriate.

This includes the role of offering advice to parents about child rearing. Those of us who have worked in the child-guidance model have learned how to offer parents advice about coping with children and about setting limits. Mainly we have learned to do so sparingly and cautiously, respecting the parents' defenses. Much has been written about the interface between parent-guidance work and psychotherapy (Arnold 1978). For instance, when we tell parents to try to set limits by sending a child to his room, we wait to see if the parents can do it. If they can, they are in a position to learn from the generally good results of being able to set an effective limit, and usually things begin to change for the better between them and the child. But if they cannot take our advice to set an effective limit, then psychotherapy begins as an investigation about what is interfering in the parental dynamics and the intrapsychic life of each parent that disables them when it comes to being able to make use of the guidance.

There is room for this kind of work in the general framework of our family approach. Helping the parents to parent more effectively is certainly on the side of the child as well. But in practice, it is difficult to carry on direct advice giving of this sort in the presence of latency or adolescent children who may resent it. In these cases, it is better to ask the kind of question that makes it clear that we support parental prerogatives but that does not constitute a flaunting of these in front of the child. The degree to which this can be done varies from family to family. In one instance, there will be a family-wide alliance that makes most reasonable interventions go well. In another, the assault on a reasonable alliance or holding capacity is such that the therapist is wise to remain above suspicion of even seeming to side with the parents. This question will have to be left to the discretion of the therapist. Most families will tolerate a few therapist mistakes of discretionary judgment during the breaking-in period as part of the process of learning to work with them.

When we decide it is unwise to give direct advice to the family, we can do work that is generally preferable anyway: We can ask what are their feelings about limit setting or whatever aspect the advice would have been about. This usually introduces some discussion of the child's resistance or resentment, or the parent's guilt. With probing, and a bit of luck, this may reveal the way in which the parent's own experience growing up is incapacitating when it comes to performing these ordinary parental functions. This often results in a parent's ending the exploration with a question, like this one from the mother of the balky 12-year-old girl described earlier in the chapter.

Mother: "You mean it's all right if I tell her I won't help her with her homework if she's going to yell at me? And just let her fail her test?"

Therapist: "Well, what do you think?"

Mother: "I guess if she does fail, she won't yell at me the next time. Or maybe she'll pass, and she won't need me to help her with homework at all! Huh! I never thought of that. Okay. I guess I know what to try."

This way of working leaves it to the child to object directly to the parent, in which case we are in a position to support their discussing it. We can, for instance, support both the child in amplifying any objection, and the mother in exploring her difficulties setting limits, without taking sides. This is all the more true because the child often does not object to the parents working out a more effective and less tortuously drawn out method of parental functioning. In fact, if asked directly how he or she feels about it, a child will often support the parent's need to set limits but ask for some reasonable modification that can be incorporated, thus giving the child a hand in the process.

To sum up, we can say that it is best to first try to use the family setting to work these matters out in the usual exploratory way. If this is inappropriate for some reason, such as the age of the child or the child's refusal to cooperate, then guidance can be provided, preserving the framework of the therapy even while giving advice. Chapter 12 gives an example and further discussion of this issue.

FACILITATING COMMUNICATION

One of the intermediate goals of family therapy is improved communication. We do not actively facilitate this by asking questions or directing individuals to speak to each other. We would not use techniques such as having a poorly related husband and wife sit back to back and tell what they disliked about each other. We facilitate communication by valuing words. We verbalize rather than act. When the emotional situation derives from preverbal experience, and words cannot be found for it, we would say so. We notice nonverbal communication and, again, try to channel that into verbal expression. In some families we find that words are used not as words but as silencers, as packaging, as weapons, as eliminatory waste, or as vomit. If we can identify this use of words and its derivation in family experience we may then be able to work toward better communication. In addition, we provide toys, paper, and markers to offer an age-appropriate expressive channel for children and some adolescents.

UNDERSTANDING: JOINING THE FAMILY EXPERIENCE THROUGH INTERPRETATION

The use of interpretation in family therapy has been attacked as ineffective; families do not want to know the truth and will not hear an interpretive comment in any effective way. This charge represents a fundamental misunderstanding of the interpretive process and caricatures interpretation as a set of intellectual ideas imposed on a family from a safe distance. This section can only frame an answer to this charge, relying on the material contained in the book at large and on the reader's experience or willingness to try to work with families in this way to test out the power of understanding within the family.

Interpretation is central to the process of any psychodynamic therapy. We have already made it clear that we are talking about a process of sharing understanding with the family, not of imposing conjecture whether it fits or not. This means that interpretation, at whatever depth it is being attempted, is not a single discrete sentence that opens a logjam in an oracular way. Sometimes something a therapist says may do that, but this is an unusual event. It is just as likely that something a family member says will constitute a piece of interpretive work that opens a logjam for the family. Indeed, when the family is working really well, this will be the rule.

The interpretive work is, as we have emphasized, part and parcel of joining with the family in the process of understanding, and of sharing our own efforts to understand. It constitutes the principle work of the holding process that the therapist contributes and is, therefore, comparable to centered relating and centered holding between a mother and child. There is no reason to think that what we say has to be right all the time. It is part of the process that family members should be able to "set us straight" a good deal of the time, and that we should work with their modifications of what we have to say. Nevertheless, the clues we use to validate what we say are not primarily the ones of conscious and overt agreement or disagreement. They are the affective tone and associative content of what follows, including the disagreement of the family members among themselves. In the following example, the parents' prompt denial of the therapist's comment suggests that the therapist is probably right, as confirmed a moment later by the son.

Therapist: "I think the family is saying that John is speaking for the shared reluctance to come that everyone feels."

Father: "I think you're wrong. I want *them* to come and get this solved. I'm tired of the grief they give me about getting here."

Mother: "Oh, I think my husband and I are together on this therapy."

John: "Well, on the way here Mom and Dad were arguing, and Dad said, 'I wish you didn't speak like that to the kids. That's why we have to go to that goddamned family therapy anyway.'"

Interpretation is the workhorse of the object relations approach. An interpretive comment is not a single theoretical notion, nor the imposition of technical terms on the family. Although these may be guides to us in our attempts to understand, that is all they are. And our language avoids theoretical terms, even if we find them personally useful. We use ordinary language, preferably one that is close to the family's experience, uses their symbols, and is clear to them. This may mean borrowing their terms, especially terms that give life to matters important to them. Minuchin (1974) has described this as "tracking." But what matters most is that the language be clear and direct. And this usually means simple and short. Often it is better to say a few things briefly over a few minutes than to give a speech, but there is no rule about this. What matters is being clear and getting things as clear as possible over time with the family. The presence of young children, or a family member with an impaired capacity to understand, changes the language that has to be used. Indeed, with very young children the language will include some play, as will be illustrated in the section on working with families with very young children in Chapters 13 and 14.

Interpretation in this way plays two roles. It speaks to the direct problem of the moment, to one person, to the relationship between two family members, or the family as a whole. At the same time, interpretation expresses the "metacommunication" about us, namely that we are there and trying to understand. The more we have a perspective from outside the process of the family, even while we join with them, the more we stand for the living oscillation between mirroring back to them who they are and offering the container that they need to further their own exploration.

In the model we propose, the primary focus of interpretive efforts is on each family member's holding situation with each other, and on the family's difficulties in providing the container necessary for the holding situation. There are many components of this: the shared anxieties about being abandoned, damaged, or unloved that lead people to become defensive and angry; the way people become controlling when they are afraid their objects will misuse them or fail to love them for themselves; the previous histories of family members that result in these situations; and the way people relate to each other as though they were yesterday's objects instead of today's real family members. All of these may be the material of the comments we make on the way to helping the family establish a better shared holding capacity. But that is the overall aim, and often as not, it is not the actual content of what we say. Instead, we work toward the goal. In the previous example, for instance, the therapist followed up on John's disclosure that Father was also having feelings about having to come to family therapy.

Therapist: "I think John has been speaking for this feeling on behalf of the whole family. It's safer for the family to let him do it because it seems OK for a child to hate coming. But when it's as though he's the only one who hates having things said about him, he is even more isolated and has even more trouble feeling people understand him. If we think about him as speaking for each of you in part, then everyone can help each other figure out what's tough about being here."

THE BEHAVIORAL INTERPRETATION

Not all comments are made in words. Some we make by maintaining our position without words, or by an action that gives a message. An action mode of intervention is at times more effective than words. For instance, a parent who could not set limits out of fear of a child's retaliation subsequently attacked the therapist for charging for missed appointments and insisting on ending on time. The therapist elected simply to hold the line in a steady, nonretaliatory way because she felt that to try to explain too much in words would either seem defensive or might humiliate the parent.

In another case, a parent repeatedly admonished his 6-year-old boy for fiddling with the toys the therapist had made available. Instead of directly challenging the parent's idea that the child should sit still, the therapist took a later opportunity to engage the child in play with the toys, giving a message through his behavior that play was a natural activity for the child and demonstrating the way this might defuse the tension between child and parent.

There are other terms we might use for this kind of intervention, for instance "modeling." But using the term "behavioral interpretation" makes the point that our aim is to increase understanding, even if it is often understanding without words. The term also reminds us that we can formulate these interventions in the same ways we formulate verbal interventions.

THE "BECAUSE CLAUSE"

Interpretation should not be a spear aimed for attack. It takes a while before we can safely speak to defensive behaviors of many individuals and families without their feeling misunderstood. Although language and tone have a good deal to do with our ability to get it across that we are not against them, successful interpretation also depends on waiting for the moment when they are ready to hear certain things.

Right from the beginning, the more we can offer a reason why people do what they do, the easier it is for them to accept it. We offer what Henry Ezriel (1952) called the "because clause," which we mentioned earlier and discussed in Chapter 7. Ezriel's specific meaning for this term can be expanded to include all attempts to explain why it would make sense, from the family members' perspective and experience, to do things—including relating to the therapist—the way they always have, even if there are shortcomings to the chosen method. Ezriel noted that a group relating to him as therapist would demonstrate three aspects of relating: a "required" relationship, an "avoided" relationship, and a dreaded "calamity."

These are three parts of the group transference that are parceled out among group members and that have to be understood together in order to understand the complete group transference. We have reintroduced them here to indicate that they present a level of interpretation that offers depth and comprehensiveness and guides the therapist to understand the transference specifically along object relations lines. The difficulty with this guide for interpretation is that it holds out the promise that the therapist could respond in such an embracing manner all the time, when in fact an interpretive contribution of this magnitude usually represents the end product of a great deal of work and of many partial offerings. Sometimes we can do no better than to say, "This troubling pattern that we have identified occurs for a reason that we need to look for." We invite the family to join us in seeking to establish the "because clause."

At other times, we will have an explanation that broadens the family members' tolerance of one another and their capacity to communicate. At these times we should certainly offer it. Often we have explanations because of the broadened perspective we have gained by observing them as a larger group, from asking ourselves the broad questions of "what has gone wrong between and among them?" and "what is wrong between them and me?" rather than the narrower question of "what is wrong with this individual?" We can derive information from several sources for this enlarged perspective: from our attention to the containing function of the family, from an understanding of group process in which the family as a group has a problem that different individuals speak for, and by our receiving and processing of transference. So the "because clause" will vary in specificity, depth, and comprehensiveness.

For example, the work in the beginning of the session with the Roberts family, described early in this chapter, was exploratory. The family was able to extend empathy for each other within the holding environment of the therapy for some considerable time. In so doing, the mother offered a partial "because clause" when she said that if her daughter had felt hurt by her, then she could see why the daughter had not wanted to help by doing the dishes. A moment later, their capacity to treat each other this way collapsed, and the mother lashed out, demonstrating the calamitous relationship. Investigating that failure enabled the therapist to say that sometimes the mother lashed out at the daughter because it was less painful than feeling openly angry at her husband. Here the explanation took the family toward the fear that if the mother expressed the anger directly at the husband, a calamitous collapse of the whole family might occur, but the therapist did not take that step in one leap.

His interpretation enabled the mother to say that the more specific reason for venting her anger on her daughter instead of her husband was that she was frightened of him but not of her daughter. This took the family one step closer to the fears underlying her attitude toward her husband, both within the current family and in her internal objects projected onto him. This let all of them understand more about this repetitive family scene and put them in a position to move to yet more understanding in the future. Before the next level of explanation could have emotional impact, the current situation needed to be linked to the mother's long experience of rejection with her own mother and, later, with her feeling that her daughter was like her sister, who had seemed to get more than she did. This added an enriched context to her personal reaction, one with which the daughter could actually sympathize and so become more like the longed-for mother.

TRANSFERENCE AND COUNTERTRANSFERENCE

Interpretation is most useful to the family when it arises from our experience of the family's use of the therapeutic environment as a holding situation. This takes us into the realm of transference and countertransference. We have learned to use transference differently in family therapy than in individual or couple therapy. This difference helps us adapt technique to each situation. The use of transference and countertransference in family and couple therapy is so fundamental to the technique of psychoanalytic family therapy that we devote to it much of the next three chapters.

WORKING THROUGH

"Working through" is a term Freud (1914) used to describe the efforts at continuing analytic work in defiance of the tendency for resistance to increase as the work progresses. In 1926 he wrote, "After the ego has decided to relinquish its resistances it still has difficulty undoing the repressions" (p. 159). In other words, naming the resistance is not enough, and the task of undoing the ego's preference for maintaining repression despite new knowledge calls for "strenuous effort." It is arduous for patient and analyst, both of whom may feel gloomy about the prospect of change. If the work is continuing reasonably well, they need not; for at such times layers of repression are being peeled away, and piecemeal resolution of the conflict should follow.

So, too, in family therapy: we do not simply name the resistances and expect derepression of unconscious family material. Families are suffering from a defensive system of object relationships that can be seen in the ways the members relate to each other and in the manner the family relates to us. These relationships are complex, deriving from multiple experiences and compromises in the face of conflict, and mutually reinforcing because they fit together. Thus they maintain a system that stays the same, and so there is resistance in the system against change. All family therapies breach the system, but in analytic family therapy we explore the motivation for its being as it is. The many determinants have to be worked out over and over again in their various forms and at the different developmental levels to permit fundamental change. That is why we expect most families to require prolonged treatment.

At the time of elaborating on his ideas about working through, Freud, (1926) had developed a more sophisticated view of the neurotic symptom than earlier. He viewed the symptom as a compromise between the id seeking expression and gratification and the ego seeking to repress these. It was also a signal of anxiety experienced by the ego when threatened by the derepression of instinctual material.

In the family, the symptomatic individual may be viewed as holding a compromise between his individuation and the solidarity of the group. Symptomatic family patterns can also be viewed as a compromise between the family's goals and those of the previous generation. And symptom formation can be seen as a signal of anxious unrest in the family system as it seeks and resists a new equilibrium appropriate to its current developmental phase. In object relations terms, a symptom in an individual or in the family group is a crystallization of previous family experience with relating. It represents multiple microscopic projective identifications distributed among the family members in a particular pattern. These are the results of many mutually reinforcing combinations of ways of relating. They are perpetuated for the same reasons that they arose, holding together and held *in situ* by faulty relationships in place of a family holding environment that would support mature interdependence.

The period of working through feels laborious, sometimes boring, frustrating, or hopeless. At such times we remind ourselves that such resistance is to be expected, occurring at the intrapsychic, interpersonal, and intergenerational levels. This is analogous to Freud's realization that resistance comes from many sources—from the ego against accepting new knowledge and derepression, from the id against renouncing instinctual gratification, and from the superego against permitting success. We also remind ourselves and our students that when the working through seems most hopelessly bogged down, we are usually closest to the repressed material. This does not consist purely of instinctual sexual or murderous urges but includes all kinds of infantile forms of relating in the family. What we work through is the family's persistence in holding on to these infantile forms of relating in order to gratify the fundamental need for attachment in the absence of more mature patterns that could more adequately satisfy the basic human need for relationship.

Family therapy has a significant advantage over individual therapy. When one member in a family changes, the effect on the others means that the whole system tends to change. This applies pressure on the others to accommodate, which causes a ripple effect that may be dramatic and intense. The power of new insights and of changes in one part of the family is such that the speed of working through can be accelerated. A change in one part of the family system can effect change in the family system as a whole, an effect that has been described by many nonanalytic family therapists. For instance, Bowen (1978) uses this phenomenon as the reason to conduct "family therapy" with only a couple. He finds that improved differentiation of self takes place only in the triangle of marital partners and therapist, and that other family members automatically change in response to that. This route for change does occur. But it also happens that resistance sets in from other corners of the family to counter the change, and the family goes back to its old equilibrium or works out a new one that minimizes change. This is the reason we assume that most families will have to cover overlapping ground many times in the process of working through.

This speaks to the question of short-term versus long-term family therapy. In a recent survey reported to us informally, Alan Gurman found that the average length of a family treatment was four to seven sessions, with twenty being the usual maximum number. Stierlin (1985) presented a telephone follow-up study of family therapy lasting eight to ten sessions with the families of anorexics, in which he reported that cure or great improvement was achieved by 80 percent of the cases. But careful examination of the data revealed that 90 percent of the improved cases were of very young adolescents with short-term anorexia. The improvement rate falls off with increasing age of the adolescent and with chronicity. We would want to offer long-term family and individual therapy to families with more severe pathology. We agree that family therapy is a powerful format, but it is not a miracle. It provides some foreshortening of the process of change, gained by working with the family members who consitute the present experience of objects for each other and the past experience on which are based the internal objects that need to change.

We are aware that our recommendation for weekly family work

lasting one to two years runs counter to the general trend in family therapy. Many of the other forms of family therapy claim to achieve their best results with few, widely spaced meetings. Psychoanalytic family therapy is an in-depth treatment in its basic format, often intensified by the collateral use of individual or couple therapy, or occasionally by increasing family sessions to more than once a week, as in the case of the family of a withholding preadolescent, which met twice weekly for an extended time. Jack Graller has told us that he increases couple sessions to twice weekly to move the treatment to new depth. Most families begin treatment with a limited goal in mind, but they can be helped to enlarge it as their understanding of the links between current difficulties and underlying issues grows.

On the other hand, there is a definite role for short-term family therapy. This may take the form of a planned brief treatment or a foreshortened therapy terminated when goals are achieved earlier than expected. Some examples will be given in later chapters. Some families maintain more limited goals, at times for defensive reasons that can be understood but not altered, at times because their holding capacity is strong despite their failure in the current crisis. Often these are families that have gotten stuck at a particular developmental stage and are good candidates for brief intervention. Once the crisis of that stage is addressed, they have gotten what they need and they are off. There are yet other families for whom practicalities of the situation rule out all but brief intervention, because a child is going off to college or the family is about to leave the area. In these situations we use our longer-term assessment of the situation as a context within which we can focus on goals that are possible or appropriate to the circumstances. With this view, we do not need to feel helplessly or omnipotently bound to attempt fundamental change in a few sessions.

Some therapists work in settings that will not support long-term work. Many health maintenance organizations, insurance companies, clinical departments, or student health services either proscribe long-term work for financial reasons or make it difficult because of the size of the patient load. Other institutional settings may limit long-term work because the patient population is mobile, as for instance in the military setting, or because it may be difficult for hospital-based family therapists to continue with families after the index patient is discharged. The question arises whether an analytic approach is helpful under these circumstances. The analytic approach cannot produce prompt symptomatic relief to satisfy an institution's need to provide service under budgetary constraint. It can only broaden the perspective and clinical acumen of the staff who work in brief therapy.

Ancillary Techniques

We have said little in this chapter about the use of specific ancillary techniques, such as the use of play in families with young children, the use of art and drawing in family evaluations and therapy, or the use of dreams and other vehicles that offer screens for projection in the course of family work. These are illustrated in examples elsewhere in the book. Although some specific familiarity with them is useful, the use of these vehicles depends primarily on the way of working we have been discussing in this chapter. For instance, when a dream or a drawing is presented in the family, it is there for investigation in terms of its shared meaning to the family and to each of the individuals. It is useful to ask the presenter of the dream or drawing to comment on it first so that he or she does not feel attacked by other family members' responses. Then we can turn to other family members for their reactions, which have the status of unconscious associations. Sometimes there is no need to ask for reactions, and instead we use whatever material develops as constituting the associations. From this point on, the discussion has the same standing as any other topic—it is available for study and understanding. Examples of the use of play and drawing are given in Chapters 1, 6, 8, 12, 14, and 19; the use of dreams is illustrated in two cases described in Chapter 19.

Cotherapy

The use of two therapists to treat a family is an established tradition in psychoanalytic family therapy. It is especially helpful in training settings or in research, where the two therapists can share their reactions and observations to enlarge their understanding of the family. The NIMH group that developed family therapy for the treatment of borderline adolescents paired the adolescent's therapist with the parents' social worker as cotherapists to represent both the adolescent's and the parents' points of view when working with the whole family (Berkowitz et al. 1974). This way of working continues to be valuable with difficult families, in which cases the added expense is justified.

From our point of view, any of these rationales justifies the use of two therapists. It enlarges the possible field of observation for us by enlarging the screen upon which the family can project its internal world, that is, its transferences. Nevertheless, there are only a few illustrations of cotherapy given in this volume, because we do not ourselves currently tend to work in cotherapy. Both of us have done so in the past, mostly when we were in stages of our own training, and David Scharff (1982) used cotherapy extensively when developing a psychodynamic treatment method for sexual disorders. From our experience of supervising students working in cotherapy, we have found that it is best to use two therapists of approximately the same level of experience. Otherwise, the less experienced therapist tends to be overshadowed.

Having two people to enlarge the field of observation and to absorb the transference offers an opportunity to enrich the understanding of the family, but this requires active discussion between each session. Without this processing, unnoticed splits will almost inevitably develop as the family parcels out "good" and "bad" transferences, and the cotherapy will no longer feel useful. Beyond its use to avoid this pitfall, the processing of the cotherapy experience is the work of understanding the family's projections.

Although we value cotherapy, recommend it when necessary, and teach it to students, we do not work together as cotherapists ourselves. This position derives from our experience that when we have done so, the time and space needed for processing the family projections have been greater for us than for a cotherapy team that is not married. This happens because the family projections that we absorb stir up not only each therapist's inner object system but resonate as well with our shared object relations. Much can be gained from this, both toward understanding the family and toward understanding ourselves. But at a certain point, we have to draw a boundary so that clinical work does not invade our marital and family space, and so that we do not exploit clinical experiences and technical problems by using them as the basis for our continuing marital renegotiation. To put it less theoretically, dinnertime is for enjoying being together and with our children, not for mulling over difficult countertransferences.

Limitations of Psychoanalytic Technique in Family Therapy

Because much is written in the family therapy literature about why psychoanalytic techniques are not effective, we want briefly to give our own assessment of their limitations. Are there families or types of families for whom they are ineffective or irrelevant? In a general sense, there are some families that are easier to treat because they bring the capacity for therapeutic alliance. We might think this would be more likely to be true of educated, verbal families, and perhaps it is partly so. But it is also true that these families can mount a more effective verbal resistance than less verbally proficient families.

Yet many less educated or uneducated families have been able to work with our reflective way of working. It is not verbal proficiency that determines a capacity for insight but a sense of trust and alliance. It is true that there are difficult-to-treat families, including ghetto families, multiproblem families, or families of substance abusers with impoverished capacities for delay of gratification. But there are other families in these categories who take readily to building understanding and taking back projections as a way of improving their holding for each other. We must not assume that because they fall into one of these socioeconomic categories they cannot profit from our work.

Some families are harder to treat than others. When families have multiple deprivations and impoverished symbolic thinking, our tools will often seem inadequate, and our resources will be stressed. For some of these families, more concrete methods of intervention may be helpful. Even so, the therapist's training in an analytic approach, and the way of conceptualizing the family's problem in developmental and transference terms, will be helpful in the conduct of the case and in understanding the countertransference.

The qualities that render these techniques ineffective are those not of impoverished symbolic thinking but of a lack of openness to exploration and to taking back projections. There are poor families and there are also well-educated or wealthy families that cannot manage. Any therapeutic endeavor will have difficulty with such families, but some of the more directive approaches may allow temporary resolution of an impasse when a family will not permit more thorough work.

Ending

It is likely that change will occur after months of preparatory work has let the family advance and retreat on its issues, much as children grow, learning through repetitions over time to reach progressively higher levels of emotional and intellectual development. Not that the work goes on forever. Termination is not focused on as a time limit to pressure change, as in brief therapy, but it is kept in mind during every session. In the practical sense, the session as a sample of treatment is not endless but is finite. We are aware of the practice of many family therapists to make family sessions long, perhaps two or more hours. We tend to see families for a defined amount of time, between forty-five minutes and an hour.

No matter how interruptive it may be to the discussion, we end the session on time. This demonstrates our commitment to the family as consultants to its process, which continues before and beyond therapy, just as the individual lives have reality beyond the family boundary. In the philosophical sense, we link the family past with its present system of object relationships with a view to enabling the autonomy. In working with issues of separation and individuation among family members, and between the family and ourselves at the end of the hour and at vacation times, we also prepare for the family to leave us. Our work with a family's reaction to the end of the hour constitutes work at the boundary of the session that begins the preparation for termination.

Termination takes so many forms and poses so many challenges to our way of working that we devote the final chapter of the book to it. Here we can say that just as the final termination offers a period of reexperiencing and reworking the family transferences in modified forms, so the nature of the ending of many sessions brings to the fore the need for interpretation and working through of issues of separation and mourning.

CHAPTER 10

Transference and Countertransference

Working with transference and countertransference is characteristic of object relations family therapy. Object relations and group analytic theories permit us to take the broadest view of transference. Transference occurs between family members, between each family member and the therapist, and between the family as a group and the therapist. We work with transference whenever it reveals itself, but our most constant focus is on the family–therapist relationship, which is defined by the family's shared group transference to us and which we detect by recognition of our countertransference responses, which include emotions, fantasies, thoughts, and behaviors. We describe the way we process and review our countertransference in the clinical setting in detail because we feel it is essential to communicating the technique so that students can learn our approach. We study it to pin down the evidence for our hypotheses about the family's experience so that it does not remain at the nontransferable level of intuition. We think this study might also be helpful to students of strategic and structural family therapy in their attempts to learn the skill of "working with the person of the therapist" (Aponte and VanDeusen 1981).

We begin with a theoretical review of the historical development of transference and countertransference concepts in the individual analytic setting. We aim to show how object relations theory has broadened Freud's early concepts. Then we show how these experiences allow for the development inside the therapist of an edition of the internal object world of the patient that corresponds to the patient's view of his or her family. From this we move on to demonstrate the application of our learning about transference and countertransference to our psychoanalytic work with families.

The Concept of Transference: Freud

The concept of transference was introduced by Freud in 1895 and modified over the years. He noticed at first that patients were inclined to make false connections between ideas and feelings to defend against awareness of memories of real situations that had upset them. Similarly, they might make a false connection between their feelings and the physician, when the real connection would have been between those feelings and important people from the past. Freud called these types of false connections *transferences* to the psychoanalytic investigator. He gave examples of women who began to resist treatment because of a transference toward him of forbidden feelings that had originally applied to someone in the past. He also noted that some patients were afraid of being influenced by and made dependent upon the physician who was treating them, at this time by hypnosis and rudimentary analysis. He thought these transferences were to be interpreted as resistances to accepting treatment.

Ten years later, Freud (1905b) described two kinds of transferences. In one type, the patient presented a facsimile of the original forbidden impulses, now directed unchanged toward the physician as a direct substitute. In the other type, through the process of sublimation, the patient presented more "ingeniously constructed" modifications of the forbidden impulses, which Freud called "revised editions." These could even become conscious, "cleverly taking advantage of some real peculiarity in the physician's person or circumstances and attaching themselves to that" (p. 116). These transferences, a recurrent and inevitable accompaniment of the psychoanalytic situation, needed to be detected and disconnected from the physician by interpretation that reconnected them to the earlier sources. In other words, transference was now viewed as a repetition that needed to be converted to a memory by interpretation, in order to free the psychoanalytic process.

In 1895, Freud had viewed transference as a stumbling block. By 1905, he saw transference as "the most powerful ally" of psychoanalysis. He had become convinced that it was "only after the transference has been resolved that a patient arrives at a sense of conviction of the validity of the connections which have been constructed during the analysis" (1905b, pp. 116–117).

Twelve years later Freud (1917b) realized that these transference manifestations became more frequent and compelling until the original psychic situation was repeated exclusively with the analyst at the center. This development he called the *transference neurosis*. Because it involved the analyst so totally, he would have ample time to examine the transference neurosis. But now he would interpret it not in hopes of getting rid of it but, rather, to discover its full nature and eventually to reconstruct its connection to past experience. The development of Freud's writing about transference follows the path of development of transference in an analysis.

Although fully aware of the importance of early relationships, and exquisitely aware of the patient's relationship to him, Freud (1905a) remained close to the libido theory. He was careful to refer to transference not as the repetition of a relationship but as the repetition of a psychological experience from the past applied to the person of the physician: The physician is simply the present site for the distribution of the libido, or sexual energy, of the patient (1917c). Freud (1912b) recognized that positive transference promoted the psychoanalytic relationship and, because it furthered the treatment, required no interpretation. However, erotic transference-love, or as we might say, an excessively positive transference, just as surely as a negative transference, served the patient's resistance to the emergence of the original edition of the conflict based in early experience (1915). Because a fresh repression was not necessary in the protected psychoanalytic situation, the transference could be worked through. The analyst had to help the patient understand his or her unconscious resistance to facing reality under the domination of the pleasure principle and to dealing with the authority of the physician in the task of psychoanalysis.

Transference: Object Relations Theory

We turn to object relations theory to extend this concept of transference to include the repetition in the therapeutic relationship of early relationships and even earlier part-object relationships. We think of transference as the living history of ways of relating, influenced by the vicissitudes of infantile dependence and by primitive emotions of a sexual and aggressive nature that arise in pursuit of attachment. The analytic situation is designed to evoke such transference because of the analyst's abstinence. Abstinence is a "fundamental principle that the patient's need and longing should be allowed to persist in her in order that they may serve as forces impelling her to do work and to make changes. We must beware of appeasing these forces by means of surrogates" (Freud 1915, p. 165).

Using an object relations theoretical base, we can now think of abstinence as producing "object hunger" in the patient. The intensity and clarity of the transference are due in large part to the way the analytic setup provides such a large gap between the patient and the analyst that the patient is forced to move toward the analyst for an attachment. Because the analyst remains at more or less a steady distance, the patient is pulled forward, out of retreat. This could be thought of as a manipulation, except that it seems to be the necessary condition for getting the internal world out into the open, for giving it a kind of psychological breathing space in which it becomes full-blown in the gap between the patient and analyst, and in which it can then be brought to life again and reexamined. When this happens, it is a matter of reliving old events from various periods of development, of which the most important, or at least the hardest to get at, tend to be the ones from the preschool years. But they are relived in the present, where the appropriateness and inappropriateness of the patient's responses can be observed not only by the analyst but, more important, by the patient, who can then see which events in current life tend to trigger old responses—responses that treat the current person (the analyst) as though he or she actually were the internal objects.

The diverse members of the British Object Relations School shared the intrinsic belief that the relationship to the therapist was at the center of their clinical work. Thus, in the tradition of British empiricism, the theory developed from their work with the relationship between the patient and the therapist. Guntrip (1969), coming late in the history of this group, wrote:

If the development and maintenance of the ego has come more and more to be seen as the fundamental psychodynamic process, and an ego can only develop in the medium of personal object-relationship, it follows that psychotherapy at any level, but particularly at the deepest level, can only occur as a result of a personal therapeutic relationship. . . . the more we are concerned about the "person" and the less about the "symptom," the more the personal therapeutic relationship comes to dominate the entire situation [p. 310].

This overall situation of the therapeutic setting pushes us toward consideration of the transference not as an isolated phenomenon of the patient as he or she exists in an impersonal situation but in context, in the culture medium of an observable personal relationship with the therapist. We agree with Bird (1972) that the transference occurring in the therapeutic relationship is unique, but like him, we, too, are taken with the "as yet unexplored idea that transference is a universal mental function which may well be the basis for all human relationships" (p. 267). We go a step further to say that the latter sort of transference operates between family members where any present relationship is colored by earlier editions of the relationship, based in turn on layered experiences at earlier developmental stages when perception, cognition, and the management of affect were more primitive. These sort of transferences in an individual operate as valencies to engage with others who have similar or complementary tendencies to relate in certain ways characteristic of stranger groups (Bion 1961) as well as of family groups (see Chapter 7).

Resistance to the Return of the Repressed Bad Object Relationship

Freud (1926) defined resistance as originating in the repression by the conscious, executive part of the mind—the ego—of the unconscious part—the impulses of the id. In addition to this repression resistance, Freud also described the resistances due to transference and secondary gain from illness, both ego resistances as well. To these he added the id resistance that necessitates working through and the superego resistance that originates in the need for punishment to expiate guilt and that blocks success and recovery. Such concepts of resistance are useful but insufficient for family work.

Fairbairn (1952) may be read as having defined the motive force of the self to create fundamentally split and repressed areas of the self as the need to get rid of ways of relating that were too painful to be borne in the central and conscious ego. Resistance now becomes different: it is the reluctance to allow a painful relationship into awareness. Guntrip (1969) added the logical extension—that resistance operates against allowing the pain of earlier experience to be introduced into the current therapeutic situation. It is the therapeutic relationship that is the motive force for the therapeutic resistance: As he explained, "My own experience leaves me in no doubt . . . that the adult in the patient finds it so disturbing and humiliating to go back to having to experience himself on the level of a child with another adult" (p. 314).

Resistance, then, is the difficulty that patients have in revealing the difficult and painful parts of themselves to themselves and experiencing them in relation to us. In the beginning, they identify the therapist with their own critical internal objects, and it becomes increasingly difficult to show parts of themselves of which they no longer approve. What gets them by this as treatment goes on is the confidence that they can be less judgmental of themselves because they borrow our acceptance of them. This is to say that the patient moves from a projective identification, in which the therapist is felt to be the patient's antilibidinal object, to an introjective identification, in which the antilibidinal object is understood and then has less need to declare itself in the usual harsh and critical way.

Miss Harvey, a 33-year-old graphic artist in her third year of analysis, formed a new relationship with a man a week after she made a suicide attempt. She came in saying that everything was now fine. When the analyst suggested the relationship and the speed of its formation might have defensive functions, probably to ward off her fear of depending on him so completely when he was soon to be away, she became furious and said he seemed not to be able to understand anything at all. He was just like the rest of the world. The proof of that lay in the fact that other people were saying the same thing to her. His questions about early sources of her anger were rebuffed staunchly. She told him to shut up: it didn't matter whether he understood or not. When she got up off the couch at the end of the hour, she straightened her hair and said, "I'm sorry for being such a bitch. I know I have to do it, but I'm sorry you have to put up with it!" The next day, she came in and said, "It's not easy to say. As soon as I got to the car I knew you were right. I think I have been mad at you for going on vacation. You are my father deserting me, and I can't stand to have you leave when I need you so much. And I can't stand to say it to you. I mean I can now, but it's still not easy."

Transference and resistance, then, can be considered to be interpersonal phenomena, deriving from internalized object relationships recreated in the therapeutic relationship.

Countertransference

Countertransference received little attention in Freud's writing, perhaps because, as Strachey (1958) suggests, he did not want patients to read too much about his technique. In 1910, Freud described the countertransference as a reaction to the patient's influence on the analyst's unconscious feelings. He warned later against a countertransference feeling that it is the analyst's charm that has caused the development of the transference of infantile love to his person. Freud (1915) saw countertransference mainly as a feeling of temptation against which the analyst must be proof. Freud (1910, 1912a, 1937) maintained his view that countertransference arose from the analyst's resistance to the emergence in him of unconscious infantile complexes, and that the remedy was self-analysis or training analysis.

In the early history of psychoanalytic technique and in a significant group of modern analysts, countertransference continued to be considered as the reflection of difficulties the analyst was having managing his own unanalyzed conflicts as they were evoked by the patient. For instance, Greenson (1967), in his landmark text on psychoanalytic technique, wrote "Countertransference is a transference reaction of an analyst to a patient, a parallel to transference, a counterpart of transference . . . countertransference reactions can lead to persistent inappropriate behavior toward the patient in the form of constant misunderstanding or some unconscious unrewarding, seductive or permissive behavior by the analyst" (p. 348). In this line of psychoanalytic thought, countertransference was therefore seen to represent essentially the analyst's own transference problems as evoked by the therapeutic setting. Tower (1956) held that "countertransference should be reserved for transferences of the analyst—in the treatment situation—and nothing else" (p. 253). She wrote that countertransference was a normal feature of being in relationship to the patient, but that if it became abnormal in degree, it could impinge on the progress of the analysis.

The British group, however, led the way in extending the concept of countertransference to a more sophisticated level in beginning the study of the responses of the analyst as the internal registering of the projections of the patient onto the analyst. This advance followed from the ideas of projection (Klein 1936) and projective identification (Klein 1946), as studied in detail by Klein and her group (Segal 1964). They suggested that the situation began with splitting and projection of drives, of libido and the aggressive derivatives of the death instinct, onto the primary object prior to more organized ways of relating. However, they also spoke of the externalization of the "good mother" or the "bad mother" onto the person of the mother, and explored the vicissitudes of the splitting of the image of the mother into parts, initially because the baby could not process the notion of a whole mother who was both good and bad. Fairbairn (1952) formulated infantile mental organization as the taking in of the experience with the mother in a way that protected against bad object relationships and that maintained order. But it was the Kleinian group that most thoroughly explored the use of the analyst's experience as the fundamental tool for understanding the patient's situation. Winnicott (1971b) and Guntrip (1969) in Britain and Searles (1979, 1986) in the United States have contributed substantially to this literature in ways that have been appealing to a broader audience than did Klein's original language.

THE WORK OF HEINRICH RACKER

The clearest theoretical formulation of countertransference, which has a direct inheritance from Klein, is that of Heinrich Racker, a Kleinian analyst in Argentina. In his 1957 paper "The Meanings and Uses of Countertransference," Racker described a clear set of transactions involved in countertransference. His ideas carry us into the area that is most useful to us in family therapy. Racker began as others before, by discussing the varying contributions to countertransference both from the patient's projection and from the therapist's difficulties. These latter contributions, the ones introduced by the therapist's difficulties, he explicitly said represent not true countertransference but the therapist's transferences to the patient.

He now introduced an entirely new idea. He said that the countertransference represented a fundamental condition of receiving the patient's projections, which became organized into projective identifications. This could only happen without the therapist knowing it was happening. He had to be available to receive these projective identifications, to allow them to take over, then to become aware of them, and to process the experience. Only in this way could the patient experience being deeply understood. The blocking out of this experience left the patient feeling shut out and treated mechanically, at a distance. In this formulation, the willingness to be available to receive these transferences (a word we can use here interchangeably with projective identifications) meant that the therapist would by necessity be working with countertransference as a fundamental means of understanding the patient's internal world.

Racker then went on to examine the varying sources of these

projective identifications within the patient's object world. These exist because the patient's internal condition is, as we have said, fundamentally split in a number of ways. The most fundamental split is between self and object, but there are splits between various parts of experience with the object, depending on the kinds of painful experience.

CONCORDANT AND COMPLEMENTARY IDENTIFICATIONS

Most fundamental to our work here is his formulation that the therapist could feel identified with two parts of the patient's own experience, with a part of either the patient's self or object. If we hear from a patient with whom we have a reasonably good alliance that her husband was drunk the night before and threatened to beat her, we might feel angry on her behalf at the husband and frightened for her welfare. This identification with the patient's self Racker termed *concordant identification.*

If, on the other hand, that patient grows slightly verbally abusive in the hour and accuses us of beating on her with our interpretations, or of imposing things on her without caring if they upset her, we may feel attacked and identify with her objects when she is displeased and angry at them. This identification with the patient's objects Racker called *complementary identification.*

It now becomes possible for us to think about the sources of countertransference in complex ways. Many of the clinical contributions of Searles, Winnicott, and others have also helped us to do so. For instance, in the situation in which we feel treated as the patient's object, presumably the patient is being a part of her self. However, when we feel treated like a part of herself, then we need to think about which person in her object life she is being, in order to be able to say to her, "I feel I am being treated by you now as you felt treated by your father, perhaps to let me learn what it was like for you and perhaps to avoid the possibility that I might become abusive to you." If we do not get caught in the terms, which introduce a level of sophistication but are not important in themselves, then we can use Racker's contribution to move to the general position that our role in the patient's life becomes a complex one in which we receive and absorb changing projections of self and object. The understanding and clarifying of the conditions under which differing images are transmitted into us constitute the work of therapy.

The Growth of "Negative Capability"

We can put all of this together to say that over time, in a sufficiently comprehensive therapy, the therapist ought to be able to
reexperience the family experience of the patient growing up. And
because this is done between the two of them in a situation of
emotional exchange, the therapist and the patient can build a
shared conviction over time about the emotional validity of this
experience. The language used between patient and therapist, and
indeed the way the therapist thinks about what is happening, need
not and should not be shot through with technical terminology or
with attempts to make the experience fit some theoretical grid.
Rather, the therapist has to be in the kind of receptive position to
create a space between therapist and patient and a corresponding
space within the therapist that can be filled up with experience
from the patient's object world. To get to this position, the therapist needs to develop a personal quality of "negative capability."
This term, first used by the poet Keats to describe a quality of
Shakespeare's poetic character, is defined as a capacity for "being
in uncertainties, mysteries, doubts, without any irritable reaching
after fact and reason" (Murray 1955, p. 261). The idea was taken up
by Bion and used in his teaching. We learned how to relate to the
concept personally from Arthur Hyatt Williams at the Tavistock
Clinic in 1973. What Williams meant by this was the capacity to
tolerate "not knowing," and to suspend the need to know for long
enough to let the meaning of an experience emerge from inside the
experience itself. When we are able to do this successfully, the
countertransference experience tells us, eventually, everything we
need to know about our relationship with our patients, and with a
depth we cannot have if we impose theory as a way of understanding. "Negative capability" is an example of object relations being a
way of working rather than a theory.

Contextual Transference and Countertransference in Individual Treatment

As therapists we create the major part of the therapeutic holding
situation when we create inside us the space for the development of
negative capability. This, along with the overall provision of the
therapeutic situation, forms the holding situation in individual
therapy. Within this holding context, the individual patient has a

transference to the holding situation itself. In this transference, the patient brings expectations of the therapeutic relationship based on internal models of the way primary figures provided holding. We call this the *contextual transference*. The therapist has a response to the patient's way of using the therapeutic environment that the therapist provides. We call this the *contextual countertransference*.

In individual therapy and analysis, the early relation to the therapist does not yet involve the process of deeply interpenetrating object worlds. Rather, the patient expects the therapist to provide a context for a certain kind of work, which may or may not correspond to what the therapist expects to offer. The first transferences are to the therapist's provision of such a working space, comparable to the adequacy of the parents' holding to sustain the growth of the child. In terms of the early mother–infant situation, the contextual transference corresponds to the infant's response to being in its mother's arms, to her physical qualities and activities that make up the envelope within which the eye-to-eye, centered relationship develops. In most weekly individual psychotherapy, the transference to the "arms around" holding aspects of the therapist is most prominent, and most of the countertransference will be generated here as well. This is also the major organizing transference in the long first phase of psychoanalysis, before the crystallization of the transference neurosis.

Once we recognize that the contextual transference is the one that is more closely connected to the patient's affect in the early work, we are in a better position to understand its vicissitudes and to work with it as a different matter than the more focused transference that characterizes the later phases of psychotherapy or psychoanalysis.

EXAMPLES FROM INDIVIDUAL TREATMENT

A woman called to ask for a consultation but asked first if the therapist's office were in his home. She had a previous therapist whose office in his home had exposed her painfully to the richness she saw in his family life, and she felt she would not be able to stand dealing with that again. When he said that his office was in his house, she asked for another referral.

In this example, the ready-made contextual transference to the holding situation around the therapy prevented a beginning. The contextual transference also shows up later in therapy.

A woman who had been in analysis for two years mentioned in passing that she still let her young daughter sleep in bed with her and her husband on occasion. The analyst had known of this practice and had felt all along that this matter could not yet be considered analytically, because for the patient his acceptance of it stood for his acceptance and understanding of her as a person, and thus for his ability to hold her contextually as she felt her mother could not. On this occasion, the analyst was, without knowing it, feeling annoyed with the patient because she had been discussing her ambivalence about continuing the analysis. He made a pointed inquiry about the sleeping arrangements and got the response that he had predicted all along—that he was not to be trusted. The patient said she had thought he had accepted her wisdom about the sleeping arrangements, and now she felt betrayed.

Although the analyst's intervention could be seen to represent several kinds of countertransference, the most important seemed to be the patient's turning him into her critical mother. But this was done so that what was challenged was the way in which the mother's criticism constituted proof that she could not hold the patient safely. This in turn could be seen to be invoked at a point in the analysis at which the patient was about to chance using the analyst in a more focused way. This felt so risky to her that she mounted a transferential challenge to the analyst's provision of holding and safety in the contextual transference. His countertransference to this failed, in the first instance, to meet the test, but it did provide information in an intense way about her fears concerning the failure of the holding environment.

Focused Transference and Countertransference in Individual Treatment

Other aspects of the transference derive from the individual's experience of the centered relationship to the parent, built up during the sequences of centered relating when mother and baby communicate at the core of their minds and bodies during the early psychosomatic partnership. In individual therapy, over time, these aspects of the transference are seen when the patient projects parts of inner objects in more or less detail into the therapist. We call this the *focused transference*. The therapist receives and is affected by this transference through the process of projective identification.

The focused transference can sometimes be detected by an intellectual review of the patient's object relations as projected into relationships with significant others. But its form is most exquisitely understood when it is experienced in the countertransference, at which point there is a recreation of the patient's inner object system in the present therapeutic relationship, which by now is capable of the kind of centered relating that took place between the patient as a child and the early mother. We call this the *focused countertransference*.

Having carefully tried to differentiate the contextual and focused transferences, we now have to remind ourselves that there is overlap. Just as the baby experiences centered relating within the holding context provided by its mother, so its experience of the mother-at-the-core is linked to its experience of the environmental mother. Reexperience of the one cuts to the other, and there is an aspect of holding that derives from the immediacy of the centered relationships and contributes to the strength of contextual holding. Thus, there is back-and-forth movement between these aspects of relationship and between these two aspects of transference. In health there is a congruence between the two transferred images as mostly ideal. In pathology there may be congruence between the two images as not ideal, or there may be a dissociation of the one from the other to protect at least one aspect of the relationship. In either case, the therapist takes in these two aspects, which are more or less differentiated by the patient's construction of early experience and which are further differentiated in the therapeutic relationship, depending on the type of treatment and the phase.

We have found it helpful in practice to distinguish the two types of countertransference by referring to them in shorthand, using bodily terms. The contextual is the "arms-around" countertransference, whereas the focused is the "eye-to-eye" countertransference. This shorthand carries the usual risk of simplification, so we have to remember that these are to be taken not literally but, rather, as visual images that help to fix the ideas, and that at any point the one may dissolve into the other, because each experience is differentiated from, but also contains, the other.

AN EXAMPLE FROM PSYCHOANALYSIS

This leads to an example of the work with the focused transference and countertransference. It is not possible, however, to discuss these without including the contextual transference and countertransference that contain them. This example elaborates upon a transference vignette about Miss Harvey given in Chapter 4 and mentioned again earlier in this chapter. To enable us to illustrate the role of countertransference, we have chosen the same issues illustrated in work with her.

A few weeks after the analytic session reported earlier in this chapter, Miss Harvey began a session by saying, "I'm too tired to talk today. I've been up all night on a project deadline, and if you want me to do anything here, you are going to have to ask me the questions. You know I don't agree with the way you try to get me to talk."

As this was a recurrent motif in her work, the analyst felt a bit annoyed, with a "here we go again" feeling, but he responded to his wish to be helpful, too, with a question as to whether she might now have any thoughts about the situation of being questioned.

"That's not the right question, you dolt!" she said. "I've told you and told you that if you want me to tell you anything, you have to ask me specific things." And she began to rant and rave, eventually telling the analyst about a situation at work where her boss had called a staff meeting. When he asked people about their projects, she had felt dumb and unable to speak. She was so mad at him for "quizzing her" that she wanted to be able to yell questions back at him.

The analyst realized that he had been feeling grilled and harassed himself in the first part of the hour and that Miss Harvey was far angrier than she had been earlier in the analysis. This association helped him to realize that he was being treated as the patient felt treated, and he now realized that he often felt "abused" by her in this way. This would result in struggles in which he felt pulled into a sort of fight with this patient, which left him feeling contentious and dissatisfied with his way of working. He would then grow silent for a few moments, only to have the patient say, "Where are you? I need for you to ask me a question. What do you think about what I have just said?" His feeling "dissatisfied with his way of working" seemed relevant now to the way he felt badgered and silenced by the patient. He tried again, using his own sense of being badgered and the inner dissatisfaction that followed in its wake.

He asked, "When I don't answer your question the right way, who do you think I might be acting like from your past?"

This time she responded. "The person you're acting like is *me!* And I'm acting like everybody else: my sister, mother, teachers I hated as a teenager, my ex-husband. I would never fight. When they would ask me questions, and I got confused, I would get silent. I would tell myself that the thing to do was to not get in a fight. But I wanted to yell.

"Look, I've told you this before, but I'll tell you again. You know my mother used to sit me in a chair and try to teach me to read. And she'd yell at me if I got words wrong. She'd say, 'You're not performing up to your potential. You'll never amount to anything if you keep going like this.' And she'd be screaming at me. I was 5 years old, for Christ's sake! I'd get so quiet, and she would shout, 'Don't sit there! You better talk or else!' And I'd want to yell at her, just so she'd know how it felt—what she was doing to me."

The analyst now felt relieved. The patient had begun to share a painful part of her own internal experience, and he no longer felt taken over by the feeling, familiar in work with Miss Harvey, of becoming someone he felt was a strange and unlikeable part of himself, the victim of badgering who became contentious and silenced.

In the same hour, the patient went on to tell the analyst about the new relationship with a man in which she felt more trusting and loving than in any she had ever been in before. It was so different from her marriage. She was able to relate her attack on the analyst to her feeling that he did not have confidence in this new relationship. She noted that she was now ready to admit that if he had been suspicious that her previous relationships with lovers were not mature, he would have been right, but that previously she did not trust him enough to admit it. In fact, she would insist that they were mature even while knowing that if he saw her with these men, he would have been dubious right away. "I never could have told you that before. You know, I can only yell at you like I have been because I trust you. And I've never trusted anyone enough to yell at them, no matter how angry or upset I felt. But then I can also tell you about this new relationship. I do appreciate it that you've forced me to keep going tonight although I was tired. You've been a prod to me, keeping me going."

The word "prod" resonated for the analyst, for he realized that that was a function he felt made to perform, with the implication of punishing, teasing, or goading the patient in a pseudo-phallic way. It made more sense now, with the patient's help.

In this amplified example, the analyst spent quite a lot of time in an identification with the patient, being persecuted by a critical maternal object. When his interpretive question led her to recognize this projection into him, the meaning of his questioning could also be understood as the "prodding" that the patient experienced with mother as well. With this work by the patient, the analyst felt relief from being captured by the projective identification, or focused transference, from her persecuting object, which had partly taken him over, and he felt restored to being a good object for the patient. This happened as she trusted him enough to tell him about her new relationship, at the same time that she confirmed the previous lack of trust that had been the antilibidinal element of the contextual transference from early in the analysis. In many of the hours in which the analyst had felt uncomfortable with the patient's behavior and with himself, he had had to tolerate "not knowing" where the discomfort came from in any definitive sense in order to let the patient work toward discovering it. This is not to say that he did not have any idea of the origin. As the patient said, they both knew in a sense. But he also had to let the moments grow by tolerating being taken over by her projective identification without throwing it back at her or shedding it. In this way, he had to relive what she was fearing and needing to relive. When she could then relive the experience with her objects, he and she had suffered through it together.

This meant that the analyst had to tolerate feeling attacked and badly treated. The patient did attack his ability to contain the work, and she did it repeatedly. But, as she made clear in this hour, even that attacking in the contextual transference represented her new capacity to trust in the context, an ability that she had given up early in her life, or perhaps had never had at all. Fundamentally, her ability to be angry at him represented a heightened trust in the contextual transference, while his overall capacity to contain these assaults drew on his trust in their relationship over the span of the work together. The growth of trust gave the patient faith in being held. The hour validated this shared conviction in the strengthened container, allowing the work with the focused transference and countertransference to proceed.

There has been some confusion about the role of transference in individual psychotherapy, because the quality of the transference seems less intense than in analysis. This has generally been taken by analysts to mean that this transference is less useful. It has certainly been seen as more diffuse. Discrete parts of an oedipal conflict with the therapist may come up in the transference, or events around vacations or something the analyst says may trigger a response in which he or she is seen by the patient as a rejecting object. But these events do not gather force like a rolling snowball. Rather, the patient comes in with a way of treating people and treats the therapist more or less like one of the internal objects. If the therapist is more benign than some, he or she picks up the cast of the more benign objects. From the beginning, the role of these objects is to provide a climate in which a kind of problem solving and self-discovery can go on. So we conclude that in individual therapy the most heartfelt reactions to the therapist mainly concern the success or failure of the holding or context-providing function.

BUILDING AN INTERNAL IMAGE OF THE INDIVIDUAL PATIENT'S FAMILY

A final point made in the example of Miss Harvey is a crucial one for family therapists and for individual therapists interested in families. The transference allows the construction in the therapist's understanding of a view of the patient's family, one that can be fully and accurately understood only through the use of the countertransference. Parts of the patient's childhood experiences with her mother came to light in this session. In other sessions, reenactments came up that conveyed her experience with father and siblings. With the benefit of many such sessions, the therapist gets a rich picture that eventually corresponds to the patient's experience of life within the family, even if not entirely accurately as others would have seen it. It is a major point of an object relations approach that this subjective experience of life in the family is just as valid as a so-called external view of the family. Both have equal standing, and one cannot replace the other. In a similar way, the family therapist can eventually get a view of the internal reality of the individual family members that is just as "true" as the interactive reality among them that is seen in the room (Winer 1985).

Transference and Countertransference in Family Treatment

This leads us to a consideration of the relevance of transference and countertransference to work with families and couples. In family therapy the patients enter therapy with intense, lifelong focused transferences to each other, which provide a leverage that is available to the individual psychotherapist only occasionally, and to the analyst only after the crystallization of the transference neurosis. The family, like the individual patient, also enters treatment with a transference to the therapist's provision of the holding. In family therapy, understanding this contextual transference is a tool for influencing more directly the several focused transferences. It is our hypothesis that the contextual transference and countertransference are the major organizers of the therapist's understanding in family therapy. The following example will illustrate this hypothesis and allow us to elaborate further.

This is a session with the Jansens, a family I had been seeing for almost two years in one form or another, and who are described in Chapters 4 and 12. They were referred when Tom, then 9 years old, broke into an electrical store and destroyed some equipment. He was regularly the butt of teasing at school and fought endlessly with his two older brothers. After an initial family session in which Tom erupted at his two brothers and then ran out of the room to the car, the father would not allow Tom's brothers to be seen in family therapy. He said, "One of our sons has gone to the dogs; we aren't going to let him contaminate the ones who are OK." Father's own defensiveness was apparent in this stance. It was clear to me, and incidentally to Mother, that Mr. Jansen could not be persuaded to attend at that point. However, after about six months of individual work with Tom, along with parent work that the father ruled was "specifically not to be therapy for us," Tom's behavior improved enough both at home and in a trial family session that Father agreed to expose all the children to family therapy. This session occurred about a year after beginning regular family sessions, a few weeks after the one reported in Chapter 4, at a time when the two older boys were at camp.

The three came in and sat, with Tom in a red swivel chair in which he rotated during much of the session, to Mr. Jansen's annoyance. Mrs. Jansen said they had not fought this week in any way, referring to last week when they had fought on the way to the session. Tom had used this in the session against his father. Mr. Jansen said that all of them, even Tom, were missing the older boys. "Sure I am," said Tom. "They're my brothers." "But you used to fight so much!" said Mrs. Jansen.

"Well, we love each other. That's just the way brothers are," said Tom. "But I also like having the house to myself."

So far, I felt this was a sort of interesting by-play, and I noted that Tom did indeed seem fonder of his absent brothers than he would have admitted to being a year earlier. I felt the parents were getting him to show off his progress, and I appreciated it partly, too, as if it were a credit to my helpfulness to them.

My idea that this was a "report card" on Tom's improvement was confirmed a moment later when Mr. Jansen said that they had gotten Tom's school report card. As he said this, Tom began to get silly and blow in the air, making noises and turning in his chair. Both parents got angry at this, telling him to stop, but he did not stop for some time. They noted that this was the kind of thing that made them mad at home. Finally, Mr. Jansen said, "Tom, no ice cream if you don't stop." "That's blackmail," yelled Tom. "Sure it is," said Father, "and I mean it." Tom now continued the behavior, while also beginning to pout. He was daring his father, who said again, "Tom! I mean it. No ice cream!" He said this in such a manner that I felt it was a dance between them, in which Tom would give in just in time to get his ice cream. I felt both frustrated for Mr. Jansen that Tom would not stop and annoyed with him for setting Tom up in the first place. I had confused and contradictory feelings about the "report" on the report cards and on Tom's growth: it seemed to me that Mr. Jansen had gotten away with showing off Tom's increased ability to express love for his brothers. Why did he have to rub it in about school? And I thought that there must be some genuine embarrassment on Tom's part about doing well at school. Though I could not quite formulate it in the hour, afterward I realized that Mr. Jansen was doing just the kind of showing off and flaunting that probably got Tom into trouble at school. Tom was doing the clowning, which probably accompanied his own wish to show off his "brilliance," and partly he was improving and now knew better than to do it but was being provoked to do so by Father.

At this point in the hour, I was feeling unsure of what was happening, and vaguely uncomfortable both with Mr. Jansen and with Tom. My discomfort was partly with Tom's clowning, which I did not believe at that moment was due to discomfort. All I could feel was that he was showing off. And I was uncomfortable with Mr. Jansen's persistent use of threats, which felt to me to be retaliatory and empty instead of constituting effective limit setting. I now recalled that I had been feeling annoyed with Mr. Jansen for urging Tom to go around slugging kids. I would start out feeling sure that was not the best solution, but Mr. Jansen and Tom managed to present these situations in which Tom was picked on in such a way that I could no longer quite tell what I thought. I knew that my own history of peer relations in latency and early adolescence made this an area in which I am a bit vulnerable, which means that I have to think through a solution in the area each time rather than relying on innate sense as I might in other areas. So I had ended up slightly confused and thinking, "Well, perhaps it is the thing to do after all."

I knew, however, that my discomfort was a time-tested sign that there was conflict and confusion in the patients, and that this was the time to intervene as long as the family was ready. I knew that my anger at Mr. Jansen was in the context of my growing liking for him overall. I noticed that Mrs. Jansen was sitting by and letting this go on, as she often did. At that moment, I thought of her as leaving things to Mr. Jansen but slightly smirking as she did so. As I thought of these things, Mr. Jansen was going on to tell about the achievement in the report card anyway, which was excellent after Tom's shaky start at the beginning of the year.

I now felt ready to use my discomfort to therapeutic advantage. I interrupted him to ask about the blackmailing and the difficult behavior. I said, "Is this exchange in here, right now, anything like the being picked on at school—which Tom really doesn't like you to discuss?"

Mr. Jansen said that perhaps it had a relationship, but he was thrown off stride by my question, because it interrupted him as he was charging ahead over Tom's objection. I could see by the way I had confused him in the process that my own discomfort had led me to intervene less smoothly than I would have wished. Mr. Jansen, however, was not too thrown off to respond, so we got by this moment.

He said, "I 'blackmail' him because I don't know what else to do. How do you stop him?" he asked. "But I can see that it might relate to school." He paused, looking down, then he looked at Tom again and said, "Did you know that I used to get in a lot of fights when I was a kid? And I used to lose!" And as he said this, Mr. Jansen's tone relaxed and he seemed to change from being in a head-on collision with Tom to being in a loving, fatherly position.

I could hardly believe the tone of Mr. Jansen's sharing. It was spontaneous and earnest, a new way of presenting himself. I felt a wash of relief at the breakthrough.

Tom said, "No! I didn't know that. Did you?" He then stopped playing with the cards he had been fiddling with after he gave up swiveling the chair, and he looked straight at his father.

I felt a kind of internal "tectonic-plate shift." Something about my feeling for Mr. Jansen was moving. I realized, again more in retrospect than I could consciously get a grip on at the moment, that I had felt slightly bullied by him right from the beginning, when he took such an outrageous stance about the "contamination of his good sons" and had used that as a front to avoid any investigating or sharing on his part. Although I felt sympathetic on one level with Mrs. Jansen's tolerance of his bullying, my going along with her in not pressuring meant I had felt vicariously bullied by her, too. But with this small evidence of willingness to share, I felt I was liking Mr. Jansen better, and because I knew how hard it was for him to let down his guard, I felt once again that I respected him and his courage.

So I asked him to say more, and this time he elaborated, slightly sheepishly but willingly: "I was athletic, which helped. But the older kids would come by, and it would always be me they picked on, and I couldn't beat them up. It wasn't quite like with Tom. It wasn't the kids my own age, but I did get beat up—often!"

I was thinking, slightly angrily still, that I understood something about how he got them to do this so regularly—that is, I was assuming he must have been provocative. As he made the brief statement about the older boys picking on him, I had a brief scene pass through my head in which I saw him taunting some older boys and saw them ganging up on him. In having this fantasy, I was identified partly with him and partly with the older boys, and partly I saw it from the perspective of my childhood self. I had some sympathy for him, and some for them.

As I was pondering this, Mrs. Jansen said, "I wonder if you didn't do something to provoke them?" I followed her by saying I had been thinking that he often seemed to be wanting Tom to fight as a ready-made attempt at a solution to being teased. Because we had been thinking together about how Tom might be provoking the other kids, I wondered if this might fit with his encouraging Tom to get things started, even though he was worried about it. Mrs. Jansen smiled and said, "Oh, he can be provocative himself, you know. Of course he does it with me, for a start."

"Can you give me an example?" I asked.

They agreed that the last big fight had been one such time, but they smiled knowingly at each other and didn't want to talk about it in front of Tom because it involved their intimate, that is sexual, life together. I noted to myself that we seemed to be very close to the emergence of material about the two of them that had formerly been ruled off-limits by Mr. Jansen. But at this moment I did not want to encourage them to invade an appropriately private boundary around their marriage. I asked if there were other examples they could share in this setting.

Mrs. Jansen thought for a moment and said, "There was the time you were supposed to pick me up and we got our signals crossed." Mr. Jansen filled in the story: she had come home in a blue fury after having to walk a good deal of the way because she had no money with her. He knew she was mad when she walked in the door. "Yes," she said, "but instead of even saying you were sorry I had to walk, you accused me of stupidity in not knowing which corner was which and said it served me right. I was too mad to begin with, but that's not the point right now. You used it to provoke me." And she smiled quite fondly to let him know she was not attacking him, and finished, "And you know it, honey!"

"It's true," he said. "I do that to her, and I kind of enjoy it. I shouldn't, but it's true that I do."

I felt glad that they had managed this piece of the work themselves, a "hats off to them" feeling that they could hold together to do it. Having accomplished the work of getting the fact of provocation within the family onto the table, I felt we could try to link it to Tom. So I turned to him and asked if he knew about this part of his father's life.

"Well, I know he can tease Mommy and me," he said. "But I never knew about the fights with the older kids. That's pretty interesting, Dad!"

Now feeling less distanced from all of them, I said, "I wonder, Mr. Jansen, if you think you might want Tom to pick off a few of the tormenters for you, a sort of vicarious victory over the kids who used to beat on you?"

"I never thought of that," he said. "Perhaps so." Mrs. Jansen now put her arm around his shoulder. She did not rub in the way she also often feels picked on and bullied by Mr. Jansen, something I think is part of her masochism. But I felt we could now talk about the question of feeling picked on in the family as an analogue to the feeling Tom can't handle peer relations at school.

I said, by way of summing up for the session, "The two issues of feeling picked on at home and at school are related, and understanding the one at home ought to help figure out what happens at school."

Tom was very interested, as indicated by his saying an unusually cheerful "Goodbye!" at the door.

In detailing this session, we hope to give a hint of the complexity of the working field in which the therapist is receiving a complex set of transferences from the family whose members each already have well-developed transferences to each other. There are, obviously, multiple reactions to the family as things occur within the session, and quite specific reactions to each of them as well as to aspects of their relationships to each other.

But the overall field is too complex to organize in this way. The organizing responses are more apt to come out of the therapist's feeling of the confusion that the family as a whole is conveying, or from the fantasy that emerges spontaneously as the therapist listens to the family and to the subgroups or individuals who are speaking. The ability to understand and then to organize this understanding grows out of a capacity for "negative capability."

Such therapist fantasies lead to more complex levels of countertransference response, as the therapist moves toward understanding the failures in the more comprehensive contextual transference, rather than in the piecemeal individual focused transferences. The family members have focused transferences to each other, like the one in which Tom treats his father as if he were bullying him and becomes the "taunting little kid" who represents an introjective identification with his father; or like the one in which Mr. Jansen projects the "suffering victim" identification into Mrs. Jansen, and she takes it in for her own reasons (which are not explored in this session). At many points in the session, the therapist is caught in these individual identifications; indeed, they form the material out of which a more comprehensive experience of the holding transference is built.

Using Individual Transferences to Inform Contextual Transference

Every family often speaks through one of its members at a time. When it does so, the individual transference of that member may hit the therapist with unusual force, resulting in what Stierlin (1977) called a "deviation" from "involved impartiality." In our experience, the impact of such individual transferences and the resulting countertransference deviations occur essentially in every family session. Whenever these deviations occur, they can be understood in a crucial and particular way: The family as a whole is putting forth one individual transference, in either its focused or contextual form, to speak for its shared contextual transference. With this view, the countertransference deviations from impartiality become not lapses but roads to understanding of the family's shared contextual transference.

Thus, in this session, the therapist's struggle with anger, at times at Father and at times at Tom for bullying, represented a countertransference response to his feeling bullied by the whole family, who were putting forth a bullying transference because as a group they feared he would abuse the therapeutic situation to pick on them. The deviating feelings the therapist felt in different ways and at different times individually toward Tom, Father, and Mother were, in each instance, clues to the shared family contextual transference that organized their interactions.*

In this way, even the therapist's responses to individual family members support his or her contextual holding for the family. It is to the transference to this function that he or she most usefully attends at the end of the day. At this level of organization, the individual building blocks of the individual and subgroup transference and countertransference interactions all count, just as every brick counts toward the construction of a house. But the attention to what is wrong about the placement of an individual brick aids in thinking about the overall structure and function of the house, not about individual bricks. In this family, the overall holding function could be seen to be undermined and depleted by the shared preoccupation with bullying and taunting, with who is going to be the victim and who the victimizer, which was also brought as a contextual transference to the therapist.

ENCOURAGING COUNTERTRANSFERENCE

Information about a family's transference comes in an initially unorganized way. It is organized by the therapist's countertransference to this shared family preoccupation. And as the family struggles to cope with its shared concern about the world—both the internal world of the family and the world that surrounds the family—this struggle gets inside the therapist, whose provision for the therapeutic work means that the family's concern will be lived

---

*We are grateful to Isca Wittenberg, whose comments during the presentation at the Tavistock Clinic in 1986 of work with this family helped to sharpen our thinking on this theoretical point.

out at the boundary between family and therapist, all within the holding context.

The signals from the family's struggle, by necessity, get mixed up with the therapist's own similar struggles. Through this process of internal matching, the therapist sorts out the fit between his or her own internal object relations and those the patients are invited to put into him or her. Sorting out this match, the therapist invokes memories of personal work with similar struggles as a way of making the whole process more available consciously, working toward a reunderstanding of the issues. Of course, some issues will have been more conflictual for the therapist than others. Every therapist has unique areas of past, internalized struggle. These are the areas that personal treatment and supervision are designed to bring to awareness and to a level of usefulness that is not otherwise possible. It is not that these areas are to be eradicated or neutralized so that the therapist's psyche can be calibrated as an unconscious transference receiving apparatus or countertransference generator. Once the therapist is sufficiently in touch with these areas, they become even more useful than the areas that never represented much of an internal struggle. For they are now the areas in which the therapist can best empathize with patient families as they struggle. We want our students to feel free to work on these issues in supervisory or continuous case settings without fear of being told they need more personal treatment. The hardest and most important lesson we have to teach our students is the fundamental importance of opening and investigating their own vulnerability. This is the cornerstone of the kind of psychoanalytic family therapy we are trying to teach, relying as we do on the countertransference.

The emphasis on *focused transference/countertransference* predominates in individual analysis, while the *contextual transference/countertransference* is the organizing interaction in family therapy. But there is overlap. In this chapter we have demonstrated the use of these two forms of transference and countertransference coexisting to different degrees in work with individuals and families. In the next chapter we will explore couple therapy as a model intermediate between individual psychotherapy and family therapy, with a transference/countertransference process shifting rapidly between the contextual and the focused.

CHAPTER 11

Couples and Couple Therapy

Problems in Centered Relating and Mutual Holding

The problem for marital partners is the need to be all-in-all for each other. The transferences and projective identifications they have to each other tend to be in a tightly locked system, and the contextual holding they have built together tends to form a more rigid system than that brought by a larger family, where dissent by any one person can provide an opportunity for change. The therapist, a relative outsider to this small and tightly knit system, needs leverage in order to enter the couple's situation without simply barging in. This is provided by the opportunity to join the rhythm of the oscillation between centered relating and contextual holding. This quality of providing a contextual holding around the holding the couple provides for itself is analogous to the father's role in providing the envelope around the mother's holding capacity. There, too, the father does so while also joining in the more intimate aspects of relating.

When a couple is originally bonding, yearning and idealization give an exciting quality to the whole relationship. It cannot be otherwise. If the angry rejecting qualities were to dominate a relationship during its formation, it simply would not move forward. Of course, we have to make an exception of the situation in which the relationship forms around a sadomasochistic bond. In this case, sex and aggression will be found to be fused, so that the angry and rejecting exchanges between this couple are so heavily sexualized that the two cannot be differentiated. The couple uses mutual aggression in exciting ways to produce that kind of bond.

Returning to the usual case, we have the situation of the lovers eagerly longing for each other through the courtship. The ideal relationship between them represses the rejecting objects for each of them. Their courtship represents a triumph over their individual and shared bad objects, and is held to be so powerful that it will triumph symbolically over all the forces of evil. This ordinary manic triumph of courtship cannot last. At some point, around the wedding usually, but whenever each partner feels the commitment has been sealed, he and she are each forced to bring their denied and repressed parts back into the relationship. It is at this point that hysterical patients begin to have trouble with their sexual expression, and obsessionals begin to demand and control. The relationship becomes both more problematical and more realistic. Robert Frost (1969) made the point poetically that married love is "a diminished thing" that occurs when "dawn goes down to day." But the diminishment of excitement does not mean that the relationship is the diminished thing it seems. When the fuller light of day washes out the evocative hues of dawn, the more ordinary and less acceptable tones come into view. In any primary relationship, after a time, the human personality seeks a whole object and seeks to express all parts of itself within the marital relationship (just as it would in the analytic transference relationship) because of "this inner compulsive striving to unite the original splits in the ego and its object within one relationship" (Sutherland 1963, p. 119). It is the reason the patient inevitably longs to show the therapist or the marital partner the repressed and rejected parts of him or herself despite fears about risking this, in order to be accepted by the therapist, who the patient feels has full knowledge of who he or she really is.

This change in the quality of a loving bond at the point of marriage or in the months and years that follow is common clinical and folk knowledge. It presents to couples who have been married for many years the problem of how to stay in touch with the exciting side of their relationship, the side that not only pulled them together initially but that should remain capable of giving joy during the marriage. In the good-enough marriage, one that is strong enough to weather the daily stresses and periodic storms of living and working together, the resilience of the exciting side of the attachment provides the impetus for the periodic refinding of each other, which is the basis of renewal in marriage.

This refinding usually occurs with the support of the couple's sexual relationship. The couple shares a psychosomatic partnership through their sexual life, which is the closest adult approximation to the intense psychosomatic partnership of the mother–infant pair. Not only does it supply a similar immediacy of feeling to that earliest relationship but it calls up the archaic echoes of the mother–infant bond because of its intense physicality. In sexual life, as in other aspects of the couple's life, centered relating coexists simultaneously with contextual holding. There is a more rapid fluctuation between the two functions in a couple than is true in a broader family. For the family as a whole, providing the enveloping frame for the centered communications between any two people attenuates the strain that can be put on each dyadic relationship by the need to be constantly doing both for each other at any one time.

If the couple's initial "mutual projective identifications" (Dicks 1967, Zinner 1976) with each other are in the main on the exciting side, then it follows that the rejecting "bad object" projective identifications, which have been kept out of the courtship, form the main challenge to their marriage. For some couples, the challenge will come at the point of marriage; for others, it will come at the birth of a first child, or perhaps the first boy or girl, who represent certain difficulties in object relating for one or both parents; for yet others, it will be when one child enters a particular developmental phase, such as that of oedipal or adolescent challenge to parental equilibrium; and for others, it may not come until one or all of the children leave home. Each couple has its own unique life course. Certain challenges are so frequently stressful that we expect them to produce serious strain, as in the case of couples who long for children and cannot have them, or couples with a seriously ill child or a child who dies. Nevertheless, it is a fundamental aspect of the psychoanalytic and object relations approach that even these overwhelming stressors need to be understood in the context of the couple's internal object relationships.

Our experience of couple dynamics comes from the clinical situation. When we see a couple for consultation, it is at the point when the partners realize that something has gone wrong between them. The troublesome transferences to each other in this situation will be primarily of the rejecting or persecuting sort, because the partners generally feel badly treated by each other at the point at which they come. Their positive feelings maintain their commitment while we try to figure out with them what has gone wrong. We rely heavily on their residual central relationship and capacity to provide holding for each other while we try to understand with them what is interfering in the freer expression and reception of the positive aspects of centered relating and of mutual holding. This point leads to the expansion of our model of the couple's system of object relationships as they come into contact with the therapist.

A Model of Transference and Countertransference in Couple Work

The basic model of intervention with couples was presented in Chapter 4, where we discussed the way couple therapists take an alternating view between direct focus into the internal worlds of each of the two individuals and broader attention to their shared relationship, looking both at their centered relating and at their contextual holding capacity. Our overall position is one of providing the contextual holding for the two of them, while also engaging at the core.

The basic model of couple therapy is inherited from the work of Henry Dicks, whose 1967 book *Marital Tensions* is the fundamental text for applying the object relations approach to couple therapy, and actually provides a starting point for the entire object relations view of the family. Dicks's therapeutic plan was for two therapists to see the separate spouses in two parallel individual psychoanalytic psychotherapies, which were integrated by being shared with him as supervisor. This format had a certain advantage in giving great depth to understanding the interlocking projective identifications as these were pieced together by both therapists working with a consultant. He and his group at the Institute for Marital Studies at the Tavistock had not yet discovered the efficacy of conjoint therapy. When they did, they moved to using conjoint marital therapy as their preferred mode of work. Dicks (1967) and his colleagues (Bannister and Pincus 1971, Pincus 1960) left us a legacy of the importance of grasping the meaning of unconscious communication as the essential part of a psychodynamic marital therapy worthy of the name.

This work is also summarized beautifully in separate articles by John Zinner and by Tom Main. Main's article (1966) gives a lucid case example from the vantage point of the supervisor of the two individual therapists, whereas Zinner's article (1976) condenses some of the main points with two clarifying conjoint case examples. Zinner highlights the unconscious fantasies that partners come to share out of their pooled projective identifications. He notes:

Intrapsychic conflicts that have been externalized through projective identifications must be reinternalized with the aid of our interpretations, since the process of working through can only be achieved at an intrapsychic level. Interventions that are aimed at modifying the behavior of the spouse who is the recipient of projections so that he or she is no longer a collusive partner have their parallel in individual therapy in the form of the analyzing of the countertransference. The transference in conjoint marital therapy must be closely attended to since the unconscious forces that influence the marital dyad are equally at play in the triad that now includes the therapist [p. 307].

Conjoint therapy for the partners has become the mode for work in couple therapy whenever the couple's relationship and their individual situations will allow it. This introduces the transference problems and opportunities that Zinner alludes to and that a few analytic writers have begun to deal with. (Dicks 1967, Henderson and Williams 1980, Levay, Kagle, and Weissberg 1979, Meissner 1978, Nadelson 1978). To date, the specifics of the differences between the conjoint transference and the individual transferences have not been explored. Nor has there been a way of talking about the couple's difficulty in dealing with the shifting quality of the transferences, or projective identifications, either to each other or to the therapist. It is the relationship between these important but discrete aspects of transference that we now need to clarify if we are going to make an advance in our understanding of the particular characteristics of transference and countertransference in couple therapy, and if we are to help them understand each other.

First, each member of the couple has his and her own individual focused and contextual transferences to the therapist. Although these are more dilute than in individual psychotherapy, they are nonetheless present. Then the couple has its shared contextual transference to the therapist's holding capacity. However, the fact that the spouses may be at odds with each other opens the possibility that the shared transference to their therapist will be more readily invaded by their individual issues.

Thus, the couple's transference represents an oscillation between its shared contextual transference and the individual transferences (both focused and contextual) that appear when the couple's bond is stressed. This stress is reflected by differential attitudes toward the therapist. The therapist works with the couple to understand both the dynamics of this oscillation and the individual transferences that emerge periodically.

This oscillation occurs with more regularity in couple therapy than in family therapy, because in family therapy the larger number of people increases the power of the contextual transference as an organizing factor in which the individual transferences tend to remain affective, directed to other family members rather than to the therapist. Although in family therapy the family's attempt to thrust a dominant individual focused transference on the therapist represents a breakdown of contextual transference in the session, this is not necessarily the case with a couple. Here, the more regular oscillation between the two means that the couple may join together to set up a situation in which one of them is supported to do some important individual transferential work, and that this individual work in turn leads to a new level of contextual transference. But we also need to take note next of the tendency of one or both of the partners in couple therapy to take up direct focused transferences to the therapist.

During couple therapy, one of the spouses often expresses a wish for individual therapy with the therapist. Whether or not this would be an appropriate arrangement, it represents a longing for an exciting and ideal object as projected onto the therapist. At this point, it is necessary to arrive at an understanding of possible depletion of the exciting transference toward the spouse, and of the degree to which such a request represents a splitting of idealized and denigrated projections. Such a request by one partner has important implications for the couple's shared holding situation and for the shared transference to the therapist.

The Alternation of Focused and Contextual Transference in Couple Therapy

The transference situation of the couple is complex in that it represents this alternation of two individual transferences with the shared contextual transference.

Moving back and forth between these two modes, the therapist actually has a more complex job in some ways than when facing a full family, where the field is clearly too complex to be able to take in all the individual transferences. As we have said, three kinds of transference can be discussed:

1. The focused transference from each spouse to the therapist
2. The contextual transference each has individually to the therapist
3. The shared contextual transference generated by the couple's contextual holding capacity and its failures or limitations

The levels of countertransference for the therapist derive from these same elements. In practice, the couple's sense of being fundamentally understood or misunderstood tends to resolve in one of two directions. Either each one wants to be understood individually by the therapist (to use individual transference/countertransference channels) or they join forces to be understood as a unit. It is this sliding away from the possibility that we can understand them individually and together at the same moment that constitutes part of the difficulty of the couple therapy format. This tendency of the transference to polarize either into the individual transferences of each spouse or into the contextual holding transference brought jointly to the therapeutic setting is shown in the following example.

Mr. and Mrs. Kyley had been seeing me for a year for help with their constantly battling marriage of twenty years. He was a 55-year-old magazine editor, and she was a 41-year-old lawyer who had been spectacularly successful after returning to law school ten years earlier. They have a boy and two girls, now aged 8 to 16. Their usual presentation in sessions began with Mrs. Kyley declaiming that her husband never did enough for her. He would protest or laugh her off. She would then accuse him of downplaying her needs and of getting the children to side against her. She often said that she had put up with all this for years but had been getting stronger since beginning individual therapy two years earlier.

In session, Mrs. Kyley began a tirade against Mr. Kyley. She screamed that her husband would never love her enough to make up for his years of neglect and ended by saying, "Perhaps I just can't love him any more!" In response, Mr. Kyley banged furiously on my coffee table. When I asked him to stop, he said that it didn't matter. He would pay for the table if it broke. I said that as far as I was concerned the table was not replaceable, and he simply had to stop. He did stop, but when Mrs. Kyley continued to be disparaging over the next few minutes he walked out, saying, "You deal with her!"

I felt annoyed with them both—abused, walked out on, and left with an unruly burden.

I said to Mrs. Kyley that it was clear she could hurt her husband, although she acted like nothing ever got through. I could see that in her desperation she often engaged him in such a way as to ensure he would say nothing caring.

In the next week's session, the Kyleys began as though nothing painful had happened, saying they had been getting along well.

Since I had been dreading seeing them after the previous week's blow-up, I was surprised. They were oblivious to the way they had left me reeling.

Mrs. Kyley had often wished her husband would begin the session. Today, as a gesture of appeasement, Mr. Kyley began with an unemotional chronicle of the ups and downs of their week. He ended with, "I can't remember the details, honey, so you tell him."

This provoked Mrs. Kyley to another tirade about his failure to listen. For instance, there had been an episode of his disobeying her directions about how to feed the children when she was away.

As I listened, I was overcome with an exasperated ennui at her attempts to control him from afar. I felt acutely pained that nothing was enough for her. At that moment I felt fed up with both of them and angry at her for picking on him.

Mrs. Kyley then described an episode a few weeks previously. As she was fixing dinner, the family sat down at the table, leaving no chair for her. She stood waiting to be noticed, growing angrier at the family's lack of concern.

As she said this, I initially felt more sympathetic to her. But the story of her silently standing there seemed designed to make a case against the family, as though it were more important to make a point to me than to deal with them directly.

I felt like a referee being alternately kicked and persuaded by both teams, and getting sick of the game in the process. I thought, "This is the kind of couple that makes me wonder why I do this kind of work." I felt like an exasperated parent wanting two children to stop bickering. As I sat overwhelmed, I pondered my taking in their shared futility.

My feeling battle-scarred, retaliatory, and hopeless represented being taken over by their projection of the shared failure of contextual holding. I was thinking of Mrs. Kyley's reversion to tirades that "Nothing is ever enough" and to Mr. Kyley's dismissing everything and being condescending both to her and to me. I now realized I had joined in a countertransference enactment of the individual and shared projective identifications. My wishing to "tell them to behave" represented the kind of message with which they regularly flailed each other.

I was then able to say, over a period of a few minutes, "I think you do these things to each other because you both feel futile with each other and about your marriage. You, Mr. Kyley, feel that you can never do things right. So you undercut your wife to disarm her criticism. And you, Mrs. Kyley, berate him because you feel there is nothing you can do to feel loved. You both feel desperately unloved by each other and you share the dread that your marriage will end."

My work had been invaded by the marital disability. My own struggle to get back on top of things had to precede gains for them. And as a way of offering myself holding, I reminded myself that small gains were important in this phase because any progress had to begin with small increments, which were necessary to change the direction of the feedback between the partners.

In these two sessions, I had succeeded in getting a handle on my contextual countertransference and the shared projective identification that had been interfering with my capacity to offer containment. This allowed me to begin to approach their focused transferences to me and to each other.

The next week's session was at 7:30 A.M. They again reported doing better, and in the wake of the last hour, I did not feel so burned.

Mrs. Kyley said, "Things are going better, but there are still some things to be addressed."

Mr. Kyley shook his head angrily, "You see! She gives no credit when things go well!"

I felt the "here we go again" feeling. I began to wonder if she, having done some baiting of her own, would now respond to his provocation, leading to our usual impasse.

Instead, Mrs. Kyley went on to describe their sexual life. "It has been twenty years of this pattern of my husband setting the scene for sex and then falling asleep. I like sex, and if it's good, I want more. But he doesn't care about my needs, and we only have sex every three or four days. And then he's apt to fall asleep right away afterward. Last weekend, we went to a hotel for the weekend. We had good sex on Saturday, but when I approached him again several hours later, he put me off. So I felt hurt."

Mr. Kyley defended himself at this point by saying that he liked the sex, too.

"Do you worry you won't be able to get an erection?" she asked. "Because I could understand that."

Mr. Kyley denied that was his concern, but on my questioning, he said, "When we've made love a few hours before, I'm not altogether sure I will manage. Sometimes it depends on other things. I often feel the second time she doesn't leave enough time to know if she wants it or not. Then I feel it's a demand. Her rhythms get in the way sometimes, too. She's not talking about that."

Mrs. Kyley agreed. "I don't like screwing in the morning, just like I don't appreciate being in your office at this ghastly hour."

Her gratuitous slap at the early hour of the session hit me because it had been scheduled to accommodate their needs. I felt an impulse, as I had before with them, to counter sarcastically. But I said nothing because I thought my wish to be sarcastic was an identification with the rejection they both felt.

Mrs. Kyley went on to say that they had sex the next day, and in appreciation, she had told him that her genitals were aching, but she had done so in such a manner that he had been offended.

As she reported this incident, I also felt some disgust.

She said, "He says I'm vulgar, and maybe I am. But I was trying to say to him, 'It was nice,' and he rejected me."

Mr. Kyley began to argue. "I'm more private than you, and more easily embarrassed. You just have to accept me as I am. I can't manage all the things you can."

"That kind of acceptance doesn't apply to me, though?" she challenged.

I was now filled up with the feeling of Mrs. Kyley as invasive, crude, and relentlessly affrontive. The feeling was so strong that I realized something desperate was going on again. I shook myself into thinking about what was going wrong. They were battering each other in the attempt to develop a common language. But that formulation did not do justice to the depth of the problem. I felt battered by them once again, although much less so this week.

I decided to intervene by restating what I had learned from the contextual countertransference the previous week as a prelude to some exploratory work on the contributions of their individual internal objects. I said, "I think this impasse is made up of Mr. Kyley feeling coerced and controlled, and Mrs. Kyley feeling nothing is enough. That is the version each of you has of something you share. And what you share is that you both feel absolutely and fundamentally unloved. Now, we aren't getting very far past the impasse, and it makes me wonder how this situation fits in with things from your early lives."

Mr. Kyley gave a scant answer. He saw no correlation to his family. But Mrs. Kyley said that his mother was a perfectionist and that he could be pushed into anything by her. He would not let Mrs. Kyley push him around the way he let his mother do it. All the resentment he had for his mother got put on her. He did not object to her formulation, but I regarded his agreement as weak and grudging, without emotional verification.

When I turned to ask Mrs. Kyley about her own early life, she began to cry about the relationship with her mother, who "never seemed to care enough." "My father was real special to my mother. I didn't get much of either of them. When I did get some time with him, he was a benign dictator. He was very controlling, but he cared. They had each other, but my mother took him over, so there wasn't much of him left for me." Mrs. Kyley was being helpful and giving for the first time today.

I said, "I think we can be clearer at the moment about what pushes you into these battles. Your husband is like the father you want desperately, but he is also like your mother keeping him from you. And sometimes he is the pair of your parents keeping you out, as when you feel he and I team up against you." She nodded, and continued to cry gently as I said, "Although you both feel shut out and hated, underneath that you long to be loved. But when you feel just a bit more loved, it just makes you feel the pain of longing because you're sure you won't get more. So you substitute fighting for loving, because when things start to go well, you have to live with disappointment when they go bad again. That's why you so often spoil the nice times, Mrs. Kyley, but you do it for both of you. Neither of you can stand the risk of things going better because that increases the pain of rejection later."

As we scheduled the next appointment, Mrs. Kyley turned down my renewed suggestion that they take the only free hour I had, at 7:30 A.M., as a regular time. She said, "I can't stand this time. We'll just keep it catch-as-catch-can."

As they left, I felt rejected and unappreciated once again.

Working with the Oscillation of Context and Focus

We have noted that in couple therapy the transference situation alternates between the individual transferences to the therapist and the shared contextual transference. With the Kyleys, there was a shared contextual transference of hopelessness, mistrust, and fight. They were in unconscious agreement that the world was a dangerous place, that someone might do you in or try to take things from you, and that it was doubtful if an outside person (i.e., the therapist) could or would be fair.

This left them feeling jointly vulnerable, but at the same time, it stemmed from their internal object situation, which threw them into mistrusting each other while feeling deficient enough about themselves that they were hopelessly dependent on each other. They had different ways of expressing this constellation: Mr. Kyley became condescending and controlling, while fending off attempts to get through to him. He was contemptuous of his objects while fearful they would leave him. Mrs. Kyley was more overtly suspicious, split good and bad objects more vigorously, and when spurned, turned to the attack, all the more if she felt she had been relying on someone. In diagnostic terms, we are describing a borderline woman married to an obsessional and narcissistic man. In object relations terms, they shared a sense of schizoid emptiness and attempted to get what they needed from each other in both complementary and shared ways.

In attempting to use the therapist to get more from each other, they joined forces to include the therapist in their flawed holding context. At this point, the therapist could feel slightly idealized, but soon felt covered in the mutual hate that pervaded and disabled their shared holding. The attempts to provide better holding for them repeatedly dissolved in an echo of their own usual failure: they would end up blaming each other. In the conjoint therapy setting, the countertransference echoed this. The therapist felt pulled to take first one side and then the other, caught first in alternating individual countertransferences and then in oscillation between a difficult countertransference to one of the spouses and to the pair of them.

To sum up the transference/countertransference situation, we can say that in the contextual countertransference the therapist had a negative, unpleasant identification that incorporated the failure of their own shared holding capacity. In the focused countertransferences, he felt identified with the rejecting object for each of them, the same internal objects they projected onto each other.

In each of the two focused countertransferences, the identification was what Racker would term a "complementary transference," leaving the therapist feeling hated like the hated internal object more often than he felt an empathic identification with either spouse. We can see that the effect of these two focused transferences would naturally lead to a deficit in the contextual transference and that this effect had to be interpreted to the Kyleys before they could begin to understand that their basic contextual failure was a shared one. From this point, we hope to help them make sense of the contribution each of them made to the failure.

In these sessions, comments about the shared contextual transference were not readily effective in helping the couple move from its position, because it was difficult to fashion an emotionally effective "because clause." Although the Kyleys were longing to be loved, their relationship to each other was so damaged that it almost coincided with their internal antilibidinal situation. Because the embattled part of the self is strongly attached to the rejecting object, the explanation had to penetrate to this defended level to become useful—to give the experience that the therapist could provide contextual holding by offering new understanding. In the sessions, the therapist was unable to do this for the husband until he was able to provide containment for the wife. In being helpful to her in the individual sense, he enacted the kind of two-person holding that the couple could not manage and offered himself as a model of an understanding and caring parent. In the process he had to provide containment for himself, just as a parent must often do before offering it to a child.

With this couple, a recurrent countertransference experience echoed the wife's need to spoil any positive change by her husband. Many times, the therapist had his attempt to work attacked by the wife or dismissed by the husband. The easiest way to approach this problem was to confront the wife on her spoiling and to attempt to understand the reasons she did so. One of the turning points in the therapy came when Mrs. Kyley attacked her husband when he had just tried to be kind. The therapist interpreted her spoiling as an attempt to avoid having to experience the pain of hoping for something better. It was easier to take up the way the husband had assigned spoiling to her after we had sketched out the consequences with her. In both cases, the motivation for the spoiling could be seen to lie in the hate of the envied object. The object was seen as exploiting the other person's dependency in order to take control. Envy and the attack on the envied object are frequent and powerful dynamics between marital partners. In couple therapy, the vicissitudes of envy are most usefully taken up in their consequences for the contextual transference.

Hate in the Countertransference

In this example the couple's transferences to each other are full of hate and mistrust. The countertransference constantly reflects this. Winnicott (1947) has detailed his struggles in psychotherapy with a boy who behaved in eminently hateful ways. He made the point that it would not have been possible to treat this boy without acknowledging his own hate and even at times acting on it, as by putting the boy outside the treatment room when his behavior became intolerable. This was the case for the therapist when he had to stop Mr. Kyley from damaging his furniture, and in the process supplied a container to unbridled aggression. With couples like this, the therapist struggles with dislike of the couple, of one or both of the individuals, with self-doubt and professional doubt, and a whole range of feelings of hate. This is an especially important aspect of transference in the work with couples. Occasionally, families will project this kind of shared hate in their contextual transference, but in our experience, it is far less usual, because there are more people to break the cycle of hate.

In couples with years of impasse, the hating, or antilibidinal constellation, has often taken over. This recalls Fairbairn's discussion (1954) of the way the antilibidinal object and ego together launch a relentless attack on the exciting object. It is far easier for spouses to fight ceaselessly than it is for them to bear the conscious burden of longing to be loved in return. This marks a principle interpretation. Many partners fight because they cannot stand to long for each other when they are unsure if they will ever be loved. In this sense, we can say that the fighting is indeed a sign of longing, but it is also armor against feeling its pain.

The Externalization of Internal Objects

This brings up the importance of the externalization of internal objects. Often what is unconscious to the individual is observable when we see the couple. This is true because of the way projective identification occupies space both in the communication between the partners and inside the one who received the projection. The point is that the projective identifications take over. These are not abstract ideas but ways in which each partner lives out a rejected and projected part of the other without any awareness of doing so. In the conjoint setting, the unnamed sense each partner often has of being taken over by projections against his or her will changes the meaning of "the unconscious." The unconscious is lived out between the spouses and before our eyes. Our capacity to observe it in this setting is what gives us the leverage we often lack in individual work, at least until the focused transference becomes intense enough to illustrate it.

The Internal Couple

An important addition to the model of transference and counter-transference is the therapist's own possession of an "internal couple" in his or her repertoire of models of internal objects. As we discussed in Chapter 6, the baby is concerned about the shared life of its parents from at least the age of 7 or 8 months, once it can hold on to a view of a single, ambivalently regarded object. This growth of the ability to tolerate ambivalence about a whole object is what Klein (1935) called the capacity for the depressive position. Ever after this, the child has an internal image of his parents together, which emphasizes a sexual version of their pairing during oedipal development.

This object relation to the parents' pairing can be seen in individual analyses when the patient recreates in the transference the parental relationship. We first learned of this idea from Harold Searles, but we cannot find it in his writings. Instead of projecting into the analyst a part of the ego or of the object, as is commonly described when the patient invokes a recreation of some aspect of the parent–child relationship, the patient projects his or her identification with the parents-as-a-couple and splits it between self and analyst. Patient and analyst then feel pulled toward a way of relating that characterizes the patient's parents' marital relationship. In couple therapy, we see the phenomenon of the projection of the internal representation of the parental couple into the present marital relationship and into the relationship between couple and therapist. Each of the marital partners has unconscious internal versions of what couples are like. As there are many versions of objects inside each of us, so there are many versions of couples—loving, hating, reasonable, unreasonable, excluding and including of a child. Let us simply call all of this the composite internal couple. The therapist's transference to his or her own internal couple informs the countertransference to the internal couple of the real life couple in treatment.

Reverberations with the Therapist's Internal Couple

In the countertransference, the therapist is constantly matching aspects of his or her internal couple with the couple in the office. Even in individual therapy, the therapist communicates with the patient's internal parental couple. This structure also exists in the therapist, and like other aspects of internal objects, we hope it will be a less rigid and less repressed internal object than the comparable ones in the patients.

What is important about holding a mental image of the patient's internal parents-in-a-relationship is that this combined internal object will represent the aspects of two fantasied adults as they are seen relating to each other, with an image of the self as an outside observer. This introduces new levels of organization that at the beginning are not yet oedipal. When the baby or toddler "thinks" of the parents as a couple, the relationship to them as a couple is not yet sexualized. It becomes so during the oedipal era, as we saw in Chapter 6. So early on, when a child "thinks" about the paired parents locked together in oral gratification or anal struggle, he or she implicitly raises the question of what kind of space they will allow for each of them to have individual, dyadic parent–child relationships and what provision they make together for containing and holding the child.

A good deal of the transference that the marital partners have to each other involves matching their estimation of their relationship to the ideals, hopes, and fears associated with their internal couples. This becomes more overt when we begin couple therapy, because the inherently triangular situation easily dissolves into a situation in which one sees oneself as being alone with two others in the room. At some times, those two will be seen as pairing to work with the therapist in what feels to be a critical or helpful way. In addition, the therapist perceives them as a couple and is therefore matching them to his or her own internal couple countertransferentially. This is part of what is to be mirrored back to them. Thus, they will be taking back in a view of themselves as a couple that, we hope, will be a modification of the image they bring.

One of the reasons work with couples can be so difficult is that they can collude to keep therapists out of their relationships. This may represent a reenactment of a time when each partner felt shut out by one or both parents, or of times when each joined with one parent to exclude the other. When this occurs, the countertransference situation is one in which the therapist feels that the couple is like his or her internal parental couple acting to exclude the child. The countertransference of rejection by the couple usually feels frustrating and painfully excluding. The patient couple becomes a combined rejecting object for the therapist, who has to work with the corresponding unconscious countertransferential tendency to enter into an antilibidinal, embattled relationship with them. If this work is not done, the therapist may act unconsciously to get rid of them.

A COUPLE WITH A GOOD-ENOUGH INTERNAL COUPLE

Pete and Sarah Masters, presented in Chapter 4, came to treatment because of a decline in their marriage after Pete's recurrent difficulty with his auto-immune disease made them fear for his health and life. Pete had become very controlling with Sarah and with the house because he worked at home. She felt completely shut out and not taken care of. Although each of them complained of mistreatment by the other in the early therapy sessions, it was also clear that they had previously had a marriage they had valued despite its flaws. This was external evidence that they must have had a shared image internally of a reasonably good internal couple despite the vicissitudes of their own lives. In addition, the therapist felt that love was still alive in this couple—that their pain had to do with the lost image of a good couple, not with its never having existed. This was contained in a quality of respect they had for each other, and in a feeling of genuine concern for each other and for their marriage.

It was hard to know where this internal sense of a "good-enough couple" came from. The history of Sarah's parents was one of an ill and damaged mother, who required all of father's attention and therefore left little of either parent to care for her. Despite Sarah's early exclusion, the image of the parents caring for each other seemed to be strong and to have given Sarah an internal sense of security about being in a couple. Interestingly, it also gave her comfort in living as a loving couple without children.

Pete's father had left when he was 6. He had felt his mother to be intrusive and denigrating of a father he idealized from afar. From his comfort and interest in his marriage, I thought he felt that a marital relationship was a good and important thing if the wife could be controlled and kept from becoming too dependent. But at the core of this relationship was a sense of a potentially loving marriage.

In the countertransference the therapist felt a hopefulness about the couple. A basic lovingness seemed present, even if they gave a sense that something was in the way of their urge to care. Within sessions, the hopefulness remained as a substrate despite invasion. This gave the therapist the feeling that his own internal couple was lovingly confirmed by work with the Masters, as opposed to its being crippled by the projected hate of the Kyleys.

So far, these two examples have presented two different contextual transferences. The Kyleys presented with a heavily antilibidinal contextual transference, whereas the Masters had a contextual transference that was "good enough," another term for one that is close to central ego and ideal-object functioning. In contrast, the next couple suffered from an exaggeration of the libidinal or exciting object constellation. This couple was seen for sex therapy, which involved a behavioral format within which psychodynamic work was carried out (Kaplan 1974, Scharff 1982).

A COUPLE WITH A NEED-EXCITING CONTEXTUAL TRANSFERENCE

Sam and Juanita came to see me [D.E.S.] and a woman cotherapist for Sam's premature ejaculation. They were not married and were both wary of further commitment. Sam was 32, and Juanita was 26. The cotherapist and I "loved" them in a parental sense, but we became aware finally that we loved them too much. Juanita had always liked sex, but underneath her love of sex was a fear of it. It was the only way to cement relationships, but she unconsciously equated a sexual union with abandonment. In treatment, we were able to tie her overvaluation of sex to the family myth of the passionate romance that had characterized her parents' courtship. Later, we could tie her fear of the devastating consequences of such a relationship to her upset when her father's many affairs eventually spelled the end of her parents' "passionate marriage" when she was 11.

Juanita had a great deal of sexual experience before meeting Sam and had enjoyed it enormously. But in moving toward marriage, she had chosen Sam as a "sexually disabled man" so that he would be grateful to her and would therefore not leave her.

Sam had suffered from premature ejaculation throughout his active sexual life. He had an image of himself as a "good boy" who always wanted to please. For him, sex was exciting, but it also threatened entrapment. He had been close to his mother, but his constant effort to please her had left untested his fear of her becoming castrating and overwhelming if he displeased her. His premature ejaculation represented the effect of his ambivalence about wanting to please the internal good mother, while feeling in danger of being smothered, taken over, and captured by the overwhelming aspect of the exciting object in the process. It represented, in other words, his unconscious solution of holding out on the exciting object.

It was the exciting image that both Sam and Juanita had of the sex that interfered in the contextual transference. They joined in presenting the excitement of their relationship as irresistible. My cotherapist and I shared their view, expressed in our countertransference covering up the threatening, antilibidinal context thoroughly, partly in collusion with the couple and partly to keep at bay the less pleasant feelings in the cotherapy team. They seemed so appealing and fond of each other, it was hard to see why Sam's psychosomatic response was to recoil. But slowly we got in touch with the way Sam felt pulled into something threatening, and the unpleasant feeling of "not being himself" that began to pull him away from Juanita. Noticing his painful response, which he could not at first articulate, helped us realize that we had colluded with the two of them in overvaluing Juanita's sexual enthusiasm. We were able to help them only when we were able to process our cotherapy issues and then to see this as a contextual transference they had been using together to cover their individual fears.

Once we saw the transferential problem, we could say to them that the fear of abandonment and smothering, the effects of a helpless dependence that they both had to face as the consequence of the intense exciting relationship, had been jointly split off and projected into Sam. He was using a psychosomatic route to express the shared contextual failure. We said they both feared an exciting relationship. Sam was afraid it would lead to the kind of domination he feared from his mother, who he felt could be scathingly critical. And Juanita feared that she would end up abandoned and lonely like her mother.

When we were able to say this, Juanita dropped her ebullience for the first time and began to cry. She said it was true that her mother had been desperately lonely after her father left, and she herself had not realized how frightened she felt that the same thing would happen to her. Sam now felt relieved, less endangered, and more sexual. The couple moved slowly forward after the successful completion of sex therapy and were married about a year afterward.

The contextual countertransference in this example involved the cotherapists jointly identifying with the couple's shared exciting-object flaw in their holding function. This was designed unconsciously by the couple to cover a shared core transferential fear that an overwhelmingly exciting object would become an abandoning object. This difficulty stems from the unconscious fantasy that the object is all-powerful and that the self is at once helpless and helplessly tied to the object (Guntrip 1969).

Our identification with the overexcited object represented the sexualization of sex. Only when we realized they had appealed to us in this way, which had gone undetected, could we help them desexualize the sex by helping them tolerate the fear of being left. We felt, in the wake of this insight, that we had been seductive— that is, we had taken on the libidinal projective identification. The countertransference liability of wanting to seduce Sam into a sexualized relationship had kept us, for a while, blind to the fear Sam and Juanita shared of being seduced and overwhelmed or abandoned, and their shared flight from this situation. When we realized this and gave up the sexualizing countertransference, they were promptly enabled to move on to a successful conclusion.

Directive Techniques in Couple Therapy

The use of transference and interpretation form the major points in the discussion of technique in couple therapy, just as they do in family therapy. The question also arises, however, as to how much the therapist should be directive or educational. Much nonanalytic couple therapy involves trying to alter interactions by prescription or direction. What, then, is the role of such interventions in an analytic framework? Do we never offer direction, or if we do, is it an error in technique?

Nothing is pure in the world of technique. It would be a mistake to rule out any reasonable area of ordinary human exchange as always constituting a technical error. There is good reason to be clear about when we are offering direction and not to disguise it. For one thing, couple therapy is itself a mixed modality, in which the transference and the therapist's point of entry shift from moment to moment and from session to session. For another, the focused transference is what makes giving advice problematical in individual therapy, but in the setting of couple therapy the focused transference is primarily between spouses. The therapist is viewed by the couple mainly through their contextual transference. Because this is modeled on the parents' holding function, it lends itself well to the giving of occasional advice. This is so because parents are vested with the functions of education and direction, so that in this transference, the giving of advice fits well.

This is not to say, however, that direction will be taken. Some of the time it will be, but as soon as it impinges on an area of individual or shared difficulty, it will be disregarded. When this happens, as it does inevitably, we will be thrown right back into the exploration of the reasons for the failure or refusal—and the exploration of these will carry us into the same transference and countertransference areas that we use generally. The most developed form of this use of direction is the format for psychodynamic sex therapy (Kaplan 1974, Scharff 1982). Here a set of directions are given for homework at the end of each session. The therapist expects that the couple will have difficulty in carrying out the directions, and uses the specific description of the failures to guide exploration of the underlying causes. These causes are then explored in object relations terms, and the therapist hopes that interpretation of these terms will allow the couple to move beyond their blocks.

In a less structured way, prescription and direction can be useful in work with couples. Most often we do not need to be directive, because when the couple undoes a block, it will be able to see new ways of functioning for itself. When a couple has been stuck for a long time, however, it may have a limited view of the options in the relationship. In that case we may sketch out together new ways of relating, which form goals for the treatment.

Other kinds of advice also have a place. There is no reason to avoid giving explicit advice about ways of dealing with children, making suggestions for the improvement of the couple's sexual life, or altering priorities, providing the therapist has considered the timing and likely impact of offering advice or education. This involves a consideration of the impact of the advice on the transference. But it is also true that never giving advice also has an impact on the transference. Once the advice has been given (or withheld), the therapist is responsible for monitoring the couple's reaction in order to understand what the transference meaning of the advice has been.

Other Techniques in Work with Couples

Framo (1976, 1981) and Williamson (1981, 1982) have both suggested bringing in the parents of adult couples as a resource in their attempts to give up the vestiges of the hierarchical relationship to parents that interfere with continued adult development and with the couple's relationship. Their work has described the need for careful preparation of the adult children, and the use of a limited number of sessions with the parents to highlight work on the growth and differentiation of the adult children. Williamson describes this as a task of the fourth decade of life as the individual needs to develop a differentiated relationship with his or her adult parents and to be free from the compelling quality of the unmetabolized introjects. Successful differentiation offers new possibilities for a peer-level intimacy for all concerned. Although we have no experience with these formats, we have frequently included parents and other members of the extended family in order to address a variety of issues over varying periods of time. Framo's and Williamson's contributions are of interest to us as being in some ways consistent with an object relations approach, which can inform our own work with families of adults.

Treating Couples Involved in Extramarital Affairs

As couple therapists faced with the question of how to treat extramarital affairs, we frequently find that the special circumstances make it difficult to get our bearings. The fundamental stance of the therapist working with marital partners should be neutral concerning investment in the marriage: it is not our marriage to try to save, but theirs to work on if they choose to do so. When a couple comes to us with a troubled marriage, however, the revelation or discovery of an extramarital sexual affair points to a failure in the holding context of the marriage. We do not make this argument on moral grounds. Couples are entitled to the cultural and ideological settings they wish for their marriages. But on clinical grounds, we believe that in our culture and at this point in social history, it is hard for a couple to manage a firm holding context for a marriage without the concordance of its sexual holding, for it is the sexual bond that ordinarily offers the necessary psychosomatic cement. In addition, the couples come to us only when there is significant difficulty, so we know that by their own definition, there has been a significant failure in the partners' holding capacity for each other (Scharff 1978, 1982).

An affair always means that, for at least one of the partners, the marital holding has been inadequate. The job of the therapist is to discover the specific meanings of the affair within the life of the couple. The overall contextual problem concerns the degree to which commitment still exists for the couple. At times, an affair comes to light within the overall context of partners who are stuck but desperately trying to pull together. It is a tragedy if such a couple falls apart over the way an affair comes to light. At the other extreme, an affair may be the final sign of deterioration in a marriage beyond salvage.

We consider the marriage in its shared form to be our primary focus in marital work. In this focus, the affair represents an externalization of the splitting of object life. Sexuality is split apart from the centrality of the marital relationship, whether this is done by shutting down of the marital sexual life, or by the dividing of the emotional and sexual bond among two or more people. At the individual level, this implies that the person is having difficulty with the achievement or maintenance of the depressive position—with maintaining a loving and ambivalent relationship with a single person. It may be that such a partner would have the capacity to do so in different marital circumstances, or it may be that he or she would not manage with anyone in any situation. The determination as to which of these situations is more likely to be true needs to be part of the diagnostic assessment by the therapist. If the splitting of objects seems to derive primarily from the dynamics of one individual, then a developmental assessment will shed further light on this.

The affair represents an event in the projected internal object situation of the betrayed spouse just as surely as it does for the one who lived out the affair. For instance, a sexual disinterest on the part of a husband, which forms part of the wife's motivation to go outside the marriage, means that she is carrying the husband's fear and avoidance with her in an introjective identification. Both partners may unconsciously agree to try to preserve their marriage by putting the sex outside it rather than risk confrontation with each other. The life stages of each of the partners and of the family are important influences in this unconscious partnership.

AFFAIRS IN RESPONSE TO THE FIRST PREGNANCY

Jim Marantz was afraid of being abandoned by his maternal object. He began to have multiple affairs when his wife became pregnant with their first child. The threat of an infantile rival shook his confidence in her love and availability. He unconsciously assumed that at birth the child would take his wife away from him. In defense, Mr. Marantz set up a series of external objects so that he was not forced to depend on any single one. That way, none of the women could leave him exposed to the feared abandonment.

However, Judy Marantz had a complementary unconscious fear that the husband would team up with a child, especially if it were a girl, to leave her in favor of an oedipal bond with the daughter. In terms of her unconscious fantasy, her husband's affairs protected her from this more dangerous alternative by pairing him with several less important objects so that she could pair with the child. In this sense, Jim's affairs had to be seen as protective of Judy at the same time that they undermined the holding capacity of their marriage.

There is, in addition, the effect of the secret on the dynamics of the couple. The handling of the secret, either by covering or revealing it, has dynamic effects on the marriage. Secrets and the keeping or sharing of them have an important developmental line in the history of the individual and of the couple (Gross 1951, Scharff 1982). In addition, we have to ask how the secret affects the couple's difficulty maintaining its boundaries and providing holding for each other.

Finally, we may be interested in the question of what is projected by the couple into the third person in the affair, the outside lover. Although we do not usually see third parties along with the couple, we see many such third parties in individual treatment— often men and women who cannot set up relationships with available partners. For these patients, the crucial question concerns the projections they have allowed or encouraged. Furthermore, if a third party *does* end up marrying the person from the affair, the extruded dynamics from the first marriage become the substrate of the next marriage.

Treatment of a marriage goes far beyond the management of an affair, but understanding the extramarital sexual activity is part of the overall treatment. The failure of the holding context and the contributing core failures need to be explored and integrated. This means that when an affair comes to light, this process is apt to provide for more working through if the knowledge of the affair can be shared. Not that it is always possible to do so. One partner may feel unable to make a revelation or may think that the other partner will be so hurt or outraged that the marriage will not survive. Often, working with this partner to understand the meanings of the affair will result in sharing it subsequently in a way that, while rocking the boat, is nevertheless fundamentally helpful.

Some years ago, one of us (D. Scharff 1978) published a paper advocating the nearly universal revelation of the affair, at least in the situation of the beginning of sex therapy, and in most instances of conjoint marital therapy. We still think that, all things being equal, marital partners will be in a far firmer position to rebuild if they are able to share the facts and explore the consequences of any affairs. But we can no longer be so completely committed to revelation when it is over the resistance of the patient, for it has not always been possible to follow this path.

AN EXAMPLE OF TREATING A COUPLE WITH AFFAIRS

James and Maryruth Shaw had been married twenty years. They were in their early forties and came to treatment with a woman therapist supervised by one of us, because of James's loss of interest in sex and his feeling of not being appreciated. They agreed that their marriage had been ravaged by James's insatiable ambition. He was a doctor whose career had always come first and who still worked long hours in research and teaching. Initially, Maryruth had shared his sense of idealism and mission, but over time she had worn down. During the last eight years, she had absented herself from him emotionally and had a number of affairs that had let her feel more appreciated.

Two years before coming to the therapist, she had confessed her affairs to her priest and felt she had obtained absolution and a new moral beginning. Although she felt uncertain about the marriage, she felt clear she would have no more extramarital involvement. She was willing to tell James about some of the affairs but felt that disclosing one in particular would be too painful because it involved a family friendship she was unwilling to lose.

The therapist struggled with the maintenance of this secret and the possible invasion it might represent in a renewed marital holding capacity. Transferentially, she [the therapist] felt that Maryruth was using this nondisclosure to remain in control of the marital therapy, and by doing this would remain in control of James symbolically. However she tried to work with Maryruth on the meanings of the secret, a block remained. The therapist felt painfully excluded and controlled herself. She decided to work with the couple, nevertheless, because they did seem to have a potentially loving commitment to each other, and because it looked as if the blockade initiated originally by James might now represent the mutual sense of rejection.

This meant that the therapist had to bear not only the painful exclusion by the wife but the rejection she felt from the compromise implicit in the reworking in this manner. Her sense of being manipulated dominated the countertransference through the early hours. The therapist gradually understood how this represented the control struggle between the couple. Maryruth had originally felt controlled and compromised for years as she tolerated James's lack of regard for her. Gradually, however, Maryruth's willingness to work in every other respect made inroads on the pain and deprivation of this countertransference.

James, too, as he looked painfully at the self-centered preoccupation that had driven her away, was able to face the anger he had both expressed and engendered. Maryruth was able to explore the way she had turned to her idealized father, both literally and in the displacement of her affairs, to control and replace James. And James was able to look at the way he had reinstated a denigrated image of his mother in taking Maryruth for granted. Despite the sense that the maintenance of the secret held something important right up to the end of treatment, the couple did well and emerged with a marriage that seemed restored to a loving, resilient situation.

At the end, the therapist felt that the most important countertransference work had been in the growth of her capacity not to have to be in control, since it was this which seemed to counter the mutual use the Shaws had made of each other before therapy.

Working with the couple "where they are at" takes precedence over any other policy in our work with couples. The extensive examination of the difficult countertransference in this situation is an integral part of the work. In most cases, we continue to recommend working with patients to understand, and if possible to share, the meaning of the infidelity, in order that it be maximally integrated. In cases where the patient is at the point of deciding to leave a marriage, we do not recommend sharing inasmuch as there is no longer any intention to rebuild. But where the couple seems to have a resilient holding capacity and there is a good chance for refinding love, then we recommend the revelation of the secret infidelity, done in the spirit of clearing the decks of wreckage so that a new superstructure can be built.

In the case of Mr. and Mrs. Marantz described earlier, Jim Marantz made a full and painful revelation of the secret affairs, which included Judy's best friend. She seriously considered leaving him, but in the wake of a decision to rework their marriage, they were able to build a kind of mutually respectful relationship they had never previously known.

A Treatment Format

We can now outline a treatment plan for the situation in which an affair is an important part of a couple's difficulty.

1. Early in the assessment, the couple's current and potential commitment to each other gives the best index of likely therapeutic success: Spouses are likely to do best if they are committed to each other despite the affairs and strains. Many couples can work successfully therapeutically without knowing initially if they will stay together, but a couple is not likely to survive a feeling of irretrievably lost commitment and a predominance of hate.

2. Therapy of the extramarital affair begins with an exploration of the meanings of the events and of the secrets in object relations terms. It then proceeds with their full revelation whenever possible. This revelation usually tests the level of commitment and puts the two spouses on equal footing. They now have equal knowledge of the failures in their relationship. It is therefore usually a way of helping the couple correct power imbalances, share vulnerability, relinquish postures of self-preserving protection, and establish a firmer foundation for rebuilding.

3. The major therapeutic task is, as always, for the couple to reintegrate the feared, denied, and split-off aspects of the relationship, which have been projected into the affairs. Help for sexual difficulty may form a crucial part of this repair.

4. In this process, the transference/countertransference interactions are central. The treatment itself absorbs the character of the affairs and of the marriage whose failures led to them. The therapist, taking in the secret, may well feel anxiety about its illicit quality, and in the process further isolate the unknowing spouse. Or the therapist may identify with a sense of moral outrage while struggling to understand. The attacks on the therapist's holding capacity are likely to be forceful and sustained, as the errant spouse tries to ward off the humiliation and loss of control of the object, which is part of making a disclosure. Nevertheless, these are to be understood and treated as transference to the contextual holding capacity.

As the therapist works in this fashion with a couple, he or she begins the process of reversing the likeness of the treatment situation to the couple's sexual affair. By refusing to go along with the splitting of objects and by not increasing the force of exaggerated and polarized projections, the therapist makes every effort to integrate split-off parts of the relationship. This enables the couple to express to each other mutual frustration and conflict. In the process, the therapist, while modeling a holding situation that will support a different kind of relationship, helps the partners toward building their relationship. If the therapist's efforts are successful, the affair's threat is countered by the understanding that gradually integrates the marriage.

CHAPTER 12

The Integration of Individual, Family, and Couple Therapy

Combined and Concurrent Therapies

In the object relations approach to family therapy, the integration of the modalities of family and individual work is common. Both of us began doing family work in settings in which it was usual for an adolescent to be seen in individual therapy, while the parents and/or the whole family were seen by a cotherapy team that included the adolescent's individual therapist. Our current working group in the Family Therapy Program of the Washington School of Psychiatry includes several members of the group that worked with Roger Shapiro at the Family Studies Section of NIMH Adult Psychiatry Branch in the 1960s and 1970s (Berkowitz et al. 1974, Shapiro 1979). They described routinely arranging for the family to be seen as a whole, the couple to be seen by one therapist, and one or more children to be seen by individual therapists. Usually the therapist of the index or hospitalized adolescent and the couple's therapist would be the cotherapists for the whole family.

Although this was a common model for an inpatient team or a crisis unit, a "derivative form" of family work seemed to fit in outpatient settings: seeing the whole family as the only therapeutic approach. It seemed less usual in the outpatient setting to use multiple approaches, although some of the early innovators in family therapy did so. For instance, the group that developed multiple impact therapy used every modality of interviewing during brief, intensive bouts of therapy (MacGregor et al., 1964).

Kramer (1968), a child analyst, was among the first to address this issue in work with children. He suggested that assessment of a child should include a family diagnostic workup. He presented three cases in which a family-wide neurotic pattern prevented a child's progress in analysis, leading him to recommend preliminary psychoanalytically oriented family and marital psychotherapy to enable the family and the parents to interrupt the neurotic family pattern sufficiently that psychoanalysis could then hope to be effective for the child.

Working with adults, Graller (1981) found that psychoanalytically oriented marital therapy was useful for analysands with the kind of self-pathology described by Kohut (1971). "Their spouses are frequently transference objects," he writes, "and often have complementary or reciprocal archaic pathology" (p. 175). When the transference was split between analyst and spouse, marital therapy, Graller suggested, could extend the applicability of analysis to these personalities with more archaic elements, by freeing the split transference deadlock.

Nonetheless, the models that developed in the field of family therapy at large tended to favor one or another fixed arrangement. In a recent conversation, Madanes confirmed that the Haley-Madanes group prefers to work with the whole family present, although they do not reject families that cannot get all their members to attend. Others, such as the Bowen group (1978), may work with one or both parents without the children but using a family systems viewpoint. Probably it was Nathan Ackerman (1958) who most rigorously recommended seeing the whole family in the early years of family therapy. Analytic understanding pervades his writing, and his depth of understanding is demonstrated in his interviews with families, some of which are still available on videotape. Ackerman (1966) also described a flexible use of family therapy either as the main mode of treatment or as an adjunct to individual therapy.

The fervor about viewing the family as a whole was to discourage the practice of concurrent individual therapy. Combined therapy received a further blow as the field of family therapy moved toward methods based more heavily on systems and communications models. Although combined forms of therapy have continued to flourish in hospital settings, they have not necessarily done so in outpatient settings where the press of crisis is less. And in at least some hospital settings, even while both forms of therapy have gone on, it has not been possible for the therapists to use the same or compatible language about the two forms of therapy, with the result that a serious discontinuity of approach develops. To a large extent the patient is left to deal with it. This difficulty has had some serious ramifications, as workers who have felt intuitively that family therapy and individual therapy both make sense have worked toward an integration of the approaches (Pearce and Friedman 1980, Sander 1979, 1987). Sander (1985) noted historical, cultural, economic, and dynamic reasons why therapists often abandon one or the other modality. Therapists tend to avoid a feeling of irreconcilable inconsistency between approaches.

It is a fundamental tenet of the object relations approach to family therapy that treatment of the family and treatment of the individual are theoretically and therapeutically consistent with each other. Object relations theory and its therapeutic approach regard the individual's inner world and external family as components of an open system. In this approach, the inner world of the individual is one subsystem, with its own boundaries that are biologically and interpersonally semipermeable. This internal object world contains a number of subunits of organization, each in relation to the individual and to the subsystems of other family members. Beyond his own personal boundary, the individual in turn is part of the larger family, which has its own boundaries. And the boundaries around the family members, with their varying degrees of permeability, determine the nature of the family's interactions with the community and the larger world.

These levels of organization are in a constantly dynamic relationship with each other as fundamental components of an overall biological and social system. Some of the components of the operating family system have been described by Reiss (1981) in a way that is consistent with but not restricted to a psychoanalytic view of the individual.

Setting the individual in the context of the family enables us to view our varying therapeutic approaches on a continuum. Even more important, we see the approaches as consistent with and related to each other, even if our therapeutic techniques vary with the dictates of the setting. The empirical altering of our therapeutic stance is determined by which aspects of the family and individual holding capacity and which aspects of transference are highlighted in different therapeutic settings. Using this formulation, we can now describe how these different emphases relate to each other. And we can begin to discuss the theoretical relationship of one kind of therapy with another, namely the interaction of individual psychotherapy or psychoanalysis with family or couple therapy. We can also examine some of the vicissitudes of the use of couple therapy along with family therapy.

One of the objections that has been most steadfastly raised to the concurrent use of family therapy and psychoanalysis has been the "dilution of the transference" that child and adolescent analysts have insisted is the almost inevitable outcome of combining these two types of work. At a general level, it is important to raise the alternate possibilities: that the use of family or couple therapy in parallel increases the breadth of approaches to the various transferences, and that it may clear the air of some extraindividual interferences. The fact is that the child's transferences to his or her parents develop ceaselessly no matter what settings he or she encounters with them, and the same is true for the child's transference to the analyst. In any event, the transference in child psychoanalysis is held empirically to be less intense and less often a focused transference neurosis than is usually the case in adult analysis. This is explained by the child's necessary, continuing real-life dependence on family.

As we explore this issue, it appears to us that the argument can equally be made on theoretical grounds that the child's transference to the analyst is apt to be more complete and comprehensive if the analyst is in interaction with the child's family in such a way that the child has access to it therapeutically. Commonly, the analyst will meet with the parents in any case; this is frequently required for the maintenance of the case. It is our contention that the severing of the connections between the child and his or her family is often, although not always, done for the benefit and comfort of the analyst, who feels the situation to be simpler. Sometimes this is indeed indicated because of the particulars of the case, but just as often, the details of the child's situation in the family argue compellingly for an integrated approach. If we did this more regularly, we would then be in a position to discuss more knowledgeably when and under which circumstances the combined approach offers an advantage, and when there are significant disadvantages.

The first example we discuss takes us into the workings of a combined individual and family treatment. The 9-year-old boy who was the index patient was seen initially, three times weekly, in individual therapy, which had the aim of extending the work in analytic depth. An initial family visit was so devastating to the family that the father became particularly resistant to further family meetings. With individual progress on the part of the boy, supported heavily by traditional parent-guidance work by the same therapist, however, the parents later were able to tolerate, and then to value, the family therapy, which became a weekly feature of our work.

Combined Child Therapy, Parent Guidance, and Family Therapy

This combination is illustrated by the Jansen Family I saw some time ago. Later sessions were described in Chapters 4 and 10. The present material from earlier sessions illustrates the interaction of individual and family therapy catalyzing each other as both treatments get off the ground.

Father was an architect, Mother a lawyer, and they had three boys: Shawn, 15, Lloyd, 13 (both high school students), and Tom, age 9, a fourth-grade student. Shawn was moderately depressed and preoccupied with himself, while Lloyd seemed to have pretty smooth sailing. Tom was the symptomatic boy, referred a year before the sessions I will report here. He had broken into an electronics store and stolen some equipment, and had gone out of his way to vandalize a particularly interesting electronics diagnostic instrument.

THE DIAGNOSTIC PHASE

First let me summarize the early work. In diagnostic interviews, I had found Tom to be quite depressed and full of rage. He was angry at his mother for her depression and at his father for his rages and preoccupation with architecture. Tom was the butt of his classroom, where he labeled himself "nerd" because the other boys called him that anyway. He had significant internalized difficulty. His parents were desperate to have him treated, especially Mrs. Jansen, who as a lawyer felt shamed by his delinquency. The parents did not get along very well, especially around Mr. Jansen's being something of an underachiever who, although preoccupied with architecture, was passive and lackluster about his practice, claiming that external circumstances got in his way. At home he was stubborn and domineering, and he weighed in at 275, a matter of extreme frustration and disappointment for Mother.

In the evaluative family session, there was enormous bickering between Shawn and Tom, while Mr. and Mrs. Jansen sharply debated who was at fault for the endless fighting at home. The real difficulty was the parental bitterness in which Mrs. Jansen felt unable to comment on her husband's infuriating passivity about his weight and his bossiness about everything else. She was in treatment and felt he should be willing to discuss their marital problems, which I inferred included some sexual difficulty on the basis of the weight, their suppressed rage, and the battles that broke out between them. Just as she seemed to be on the verge of discussing these matters, a fight broke out between the younger two boys, and Tom ran from the room and hid in the car.

Mr. Jansen was angry when they came to the interpretive and planning meeting. He said that they already had one casualty in the family—Tom, who clearly needed help. They were not going to sacrifice their healthy children to Tom's needs. There would be no more family meetings until Tom could behave himself and be less hateful. Mrs. Jansen said she had to go along with her husband despite her disagreement. She also said that although their marriage badly needed help, out of deference to her husband's position we would have to concentrate on Tom. The couple agreed reluctantly to periodic family meetings as benchmarks until Tom could tolerate such regular family meetings.

PARENT GUIDANCE

In the beginning, I met weekly with Mr. and Mrs. Jansen. They presented their difficulty with Tom's refusal to go along with the limits they set for him. It turned out that the worst of these refusals were usually at times of parental fights. Either the parents would be arguing and Tom, often in a squabble with Shawn, would become so disruptive that they would have to interrupt their fights to deal with him. Or one of the boys would misbehave, and a parental fight would erupt over the proper handling of the blame and punishment. Mr. Jansen tended to be more severe with Tom than Mrs. Jansen could tolerate, while she seemed to come down harder on the other boys.

We examined the parents' divided loyalties between the boys. Mrs. Jansen was identified with Tom as a victim, whereas Mr. Jansen felt Tom victimized his older brothers. Nevertheless, the leading edge of the work here was to help them understand how the fights between the boys became fights between them. I asked them to back each other vigorously in setting limits, and never to argue about the justice of a limit in front of the boys. They were able to do this and became relative experts at collaborative limit setting in two months. Then we worked at the parental coalition in the displacement of the guidance work about the children. I showed them how the regular pattern of the boys' interruptions seemed to be aimed specifically at distracting them from their own battles. They saw that these battles were extremely anxiety-provoking for the boys, and without our touching on any of the actual issues between them except the children, things improved markedly.

Over a period of a few months, Tom became calmer and able to accept limits. They then said that the other boys were much better and that they were getting along better, too. The whole family was warmer and calmer. They thanked me warmly, and said that they did not feel they needed to come with the same regularity but wanted to keep coming once a month while Tom's individual treatment continued.

INDIVIDUAL THERAPY FOR THE CHILD

Tom's early individual meetings with me were repetitive. He always represented himself as a bad spaceship or car. Most often he was Darth Vader's fleet, who could pretend to be good but would invariably defeat the good guys. One by one, his bad guys would dismantle my good guys, absorb their energy, and take over the universe. I felt bored and defeated. If we played checkers, he would play with a vengeance and win, or change the rules just as I was about to wipe him out. At school, he continued to get picked on and victimized, but he never discussed it with me.

As Tom began to shift, he introduced new characters. At first they would pretend to be good guys and then doff their masks to conquer sneeringly once again. Later, they condescended to help the good guys for an enormous price. And finally, he introduced Han Solo, a bad guy who had become a truly good guy. Han helped the weak forces of good protect the universe.

One session after I was away for a week, Han began to help and offered to work, as was his habit, for the reasonable price of $100 million, payable in advance. He began to clean up the usual criminals but went haywire and wreaked havoc on Earth, releasing all the evil forces. "What's gone wrong?" I asked in despair. "You have to call Dr. Tom Jansen for emergency help!" said Tom. I ran for the intergalactic laser communicator, and he rushed over in his repair ship to say that Han had contracted an interstellar infectious virus. "You know, like a mouse loose in a robot's circuits! It ate away his neuronal system, but I can fix it with a galactic antidote."

I said, "Tom, I think something like this happened to you when you broke into that electronics store last year. This time, I was away and Han had a serious relapse to being very mad. How about when you did all that stuff? Were you mad about something?"

He tried to brush me off and then, with the first insight of our work together, said, "I think my mother had just been in the hospital for her heart murmur. I wasn't worried, though."

"You weren't worried about what?" I asked.

"Oh, just not much—except about who would cook for us."

"Meaning what?" I asked.

"Kaplooey for her!" he said, admitting now that he had been very worried that she would die.

In reaction to this link now made, Tom ran away from his house before his baby-sitter could bring him to the next individual hour. The next time I saw him was at our now regular family session. These had been reinstated two months earlier, because Shawn, the 15-year-old, was now seen as depressed and having almost no friends. By this time, Mr. Jansen felt so grateful for the help in setting limits for Tom that he would do whatever I suggested, almost obsequiously. Meanwhile, Mrs. Jansen had begun tentatively to introduce aspects of their disagreements whenever she could make them relevant to Tom and Shawn's upset.

FAMILY THERAPY

Tom and Shawn came in fighting for the swivel chair, which is the twin of the one I claim for myself. Tom said that Shawn owed him money.

"It's not fair," Tom said, "because Shawn has $500 from confirmation and I only have $40. Anyhow, Shawn gets more new things, and he'll probably get to drive the car soon."

Shawn now said that since Tom's difficulty, Mother and Father were too involved with him, and Shawn got very little from them. Lloyd sat imperiously and seemed immune to all this.

Tom said, "Mother works too hard! She didn't work when you guys were young, and that's unfair. Other kids my age get someone waiting at home, like to say "Hi!" to them, and they get snacks and a big bowl of ice cream! It's just not fair!!" And he began to cry.

I said, "Things seem in short supply for several people." The boys agreed. I asked, "Does everybody in the family feel deprived?"

Lloyd said, "Yeah, why isn't there enough money, Dad?"

I asked if there was an implication that Mr. Jansen used his bluster to cover not pulling his weight. This was acknowledged as a tension between the parents that had been loudly debated at home in front of the children. Shawn said that one reason there was not enough to go around was that money went to me and to Mother's therapist.

Mrs. Jansen now said, "I think my husband's overeating and his being so stubborn come from his feeling that I don't have enough time for him and I don't feed him well enough."

He agreed grudgingly and said, "I grew up with a crazy mother, and I was an only child. My father ran off with a woman when I was 2 months old, and I was my mother's sole comfort. I was indulged and smothered, but I also felt deprived and often lonely. At home now I often feel forgotten. When I feel like that, I sometimes have these fantasies of taking revenge on my father for leaving me and my mother to fend for ourselves. Once when I was a boy, I got into a fight with a boy—the main thing about him was that he was the son of a male teacher and this boy had teased me for not having a father. I think I can understand something of Tom's sense of deprivation, although partly I can't. Because even with our marriage problems, Tom has had it so much better than I did."

For the first time during a session, Mrs. Jansen now reached over and touched her husband's hand. The session was over, and the family walked out in a subdued mood but seeming closer.

The family meetings now became a place where both children and parents could work increasingly openly, and where my counter-transference was less subject to angry flurries of taking sides, or of resenting the compound resistance as projected into Shawn and Tom. Mr. and Mrs. Jansen soon put Shawn's depression on the agenda, and even their marital difficulties slowly moved into the work.

INDIVIDUAL THERAPY CONTINUED

In the next individual session, Tom asked if he could bring in his mother to help him tell me about the terrible day at school, in which he had been teased for the first time in several weeks. This let me wonder out loud if he were trying to get his mother to protect him from me. I felt that he was experiencing me in the transference as a powerful father. I had in mind a similar position his father had enjoyed with his own mother and with Mrs. Jansen. Tom rejected my interpretation out of hand.

In the next session, he took me on fiercely in checkers. Our men got into gridlock. After a long, tense buildup, I made the first mistake and was almost instantaneously annihilated. I was angry and felt sheepish for competing so unrestrainedly but said nothing. But beginning in the next hour, the quality of our games changed completely. For the first time in our year of meeting, he played honestly and fairly, generously complimenting me on good plays or good luck. While enjoying his own successes, he seemed to stop gloating. I began to enjoy the individual work with him, a quality that endured over the next months of the individual meetings. The games now moved into a latency mold, with attention to skill and rules.

In the transference, Tom began to emulate and idealize me in a way much more fitting to a boy moving away from an open oedipal attack on his father. He seemed to give up the notion that he could get my power only by repetitively stealing it from me and instead began to enter into honest competition with me.

Countertransferentially, instead of feeling resentful and constantly battered by him, as I often had by his parents' former resistance to me, I began to feel a more flexible range of emotions. I enjoyed it when I won, and I suffered (as I usually do) when I lost— but I no longer felt Tom had cheated me. I felt I had a clever, although sometimes boring, latency-aged competitor who could teach me a thing or two.

A few weeks later I wondered aloud if he had any idea why he used to like to change the rules when he was about to lose. Tom said, "Oh, sometimes I still would like to do it, you know. I feel like I'm going to lose everything when I'm about to lose. I feel in a corner, and I start to get mad. Then I think, 'Oh, well! There's always the next time.' But I used to feel I had so little, that I thought, 'At least I deserve to win this game.' I don't feel that now. I get along with the boys in my class better, too—not perfect, but I think I'll lick it before we're done here. That's what therapy is for, you know!"

MUTUAL ENHANCEMENT OF TREATMENT MODALITIES

In this example, Tom's individual transference evolved in a series of steps that illustrate the sequential modification of his internal objects and the harsh, antilibidinal object with which he has been in intense relationship. The phase of his individual treatment that occupied the first year involved my accepting a painful transference role as a punitive object he despised and envied, and whose power over him he resented deeply. He was heavily identified with this object, in a fusion of libidinal and antilibidinal ways. He repeatedly tested the reliability of my contextual holding in the transference.

Slowly, we were able to see the core issues emerge, and the transference/countertransference issues began to feel more flexible. At first he tried on my "good object" quality, borrowed from my understanding holding of him. As he did so, he began to feel centrally understood and held, and he began to introject some of my qualities, now useful to him: reflection, the capacity for delay while understanding vulnerability, and the ability to compete without feeling devastated.

At the same time, the family work became possible on two counts. Father felt both held and understood by me as I supported him in being a father to Tom. Not only did he feel less humiliated and alone once he was able to set limits, but he felt reassured that I had respected his own limits without derision or attack. Mrs. Jansen also felt supported by my help, both with the boys and by my being able to offer it without forcing her to choose between Tom and the rest of her family. In effect, my offering a container to the couple allowed them to modify the shared transference of resistance they had to my holding capacity—which in the beginning was suspicious and guarded. Tom's improvement fortunately reinforced this and served as evidence that I could lend them a more effective envelope for the family with which they could identify and could then themselves provide for their family. But I think it is possible that even without Tom's tangible improvement, Mr. Jansen would have felt able to move back to family work as my relationship with him solidified.

When we returned to the family work, a mutually catalyzing relationship between the two ways of working finally became possible. The fact that Tom had become a typical latency patient in the individual psychotherapy made his individual work terribly slow. In the family sessions, however, his parents could point out that he still had trouble with being teased, and he was able to take it from them without resenting the questioning I would have had to do if they had not been able to say it in front of both of us. Thus, I was actually preserved as a nonintrusive, benign object, whose good intentions were confirmed at weekly intervals by his parents' increasingly helpful behavior.

Because I never betrayed Tom's confidence, he could feel I respected him and his inner world as well. It is important not to carry information back and forth between the two modes of therapy unless there is a compelling reason, such as risk of life or serious abuse. The holding of boundaries is one of the crucial functions that most families who see us have not been able to accomplish. We can and should stand for appropriate boundaries for the family.

In the family, I was able to turn a number of individual holding situations into a context for the whole family. In this endeavor, I countered the way they had been forced to splinter their holding capacity as each member felt compelled to defend against the intrusion and control of others—against the projective identifications that were so destructive. Thus, Tom and Shawn could begin to return the projections of vulnerability and deprivation to their parents, and the parents could begin to accept them. In turn, Tom could give up the identification with his father's greed as the only answer to deprivation, after his father could talk of his anger at the deprived sense he carried. The "bad" or "evil object" identification with which Tom had come to treatment could now be seen partly as an identification with his father's privation and anger and partly as a satanic pact, a case of "If I get no love from the good, then evil be thou my good," which Fairbairn (1940) refers to as a decision to wholly embrace the bad object when all hope of loving from a good object is lost. This could be modified only when the containing transference felt secure enough to let Tom expose the vulnerable hopelessness long enough for reworking to go on. In this task, his individual focused transference/countertransference relationship and the increased contextual holding that his family could provide played synergistic roles. I was unable to discover, in this family, any sign of their interfering with each other.

This case illustrates the way child-guidance work with parents can pave the way for family therapy. This way of working allows the parent worker to respect the parents' use of displacement or projection of their issues onto the child—something that many parents need if they are to be able to work with us at all. In play therapy, we let the child reveal the conflicts, wishes, and anxieties in the displacement of play until the child is ready to own them. Similarly, we let the parents speak of their own issues through talking about their child. For many parents and children, the work has to stay in the displacement. In other cases, the parents are able to move progressively to the recognition of their own role in a family difficulty, or to consider directly the way a child's symptomatology may reflect their own marital difficulty. At that point they become treatable directly, and a shift can be made to a more direct modality. Which modality this will be and when this might occur will depend on the therapist's assessment of the family's need, some practical considerations, and the phase of the work the family is in at the time.

Combined Child Analysis and Couple Therapy

In this case we note that couple therapy supported the analysis of the child, but with a mixed result for the couple.

Adam Taylor was referred just after his twelfth birthday because his parents felt he was depressed and was, for the first time, showing sporadic fits of anger. Recently, his school performance had fallen off markedly, and he had accelerated the usual amount of jealous scrapping with his 9-year-old brother, Sam. We want to mention that D.E.S. was the therapist, since therapist gender and name are significant in this case.

When I saw him alone in a diagnostic interview, Adam was a smiling, articulate, and pleasantly sardonic fellow who could describe his difficulty well. He confirmed what Mr. and Mrs. Taylor had said: that he had been unhappy since his mother went to work full time two years earlier. He missed her and had grown to resent the time she gave to his brother, whom he felt got more than his share. After we had discussed some of these matters, I asked Adam to draw pictures of himself and of his family in some activity. Figure 12.1 is a picture of himself, a rather obsessional, hardworking young man. Figure 12.2 is a family picture, showing the family at the beach. Adam is playing ball, Sam is in the water, and Adam's parents are lying on the sand, with Father encased in his scuba gear.

"What's Sam doing there?" I asked.

"Oh, he's drowning and he's calling for help," said Adam.

"What happens, then?" I asked.

"He shouts, but they're asleep," he said.

"So what next?" I said.

"Too bad for Sam!" Adam quipped, and grinned.

Adam could recognize his anger, and he knew he missed his

Fig. 12.1 Adam's self-portrait.

mother. But he had no explanation for his falling school performance, his difficulty with peers, or his passivity. Analysis was indicated because of the internalized nature of his difficulty, and because of his many assets, including his psychological curiosity. In addition, his father was unwilling to participate in family therapy, although he did agree to parent counseling.

Adam got himself to his analytic sessions, walking or bicycling quite a distance, rain or shine, four times a week. Nevertheless, in sessions he ran into the brick wall of his own internal resistance to looking at his anger, at first the anger toward his father, and late in the analysis the anger toward his mother. We quickly discovered, however, that the anger toward his brother Sam was displaced from that of his parents, and especially that Sam was a stand-in for Father in getting Mother's favor. The stance that Adam had adopted was that of a passive inability to take care of himself in competitive situations. The stauncher the passivity, the more he would appeal to a woman to rescue him—his mother, a teacher, or a girl his own age.

Fig. 12.2 Adam's family picture.

He avoided competing with boys, although he had some neighborhood boy friends he was willing to play competitive games with. Thus, his resistance in the analysis showed the same passive plaint that I rescue him by doing the analytic work for him.

At these times, despite my overall fondness for Adam, I found myself gritting my teeth, feeling bored, and wanting to bail us both out by "just getting us over this hump."

Only slowly did his more openly angry reluctance surface, at which time it became clear that he was frightened to confront me directly for fear I would retaliate. In this role, I was his father of whom he was fearful, largely because of oedipal rivalry.

Meanwhile, Mr. and Mrs. Taylor had told me a good deal about themselves. Mrs. Taylor had converted to Catholicism in order to marry Mr. Taylor in church and had risked her Methodist family's displeasure. Surprisingly, he had been warmly accepted by her family, which he felt was much warmer than his. He had gone into the Marines at 18 to get away from a domineering mother and a father who never had time for the family, and although he valued the warmth he felt he got from his wife, he was suspicious of her wish that he "open up and be more loving." He said he needed his anger to get ahead in the military, where he had become a successful pilot and squadron leader. "I don't like the idea of therapy, and besides, I need my aggression for my job," he said. "It's OK, though. You and my wife can do whatever Adam needs."

Mrs. Taylor was extremely unhappy about her marriage. She felt that she had done all the accommodating through the early years, and, feeling that her husband was walled off from her, she had turned to the boys excessively. She had come from a family in which her father was successful and aloof, and she felt she had picked Mr. Taylor because he was in her father's mold. But through the years, she began to wish for more. Finally, she went back to work and got some therapy as well. Now she felt that she had changed enough so that the marriage was not going to survive without help. She said openly to Mr. Taylor and to me that she felt Adam had picked up some of her own depression, and she asked if there were a way of helping her and her husband communicate more openly.

I would have liked to refer Mr. and Mrs. Taylor to a colleague for couple therapy. As I noted, Father forbade any family therapy, with his notion that he could not afford to be brainwashed by therapy and that Sam did not need it. He would agree only to parent work with me around Adam's analytic work. I was worried about Adam's attitude about my working so closely with his parents on a regular basis, inasmuch as many adolescents object to this arrangement, and it is often necessary to have them seen by a colleague. But not Adam! He said, "I figure they need all the help they can get— with themselves and with me! And they like you, so I hope you can help them."

So we began. Gradually, the way Adam withdrew and asked to be rescued could be seen as a parallel to Mr. Taylor's behavior at home, and Mrs. Taylor's penchant for rescuing could be seen as coming on the one hand from her own guilt and longing, and on the other as playing into the dynamics of both father and son. Mr. Taylor was able to begin to discuss some of his own difficulty being directly angry at his wife until he blew a fuse, at which times he would rage. This set the family to fearing these rages enough that everyone avoided provoking him, and it was part of the context of Adam's fear of competing openly with Father. As they discussed this pattern, they were able to take up more directly the underlying and more pervasive pattern: that usually Mr. Taylor was frightened to anger his wife because of his desperate dependency on her, and so he appealed to her passively. It was this pattern that was typical of Adam, and we got to it by considering Adam's behavior and then asking who he was like in this regard. After this, Mr. Taylor became a more openly cooperative patient, and the work began to move into direct work on the couple.

The effect of their working on this also seemed to free Adam to move into directly oedipal competition with me. At first he dreamed of being sent on an exciting space mission by a woman but shooting his little laser gun at a male foe during the mission. Later he dreamed of a version of the movie *Jaws* in which the shark was going to get a man named David, while Adam was in possession of the equipment to capture the shark. In this work, I represented at various times the mother who offered to rescue him and whom he longed for (the libidinal self and object), and the powerful and threatening father whom he feared and wished to defeat (the antilibidinal object). We noted that he tended to split good and bad objects along sexual lines, and he was able to give up the excessive idealization of Mother and the denigration of Father. Through the transference to me, and through my struggles with such countertransferences as feeling attacked from under the cover of his dreams, Adam was able to modify his internal object images of his parents so that they became at once more realistic and more benign. As he did so, my fondness for him became deeper but also more realistic concerning the trials he could put me through.

The parent therapy in this case was not smooth, however. At a point in the second year, Mrs. Taylor announced that she felt that her husband had tried to do what she had asked of him but that she was not going to be happy in the marriage. Over a painful period of weeks, she made the tentative, and then the final, decision to separate. Mr. Taylor was devastated and at that point decided to enter individual therapy on his own, so I referred him. Important for my analytic work with Adam, both parents were able to support his growth so that he was able to absorb and process the blow and to maintain allegiances to both parents while not leaning on them to be rescued. He had fantasies and dreams of rescuing them, but he was able to mourn his parents' marriage and finish his own work. At the end of two and a half years, he was doing well in school, had made friendships with boys in several settings, and maintained good relationships with both parents. Mr. Taylor was turning to Adam to rescue him from his loneliness at times, but Adam was able to maintain his friendliness without being pulled into doing so.

Every form of therapy has to take note of its failures and its partial successes. From the point of view of child analysis, this case is completely successful, never mind the divorce. From the point of view of the marital therapy, the case is a failure, never mind the child's return to a normal developmental path. From the point of view of the overall family, the success is mixed. Two of the individuals grew a great deal—mother and son. The second son got the benefit of improved parenting before the divorce, and the father grew somewhat, but could not go further.

Would the case have done better if conjoint family therapy had been added? Of course, we cannot know, but it seemed unlikely that Father would ever agree to this arrangement in any meaningful way. Nevertheless, the question remains.

We must admit that all treatment modalities have to reckon with the fact of problematic outcome. This case presents a mixed result. The question has to be raised whether part of the difficulty has to do with the arrangement or conduct of the case. Not all family or marital work leads to happy endings, and if we imply that it does, we will be providing an impossible model for therapists. In marital work, we treat the marriage as if it were the patient. We must not insist that marital partners stay together for our sake, and we must expect that a certain number of our marital therapy cases will end in separation. When this happens, our goal is the growth and individual well-being of the individuals in the family. It matters that they not carry forward an unmodified internal history of scarred objects.

In this case, the marriage was probably not capable of surviving regardless of the therapeutic modality. The father's reluctance to engage in any kind of therapy, although eventually tempered, nevertheless represented the kind of holding out that his wife no longer felt she could tolerate in her husband. At the time of their parting, each parent was better able to tune in to the needs of the children, although the wife had grown more in this respect than the husband. Adam had grown enough that with each parent he could maintain his part of the holding relationship staunchly. That is to say, he was more than able to make up for some of his father's penchant to lean excessively on him, tolerating it at times, and setting limits that did not alienate his father at others. We felt at the end of this treatment that Sam might well need intervention in the near future to help with his adjustment to the divorce but that we would watch and see.

We now turn to an examination of the interplay of the transference and countertransference in this case. Our reason for presenting this case is to speak to the argument that the work in depth with the parents might interfere with the child's analytic work. There was never any evidence that it did so. Adam's contextual transference to me was one of trust and confidence in the holding situation. He was able to extend this to the situation of hoping I would be helpful to his family. When he reflected on the breakdown of his parents' marriage, he eventually decided he could not hold me responsible any more than he could finally hold himself responsible. He was able to develop a well-formed transference neurosis—that is, a focused transference of intensity and specificity in which I embodied the qualities of the libidinal and antilibidinal objects. And he was able to work through the neurotic elements of that focused transference with me. Finally, he was able to separate in a timely way and be off on his own life's path.

For the parents, the contextual transference to me as a person who shared their interest in their problems as parents enabled the two of them to join with me in this task when they could not join in other tasks. This gradually allowed the growth of the elements of the more focused transferences, which are necessary to couple therapy, in contrast to parent guidance. Mrs. Taylor brought one version of a wish for the rescue of her marriage, while Mr. Taylor brought into our therapy the passive resistance with which he usually handled relationships. The therapy did permit some work on these elements. Although it was not enough, ultimately, to make the holding situation in the overall marriage adequate, work had gone on that was felt to be important to each of the individuals. One of the points to be made is that this work was possible, regardless of the final outcome of the marriage.

Phasing Treatment Modalities

These two cases make the point that while the integration of family and individual work is entirely possible, it is not so in every case. Once we consider the possible application of family therapy and of individual therapy to the treatment of our patients, there are many decisions to be made. The decision about which therapeutic modality to offer will involve more complex planning than if we only offer a limited range of services—for instance, only family therapy or only individual therapy. Treatment planning can be thought of as our joining with the individual or family to consider their needs. We are struggling together to find the best ways of working, and if something works for a while and then does not suffice, it can be changed. What runs through the work is an approach that has a strong common thread. It is not necessary to keep the surface arrangements as a permanent structure if they no longer serve.

In thinking about the concept of working with the family in several ways over time, we find it useful to think of the concept of *phasing*. We use different modalities as certain issues seem to dominate the work. As the issues change, the appropriate "frame" for the work may change. Thus, a couple may come for marital work and after some time get to a point where their holding capacity is much better. At that point, one of them may have individual work to do. Later, through the individual work, it may become clearer that the other spouse now has individual work to be done. Or the developmental crisis of a child may now make family work the most useful way of proceeding.

Phasing must be differentiated, however, from the very different process of letting the therapy drift without a frame that provides a context for its structure. Thoughtfully changing the structure of the work is consistent with an in-depth understanding of the needs of the individual patients and of the family. This means that such shifts must be thought through in terms of the ramifications for the family and for the individuals. Of course, mistakes will be made, but they can also be considered to provide evidence of the need for a better plan. In any event, it will just as often be a mistake to continue with a rigidly unchanging plan when the circumstances no longer suit the original structure.

The constructive phasing of various forms of treatment can maximize the flexible use of a family approach as an integrated tool. The following vignettes illustrate some examples of the constructive use of phasing.

FAMILY THERAPY COMBINED WITH INDIVIDUAL THERAPY

A 23-year-old woman, Robin Wagner, was referred with her parents by the woman's individual therapist. She had a history of multiple drug abuse during adolescence, fights with her family for several years, and recurrent depression. The present family conflict arose because her parents were irate that she was living openly in a lesbian relationship while going to college, for which her parents were paying. The parents and the child were at such odds over her homosexuality that they were on the point of not speaking. Additionally, the woman was only marginally motivated for therapy.

Mr. and Mrs. Wagner agreed to come to conjoint meetings in order to try to repair their relationship with Robin but quickly told the therapist they hoped to motivate her to investigate her homosexuality, which was very painful to them. During a series of six meetings, Robin and her parents were able to review the history of their stormy relationship, Robin became less demanding for "total acceptance," and the parents were able to share the history of the early period in Robin's life, which had been traumatically deprived. Father had been alcoholic and verbally abusive to Mother, who had become severely depressed over several years. Although it was helpful for Robin to hear this, she began to use it against her parents in the sessions. They said that although they felt profoundly responsible for Robin's early suffering, they felt they had to limit the amount of abuse they were willing to take for their mistakes. Both had worked exhaustively in therapy to get on top of those early issues; Mrs. Wagner had recently begun psychoanalysis for her own recurrent depression, while Mr. Wagner was finishing a therapeutic effort that he felt had been necessary to rework some of the remaining issues about his past drinking.

After this series of sessions, the parents said they now felt they could accept Robin's decisions about her sexuality without needing to ostracize her. When we stopped meeting, she planned to reintensify her individual work to look at the provocation she periodically levied at her parents and at others in her life, and perhaps to explore her sexual choices. Her therapist confirmed that she had moved into therapy with renewed energy and interest.

INDIVIDUAL THERAPY COMBINED WITH SEX THERAPY

Mr. and Mrs. Venuto, a couple in their forties, were referred by Mr. Venuto's individual therapist because of a long-standing sexual dysfunction that hinged on Mrs. Venuto's lack of sexual desire. She also had a history of anorexia and depression, neither of which had been symptomatic in several years. The Venutos spent several months working in the sex therapy format, during which Mr. Venuto continued in his individual work. Sex therapy and individual therapy can coexist helpfully when both derive from an object relations framework (Scharff 1982).

In sex therapy, they were assigned a set of exercises designed to highlight aspects of overall functioning while lowering anxiety. These exercises also provide a vehicle for bringing to the surface aspects of internal object relationships and projective identifications that are being expressed by the individual and within the couple by the psychosomatic route of their sexual life. At the end of a successful course of sex therapy, Mrs. Venuto was capable of enjoying their sexual relationship and Mr. Venuto was less demanding of her. Nevertheless, she now felt that she had issues that made it painful for her to be fully available sexually and emotionally to her husband. She felt the sex therapy had clarified for her that the difficulty was not primarily in anything he was doing to her or failing to do for her, but rather that she had work to do on her own, and she requested referral for intensive psychotherapy.

The next example illustrates an integrated approach in the treatment of a young adult. In this case, psychoanalysis of the young adult "child," family therapy, and couple therapy for the parents became ingredients of a difficult treatment.

Psychoanalysis Combined with Family and Couple Therapy

Reverend and Mrs. Barnett brought their 24-year-old daughter, Sue, for further treatment of depression and suicidality. Previous treatment included individual and group therapy and three hospitalizations in the Boston area since leaving home after college. She said she valued her most recent individual therapist, but during treatment with him, she required hospitalization again and became chronically suicidal. She and her parents decided that she would be safer living at home in Virginia, where she could return to her former place of employment as a computer programmer.

The parents were disappointed in therapists they had met and related to me in a challenging way, as if to make me prove I could manage what others had not. Despite continuing distrust of my competence, they agreed to individual psychoanalysis for Sue and weekly family therapy. Sue took to her analysis readily, talking in that setting of feelings of depression and emptiness, poor self-esteem, difficulties in organizing her computer work, and discomfort in dealing with her father. Early family meetings focused on the parents' anger at Sue for not reassuring them that she intended to live, and at Abby, their 18-year-old, for being rude and inconsiderate when at home and for preferring to be out every night.

AN EARLY FAMILY MEETING

Abby had been so rude that Mother said she could not go to Georgetown as planned, but Father permitted her to go, because he did not want to join with his wife, who tended to be angry about everything and excessively punishing. Mother was hurt and silently angry about his failure to back her. Later she saw Father "cozying up" to Abby, admiring the silk shirt she had bought at a boutique in Georgetown. As she described this, Mother became upset again, her anger inflamed by her husband's response. Reverend Barnett affirmed his right not to discipline, not to feel angry, and not to be told what to do or feel by his wife. He felt there was so much anger it had to have come from the past. Mrs. Barnett felt he was weaseling out of recognizing how he had caused her anger in the present. Meantime, the children remained quiet, Sue looking worried and occasionally clarifying a point, and Abby looking bored.

I said that Mother resented being left to do all the disciplining, but that, having accepted the responsibility, she now resented help with it, whereas Father was so identified with the child's objection to being controlled that he could not discipline her. Father amplified his dislike of control by Mother that led him to feel sympathy for Abby, and Abby began to say that none of this was her fault. Mother looked angrier than ever. I said I thought Mother was angry for the further reason that Father's bond with Abby seemed stronger than his bond with her. Mother was furious at me for not understanding, whereas Father insisted I was right. Mother said that what bothered her was his interference in her management of Abby.

My interpretation was wrong because I had assumed the family was dealing with jealousy at the oedipal level. Instead, they were dealing with the parents' envious competition to be in relation to a child, in this case Abby, who represented the exciting object for both parents. At the end of the session Abby said she could not stand to feel so guilty and would never return to family therapy.

SUE'S SUBSEQUENT ANALYTIC SESSION

In Sue's individual session following this family therapy meeting, she told me she felt terrible to be causing rows by being the one whose illness called for family treatment. She felt upset by the depression at home and by her father's agreeing with my interpretations as if he were just "cozying up" to me. In the transference, she identified me as the exciting object like Abby, and identified herself with the rejecting object like Mother.

THE NEXT FAMILY MEETING

In further argument over disciplinary issues, the parents again demonstrated their opposing views about the children. Father said, "It's hopeless. We always deal with Mother's relationship to the children, when I want to talk about our marriage." Mother said nothing. Sue said she wanted to work on problems of relating to her father. She felt she was an anxious person to be around, but she did not believe that was the only reason her father was uncomfortable around her. He replied that it was true he felt anxious dealing with her and, indeed, with both girls as soon as they got to be adolescent. He had not figured out why. Sue felt very relieved by his admission. She said it had been difficult for her to bring up her relationship to her parents here, but now that she had done so she could also say that her father sometimes treated her as a substitute for her mother, looking to her to tell him what to do, perhaps because she had some of Mother's organizing qualities. However, she was also not like her mother and would rather be treated as herself. I said that we had begun with their sense of hopelessness about focusing on their marriage relationship instead of on their dealings with the children. Yet the work Sue did on her relationship with her father was connected to that topic, because her difficulty stemmed from insecurity about the husband–wife solidarity.

Sue's taking the initiative to pursue her own goal, the parents' tolerance of her effort, and her father's working with her might have seemed to be following the defensive pattern of avoiding the marital relationship. But a few days after the session, the parents asked for couple sessions with me.

SUE'S NEXT ANALYTIC SESSION

In analysis the next day, Sue reflected on how my presence helped her to work with her family and to share in mourning lost relatedness. She said, "Having you there helped. I guess I was afraid of what my Mom might say. I didn't want it to seem like an attack on my Dad. I knew she was partly on my side, but I didn't want her to go to my side. It's easier here, because I feel, since you are here and you know I've got the problems I bring up in individual therapy, you know it's on my mind. That's an impetus to bring things up. It's so hard for me. I feel mean and afraid I might be wrong. Also, I can be just as extreme as my Mom. I said to my Dad, 'Well, I don't agree with that *at all.*' I sound like, '*No, not at all*, what I think is *completely different!*' even if it's just a small difference. I'm afraid of myself like that, and you help that. You would ask me to be more specific and get me to say what I mean and not just attack him. Before we came last night, I really wanted to say, 'Forget family therapy! It's too hard! It's so delicate and touchy!' We are so anxious. It's hard to change my Dad. I'd rather live with him. At the same time, it really bothers me. And how sad for my Dad to have Abby and me bother him as soon as we become adolescent. He got along so well with us before then."

THE COUPLE'S MEETING

Reverend Barnett had been angry at Mrs. Barnett for being angry at Sue for breaking her leg when she slipped on the ice in high heels. Mother earnestly tried to explain why a mother might feel anger as well as love and concern, but Father brushed this aside. I said that Mrs. Barnett seemed eager to have Reverend Barnett validate her emotions, but before I could go further, she furiously scolded me for being "dead wrong." She had simply been trying to ensure against his anger being dumped on her unfairly. *I felt stunned and disabled, so that the differentiation I had been making between her anger and some kind of striving for validation got wiped out of my mind.* Father began to discuss how confused he became when she attacked, and I recognized my experience as close to his. This helped me to recover and try again.

I said that sometimes she appeared to be angry but that I felt this was a misreading of her emotional state. It seemed to me at those times she was closer to a feeling of anxiety and potential rage that I would misconstrue her. She nodded, and I continued to say that I thought that there had been early life relationships in which she had been upset by being misperceived to the point of abusing her identity. She said, "You're absolutely right!" but the next moment she turned on me accusingly for agreeing with her husband that her anger came from the past. *Again, I felt stunned, confused, and incompetent—this time in an aggravated form when her husband supported her and berated me on her behalf.*

This countertransference experience enabled me to experience and understand the desperation about feeling understood. When my understanding was off-target, they felt frightened by my incompetence. When it was good, they had to attack me and spoil it. I could sense why, as a couple, they could not provide for each other a holding environment. Instead, their shared internal object relations were not steady but were subject to violent fluctuation. The attempt to dispel this unsteady feeling of destroying wholeness or goodness led to their projection of confusion into me. From this, I understood that Sue's confusion and inability to get organized had arisen from her valency for receiving their projection.

An Integrated Approach to Families with Holding Capacity Deficits

The work with this family demonstrates the usefulness of the integrated approach in a family with major deficits in their capacity for containment. These deficits have contributed to the difficulty in the index patient's ability to become securely autonomous as a young adult, to her depression and suicide risk, and to her deficient personality structure. The inability of the family to get both daughters to the family meetings is also symptomatic of their failure to provide a holding context.

Sue could form an attachment in the analytic situation that was sufficient for her to work, but it is doubtful that she could have approached the most difficult of the internal object issues without the family meetings. Her tendency without this setting, as in her previous individual therapy, was to split objects. Her previous therapist could not provide an adequate holding context because he was idealized while Sue was destroying herself. Without the family therapy holding context, this could have been repeated in her psychoanalysis.

Sue's depression provided an avenue through which the parents began much-needed marital therapy, which they could not ask for directly until some of the family work had been done. Psychoanalysis for Sue relieved the parents of the burdensome task of providing holding for a child who should no longer need it and protected her from their tendency to project destruction into her. Meeting with the family helped them to provide a holding context for Sue's analysis. In the couple therapy begun on behalf of the family and with their knowledge and support, I took on the arduous task of containing the couple's projections without being damaged by them. Sue was there to learn from repetitions of this work done in the family setting. I functioned as a holding environment for the family, which could then support the couple's work and the family work. Sue's individual work and the umbrella of my presence at the family meeting protected her as she faced the threatening aspects of her parents. Experiencing Sue's family with her accelerated my understanding of Sue's confusion and self-destructiveness and advanced the work on Sue's inner object relations. The transference was affected both positively and negatively as the index patient would alternate between feeling supported by me or feeling, as her parents did, that I would never understand.

There are many possible combinations in working with families, once the therapist investigates the integration of modalities. Contrary to the idea that the differing modalities interfere with each other, psychodynamic therapists who are able to work comfortably in family and individual work have found that they catalyze each other and make a depth and breadth of work possible that minimizes the sacrifice of one part of the family for the other. The several combinations illustrated in this chapter make the point that each treatment plan should be tailored to the specific needs of the family.

PART IV

Life Phases in Family Therapy

CHAPTER 13

Family Therapy with Very Young Children

Why Work with Children?

Object relations family therapy, which draws on individual psychoanalytic and small group theory, values the unique individual contribution of each family member as well as the shared participation in the family group. This approach requires that all members be present—not only those who can speak effectively. We want to include infants, toddlers, and play-age children so that we can learn about their contribution from observing their presence and listening to their play communication. In fact, we find their presence particularly important because they cannot speak for themselves. Yet there are not many teachers who focus on young children in family therapy, and there are few resource articles in the family therapy literature that describe the techniques for including them.

An exhaustive literature search was made by Zilbach (1986) whose findings confirmed our impression. She told us that she found only four direct references to the inclusion of young children in family therapy. Our own teaching has made use of contributions by Ackerman (1970, 1982), Guttman (1975), Zilbach (1974), and Zilbach and coauthors (1972), supplemented by references from the individual child therapy literature, which we modify for family therapy teaching (Beiser 1976, Peller 1954, and Winnicott 1958, 1960a, 1964, 1965b, 1971b). Zilbach (1986) concludes that young children have been excluded from family therapy because of therapist or parent discomfort. She reminds us why it is so important to include them: Often a child is the one whose symptoms call attention to the family's problems; other children in the family may have more subtle difficulties that can be detected early if all are seen; children may act as allies and cotherapists as they speak and play to express emotion and clarify the unconscious themes; and in general, they complete the whole picture of the family that is essential to "whole family understanding."

We find that children between the ages of 3 and 10 do not seem to know enough of the family's defenses to know when to keep quiet and what not to say, so they frequently blurt things out, and no one seems to object. Kwiatkowska (1971), who developed the technique of family art evaluation, taught that the youngest child was often the best informant about the family. Children under 3 who cannot speak well nonetheless may speak occasional words or sentences that cut through to the issues, as the following vignette illustrates.

When a mother and father were arguing in the session about which of them was going to give in and move from their stubbornly held positions, their 2-year-old boy put two figures side by side, one on a chair and one on a toilet, and said "Potty!" The parents laughed, and the father said, "Right on!"

This fresh and naive "Emperor's New Clothes" capacity is valuable to us, but it is actually a minor reason for having young children in the room. The crucial reason to include all ages of children is that, because the family is organized as a whole, the absence of any of its members changes the overall matrix of the family. It is not possible to see and hear what it is like for the family to have its infant among the other family members unless we observe it. If the couple just mentioned had been seen alone, the therapist would not have noticed their reaction to the toddler.

The father nodded ruefully, saying that someone would have to get off the pot, while the mother delightedly started to play with the clever child. The parents who gained insight from their child's play did not, however, apply this to solving their argument. Instead, they were diverted from their battle, with the consequence of mother and son pairing as a solution to stress in the marital relationship.

If we see the family without the baby, then we basically see a subgroup, and the dynamics are usually fundamentally different. So having all the members present is essential for the therapist to get "whole family understanding."

An Overview of Young Children in Family Therapy

THE CHILD FROM ZERO TO THREE

We begin with the question of the usefulness of family therapy to the very young child. It does not seem that the words we say to the family can be understood by the young child with limited verbal capacity. If, then, we are going to conduct family therapy primarily through words, some might say that it would seem logical to draw the conclusion that the young child will not be able to understand and will therefore be extraneous to the process. This opinion is advanced by parents and therapists who feel uncomfortable about including children.

There are a number of ways in which this argument misses the point. For the very young, preverbal child, the direct effects of what we say are extremely limited. The young child is exquisitely cued to the parents' affective tone, even more than to their words. A good deal of the impact of what the parents are saying is explicitly observable by watching the child. Sometimes, for instance, while the parents have a brief angry exchange, the 2-year-old will immediately come between them and begin an interaction designed to keep them from fighting. The adults are usually unaware of this kind of interaction. If we are able to share this observation with them, their heightened awareness may help them notice what they were actually doing (i.e., it may increase the powers of their observing egos) and it may increase their understanding of what their life together means to their child.

The impact on the parents of realizing that their fighting does something immediate to their child is often far greater than our simply giving them a verbal interpretation about it. As therapists, we also need other observational data derived from seeing the whole family. If something begins to shift for the parents, having the whole family there allows us to observe how this affects the entire set of feedback loops in the family. We cannot see the full effect of our interventions without the changed, or unchanged, part played by the child. Many of the instantaneous effects the child demonstrates are extremely helpful in orienting parent and therapist.

We consult to the holding capacity of the family, not primarily to the individuals and their intrapsychic life. There is therefore no essential difference when we work with families with young children. We do not need to speak directly to the young child, although we may do so at times if it seems to work. We are speaking to the whole family and especially to its ability to provide holding for its members. But to do so effectively, we need the whole family there. And the family is complete only when the young children—including infants—are present. With children from infancy through the preverbal era, the therapeutic input to the child comes by the mediation of our contribution through the parents. This means that speaking to the parents constitutes speaking indirectly to the young child, especially the child under 3.

We know that there are methodologies for direct therapeutic work with infants and young children, such as those developed by Greenspan (1981) and his colleagues. This work is of interest to all mental health workers, but it is not immediately germane to psychoanalytic family therapy. We draw support for our way of working with infants and toddlers more directly from infant researchers who work with mother–child dyads (Fraiberg et al. 1975). They stress the importance of having the infant present during psychoanalytic psychotherapy of the mother. Thus, the information and the transference are generated by the mother–infant pair, and the therapist, while interacting verbally with the mother, is *reacting* to her and her baby. There is also the possibility for the therapist to actually hold and handle the baby if this seems useful, which it may well be in experienced hands, either diagnostically regarding the baby or as a way of being in a physical conversation with the mother and baby but with more emotional impact than when "just talking about it."

In summary, our way of working does not rely exclusively on verbal input. The direct participation of the infant or toddler is all the more important because so much is lost in putting the infant's behavior into a report. Being able to describe to parents the emotional import of the family interactions that occur tends to expand their holding function and to promote centered interactions with the infant. And the infant's changed response needs to be fed back to them for further understanding and elaboration of their behavior and feelings.

The child's experience with parents is being transmuted into internal objects by the young child during the time they consult us. Parents have a dual role as managers of a child and as the "material" of the child's growing internal object world. This gives what they do now an importance that is greater than that of later interactions when the child is older. When we speak to them, we are addressing the child's internal world as it is forming. It is important that what we say to them be fundamentally informed by the most we can know about the child.

THE CHILD FROM THREE TO SIX

Once the child is over 3 or so, the problem is easier in many ways. All that we have said still applies: we need the whole family to be in the room with us if we are to understand them as a whole. But in addition, these children can tell us a great deal directly, and they can absorb a great deal of what we have to tell them. They do so most often through the medium of play. The parents can also be taught to understand what the child is saying, at least to the extent that they can see where the therapist's information about the child's experience is coming from. It is not necessary to train the parents to become surrogate therapists, for that is not a helpful role for parents. But we can use our work to help them to observe and take in what the child is saying, and often to speak or communicate more directly with the child. Here the child therapist has an advantage in being comfortable and familiar with the way children use play as a medium for the expression of their internal worlds.

For the therapist without child training, however, there is hope. To begin with, the use of play is not the only source of communication. Because the information from the child about the family is largely nonverbal, or "metaverbal" (that is, beyond the literal meaning of the words) the analytic family therapist is already in a position to be observing affective interactions rather than mere manifest content of play. Furthermore, the acquisition of a limited amount of play material and comfort with using it comes readily to those who are interested. Some training and encouragement provide the therapist enough support to begin incorporating a limited number of play materials into the family sessions and letting the children play while the whole family is talking. Occasionally, we find it useful to signal to the adults that we are going to interrupt in order to talk or play directly with the children. We may then get on the floor to join the children or to engage in getting a particular child to elaborate on a piece of play. If there are cotherapists, it is extremely useful to let one tune in on the play while the other keeps the conversation going with the older family members. The one playing directly with the children can then keep track of the parallels between the play-conversation and the word-conversation. There will invariably be many parallels, and they will be among the most informative pieces of material about the underlying life of the family. It is not essential, however, to use cotherapists for this situation.

The primary data for understanding the family comes from the combined process of observing and absorbing. The absorbing process is the process of taking in the transference at large and allowing it to enter the therapist's inner world. There it makes contact with the therapist's internal family, where it triggers the countertransference. This process of the exercise of the therapist's "negative capability" requires neither a knowledge of play therapy nor a singleminded concentration. It does require the capacity to absorb and reflect, allowing fantasies to form in the process. One does not have to be a child therapist to do that, for each of us has an inner child to fall back on in the process, and that is the fundamental internal tool. What is needed is a willingness to be open to the play and, at the practical level, to provide a few toys.

THE CHILD FROM SIX TO TEN

Older latency children may or may not need to play. Play is a normal, age-appropriate way of dealing with anxiety at this age, and children may play to bind anxiety while they talk of their issues. Play may also be used to express their concerns in displacement, or it may be used overdefensively, which can then be interpreted by the therapist. But the most important reason for offering toy material for these children, who do have adequate verbal capacity to participate, is that the child of this age, still so rooted in body and in action, does better in the session with something to do that enables constructive movement. More or less can be made of play with these children, but they feel substantially more comfortable while engaged in some action. They also listen better over the period of a session and become better participants. And the content of the play, even into early adolescence, may be informative with an impact that words alone cannot offer. This will be especially true with the inhibited or inarticulate child.

The Developmental Level of the Child

Underlying the differences in our approaches to families with children of these various ages is an understanding of the development of the child. It is not our intention here to describe detailed developmental sequences, but we do think the family therapist needs to read about this in Freud, Winnicott, Erikson, Bowlby, Mahler, and so on. Some modifications of our view of development that were introduced by recent infant research and by object relations theory have been spelled out in Chapter 6 and in a previous book (Scharff 1982).

Here we can say that one of the most important things to assess is the quality of relatedness of the child to the parents and family, and the appropriateness of this for the child's stage of development. Assessment of the amount of anxiety or detachment in the various bonds to parents, and the degree of appropriate or inappropriate reliance on them should be included, along with an assessment of overall cognitive and emotional development. We do not mean to contradict our assertion that the family therapist need not be an experienced child clinician. If a therapist does not have child training, an evaluation by a skilled child therapist or pediatrician can be used adjunctively.

Once the level of development of the child is documented, the therapy can proceed. Any other interventions that seem to be required can also be instituted, such as tutoring for a learning difficulty, nutritional supplementation for an infant who is failing to thrive, or individual psychotherapy for a child with severe internalized difficulty. These interventions are all compatible with analytic family therapy. Although the pediatrician or teacher may even see the other interventions as primary, we know that they often do not work without the family therapy. It is not that the therapist needs to know everything about child development, but he or she needs to see the family—and that means the whole family. It is not difficult to arrange consultation to cover areas in which the therapist is not experienced. But no one else will do the assessment of the family situation, and there all that is required is the willingness to relate to children and the confidence that the meaning of the interactions will emerge from the experience of the family.

The Relationship between the Developmental Levels of the Child and of the Family

In discussing assessment in Chapter 8, we described the process of making an estimate of the developmental level of the family's mode of functioning. Of course, the developmental level of the family is ordinarily carried forward by the growth of its children and the chronology of its external development. Thus, the family with its first newborn will be characterized by the processes of adjustment in moving from being a couple to a threesome, and particularly to a threesome with a maternal–infant preoccupation. The family with three adolescent children will be dominated by sexual and assertive aspects of adolescence, and we can expect that the parents will have aspects of their own adolescent issues recalled with some frequency.

How this aspect of the "developmental level of the family" fits with the overall psychosexual developmental level of the family will vary. Some families are particularly challenged at one stage, others at another. For some, it is the oedipal challenge that is too much for their holding capacity, and for others it is the first onset of preadolescence with one or another child. Thus, the level of functioning of the family may or may not correspond to the external markings of its "chronological" development, just as the internal development of the individual may be out of synchrony with actual chronological age. Just as these differences are important in the assessment of the individual, so are they with families. It is not unusual to see a family with a toddler that is concerned with principles of development appropriate to latency children. Such a family might be inappropriately concerned that a 3-year-old be able to face things and manage alone. Nor is it unusual to see the family that protects an older child, rather as an infant in need of safety.

This monitoring of levels of development is not just a matter of the first session; we are also interested in times the family might regress to an earlier mode of functioning under certain stresses. One goal of treatment may be to help the family understand the way its level of functioning alters during differing circumstances.

Family Therapy with Infants and Toddlers

As we have said, young children have often been excluded from family therapy. We have found that, among family therapists who do work with play-age children, there is a further subcategory of exclusion, namely that of infants and toddlers. This is such a loss because the role of being the youngest permits this child to say or show what others find unsayable. (We have found this to apply even when the youngest is an adolescent.) We think that the family projects much of its childlike spontaneity into the youngest and then simultaneously disavows and cherishes it there with as much determination as it uses to keep its last child a baby. So to exclude the little one is to collude with this process. The therapist then misses out on a therapeutic opportunity for understanding the whole family and for effecting a reintegration of projected capacities.

For instance, an older boy may welcome the interview in which the baby is not present because he gets his parents to himself, and so, although reporting that he feels jealous of his new sibling, he may look and act happy as a clam. But either telling us about jealousy, or denying it when the parents report it, is qualitatively different from the alternating aggression and depression we may observe when that same older child and the baby are there together. Furthermore, we may be able to observe that despite the parents' concern for the older child and their sensitivity to his jealousy, they are unable to describe something we can see and feel when the baby is with us: that the whole family revolves around the baby whenever it is awake, and even for substantial periods when it is asleep. These observations also apply to the way a couple's interactions are altered when their infant is present. For this reason, if we see a couple alone, we will not know how that child's presence alters their family fundamentally. In the examples that follow, we get a chance to see ways of working with families with infants and toddlers. Two of the families had only young children, while the third had three older children and a baby, but the presence of the baby was crucial to understanding the family.

A FAMILY WITH PRESCHOOL CHILDREN

Charles, a 30-year-old man, had previously consulted a male colleague because of mounting depression that was affecting his work as an accountant. He had placed first in his graduate school class and had been hired by a prestigious accounting firm. Now he was supposed to study for the extremely competitive qualifying exams while beginning his job. In the last five months, however, he had been unable to study because he felt more and more depressed. Recently, he felt that it was becoming difficult to keep up his performance at his job, although no one had yet criticized him. When his psychiatrist left for vacation after the first interview, Charles said that he wanted to transfer, preferably to a woman therapist.

The story he told me (J.S.S.) made sense of his depression. He and his wife, Abigail, had been married eight years. She was about to deliver their fourth child. They had three boys, aged 5, 2½, and 1½. Although they had planned the first two children, the third child and the present pregnancy represented birth control failures. Charles said that he felt guilty for being preoccupied with his exam preparation and not available to support his wife over the past six months.

Charles had come from a large family, and although he and his wife wanted a number of children, the way it had happened made it feel out of their control. Furthermore, Charles's father had gone to Vietnam for a year when Charles was 5 and had come back a changed person. The family seemed to disintegrate from that point on, although they kept on having more children. He felt the pressure he was under to study for his exams might constitute a "Vietnam" experience for his family and for his oldest boy, now aged 5, and that he might be abandoning them, as he felt his father had abandoned him.

That, however, was not all. His 1½-year-old child, Todd, had been having breathing difficulty. When his wife had seen the child turn blue and pass out, she had called the pediatrician, who told her he thought it was nothing to be alarmed about and that it would pass. This had gone on for four months, until a month ago when Charles had finally seen an episode. He rushed the child to the emergency room, where he obtained the diagnosis of atypical asthma. The pediatrician was, however, very tight-lipped. Although the boy was begun on medication, Charles and Abigail were given no information or counseling about his difficulty. The consequence was that they had spent the last month worrying about their son's health and prognosis. When I heard this story, I began to feel that Charles's depression was more likely to be reactive to the current stress in the family than to be deeply neurotic, and I asked him to come in with his family.

The family arrived with the three children parading energetically up the driveway to my office. I thought at first glance that Todd, the 1½-year-old, might have an odd appearance, but as he spoke to me, I quickly realized that he was not abnormal and that it was the developmental history of prematurity that had alerted me to the possibility. He had a round face with a double chin and was enormous, but his brother was large as well. I was relieved in the first few minutes of the family session to discover that he was bright, verbal, and engaging. Both of the children explored my office energetically in the rambling way typical of 1- and 2-year-olds. They pulled out toys, showed them to their parents and later to me, dropped them, and continued on. During the time I talked with the parents, I occasionally interrupted to tune in on one of them, or to ask the parents how common a certain behavior was.

The parents described their children, Abigail talking more than Charles. They said that Todd had been premature by two months, and it took him a long time to leave the hospital. Once he did, however, he had shot up, and by 8 months was so huge that he was slow in learning to walk. But he had been advanced in verbal development, with a vocabulary almost as advanced as John, his year-older brother. John did show the beginning of sentence formation, indicating to me that he was on track verbally, while Andy, the 5-year-old, played quite complicated games with armies of toy cars that illustrated appropriate prelatency skills.

While I conducted a family interview, I observed the children out of the corner of my eye, making a general developmental assessment and getting an idea of their relatedness while I talked with the parents. Abigail told me that she liked having the children and wanted more. She had come from a large family and had done a considerable amount of caretaking of younger children, so she knew what she was getting into. I noticed she was alert to her children's needs, helping them negotiate toy trades while talking to me. She was a competent, experienced mother. On the other hand, she and Charles felt pretty overwhelmed just now. She told me that each time she had to wait through Todd's "breath-holding episodes," she was alone with the fear that the child would die. She felt it was especially difficult while waiting to have this fourth baby. Not only was she uncomfortable with the pregnancy but there was something about having a sick baby while being pregnant with another that got to her. She had gotten pregnant while nursing Todd and was angry this had not protected her against another pregnancy. However, because she liked children, it was not the fact of the fourth child that bothered her but the sense of being overwhelmed. In this interview, she said that she felt guilty that she had not been able to be more supportive of Charles in his job. I felt touched by the parallel to his wish to do more for her.

Meanwhile, the children played with various toys in age-appropriate ways. Todd played with a gun, and on a couple of occasions looked as if he might hit someone with the butt handle of it. Once he started to tear a child's picture off my bulletin board, and his father stopped him by taking him on his lap. Andy roamed, played with miniature cars, and built with blocks with John. Toward the end of the interview, the little ones got a bit fractious, and two bottles came out.

By the end of the interview, I had the impression of a well-related family who cared for one another and managed well. There was a good level of cooperation. The parents related to each other and to the children in a fluid and supportive manner. I thought that the two older boys might be relatively slower developmentally, although still well within normal range, but Todd's verbal development was stunning. His other behavior seemed entirely appropriate, although he seemed a bit wound up. His parents confirmed that he acted in a slightly driven way since being placed on the medicine for his asthma but felt he seemed to be returning to normal.

I thought the times the parents had held hands when one of them seemed to need support had not caused a reaction from the children, and that there was a remarkable absence of anger in the family, even toward doctors. On the other hand, I did think that both parents were depressed, visibly sad, and low on energy. This did not seem to be transmitted to the children, but perhaps I had not been free enough to detect it in this session.

When I was scheduled to see the family the next week, only Abigail and the children showed up. I met with her briefly while she gave Charles's excuse that he had needed to study. She confirmed that she did feel he was depressed and had been ducking out on things. I worried about the family's reluctance to come and set up another appointment for them two days later.

Abigail came with the younger boys only because Andy had gastric flu. Charles joined them from work a bit late. During the first part of the interview, I listened to Charles talk about external causes of stress. While I did this, both children played with small movable human figures. John had the mother doll doing splits, rather painfully I thought. Todd had a pilot figure doing less organized bodily movements. Throughout the session, the children toddled around the room and got into the toys. Todd was the more active explorer, playing with my telephone several times, handing me the receiver and then saying "thank you." He worked at imitating words that I said to him. I was impressed that he no longer seemed driven and that any signs of hyperactivity were gone. Later in the hour, when Charles was finally able to discuss further reasons for his depression, the children seemed suddenly to get fractious and whiny.

At first, Charles talked about his depression rather superficially. He played down the role of Todd's asthma and even of having the three children so quickly. He said that as far as he was concerned, his major stress came from his accounting firm, which seemed to have gone back on its promise to give him the time he needed to study. Instead, just as his Certified Public Accountant exams were coming up, they had insisted he double his workload. One effect had been that he had begun eating an enormous amount. He felt the firm was jeopardizing his career, and he felt betrayed. He said that despite all this, he really was not mad at anyone and that it just seemed to be a fault in the system: of course they needed the work done, and the exams just happened to coincide. He said again that all this had meant that he had been so preoccupied that he had not been supportive of Abigail as she went house hunting, and this time she confirmed that she felt it was true.

It now emerged that they were having to move because of the enlarging size of their family, and that after house hunting the last few days, Abigail had found a new apartment located near her mother-in-law. They would move there two months from now.

This topic finally led to Charles being able to speak of issues that related to his depression. His parents had divorced when he was 10. He had lived with his mother, and the relationship with his father had always been tenuous. (I now understood why the first referral had not worked out. Charles must have felt quite rejected by my male colleague and looked to a woman to be more reliable.) Father was remarried and involved with his second family. Charles was much closer to his father's father, and this grandfather had died six months before.

"My grandfather really was a much better father than my Dad, so I miss him a lot!" said Charles. "Plus the fact that while my grandfather was alive, my Dad kind of made a show of keeping things going with me to please his Dad. But since Granddad died, he has stopped trying."

As Charles said this, both children suddenly stopped playing and grew whiny. While Charles talked, and over the next minutes, Todd headed right for him and put up his arms to be lifted onto his lap. He sat there and began to cry, without an apparent explanation for his distress. John now wandered listlessly around and seemed unhappy. After a moment, Abigail reached into her bag and handed them both bottles, and they then sucked in a somber way.

After a moment, Abigail continued. "It really is hurtful," she said. "They will write cards to me and the children and leave Charles's name off the card." And she touched his arm as she said this. I felt much more let into Charles's and the family's depression, and at that moment felt a sense of sadness such as Charles may have felt when his "good father" died, removing the vehicle for relating to his own father. It was at this time that his son suddenly began to have the episodes of asthma. For a moment I felt identified and caught up in Charles's sense of loss and of being overwhelmed, kicked when he was down. Then I felt this had spread to the whole family. In Charles's own loss of a father, he had suddenly felt unable to be a father to his own family, and this was the issue of his personal depression and of the family's depletion. The last part of the session was spent discussing these observations and their family-wide implications.

This session and the ones that followed confirmed my impression that this was a family that not only was basically healthy but was actually quite strong. They were going through enormous stress, which quite reasonably depressed the adults and at least the oldest of the children. In the process of working with them, it was possible to see that they dealt well with their children and cared for each other. The depressive issue of Charles's loss of his intact family during latency, plus the strain from the earlier family tension as he was growing up, left him vulnerable to feeling loss of competence as a father. Thus the phase of family growth, the loss of his grandfather, and the illness in the toddler triggered a family-wide crisis. The prognosis for being able to move past the depression and cope with Todd's illness seemed excellent, because the family's vulnerability seemed to surface readily into the shared space where we could examine it, and because the parents were not defensive.

With regard to Todd's asthma, I was able to strengthen the family's connection with their pediatrician, who could then better offer the medical support and attention they deserved, and could evaluate the contribution of emotional triggers for the asthmatic episodes. In short, it seemed to be a family in which the relationships, the object worlds in formation, and the levels of development both of the children and of the family's overall mode of function all seemed to be safely within normal bounds ordinarily. The history of early losses seemed to fall heavily on Charles's side, but the combined assets and trust of the couple looked adequate to the therapeutic task. The job was to help them with their adjustment to their unfortunate medical situation and to help them with current multiple stress. Except for my helping them get better medical care, however, they were able to assume the work of managing a better adjustment themselves, once they could get on with understanding the meaning of their multiple losses and the vulnerability these losses had tapped.

The next vignette is presented to give another example of brief developmental assessment in a couple whose capacity to cope was threatened.

A FAMILY WITH ONE-YEAR-OLD TWINS

The 18-year-old wife of a 21-year-old mail carrier came to her family doctor because she felt completely overrun by her identical twin sons, aged 15 months. She had been married only eighteen months because her husband had been ambivalent about getting married after she discovered her pregnancy. The doctor thought the husband was continuing to be quite negligent of his wife and family and suggested the wife consult a child psychiatrist to help her with the children. Of course, I thought that was the husband's job, and so I asked to see them as a family.

Despite the description of the husband as slippery, he proved to have more motivation than was first apparent. In the meetings with the wife and twins, he was interested and helpful with the babies, who indeed were into everything nonstop. He was able to admit his difficulty with being "trapped into a family" but said that he fled the house partly because his wife became so passive and depressed. She agreed that she tended to throw up her hands and blame him, and that she was frightened to leave the house to become more involved in establishing a network for herself. While the parents were working toward a less blaming and more cooperative relationship, I was able to observe the twins, who were active and charming. They were responsive to the parents' emotions when they were discussing aspects of their own experience in growing up with parents who had been shaky models. I felt a great deal of sympathy for the challenge to these young parents posed by the daily management of the twins.

At the end of a series of five meetings, the couple seemed to be more centered on each other and working more cooperatively in the management and care of their twins. I suggested to the wife that she join a support group for mothers of toddlers, but she was unable to follow through. Although the future might well hold more challenges to their marriage, for the moment they felt steadied on their way and did not want further treatment.

A FAMILY WHOSE EIGHT-YEAR-OLD WAS OVERWHELMED
BY HER INFANT SISTER

The following assessment was videotaped and observed by a few students and colleagues, who were actually in the room at the time of the interview. The videotaping and discussion with colleagues has allowed closer observation than is ordinarily possible.

Kelly Cleary was an 8½-year-old girl who was referred by her pediatrician because she wrote two notes to 10-year-old boys and left them in her house. They were found by her 13-year-old sister, Jane. In them Kelly said that she liked her sexual play with the boys and was looking forward to repeating it. Although this incident had piqued the family's determination to get help, both parents were clear that her behavior at home and at school also warranted evaluation. In both settings she demanded attention from parents and teachers and then rejected their approach, instead making desperate attempts to curry favor with her older sisters or older peers.

When the family came in, Kelly sat at the end of a row of chairs nearest to me but farthest from her parents. Jane took baby Randi from her mother and held her. Thus, when Jane and Brooke (the other adolescent sister) sat between Kelly and her parents, all three sisters came between Kelly and her parents.

When Jane soon handed the baby back to Mother, Mrs. Cleary immediately placed the baby prominently on the floor in front of everyone. During the subsequent interview, the baby made loud gurgling noises and played. She handled and mouthed toys, scooted across the rug, and looked at various family members. Although I had made a selection of toys that might suit Kelly and the older girls (dolls, blocks, cars, paper, and pens), only the baby used them.

During the first part of the interview, the family described the referring problem, focusing exclusively on Kelly. Because Kelly herself was unwilling to speak, Mr. and Mrs. Cleary and Jane gradually told the story. Reluctantly, Jane said that she had found the notes. Kelly began to cry, and Jane took her in her arms, much as she had done earlier with the baby. When I asked why she thought Kelly was crying, Jane, too, began to cry, and said that Kelly felt terribly embarrassed about the notes. There was a long, painful silence broken by the sobbing of the two sisters who embraced each other.

All this time, the baby, Randi, was playing noisily on the floor, cooing so loudly that I was aware of her presence even when I did not look at her. Her noises seemed to dominate the room. When I did glance at her, however, she was cheerful and unperturbed. She was picking up a block, then a truck, and chewing on them. No one in the family was, at this moment, tuning in on her, but I felt we were all aware of her presence as she glanced from one family member to another.

In the session we had now seen how Kelly used the notes to get mothering from Jane. I thought inclusion and exclusion in the family might be important issues. Accordingly, I asked, "Who is closest to whom in the family?" The parents said that the older girls had each other and that Kelly had to try to interest them in her, often without success. Father said he felt for Kelly because he had grown up with an older brother and sister and had frequently felt left out. As he spoke, I saw that the baby was climbing up 12-year-old Brooke's legs and was being ignored. Putting this observation together with Father's loneliness, I developed a conviction that being left out was the pervading issue in the family, lodged in Kelly. Her sitting out on the end of the family seating pattern had been the first sign of it in the interview; in contrast, the baby seemed to be the focus of attention, although even she could be ignored.

The parents now said that they were thinking about Kelly's feeling excluded when they had decided to let baby Randi live in her room. Each girl had wanted the baby in her room, but they had awarded her to Kelly to solve the problem of her loneliness. I turned to Kelly jokingly and asked, "Was it as good as you thought, winning the competition? Isn't that sweet little thing kind of a pain in the neck sometimes?"

This brought Kelly out of her reticence. She laughed, looked at her mother as if to see if it were all right, and said, "Well, I can't always go in my room because she's there taking a nap." Randi was again making loud noises that cut across our conversation.

"Does she keep you up at night?" I asked.

"Sometimes. She wakes me up when she wants Mom to feed her."

"So it's not as great as you thought?" I said.

"Well, it's not *too* bad," she said. "I still like it sometimes."

"How do you feel about having Randi, then, Kelly?" I asked, feeling that now that we were talking, I could move into the central territory.

"I was excited at first, but not now."

"So you won the competition, but you can't go into your room?" I said.

"I have to be quiet for her to go to sleep, or my parents keep me out a couple of minutes," she answered.

"Is she a pain in the neck?" I asked again.

"Sometimes!" she agreed, laughing, and she was joined by the laughter of the whole family.

"Are you the one who mostly thinks she's a pain?" I added.

"Well, maybe Mom does, too. Because she acts up a lot."

"That little thing?" I said in a mock incredulous tone, and the family again laughed and nodded.

Randi had been sitting on Father's lap the last few minutes, eating a cracker to keep her quiet, looking quite self-satisfied. "Does she always eat?" I asked. They said she ate practically all the time. She was now drooling crackers on Father's clothes.

Mother said, chuckling, "Randi has the family wrapped around her little finger." And the family discussed the way she screamed in the car for hours on the recent family trip over Thanksgiving. They were all in quite an indulgent mood about Randi, including Kelly.

"Do you think she'll come to me?" I asked. Father handed me the baby, who turned away from me as she gave Mother a slightly anxious glance. Since she was just 8 months old, I began to ask about stranger-anxiety. They said she had not demonstrated any noticeable anxiety yet, although she had recently been choosy about whose lap she was on. The day before she had refused to leave Jane's lap to go to Kelly.

As I took Randi in my lap to "interview her" at close range, Jane put a dog puppet on her hand, and Kelly began to chew on her thumbnail. Kelly now began to whisper to Jane as Randi looked for the cracker she had dropped. Mother said that Kelly had asked for a brother or sister many times over the years and that the parents had said "It doesn't work like that."

Kelly eagerly volunteered, "We kept asking them to have a baby, and this time they called us downstairs to tell us something." Jane added, "And she got what she wanted!"

I made a face and said, "So she *thought* she wanted it! And they did all this for you? You're pretty powerful. Did they want a baby, too?"

Kelly laughed, "Everybody was excited and I was, too. Every time they called us down, I said, 'Maybe it's to tell us they'll have a baby.' And that time they did!"

"Three wasn't enough? They needed *you*?" I quipped, smiling at Randi, as if incredulously. And again, all the girls laughed.

During this exchange, I was playing with Randi, who was mainly interested in turning to stare at her mother and sisters. But as she warmed up to me, we were able to make smiles with each other. At one point she dropped her cracker and began to search for it. Jane pointed out that she had lost it, and Kelly climbed out of her chair to retrieve it for her.

Mother answered my question of a moment earlier by saying that Randi was a surprise, a failure of the thermal method of birth control. The pregnancy had been discovered just when Mother was already upset by relocation to Washington. Everyone else in the family had felt the pregnancy was "neat," except Mother. As she said this, Randi, who was still on my lap, began to cry, so I gave her to Mother, who held her briefly and then put her on a blanket on the floor.

The family went on to talk about missing the home they had to leave to move to Washington a year earlier, and about Father's absence from the family during the year before that. Randi had been lying quietly on a blanket on the floor. Now as they talked about these losses she suddenly lurched onto her back and began to cry. Without moving, Mother said to me, "Randi is spoiled. She wants to be held." At these words, Kelly went to pick up Randi, got a bottle from Father, and began to feed her.

I said to Kelly, "Randi is letting you mother her."

Kelly nodded and began to talk about her own loneliness in the family and her neighborhood. During this conversation, Randi got fussy while Kelly held her, but Father and Mother seemed impervious to her cries. After some time, Mother reluctantly took Randi from Kelly and began to nurse her.

I now felt that Kelly had become trusting enough with me that I could try to understand some things with her. So I said, "I'm beginning to get a sense of what Kelly feels she is up against. She has felt left out, and Randi has taken her spot as the baby. You used to be the baby (Kelly nods) and now she's the baby (Kelly nods more). Everybody laughs and smiles at her when she goes to them, and here you are, stuck out on the end of the family and feeling left out. And it's worse since Randi popped in the middle of things."

Kelly nodded with each point. She said, "Kind of . . . "

I continued, "You know, Moms and Dads have babies together."

"Yeah," she said, covering her mouth as she had when we discussed the notes.

I summed up this part of the interview by saying to Kelly and to the family that I thought the sexual behavior and notes had been Kelly's way to get attention in imitation of the way Mom and Dad paid sexual attention to each other and had babies together. Kelly nodded again. I asked if she had felt more lonely since the baby came along, and she nodded again, slowly and definitely.

During the rest of the interview, Brooke, the sister who had been the quietest, jumped in to say that when she had friends over, they all just wanted to play with the baby—that a great deal of family life was organized around the baby. And Mother was able to discuss the efforts she had made to provide mothering to Kelly and the rebuff from Kelly she so often felt. This let me conclude the interview, using additional information that I have not reported in this brief summary, by saying that Kelly spoke for the sense in the family that people could not get mothering, and that the baby stood for being the one who got all the mothering. Everyone felt ignored and deprived in many ways; thus they were all in the position that Kelly spoke for, of feeling lonely and jealous of Randi. In this way, Kelly's sense that she got nothing while Randi got everything stood for a family-wide problem that needed to be understood and worked with.

This assessment session shows many of the issues that are fundamental in working with families with infants. None of us could get away from centering on the baby, and thus we could feel the way the baby dominated the family, just as the symptomatic child described.

The process of the interview followed a pattern that is important with young children and infants in a more specifically technical way than with older children and adults. The therapist's first task is to help the family feel at ease and to deal with the anxieties that interfere with exploration. For younger children, this involves their learning how to speak, play, and interact in an increasingly trusting way. In this session, I had worked to see how much each child could contribute before "interviewing" the baby by picking her up and interacting directly. A face-to-face interaction is often helpful, although it might not always be possible or advisable. Here it allowed me to get independent information about how the baby related to a stranger and to the rest of the family from a distance. At the same time, as with the brief period of "individual interviewing" of other family members, I monitored the family's reaction to the "discussion" with the baby. The family's enthusiastic support of the infant as the central family figure emerged as I handled and talked to her.

Throughout the interview, each of the children was responsive to the verbal content of the interview. Nonverbal responses, however, were illuminated by the baby's behavior and were enriched by comparison of the baby's reactions and the behavior of the older children. For instance, the girls made sucking or chewing mouth movements while the baby nursed; Jane embraced Kelly just as she had held the baby. The baby's reactions were also important clues to affects the family either could not identify or actively misread. Thus, the baby cried almost every time there was a discussion of "not being wanted" or feeling rejected. In one instance, when Mother discussed the fact that the pregnancy was unplanned, Randi promptly began to cry and had to be given to Mother. Again, when Mr. Cleary discussed the loss of a home, which occurred when the family moved to Washington, Randi actually fell over on her back and began to cry. At this moment, when the topic and its affect were about loss, Mother misread the baby's anxiety when she told me that Randi was "spoiled and wanted attention."

From our experience in the session with this baby we can extrapolate to the early experience of the other children. When loss and depression are in the air and the infant picks it up, the mother experiences the infant as demanding of her and becomes rejecting, presumably out of a sense of feeling sad or depleted herself. When Randi and Kelly were expressing their depression, Mother accused each of them of wanting attention. The baby's presence highlights the use of projective identification in the family, offering clues to the way it has operated in the past and is now embedded in other individuals and in the family. A central part of such understanding comes from the therapist's countertransference, both to the family as a whole and to the baby. Unlike the mother, I began to absorb the sadness, isolation, and loss that affected the family at every level and from this personal base to clarify the family experience.

I imagined that there was a sense of sadness and separateness between the parents, who each felt isolated and excluded, and that this feeling was passed on to the children. I felt that the "lost home" seemed to stand for the sense of loss pervading the family, and that Kelly's wish for sexual connectedness seemed to speak for desperate longing throughout the family. And as I sat with the baby, who was happy and full of potential, I felt sad that she might be taken over by the sadness in the family. I thought, as I reflected on it, that this meant that the family had an unconscious fantasy that the baby represented hope for the whole family. But I thought that they must have an unconscious fear that as the baby grew she too would become vulnerable to the snuffing out of hope because the family was deficient. If so, it would be a fear that the family's shared deficiency would produce another lonely and damaged child. This fantasy arose from my countertransference and would have to be tested out over time before it could have lasting validity, but it represented a first hypothesis concerning the family's unconscious fantasy of itself as inevitably and tragically damaging to growth and hope.

The methods of dealing with the family with a young baby

involve many of the same elements of working that are relevant to any family. These are getting to know the group and the contributions of the individuals, taking in the experience intellectually and emotionally, clarifying interactions, and getting family members to elaborate on their experience and their understanding. With the nonverbal infant, however, we cannot rely on getting a message directly across to the baby. We speak to the older family members and study their ways of communicating with the infant as a test of the usefulness of our interventions, even as we use the infant's interactions in the family as a crucial part of the data in arriving at our understanding. The simple fact that the infant does not directly tell the therapist what he or she thinks, or cannot "understand" what the therapist says, is not a reason for excluding the infant. On the contrary: it is the reason that the baby must be there to present the information in the bodily, interactive, playful way of infancy.

These examples have described work with families with infants and toddlers. Although one of the families also had older children, the sessions with these families did not extensively rely on play. In the next chapter, we explore the use of play as a central technique in therapy with children from age 2½ to early adolescence.

CHAPTER 14

Older Play-Age Children in Family Therapy

Play: The Child's Communication

The natural vehicle of expression for the young child is play. Even the child who is verbally adept or precocious will find self-expression easier through play than words. It can be argued that an especially verbal child of 5 or 6 can manage with words in the family. But it is nevertheless true that even that child could say and reveal more of his or her internal world and observations of the family with the help of some extraverbal play material. This is true because of the way that the capacity to use words emerges out of bodily experience in the beginning, and because the play-age child is still a "sensorimotor" learner in Piaget's terms (1962), a child bound with a certain concrete set to any observations, which are more understandable when tied to something physical.

This means that the physical acts of making a swirl or a line in a drawing, or making a car go back and forth on the rug, or marching a doll from one play-space to another are closely tied to the child's internal experience of an emotional issue. They are the first substitutes for such actions as those of the children we read about in the last chapter, who physically went up to their parents or who began to cry when the atmosphere clouded over. Progressing from this stage, the child substitutes actions in a transitionally symbolic space. At first, in the child of about 3, these are the kinds of games that are closely linked to sensorimotor experience. In the beginning, drawing is primarily a matter of motor expression (using the arm to make the swirls or lines) rather than a symbolic expression. Block building is stacking, not representing, while cars are rushed about and dolls are held and fed. These are derivatives of body movement. They are often shown off to the parent, and in phallic development become things to be proud of.

Moving into the oedipal era, the child begins to employ play and games at a symbolic level. It is here, of course, that we can find the charming and rich themes that constitute oedipal fantasy—family stories, cops and robbers, princesses. Early in this period, the themes are remarkably close to the family, and we can extrapolate a direct lineage from the child's family experience. But the older oedipal child, of the age of 5 perhaps, and certainly by 6, should have some distance on the family, producing stories or drawings that have some quality of a life of their own. In fact, the absence of some distance from the child's family is a sign of the child being too caught up in family struggles.

By the age of 5½ or 6, the child will normally begin to include, and eventually to emphasize, games that mark latency: games with rules, sports, jump-rope rhymes, doll play that not only has elaborated themes but has certain dress codes or daily rituals. In individual therapy, these can dominate as the latency child uses them to defend against earlier material, leading to the exasperation of many child therapists. These games, however, do not tend to show up in the family therapy setting. Here the child will probably be content with elements that came into the repertoire earlier—versions of fantasy play with dolls or toy soldiers, cars, puppets, and small blocks.

Paper and crayons or markers constitute the most universal play equipment, and they alone suffice for many families with children, even into adolescence. The plasticity of the drawing medium is such that it can absorb the child's action-proneness (which is normal into early adolescence) and support concentration on the verbal activity in the room. Never mind that the child seems to be absorbed and "not paying attention." A young boy or girl is in a better place to be receptive when playing than when slumped on the couch, feeling constrained and restless as the parents expect "good behavior" in an adult setting. The provision of equipment appropriate to age level does more than give a message that this is a place designed for the child, too. It offers appropriate, familiar, and accessible media for a range of expression.

Setting Up the Play Space

At the practical level, we recommend that the office be large enough to accommodate a seated family and playing children. The decor needs to be fairly robust to tolerate some wear and tear. We suggest having a play table in the middle of the circle of seats so that the play can be absorbed easily at the center of the therapist's attention. To begin, the therapist needs only a few simple toys from each group suggested by Beiser (1976), catering to the children's developmental stages of play as described earlier and outlined by Peller (1954).

Paper and crayons are the basic toys for any age. There is no need to get into paint or pastels that require a higher level of expertise and more cleanup. Magic markers give a clear, bold, colorful outline that children enjoy (and that reproduce well for teaching purposes), but they should be used only by therapists who are not anxious about the vulnerability of the office furniture. Others can choose crayons and oil pastels. It is easy for the child to draw and listen or talk, and the drawings are available as projection screens for the child and for the rest of the family.

The next equipment would be a few blocks and human figures, a small doll family for girls, and toy soldiers, cowboys, or action figures for boys. Small trucks, cars, and airplanes perform the same functions for boys as the doll family does for girls— figures for the displaced play expression of personal issues. Puppets may be useful, and although they are often frightening for the child under 4, we find that older children, and sometimes parents, may insist on using them despite the younger child's fright. It is also important not to have too many toys so that the child does not get lost in them.

The Internal Play Space

This leads us to the experience of the therapist in this setting. If the therapist has even a little experience with child therapy, the suggestion that toys and drawing material are appropriate will not be strange and may even provide a welcome relief. Many therapists, however, come to family work from adult and adolescent experience and will feel the usual anxiety about playing while trying to work.

To help our trainees confront this issue, we have designed an experiential session in which we build a progression to the use of toys as an extension of one's professional personality. First we ask the trainees to join in a memory-recall experience of some events of their own childhood, as we read some questions that will bring certain kinds of events to mind: early days with family, first days in school, childhood friends, teachers, and so on. Then, from a wide assortment of play materials, we ask each of them to choose a toy and to pretend that their toys are looking for partners. Each toy-couple then "chooses" other toys from among those selected by the other trainees with whom to form a family. Each "family" meets to divide up roles and to invent a history, which they then present to the class. As the class questions them about the family relationships, aspects of the use of toys as an extension of individual personality emerge, and at the end, we ask each trainee to comment on this to the extent he or she is comfortable in doing so. This exercise is aimed at breaking the barrier between the play medium and the adult's personality—a barrier naturally built up over the years spent eschewing childish things. But for our purposes, and of course for the purposes of therapy generally, a refamiliarization is helpful. It is important to emphasize, however, that the point of the exercise is not to expose the inner life of the trainee, inasmuch as we do not expect or wish to do that in the training setting. Nevertheless, to the extent that trainees become increasingly comfortable with aspects of their internal life, they will be able to employ them both in this setting and with families in treatment.

Uses of Play

Comfort with and understanding of play is one aspect of the contextual holding the therapist provides for the family with play-age children. Furthermore, the play and the parents' handling of it gives information about the family's holding capacity. When there are two or more children, the toy materials will be the medium over which we can observe their sibling rivalry and the parents' management of it. Here there is no problem of needing to maintain a displacement. This is very like the home situation. The parents and children can tell you how this is both similar to and different from it, and we can then explore this area. Often we can track progress in the family's management of anxiety and their projecting conflicts onto the children by the amount of conflict between the children over play and play materials. In addition, we can help the parents understand the use of play in talking with their children. Many of the mothers and a few of the fathers are already used to playing with their children. Most of them, however, will be used to joining in as an active theme setter. Here the trick is to allow the child to use the play to talk to us, and occasionally to use it ourselves to talk back. For the most part, however, the therapist and parents will be talking in words, and the words can be simplified and spoken directly to the child as a way of communicating.

The play is used as an ancillary piece of information and very often is not commented on directly. Thus, if a child is making a drawing of a figure with huge teeth while the parents are fighting, the therapist might say, "I think John may feel that the fight between the two of you seems like biting with teeth—like the ones in that monster he's been drawing." We do this because the direct linking of the play to the content of the session is often too threatening to the child, and the immediate result is to inhibit the play. This is not unlike the technique often used in individual child therapy, where the play is taken as a gloss on the transference and is used to illustrate the therapist's point rather than being presented as the evidence for it.

Levels of Displacement in Play

There are four "levels of displacement" in our processing of the children's play:

1. We observe the play but do not comment directly on it. This is useful if the child is extremely touchy about the play and will abandon it if challenged. The play can still be a crucial medium of information for us.

2. We occasionally ask the child to tell us what he or she is doing and to elaborate on the theme or the story behind the drawing. It is easy to do this if the child is giving the picture to a parent or to the therapist. Again, at this level no comment is made because of the fragility of the activity and the likelihood it will go into hiding because of anxiety.

3. After getting the elaboration, or when there is a link to be made with the session content, we use the play as a metaphor or illustration. Here we might say, "That is *like* John's picture," or "That is *like* what was happening to those trucks. Maybe that is a way of thinking about what is happening in the family." With this level of displacement, the child usually will not feel that the production is being taken away from him or her.

4. After observing the play, we can say, "I think John is trying to tell us that those trucks running into each other is what happens in the family." This direct linking is possible in some families, especially with older children who are close to sensing that they are giving expression to family conflicts or at least to their own reaction to them.

Play in the Assessment Phase

This example of assessment of a family with a 2¾-year-old illustrates the typical features of play with an infant as described in the last chapter but also takes us into the area of thematic content more typical of 3-year-olds and older.

Bill and Peggy Noonan were in the waiting room with Kim, their 2¾-year-old daughter. Some years earlier, I [D. E. S.] had done an evaluation of the couple relationship, when both were graduate students. I learned that although they loved each other, they rarely had sex. I had seen Bill and Peggy together for several sessions to assess their marital and sexual relationship. Because of Bill's profound difficulty, not just in managing sexual intimacy but in developing any true personal relatedness, I felt that he was unable to benefit from couple therapy, and so I referred him for low-fee psychoanalysis. I referred Peggy for psychotherapy for her depression, poor self-esteem, and feelings of sexual rejection. Their parallel treatments were ultimately successful, and they became able to enjoy their marriage and to start a family.

Their cherished child's sleep difficulty at 9 months brought them back to consult me. In retrospect, I think it was a mistake not to see the baby with both parents myself. I referred them instead to an infant psychiatrist. They worked with him for a few months, but for various reasons, this was not very helpful. The sleep difficulty cleared up eventually.

When Peggy called me this time, Kim, now 2¾, was having temper tantrums and was masturbating excessively at home and in public. I met with Peggy for a history of Kim's development and of the current state of their marriage. At this point, although Bill was fully involved and functional, Peggy was somewhat withdrawn from him sexually. She found herself resenting the years of his sexual disinterest, but she felt he had changed and she consciously wanted to be able to respond to him. We agreed to take a look at the overall family situation, and so the three of them came for a family session.

As I entered the waiting room, Bill was reading loudly and energetically to Kim, who was on his lap. He smiled slightly sheepishly, seeing me after all this time, with such changed circumstances. As they sat down, Kim stayed close to Bill. She climbed on his lap and there was a bit of quiet roughhousing.

Initially, the mother talked about their concern with Kim's touching her genitalia. I spent the first few minutes making friends with

Kim. She was only slightly reticent, smiling from between the knees of both parents, who sat opposite me. Her parents indicated that she liked puppets, so I brought over the rabbit puppet and offered to let her have it. She told them she had a rabbit and showed it shyly but easily. Bill said she related more easily to men and would not warm up to a woman in this way. I noticed that she stayed at home base with her parents mostly and came forward to me only very slowly. I thought that was standard for her age.

In the next few minutes, Bill teased Kim slightly, then backed off. He said she was not scared by the big nose on the puppet at home, and then he reminded her about how he usually teased her, and how she responded by poking at him or putting her hand on his leg.

Over the next few moments, Bill took the lead in discussing their concern with her masturbation and cited his own lifelong concern with the adequacy of his genitals. Without being aware of it, he touched his genitals frequently as he talked. He had grown up within a family that was not only very distant emotionally but that was very discouraging of sexuality. He said he was uncomfortabe when Kim touched herself, even when he was changing her, but far more so when she did it in public. They had stopped taking baths together when Kim was 1, but she still ran for the bathroom when she heard the sound of his urinating. Peggy confirmed that Kim was very excited about these events. "Oh yeah. She really races for it. It's hard to keep her out of there!"

During this period Kim was climbing on Bill's lap and jumping off the couch. She centered on her father while casting glances at her mother and me. He tried to send her over for more toys. At first she stood by him but a few moments later went over to Peggy, who invited her to the shelves of toys. First she built with small blocks. She showed her parents a series of two- and three-block towers with cylinders sticking up. She accurately said one block was an "arch" and that her friend had such an arch in her house. She sang "We went to the Animal Fair," with the kind of distinct articulation that goes with recent language acquisition. Her language and her capacity to play alone seemed very good.

Kim next picked up some Tinkertoys. She turned to involve her mother, who followed Kim's lead as Kim put some rods into the receiving pieces and eventually built a tall, thin cylinder. She said it was a birthday cake. With some added input from her mother, she now added spokes to the receiving piece and said it was both a space ship *and* a birthday cake.

Bill meanwhile had gone on to say that he found himself doing things that were uncomfortably similar to those of his own father that he had always disliked. For instance, he would lose his patience with Kim during her temper tantrums. Peggy said his reaction was not too bad, but she knew he found it frustrating. He said he would like help with their residual sexual difficulty and to make him a better father than his own father had been to him. Peggy looked up from the play at this point and agreed that they needed help with both, although things were a great deal better.

"Oh, that's true," agreed Bill. "You know, there are tears coming to my eyes right now. If you knew the change in the quality of our life. . . . There's no comparison. I can love somebody!"

In the rest of the session, I commented on the relationship between the couple's sexual difficulty and their concern over Kim's masturbation. I drew on my observations of the overexcitement in Kim's interaction with her father, which I had felt from the first moment of the interview and which had been confirmed by history. I felt that he was deeply invested in an exciting relationship as a compensation for his fear of being, like his own father, a rejecting father. Feeling puzzled about how to approach him about this without injuring his vulnerable sense of fathering, I elected to wait to comment on the excited aspects of the relationship until another interview when I could have a better sense of how to take it up.

I noted that with Peggy Kim was much calmer and that her play, through the medium of the toys, was more appropriate and not excited. Partly, this is what I would expect for the difference between a child's play with her father and her mother, as we discussed in Chapter 6. But I felt there was an exaggerated edge to this difference that left Kim out on a limb, and that Peggy's observation about Kim's racing for the bathroom indicated that she had some idea of the excessive excitement.

I felt I should say nothing about this difference yet. In review, I realized that Peggy's half-knowing tolerance of the excessive excitement actually constituted both a projective identification and a masochistic surrender. She was encouraging an excited, prematurely oedipal relationship between Kim and her father because of her investment in vicariously reliving her own family pattern, in which she had turned excitedly to her father and away from her mother, whom she felt to be rejecting. Now, she was putting herself in the position of being the mother who was taken for granted and, therefore, was actually rejected and subtly abused, while she unconsciously encouraged a sexualized relationship between Kim and Bill.

She was about to do herself out of being a loved mother, because of encouraging a sexualized and therefore guilty oedipal phase. These matters seemed to be relevant to her current sexual withdrawal. They could not have come to light years earlier in her own treatment when they were masked by Bill's withdrawal.

During this session, I was unable to comment on the origins of the temper tantrums, but I did give some guidance on managing them with firm limits. This allowed more material to emerge about them in the next session. The tantrums were indeed linked to the sexual difficulties in child and parents. They frequently occurred when Kim was in bed with her parents in the morning. Bill would read to her, and then he would get up. One morning that week, Kim threw a fit aimed at Peggy over the incorrect arrangement of the pillows just after Bill got up. It was now possible for us to see that one contribution to the tantrums was the anxiety about the same excited situation that contributed to the masturbation. Kim's anxiety seemed to concern her troubled feeling about her mother and her difficulty managing her disappointment when the excited situation inevitably ended.

In the next session, the pattern of relationships was the same. Kim showed a consistently excited relationship with her father and played in a calmer, more organized way with her mother. Bill had been away for a few days, and Kim had spoken repeatedly of missing him. Bill reported that he was glad to see her when she greeted him at the airport. "She couldn't stop kissing and hugging me," he said. "I got a bit of a sexual rush. Not in my genitals, just in my chest. It was so great to feel such a strong feeling after being away. I can't get over it."

By now I felt our working together was on a solid enough footing that I could comment on the observations I had made concerning the overexcited relationship between Kim and Bill, and the way Peggy, in her investment in that kind of relationship from her own past with her father, could support it over her own reservations. She acknowledged that she had questioned Bill about the stimulation in the relationship, but she agreed that she had bowed to his insistence that it was fine. I said that although nothing definitive had happened yet, I could see the set of relationships verging on a repetition of what Peggy had had with her own parents: She had idealized an excited relationship with her father and denigrated her mother's role. Peggy and Bill then looked startled, but over several minutes I was able to show them evidence I had been collecting from the session and to connect it to their own misgivings.

While I was talking about Bill's excited relationship with Kim, she began to play with the family of flexible dolls, putting twin babies in bed with the parents. She had done this before in a random way, but on this occasion I noticed that the play of the babies' snuggling with the parents got more purposeful as I talked with Bill about his investment in a warm, exciting relationship with Kim. The play was not specifically oedipal, I thought, because the mother stayed in bed with the group. But it was excessively excited.

Then, when I turned to talk about Peggy's fear of setting limits on Bill because of her unconscious, self-defeating investment in Bill and Kim's sexualized relationship, Kim's theme changed abruptly. The mother doll sent the babies to their room for playing in the sink. This play between baby and mother was firmly rejecting of excitement. I joined her on the floor, took the daddy doll from the bed where it still lay, and had the daddy say, "Mommy, maybe the babies would like to play with me." With that, the babies ran from the scene with the mother, jumped onto the daddy, and began an excited romp. I said, "Sometimes the babies like to see their daddy when their mommy is mad at them." Kim said, "I like to have my daddy come home all the time. But sometimes my mommy *is* mad at me!" And she smiled at Peggy and said, "Aren't you, Mommy?"

It was only when I saw this shift in Kim's play that I was able to demonstrate to Bill and Peggy, through the play, that Kim clearly picked up the split between them, and that she would assign the painful, rejecting side to Peggy and seek the exciting side with Bill. The point hit home for them as I reviewed the play, which they had also seen but not understood, and they looked at each other with new understanding. Over the next weeks, they brought in examples of this shared tendency, and the issues behind it emerged for a reworking which went quickly because of their extensive previous therapies.

In these sessions, the play did not, at first, constitute the kind of informative material it does with older children. Rather, it provided the medium through which the child related with her parents and was the context for my observation of their relationships. Thus, the play between Kim and her father could be seen to be too direct, too bodily, and too excited for a child of this age, whereas the play with Peggy was calmer, more organized, and more appropriate. In Kim's play by herself and with her mother, I could observe an advanced level of verbal development, of symbolic manipulation of objects, and of cooperative play. I could not observe these with the interactions with the father, and that gave me a clue about the regressive and fused quality of the transactions in her relationship to him. At first I spoke to the parents rather than to Kim because of the age of the child, and because I felt the parents' commitment to providing holding would serve them well in modifying the imbalance in their parenting.

With more time, however, even this very young child began to provide more specific information through her play. In the last session reported, her play had joined in the conversation of the session and was both exquisitely reactive to it and richly informative to us. The play intervention by the therapist in the assessment phase was primarily designed to demonstrate the issues to the parents, but later therapy would involve the use of such interventions through play to request further elaboration of family themes from Kim and to speak to her directly.

Play During the Course of Family Therapy

During the course of family treatment, play assumes varying roles. It may be more or less central to the content of the sessions; how central it is will vary among families and over time. A couple of examples will illustrate this, but the variability among children and families will keep us from presenting any normative picture. At times it may seem that play has a minimal role in helping us understand the family, simply allowing the play-age child to feel comfortable while the "real work" is elsewhere. More often, the play of the child forms a leitmotif that is an invaluable part of the overall fabric of work with a family, moving helpfully as the family progresses, providing clues as issues emerge.

One such illustration has already been provided in the example of the Jansen Family, described in Chapter 12. Here, the play in the family sessions was not usually highly thematic, even though Tom's play in individual sessions was. Nevertheless, the quality of cooperation between the siblings provided a gauge of the overall progress of the family, and regressions to battling inevitably warned of an underlying crisis.

In the following illustration, the play generated a number of drawings through which the themes were expressed.

The Wolff family sought help for their 11-year-old adopted boy, Wilson, who felt he was different from the rest of the family and talked about feeling unaccepted and uncared for by them. He was accident-prone and was playing a number of mischievous pranks, including playing with matches, which made me wonder if he might be predelinquent. There was no external evidence that the family had rejected Wilson, although recently he had provoked his father into screaming at him and spanking him. Father had also moved out of the house eight months earlier, after a good deal of bitterness between Mr. and Mrs. Wolff over the previous year. There was a 14-year-old sister who was less trouble than Wilson, but she too had difficulty—in her case, with peers. She "bested" them in a way that left them furious at her.

By the time I saw them, Mr. and Mrs. Wolff had decided to reconcile and to come to family therapy together. In the early sessions, Wilson maintained that he hated his family, especially his father. He took them on about religious education, saying that they did not know if he was born Jewish, as they were, but he thought not, and so they should not force him to have Hebrew lessons. He sat apart from the family at the play table, where he acted as though he were not interested in what was said unless someone spoke directly to him. He played an endless series of smuggling games in which the bad guys tried to steal the treasure, fell off ladders or out of helicopters, shot the police or army, and were shot themselves. He drew many violent drawings during the sessions, such as one showing the violent deaths of a number of people (Fig. 14.1). Two other drawings (Figs. 14.2 and 14.3) were particularly hateful, showing the beginnings of an operation of gas chambers, clearly a direct attack on his parents.

As Wilson was drawing these pictures and playing these games, much of the content of the sessions had to do with the murderously angry feelings in the family. Mother, who had a great deal of barely restrained resentment, was openly furious at Father for leaving her, even when he was in the process of returning. Father felt angry at the many restraints she imposed on him. Much of Wilson's most violent production can be seen as an identification with their anger, and especially with an angry, murderous father who sees the whole family as his enemy.

In another family session, Wilson, at my request, drew a picture of his family (Fig. 14.4). The picture shows his family after Father has murdered Mother and Wilson, sparing Mammy, the cat and Dale, the sister. This outcome incorporates the parental fight with a viciousness added to by his own preadolescent development. It shows the fusion of sexuality with aggression in a way that was quite accu-

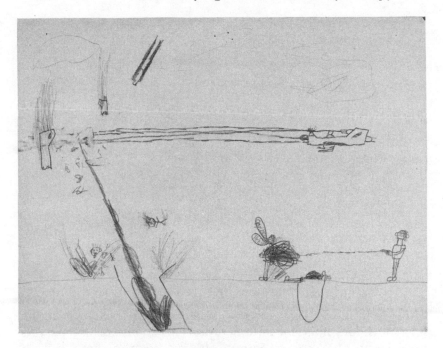

Fig. 14.1 Wilson's drawing of violent deaths.

Fig. 14.2 Wilson's "I Declare War."

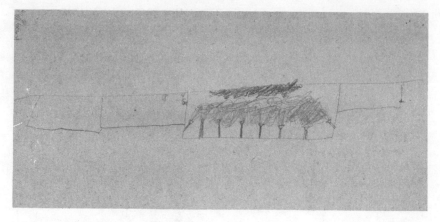

Fig. 14.3 Wilson's "gas chamber."

rate for the family. His version of an oedipal confrontation with Father is more complete than the usual castration theme. While Dale is left alive for Father, the knifing represents an intense and perverse penetration of Wilson by Father. This picture also shows Wilson's introjection of his mother's sense of being abused and uncared for by his father.

Fig. 14.4 Wilson's family picture.

In the starkness of this picture, the family was able to see a dramatic rendering of how they were feeling treated by each other. The picture formed a valuable link to the family-wide development of empathy, and by the end of the family treatment, the reconciled parents were much gentler with each other. Wilson was able to give up the aggressive core of his internalized family and to feel part of a renewed sense of caring in a reconstructed family.

The next illustration gives a case where the play was intrinsic to understanding the core issues. We conclude with this example because the material illustrates the play of the latency child in interaction with the toddler, a reminder that most families do not fall into one or another precise developmental category.

A Play-Age Family in Assessment and Treatment

THE INDIVIDUAL ASSESSMENT

Kent and Mary Dickie came to see me [D.E.S.] about their 8-year-old boy, Ian. Kent was a 32-year-old foreign service officer; Mary was a housewife. To my first meeting with them, they brought their 19-month-old daughter, Katia, who wandered around the room, pulling out toys and being quite a charming toddler, while we talked about their concerns about Ian. They told me that Ian had done reasonably well in first grade, but now the school was saying he was hopelessly behind. He frequently wandered around the classroom. When Mary tried to work with him on reading or telling time, he threw temper tantrums. Otherwise he got on well with his mother and loved to do things such as cooking with her. One additional symptom was that he complained of blurred vision and frequently had watery eyes. The teacher had suggested that vision problems might be interfering with his reading.

The parents told me that Kent was away on a secret mission without his family the first six months of Ian's life. When he got back, he was in graduate school, working hard and not seeing much of Ian. Mary was also working, and they alternated care of Ian. He began preschool at age 3½ and did well. They said that between the ages of 3 and 4½, he used to barge in between Kent and Mary to give both of them a hug. He also wanted to be included in less intrusive ways.

When Ian was 5½, they moved to Washington, D.C., for Kent's present assignment. Soon after that, Mary became pregnant with

Katia, who was a planned baby. Ian, they said, was fond of Katia and not too upset by her birth, but now he was jealous during the daily routine of allowing the children in the parents' bed in the morning.

The individual evaluation and psychological testing of Ian demonstrated that his school performance was complicated by uneven cognitive development. He was also struggling with an identity disorder with its basis in conflicts around aggression, depression, and gender role confusion. His overall intelligence was above average but was significantly lowered by these conflicts. When he first began the reading test, he could not even perform at the first-grade level because he grew anxious and confused. He said the words seemed to move back and forth across the page. This reaction seemed triggered by stress, and when the psychologist was able to calm him, he was able to read at the third-grade level with perfect comprehension.

Although these tests frequently provide us with a description of internal object life, Ian was so withholding that a clear picture could not be obtained. There was some indication that his supply of "good objects" was rather limited. He reflected on his mother as either misunderstanding or critical and punitive, while his father was a compensatory primary attachment figure who provided soothing and internal stimulation. Ian said, "He tickled me and I felt good," and "I liked it because he bounced me." This was all the more poignant because he presented Father as only marginally available, and this contributed significantly to Ian's depression.

When I first saw Ian, I worried that there was something abnormal about his appearance, with his droopy eyelids and protuberant ears. Later I thought the odd quality stemmed from his sadness and confusion. He began the first individual diagnostic session by playing with two guns. First he pointed one at me, and then put the two of them to his head and pulled the triggers. He was absorbed with the mechanics of the guns, before going on to investigate the mechanics of a number of other toys. It suggested to me a great concern with aggression, the turning of it onto himself, and then an immediate reversion to an early level of play that invested in the bodily derivatives of the toys rather than their thematic value. He said he hated the kind of darts I had because they would not stick to the target. In a similar veiled way, the two hours were filled with aggressive themes and with their denial. He said his mother did not like him to have play guns but would allow Tinkertoy guns if the play was quiet, but he stumbled over the words in telling me this. He played and described war games energetically.

His first picture (Fig. 14.5) was of "a prehistoric monster, a cross between a snake and a dragon. It killed other animals and ate them." When I asked him to draw a picture of his family doing something, he said he only drew stick figures standing still (Fig. 14.6). He drew himself of normal size between his parents, while his sister was tiny, but he gave me several names for her as he drew her and told me his mother stayed home with her all day. He denied any jealousy of her or resentment of his mother.

Through the two sessions, I felt quite shut out by him, which I felt signaled a good deal of depression. He continued to perseverate on aggressive themes, wanting guns and playing cops and robbers or battles. His identifications were with ambiguous figures like the furry Chewbacca of *Star Wars*, "who doesn't talk and is furry," or with Dustin Hoffman playing a woman in the movie *Tootsie*. Finally, he told me that he had trouble seeing because his eyes had water in them all the time, so things got blurry. I had the impression that he was frequently on the verge of tears, and that his sadness and his preoccupation with fighting and devouring interfered continuously with his ability to think and to learn in school.

Fig. 14.5 Ian's "prehistoric monster."

Fig. 14.6 Ian's family picture.

An ophthalmologic evaluation confirmed that Ian's vision and capacity to produce and clear tears were all normal. The explanation for his watery eyes did indeed lie in the psychological arena.

THE FAMILY ASSESSMENT

The family diagnostic interview was the single most revealing session of the evaluation, given Ian's guarded posture in the individual sessions with me. Kent and Mary sat on the couch, while Ian sat opposite. I noticed that Kent looked vigorous and attractive and that Mary seemed fat and frumpy next to him. Katia wandered about the room, invading the supply of toys and ferociously pulling items off the shelves, quite confident that the world was her oyster. As Father pumped Ian about school, Katia pulled the dollhouse off the shelf and unceremoniously dumped the contents all over the floor. She promptly abandoned this to move to the next thing, but Ian then began to examine the heap of dolls and furniture. He seemed to follow her lead in level of play. As Katia dumped out some blocks, Father continued to interrogate Ian about his school life and his behavior, and I noted that Ian was a bit frightened of him. I pointed to Ian's picture from the individual diagnostic session, pinned to my bulletin board, and asked if he thought of his father sometimes as a dinosaur. He said, "Yeah. He's the kind with little hands that eats meat." When his father identified this as tyrannosaurus rex, Ian lit up agreeably. Father asked if he yelled as much as he used to, and Ian said he did. Father looked disappointed, because he was trying not to shout so much, but he accepted that was the way Ian felt about it.

Ian now picked up the two guns, getting the long-barreled pistol and then the short-barreled Saturday night special, and began pointing and shooting them. Mary looked disapproving and anxious. She did not allow Ian to have guns. Kent had grown up with guns and enjoyed skeet shooting with his father. Mary's parents had been divorced when she was 10, and she later accompanied her step-father, who liked to hunt and shoot. However, he also had guns on his mind in a paranoid way and was an alcoholic who often seemed on the verge of violence. Although he had never shot anyone, guns were the hallmark of her untrusting relationship with him.

At this point, Ian was playing at shooting himself in the head and acting dead. Kent asked if he was playing that he had shot himself. Ian said he was only listening to the noise, but his denial was clear.

Mary went on to describe her parents' divorce, how much she missed her father, whom she saw alternate weekends, and how she was affected by her mother's remarriage two years later. On one occasion during a drunken quarrel between her mother and step-father, he briefly choked Mary after her mother had yelled that Mary should run away. The marriage had managed to survive, although both mother and stepfather continued to drink heavily. All of this had a great deal to do with her dislike of guns and of Ian's playing with guns, but she could tolerate tank battles or guns fashioned from Tinkertoys.

While Mary was describing this, Ian brought a toy ambulance over to show Father, as if to say he would like to help his wounded mother. When she mentioned the guns again, he brought one of the guns over to his father and asked him what kind it was. Father, despite having been an expert on guns, had given them up in deference to his wife, although when he was growing up they were one of the few vehicles to a relationship with his own father. As Kent and Ian discussed the gun, they were sitting together in the most loving posture of the interview.

At this moment, Katia wandered near with a polythene bag of doll toys, and Mary began to wrestle with taking it away from her.

She was concerned that the plastic would be fatal. Inasmuch as Katia had been carrying the bag for the previous ten minutes, I said I thought that Mary's becoming aware of it at that moment related to an emerging concern that she would fail to protect her children and harm would come to them. She would be a harmful parent just like her stepfather. She began to cry and said she was very worried about this, and about Ian harming Katia with violent play: "If Ian starts playing with something, it's as though it's going to explode. It always ends up that way!" I noticed that he was now playing with toy airplanes and soldiers, and as the hour drew to a close, he was setting up a battle. Katia grabbed a tank from him, and he gave in. Mary said that he had a choice at home to give in or not, but if a toy was Katia's, he had to give it to her. I had noticed in the latter part of the hour that he gave in to Katia rather than cause a scene when she took things from him.

As the hour closed, I said I thought Ian embodied the fear that Mary's stepfather would resurface, a symbol of the destruction of her loved real father. I noted that both parents and Ian had shared the experience of father absence and that there was anger about this that was being inhibited. In view of the role of inhibition of aggression, we might regard the gun issue as symbolically close to the main concerns over loss of fathers and fear of destructive parents, a fear most conscious for Mother. I recommended family therapy as the most effective and central approach to Ian's difficulties and to the family issues, and they agreed to weekly meetings.

In this hour, the play was rather scattered. Ian tended to use play mostly at the level of his much younger sister and as a vehicle for talking to his parents. Katia's play, with interest in the qualities of the toys and with frequent change of focus, seemed age-appropriate, but Ian had difficulty moving beyond a regressed level. When he did try to set up a thematic "battle," he was interrupted by his sister and gave it up. Thus, the play gave a dynamic and revealing quality to the session beyond Ian's verbal contribution. He used the play materials to demonstrate his relationship to his parents and sister and to illustrate some of the dynamics of his immaturity, depression, and inhibition. The link to the verbal content in the interview was direct, compelling, and enriching.

TREATMENT SESSIONS

Through the early family sessions, Ian became more available and developed more range in his play. In one hour, while Katia cataloged and named tiny animals, he built a tall "television tower" that fell over just as Mother discussed coming home from the hospital with Katia. Ian said that sometimes he thought of his parents as a two-headed monster yelling at him, and that he felt Katia was actually bigger than he was because as the baby, she got all the attention. At this point, Katia began to take down a doll baby and feed it; then she moved to her first thematic play, putting a baby in a crib together with two parents and clearly excluding any brother who might happen to exist. We discussed Ian's upset at school. To my query about his sadness at being excluded, he got teary and remained so for the rest of the hour. At the end of this hour, Ian commented that the mess Katia made in my office was nothing compared to the one she made at home. The anger was emerging slowly.

In the following sessions I commented on Ian's forebearance with Katia's destruction of his constructions, and as I did so, he became more openly angry at her. Meanwhile, the parents discussed Mother's fear that he would turn out to be like her stepfather if he were openly aggressive. It also emerged that Kent was passive-aggressive in a number of ways in the marriage and expressed this in the sessions through his lateness. As Mary, with my urging, took up her anger with him openly, he began to respond and come out from behind his role as the "good guy" to explore some of his resentment at her and at his mother, whom he held responsible for his father's absences and for dominating him during them.

Now Ian began to be aggressive in a covert way. He would set up a building and entice Katia over to knock it down. When she did so, he would react gleefully. He began to move from being resentful at her destroying his things to exploiting her to do the things he felt his mother would frown on. When I pointed this out, saying that I thought he was afraid to do it himself, he began to become more direct.

For instance, when we were discussing his "playing in the classroom," he set up some soldiers and pinned one of them against the wall with the toy ambulance. I said I thought that the ambulance was "letting the soldier have it" the way he wanted "to let the teacher have it," and that his classroom was a kind of battleground. He laughed and said it was true, and Katia joined in as things began to fly—in a mild form. Mary now recalled that at the same age, she had had school difficulty, which may have been due to the difficulty in her family at that period. This offered her a way of identifying with Ian's anger.

Mary and Kent were tolerating Ian's new open aggression much better, as Mary openly discussed her fears of aggression in men, and as Kent discussed what he had missed in the relationship with his own father and had given up in his relationship with Ian. After this phase of the work, Ian began to move forward. I had felt the quality of his play and Mary's inhibition of the feared aggression had kept this family operating at the "anal" level of the need to control its members and their aggression in order to safeguard dependency issues. As we worked on this, Ian began to move toward oedipal development.

During one session in which he sat next to his mother, I was overcome by a surprising countertransference experience of her as sexually attractive. As I sat staring at her, I began to think that under her sloppy clothes she seemed more appealing (in a Rubenesque way) than I had previously thought and that I could, after all, see what her husband saw in her.

Just as I was thinking this had to do with my identifying a better marital pairing, I spied Ian sitting next to her thrusting a little truck with a water cannon into the "V" created in the raised ladder of a toy hook-and-ladder truck. It dawned on me that here was an oedipal striving and that aggression was not the only thing that had been barred in the family. I was just thinking that they were moving rapidly as a family into oedipal development, when in the next moment, Ian turned to poking Katia with a tiny play sword. Aggression, here in the service of the sexual feelings, nevertheless took over once again. Ian began to play at an army battle with a new gusto. I thought that this related to Father and asked if Ian ever felt like taking his father on. He grinned and said he did, but that usually he got Katia to do it for him. He would say, "Go hit Daddy, Katia." When she did it in her cute little way, Father would not mind and had no notion it came from Ian.

The family play and discussion now became more consistently oedipal. In the next hour, after Ian had egged Katia on to some mild aggressive play, she turned to playing with doll figures in a model shower stall, setting up a variety of pairings. At one point the father was enthusiastically standing on the daughter in the shower. Ian took the father doll from Katia and bent its legs to sit on the toilet. But Katia arranged the father and daughter with their feet in the toilet.

As we discussed the fact that Mother occasionally showered with Katia, Katia put the father and baby in two cars and began to bang them into each other so that the baby would have flown off the table top if Mary had not blocked it. I now said that I wondered if Ian ever got mad at his sister for getting too much both from Mom and from Dad, and if he ever set her up to be punished. He grinned and said, "Sure I do!" Father was able to remember doing the same to his older sister and spying on her with boyfriends. While we discussed this, Katia accelerated the father-car bumping into the baby-car and then got a gun and waved it. Ian got the larger gun, while Mary watched with a guarded but fairly relaxed attitude.

I became aware of worrying that she would feel I was responsible for setting up this "violent scene" and felt that I was in danger of becoming her violent parents in the contextual transference. I felt this had to do with the specific inhibition of aggression at the moment, but I was feeling this was a cover for sexual issues, too, and that Ian and Katia must be living these out in their play.

Katia now waved her gun realistically and went "bang-bang" at Ian. The gun was pointed backwards, however, and Ian showed her how to turn the gun around the right way to aim it at him. He denied that he ever felt like shooting her, but Mary said she was worried Ian would teach Katia to be destructive. I commented that there was a good deal in her history to make her worry about that, and Ian piped up, "It's only a toy, Mom!" His reality testing was good, but he still denied all jealousy and anger at Katia, even while continuing to feed her play vengeance on him.

When it was time to go, Ian raced to pick up the blocks and stacked them in a tall tower on top of a bookshelf. On the very top, he placed a toy baby bottle and then stepped aside in triumph. I said that I thought he was saying that in his family, the babies were on top. His father confirmed that Ian had wanted to be carried like a baby on the way to the session. I said something about getting things by growing up instead of growing down, but I had underestimated Ian. He called Katia over to the tower, and I realized it had been designed to lure her with the bottle and then when she reached for it, the blocks would fall on her head. While we staved off the collapse of the ambush, I laughed and said that now we all knew the secret of his jealousy. Ian and his parents laughed as well, and Katia joined in with her infectious giggle.

In the following session, there was a move back to aggressive themes around Ian's jealousy at Katia. He was less compliant in giving everything to Katia as soon as she moved in on him. The result was that she "screamed bloody murder." He cast a questioning eye at his mother and said, "All right, Katia. Here! You can have it," and he gave in. I said that it now appeared that Katia "got away with murder," and that he had been mad at her ever since she came along when he was in kindergarten, but because Mother had been afraid of anger in men and boys, he had had to give in to her and not get mad. In their family, screaming seemed to be all right for girls, and then they were in charge. I thought some of this fear lay in Mary's fear of being angry and therefore being a bad person. I said that because of this she was mainly projecting these feelings onto Ian, as if only boys could be angry and bad. She accepted this interpretation and began to talk of her own fear of being a bad, destructive person, and especially that she would harm Katia. This related to her notion, which we had begun to explore, that she had been responsible for her parents' divorce and the loss of her father. Kent shared a measure of this feeling around his father's absence for a year when he was 5, which he now realized must have given him a guilty possession of his mother.

For Mary, this unconscious fear of marital disruption translated into a fear of Ian's becoming interested in and possessive of her as a threat to her marriage. She had handled this by discouraging Ian's forward movement to oedipal interest in her and his competitive stance toward his father. She had invested instead in Katia, to the point of encouraging an excessively close relationship between herself and Katia. Kent's readily surrendering a relationship with Ian had stemmed from his feeling that he had to give in to a dominant mother and from his inability to express his resentment then and even now, when the relationship with his son was curtailed just as the one with his father had been. Ian had also picked up the inhibition of aggression from his father.

As all these matters seemed to be in the process of being worked through in the family, we approached a time when Kent would have to be away. He had arranged to attend a summer institute before the beginning of therapy and was now angry with himself for leaving his family in the middle of the work. He felt he had set up the kind of isolation he hated so much. As he discussed this, Ian put a pilot figure in a space vehicle and pushed it along the table so it made a lonely journey and fell off the end of the table, while Katia began to dump things all over the floor and cover the family with her activity. She then drew an unrecognizable figure that she said was a bird without wings. I said that then it would not be able to fly away, so it expressed their wish that Father could not fly away from them in an airplane.

In the following session, Kent said he had been unable to discuss his absence because he was so mad at himself. "I feel like I put a gun to my own head," he said, "because I didn't have to take this goddamned brushup course, and I want to be with my family!" Mary was angry at him for being unable to discuss this at home. While he was saying this, Katia trampled a log cabin Ian was building, and he squeezed her leg. He said she had bumped into him, and he did not need to take bad treatment like that from her anymore. His anger was clear. He then drew a picture of a "Martian" (Fig. 14.7). He said it was scary. I asked him about the Martian: Was it a good one or a bad one?

"Well," he said, "no one likes this Martian anyway."

I said that with Father going away, there was a lot of sad and bad feeling for everyone in the family. I had noticed the family move backward a bit under the strain. Ian's picture, for instance, was very like one a 3-year-old might draw, and he was clear it was an angry "monster" that was invading from Mars. I thought that in the situation, no one felt good about him or herself.

In the last session before Kent's absence, the family was calmer and had been able to discuss the impending separation. Ian sailed paper airplanes as they discussed plans for the two months. We discussed Kent's possible unconscious wish to leave his family in order to be like, and therefore close to, his father. Katia played happily, and the two parents once again looked fond of each other.

Fig. 14.7 Ian's "Martian."

Defensive and Expressive Aspects of Play

In this therapy, play progressed in parallel with the movement of the issues. Both children's responses to the issues in the treatment could be understood through play, which formed their principal medium of communication even though the girl was only 19 months old at the beginning of the treatment. The play was useful in many ways. It gave the children an age-appropriate activity during the adult verbal exchanges; it provided a medium for communication; it enabled brother and sister to interact in a way that we could understand; it allowed for the displacement of affect too strong to be directly tolerated, but in a way that could still be used therapeutically; and it gave me and the parents a way of speaking with the children. Much of the discussion with Ian was direct, using the play as informative communication with him, to which I responded in words. The communication with Katia was carried out by speaking with the parents about what I understood about her and her role in the family.

When I first evaluated Ian, my reaction to the inhibition of aggression and sexuality in his play was to find him closed, a bit boring, and rather odd. When he and his family allowed a fuller expression, I felt in touch with him and with the family as a whole. Conversely, as they reined in Katia a bit, I felt less that she was a little terror. And through the whole process, my earlier partiality to Kent, with slight dread of Mary, yielded to an even fondness for the two of them and for the whole family.

The family's holding and containing of their young children includes specifically the way they allow or facilitate young child's play. In this family, we saw a growth in the tolerance of an aggressive boy's battle play; at the same time, the family was able to shape its toddler's aggressive play more effectively. As the therapy progressed, the quality of the relationships within the family changed, their level of relating to each other progressed, and the form and content of the play progressed. Within this overall progression, small regressions indicative of events of moment in the family or in individuals could be seen. Thus, the play was indicative both of general growth and of momentary fluctuation.

Transference and countertransference issues are communicated at least as effectively through play as by verbal means. Responses to play, to mess or play achievements, and to the use of play to communicate in the family were as immediate as with families that rely on words.

There is no need to exclude children of any age from using play or drawing materials in the course of family therapy. The work with older children, however, is less likely to have such a heavy emphasis on the medium of play. Where the children are of differing ages, perhaps ranging from preschool through late adolescence, a variety of modes of communication will be appropriate. The analytic family therapist should feel free to use all the modalities that are suitable to the family working at that moment.

CHAPTER 15

Families with Adolescents

Adolescents generally do not play with toys in therapy, although they may fiddle with paper, tissue, or hairbrushes. They work verbally, and any use of alternative expressive methods like drawing is usually adjunctive rather than central. So in some ways, work with families of adolescents is the easiest form of family therapy for the individual adult therapist to begin with.

Resistance in Adolescent Families

Nevertheless, there are special problems that can make the work in family therapy with adolescents far from easy. To begin with, there is the problem of the motivation of the adolescents. Some therapists find treating adolescents individually too difficult to attempt. Many adolescents are reluctant to risk the closeness of intensive therapy, in which uncomfortable sexual feelings may arise. They are also inclined to be intensely private about sexual issues for fear of censure, which may interfere with the individual therapist's wish to understand these matters as an important part of the adolescent's peer relationships. There are, however, many patients right through the period from 12 to 20 who are willing, articulate, and cooperative. They can offer some of the most heartening and humorous moments to their therapists; Adam (Chapter 12) and Ashley (this chapter) are such examples.

Defensiveness and lack of motivation on the part of the adolescent patient are frequent indications for the use of family work instead of individual therapy. The motivation may lie almost wholly in the parents, or in the school or other institutions that have responsibility for the care or education of the adolescent. It is not unreasonable to make a decision that the adolescent is so poorly motivated or frankly resistant that it will be both easier and more effective to work with the motivation and support of the parents in the room with us. One of the cases described later illustrates this point.

Often it turns out that the motivation on the part of the family is compromised in a significant way; for instance, one or both parents may be reluctant to delve into aspects of their own difficulties or into marital difficulties, which are the functional equivalents of the child's unwillingness to speak in individual and family sessions. A principal difference between the two settings, however, is the therapist's opportunity to address the resistance directly in the family-wide perspective. This often relieves the adolescent of the sense of being on the hot seat. When he or she gets "grilled" by the parents, it is possible to move the center of attack off the adolescent with a question about what the adolescent's reluctance represents about the family's difficulty as a whole. This changes the focus from the individual resistance to the level of the contextual transference. We can ask, "What is it in the family experience that makes it important to hold a rigid boundary against the outside world?"

When the adolescent resists, the family may feel "grilled," too. But in these cases, it is usually other members of the family who have provided the motivation to come and who thus are more ready to accept the confrontation of the issues. And in those cases where it is the community (e.g., the court) that has forced the family to come, the adults will more likely feel the urgency of the situation than the adolescent. No matter how much we, as therapists, understand this problem, it will not always be possible to convey motivational questions to the adolescent early in individual therapy, and we may find that it is more effective to work with the family than to fight an endless uphill battle in individual therapy.

Adolescent Separation–Individuation

Lack of intrinsic motivation is not the only reason that many adolescents are reluctant to work. Understanding the stage of adolescent development is a crucial part of our framework for working with the adolescent patient and with the family. We refer to the phase of adolescent development that Blos (1967) has called the *second separation–individuation*. This term is borrowed from

Mahler's studies of the toddler between 1 year and 2½ years who is becoming a separate person from his mother (Mahler et al. 1975). Blos emphasized that the hallmark of adolescent development is the move away from dependency on the primary family figures. This is accompanied by a comparable internal development that focuses on the image of the self freed from the internal objects. But because this is fragile, and because there is much in the child to militate against it, he or she is often caught up in an oscillation between increased dependency and exaggerated or impulsive independence. Of course, there is much that is normally tumultuous about adolescence, including conflicts arising from the surge of physical and sexual energy at puberty and the resurgence of the Oedipus complex that Blos described. Anna Freud (1958) held that turmoil is the natural condition of adolescence. We have learned that those adolescents who behave in a more radically disturbed way have internalized pathology and will have prognoses that reflect the severity of the acting out of their inner struggles (Masterson 1967). It is a quality of inner turmoil that can be said to characterize the movement from preadolescent dependency to later independence.

This means that one of the jobs of the adolescent therapist is to help the adolescent get a "shell" around the penchant for externalizing the turmoil and inner struggle. This shell normally derives from the family's capacity to form a container for the child, and its deficiency in doing so during growth is what is reflected in sum in the adolescent's own, now internalized, difficulty in providing self-holding.

Acting out is one of the indications for family therapy with adolescents. Johnson and Szurek (1952) provided an important precursor for looking to family dynamics to understand psychopathology with their classic description of adolescent acting out of parental conflicts insufficiently repressed due to "superego lacunae." Szurek (1974) applied this concept to the development of sexual symptomatology in adolescence. Much of the work of the NIMH group began with acting-out adolescents and their families. Drug use, running away, and the diagnostic category of "borderline" or "narcissistic" characterized most of these families. Roger Shapiro, John Zinner, Edward Shapiro, David Berkowitz, Helm Stierlin, Robert Winer, Kent Ravenscroft, David Levi, and a number of other researchers were instrumental in teaching us about the dynamics of these acting-out families (Berkowitz et al. 1974, Levi, Stierlin, and Savard 1972. Shapiro et al. 1975, Shapiro and Zinner 1971, and Stierlin and Ravenscroft 1972). Williams (1981), at the Tavistock Clinic, points out how adolescent violence results from family stereotyping to avoid intrapsychic conflict: The family's violence settles on one member while the others disapprove.

In their population, Zinner and Shapiro (1974) described the family as a "single psychic entity" with multiple projective identifications. Within this context, they described the action of "defensive delineation" as the way in which a family characterized one family member (often the adolescent) as possessing certain character qualities, which could eventually be seen to cling to that person because of defensive functions this labeling served for the rest of the family. In other words, the projective identifications were reinforced by multiple sources in the family and came to represent a critical building block of the family's shared holding capacity for each other.

This can be seen to fix the adolescent in a relationship to the family's psychological structure. It tends to do violence to the adolescent's wish and need to have an evolving sense of self as part of the route to winning freedom from encasement in the family's structure. In this case, a family holding pattern that has become more rigid out of a shared defensiveness will be felt by the emerging adolescent as an attempt to keep him or her in a more rigid internal pattern as well. This is the reason that Stierlin (1971, 1974) has described adolescent running away as a show of strength in the face of a family attempt to keep an adolescent from achieving a more flexible and independent identity.

Winnicott's contribution of "true" and "false self" (1960b) is also particularly helpful to understanding this phase of adolescent development. The false self developed to cover its true core in order to please the mother. Winnicott described the struggle to refind the true self in work with the adult, but we have been impressed that this struggle usually begins in adolescence. The adolescent, especially the disturbed one, often screams out to have his or her experience of self understood in terms other than the ones the family insists on, begging to be recognized as truly someone other than the person the family sees. Sometimes this is a conscious and open rebellion against the family's repetitive and insistent defensive delineation of the adolescent; at other times, it is an inchoate attempt to internalize a disorganized sense of inner confusion in which a wish to maintain an identity consistent with the family view, or with pleasing other family members, is in mortal internal combat with the wish to express a core of internal striving that is felt to be closer to the true self.

These true self strivings, which were covered by a false sense of compliance and congeniality, become more angry and rejecting, to the degree that there is a sense of being unacceptable to the family. But their origin begins not in the antilibidinal constellation but in the need the young child feels to go along with the libidinal urgings of the mother. That is, the false self develops in response to the message to the child not to become separate from the mother or the parents and, in not separating, to honor the primacy of an overclose, libidinal attachment to the mother and family. It can be seen, then, that the false self is a caretaker self, handling a threat of external rejection by using the libidinal constellation to quiet and eventually to secondarily repress the antilibidinal constellation; for the internalized message is that the child must not be aggressive to one or both parents. This is usually conveyed with some sense of threat by the parent, such as the coercive threat that "You will never amount to anything" or "I will reject you if you become a separate person." One of the frequent threats that can be terribly effective is the parent's threat to become sick or to die if the child becomes more assertive in wishing to become separate from the parent. The struggle against this kind of context of early family life is often what hits during adolescence, with a resulting sense of turmoil not only in the adolescent family member but in the parents as well.

This is the kind of struggle that Erikson (1962) discussed in his reexamination of Freud's famous Dora case (1905b). Basically, Dora was brought to Freud because of her refusal to comply with the family. She was a defiant and argumentative girl who had been her father's favorite but would now give him no peace. The story that unfolded was one in which she was the victim of a barely disguised acting out of parental discord. Father blamed Mother's depression and sexual withholding for his open affair with a married woman who had taken care of and befriended Dora; that is, she had been a substitute good mother and ego ideal. When the mistress's husband began to make passes at her, Dora's feelings were stirred up. Actually, if we saw this case today, there is every chance that the family and the mistress's husband, Herr K., would be reported for child sexual abuse—not necessarily to any better result than with Freud's treatment. Freud took the position that Dora had an intrinsic motivation to be seduced, overlooking the family-wide pattern of corruption that formed the context of Dora's lifelong psychosomatic and characterological difficulties (Deutsch 1957). Erikson's point was that what partly drove Dora from Freud was her inability to get verification of her experience from him. He used this to illustrate the adolescent need for getting validation from the outside world to foster the establishment of identity. No one in Dora's family could do this for her, and Freud, too, failed to understand this need. In a way, she showed considerable strength to be able to leave him as a statement of her belief in her own understanding of her experience.

This has been a considerable digression from the discussion of the adolescent's striving to be internally independent. But it sets the stage for our consideration of the role of the need for independence in the adolescent and the role this plays in the decision whether or not to offer family therapy. It has been argued that if adolescents are developmentally at the point of working toward independence, they should not be roped back into the family setting by being seen with their parents in therapy. In reality, the situation is both more and less complex.

We begin by asking if this is even an issue for the adolescent. Many are not having difficulty with moving toward independence but are having some other kind of trouble. The real issue may be the quality of the relationship to the parents. Can the child work best with them in the room, or not? This turns on several things. We can conceptualize it as relating to the quality of the contextual holding capacity of the family and the relation of the adolescent to the contextual holding. If the family has a generally benign quality of holding, then the various family members, probably including the adolescent, are likely to feel that the family and its members are generally on the adolescent's side. In this case, the family setting is a natural one of helpfulness to the child, even though the developmental stage is one of encouraging separation. In this case, the child will expect the family to be just as much on his or her side as on the side of the other family members. If there is difficulty in a developmental step, it will not be felt that it is because there is an overriding wish to stunt development. In these cases we can begin by assuming that whatever is in the way for the adolescent will represent an interfering theme for the whole family, and that the work at understanding and relieving it may well proceed smoothly among them. In other cases, it is precisely the family's difficulty in providing a holding context that calls for family therapy. Many adolescents have great difficulty taking their leave from a shaky family, and our work to stabilize both the actual family and the adolescent's view of it will help them to differentiate and become more autonomous. This is especially true for many families seen in the hospital.

The following example, from work with youngsters leaving school in England, illustrates the family members' shared difficulty with the developmental step of promoting separation–individuation. Their capacity to work well together on it illustrates the strength of their contextual holding.

A FAMILY WITH DIFFICULTY IN PROMOTING AUTONOMY

Keith Holmes, a 16-year-old boy, came to see me [D.E.S.] in London because he was shakily established in the world of work (Scharff and Hill 1976). Keith had left school earlier that year to take up an apprenticeship as a draftsman, in which there was provision for one-day-per-week work-release to attend college. If he pursued this path, he would get a diploma in draftsmanship at the end of four years. However, in the same way that he had found school difficult over the last year before he left, he also found the day at college difficult. He told me that he was afraid of being called on to speak publicly in class, an old fear he carried from high school. To his alarm, he had found that the public speaking phobia was rapidly spreading. He had become afraid to speak to workmen on the job or to use the telephone for fear he might be asked to read a letter over the phone and would be unable to do so. He began to refuse to answer the phone. Because his job involved frequent telephone calls, he grew increasingly afraid at work. So he decided he had better consult his general practitioner about the growing difficulty, which he did without telling his family of his trouble. When he got to the doctor's office, Keith was surprised and alarmed to find his father also in the waiting room.

In his interview with Leam Donellan, my social worker colleague who saw the father while I was seeing Keith, Mr. Holmes said that he had seen the general practitioner that day because of work-related difficulty. He had recently made the decision to change his job, a decision that meant a recognition that he had in part failed in his career. His depression and anxiety about his own career change coincided with Keith's difficulty in a way we shall presently describe.

In an interview alone with me, Keith was able to outline the phobia and the potential difficulty he was having from it. He also told me about the strain in his family concerning Father's career change. The family would have to make a major life move that would mean more than a job change. His father had given up a job of many years' standing as a junior executive in a food-packaging firm and had bought a dairy shop that had previously been owned by Keith's mother's parents. There had been difficulties in arranging the move into the apartment above the shop, which was part of the usual arrangement for this kind of small business in England. At the time when I first saw Keith, the family was just about to move. This would introduce a psychosocial transition for the entire family, including Keith—that is, a period of shift that had ramifications for every sector of their lives (Parkes 1971, Scharff and Hill 1976).

In addition, Keith said that his family had a secret that he was not supposed to know. His mother's father had died recently of a late stage of syphilis, and he thought the family, and especially his mother, was ashamed of the grandfather's having contracted syphilis in his youth. He was not sure why his mother was so upset about this, but he thought she was. This information was confirmed by the parents in their interview. With such striking parallels in the parent interviews and the adolescent interviews, it was natural for us to decide to meet with the family together. An interesting feature of the work with this family concerned the pairing of two men as cotherapists. Mr. Donellan was identified as the parents' worker and I as Keith's individual therapist—both of us, however, being there for the whole family.

We saw Keith together with Mr. and Mrs. Holmes, Keith's 6-year-old brother, and his 18-year-old sister. It became apparent that mother "bore all the burdens of the men in the family." They had made her set limits for them all through the years. This was important now because she knew how to manage the dairy shop, inasmuch as she had grown up living above it and working in it. She had never been able to move more than a few miles from her family geographically, and now they would be living once again just around the corner from her mother. Her parents had not gotten along very well with each other, and the late-life discovery of her father's syphilis had not only been a source of great shame but had had the effect of adding to the bitterness of the long-standing arguments between her parents. Her role as mediator between them had been an early instance of shouldering the burden for the man's difficulty.

Mr. Holmes saw himself as having had a checkered career. He had worked his way up in a food-processing business until he reached a supervisory position. Because he lacked a university degree, however, he felt there was no further opportunity for advancement. Over the past several years he had not been promoted, and recently, with the relocation of the factory to a small industrial area some distance from London, he had been commuting long hours. His interpretation of the situation was that his career growth was effectively at an end because of his lack of educational credentials. (Of course, we could not tell whether there were other factors.) With his wife, he made the set of decisions that resulted in buying the dairy shop, which could be expected to be considerably more lucrative, although less "professional."

It now became apparent that Keith's difficulty in moving into a professional world at the time the family was suffering a defeat in this area had made him a recipient for the projection of their fears. This mid-life crisis for his father had reawakened issues of the latter's own career choice at a similar point in his midadolescence to Keith's present one. At that time, Father had chosen not to go to university and had undertaken an apprenticeship like the one Keith had begun recently. The repercussions were only now being felt. The threat to the family was that they were all thrown into a combined business and personal situation that Mrs. Holmes remembered with dread. Particularly, it meant to her that she would be increasingly called on to support the men who were apt to be weak and defective, and it was this fear that Keith was living out.

There was more family specificity to Keith's phobia about speaking on the telephone and in public, however. Mr. Holmes also recounted having overcome a public speaking phobia of his own. He had been unable to speak in public in high school and early in his career. As a young man, he deliberately set out to organize religious forums in which he would be called on to speak. Only by this conscious effort had he been able to overcome a dread that was very similar to the one now confronting Keith. This could be seen to be an external part of his fear of being weak professionally himself.

Keith's growing uncertainty about work expressed itself in a crippling symptom of inability to use the telephone or speak in positions of minor authority. The family's crisis as they underwent a change of career and a change of dominance within the family, with Mother now assuming a major breadwinning role, expressed itself in Keith's adolescent developmental crisis. Father's bitterness about his own career and the general pattern within the family of "pinning everything on Mother," because the men could not be trusted, was consistent with Keith's having increasing anxiety about pursuing a new career involving learning, promotion, and a progressive assumption of independence and responsibility. The family's shared anxiety about a man's assumption of responsibility could be seen now to lead to Keith's specific phobia, which threatened his growth and individuation just at the moment the family was moving back into a less differentiated pattern where Mother was afraid she would swamp Father and sap his strength.

In this case, the parents' interest and that of the child coincided sufficiently that they worked comfortably together. They had no overt battle with Keith about his becoming progressively autonomous: They shared a conflict with him about the tribulations of being independent and of achieving. They were not invested in using him via projective identification to get rid of their bad object relations. Rather, they suffered neurotically in a way that invaded the family's overall capacity to act as a container for progressive differentiation. Keith was caught up in something that also caught them—the fear of extending himself.

In this constellation, family work was not only possible but actually set up an ideal situation for the shared exploration and enlargement of the family's shared holding capacity. Their transference to the therapeutic holding envelope was positive, and the fact that there were two male therapists seemed to reinforce the possibility of an effective male role. Mr. Holmes was able to see, in the process of the work, that the life issues he had found crippling did not need to be passed on to Keith. He and Keith began to work openly together to use some of the lessons Father had learned to relieve Keith's present anxiety at work. Keith now found himself able to use the phone, to take on more difficult tasks, and to move more confidently toward a competence at work, which included continued education. As this happened, Mrs. Holmes felt relieved of her burden to carry the load for incompetent and demanding men. Although we have not documented the participation of the other two children in this example, we may say briefly that there were comparable shifts in their understanding of family life that were useful to each of them.

Interlocking Life Crises

In the Holmes family, the issue of separation and individuation and the assumption of autonomy by the mid-adolescent were actually symptomatic of the life crisis for the whole family. This is a frequent feature of families with adolescents. The parents undergo a mid-life shift that echoes the struggles of the child and constitutes their own efforts to make course corrections for decisions made when they were at the stage the adolescent is currently in. The notion of concomitant transitions in families of adolescents derives from Erikson's description (1950, 1958) of the life crises of adolescence and adulthood. The parent is often struggling with issues of his own mid-life crisis, as poignantly described by Jacques (1965), just as the adolescent is challenging his role as a parent. The interaction of these factors leads to the dynamics of interlocking life crises seen when we work with adolescent families (Scharff and Hill 1976).

Chronic Intergenerational Interlocking

The following example illustrates midphase work with a family with less firm contextual holding for a similar kind of work that needed doing around adolescent separation. The difficulty represented prolonged family failure rather than an acute regression due to family crisis.

FAMILY AMBIVALENCE ABOUT DEPENDENCE AND INDEPENDENCE IN PARENTS AND CHILDREN

For the Browns, described in Chapter 8, the family vacation to Bethany Beach would begin next week. The parents were anxious to discuss their expectations of the children beforehand so they could arrive in a spirit of cooperation. Deirdre, who in a previous session had been very worried that her parents would go out every night and leave her alone at home, said nothing. Ashley spoke about her worry that her parents would control her too much. The parents were worried that she would be nice only if allowed to do as she wished. The parents expected to go out alone four or five times and to go to dinner as a family twice. Ashley said she would be willing to baby-sit two nights but not more. But the parents insisted that when they were gone, they expected Ashley, age 14, to be with Deirdre, age 10, as they felt the beach was no longer safe for either girl to stroll about alone.

Ashley responded in the sarcastic, contemptuous tone that her parents hated. It's difficult to capture the full extent of her demolishing effect, as she mocked their idea that they were doing something nice for her. "Yeah, that's just great, isn't it? You take me to Bethany to make me stay in a poky house every night. Well, that's not my idea of fun. I should not have to take care of that idiotic child. Thanks a lot. Why not leave me home?" Mother said they might do that and leave her at Grandma's. Ashley responded even more contemptuously. Father said that was why he just could not like her. Her mother said tearfully that she still could like Ashley because she remembered the wonderful, sweet little girl Ashley had been. Surely that person was still there. At that moment, Ashley began to show her mother a burst blister that hurt, and her mother said she'd put ointment on it, but meanwhile, Ashley should keep the bandage on. I was reminded of a 3- to 5-year-old girl showing her minor hurts to Mommy. Father said, "Let's not waste money talking about bandages."

Ashley then entertained the family by rating all her teenage friends and their parents to justify her opinion that her parents were lucky to have her. Then she rated her parents in the top 5. The smiling parents were captivated and began to talk about the other families' foibles, until I pointed out how they had been entranced and derailed. They agreed that Ashley's proof that she was just as wonderful as they thought had sidetracked the discussion of their vacation arrangements and the children's responsibilities. I asked what would they do with Deirdre if Ashley was left at Grandma's? They said they would feel safe leaving her alone. Deirdre, who had previously been worried about this, said she would not be lonely now that she had discovered the game of solitaire. It suddenly became clear that they were actually worried about Ashley, not Deirdre. I said, "So Deirdre is really baby-sitting Ashley." They agreed. The parents were worried that Ashley, although older and more able to take care of herself, was also more attractive and therefore more vulnerable. Ashley, instead of reassuring them, reacted provocatively. This inflamed their anxiety and led to their clamping down on her, which she claimed not to want. However, she also said that her parents did not do enough caring for her in general. She wished her mother would do her laundry, drive her places without insisting on a carpool, and prepare meals without her help and without expecting her gratitude.

The parents had shared a feeling of wonder about Ashley when she was born. They each loved her more than they loved each other. Their sexual relationship had been almost nonexistent since she was about a year old. Father had the fantasy that Mother would be a cute, adoring, dependent wife who would nurture him. Mother had the fantasy that Father would fulfill his brilliant promise as an architect, earn lots of money, and provide for her. She was disappointed that he had no ambition and so she had to work as well. He felt satisfied with his considerable achievement as an associate professor of architecture and did not care about earning more, but he was disappointed that he had to help around the house because Mrs. Brown was unwilling or unable to keep house, do the laundry, and transport the children. On the surface, he helped willingly, but he often dragged his feet. It also upset him that she yelled at the children for not helping and for creating messes. He tended to say nothing when he was angry, but his silence made her more likely to yell. She was furious that he could not assert paternal authority and make the children take responsibility. He was furious that she left the children feeling just like he did, so underfed and deprived that none of them had anything they wished to give.

This family also demonstrated intergenerational difficulties: Ashley's adolescent development threatened the family's difficulties not only around individuation and separation but around burgeoning sexuality, which they unconsciously imputed as a cause of adult disappointment. The mutual parental disappointments were projected into Ashley's threatened sexual interests and further complicated the capacity of this family, already hobbled in its ability to support its members to differentiate from each other. In this family there was not an acute regression under stress, as was the case of the Holmes family, but a chronic difficulty had hampered growth for years.

Concerning More Difficult Families

This chapter has not yet given examples of some of the more difficult families—those with delinquency, those with drug or alcohol abuse, or those with a borderline or narcissistic child. These families are usually characterized by intense projection and splitting, or intense overvaluation of certain characteristics or individuals at the expense of others. Such families provide an enormous challenge to therapists to hold them in the therapy, and their contextual transferences are correspondingly shot through with attacks on our function, competence, and confidence. This means that the countertransference is correspondingly subject to wider swings, more areas of doubt and despair, and wider splitting with less sure therapeutic equilibrium and poise, internal or external. In addition, the therapeutic context often requires the reinforcement of contextual holding that an inpatient setting can provide.

A family therapy trainee described her work with an acting-out girl, the daughter of divorced parents. The father was an alcoholic and the mother was unsteady in the running of her own life and in the people she chose, in addition to encouraging her daughter's acting out with drugs. At one point she permitted a derelict boyfriend of the girl to stay for the weekend. At the same time, she was refusing to sleep with her own boyfriend, who was living in the house with her and the children. She said, "I wouldn't want the children to get the wrong idea about my sexual life."

Here the work involved helping the mother and daughter explore the effects of the shoddy container that the mother was providing for the family, and the attacks the girl made on the holding the mother could provide. On the way to this, the therapist helped the mother clarify her relationship to her own boyfriend, who began to make his own gains and to join the family regularly in family therapy. He was then able to contribute to Mother's capacity to provide a more consistent home and to clarify the needs not only of the acting-out adolescent but of the younger child who was not acting out. A good deal of time was given to shoring up the mother's capacity to provide consistency. Therapy for the mother, later including her boyfriend, focused on her frequent failures to provide limits and consistency. Slight improvement in Mother's holding capacity enabled the girl to begin to discuss her feelings about being able to destroy the environment she also knew she needed.

In this way, an alternation between parent guidance and psychotherapy proceeded until the mother became firm enough to take a series of stands and to proceed with placement of the girl in the residential treatment she needed. This seemed to represent the best outcome that could be hoped for, inasmuch as the child was too disturbed to be contained in a less restrictive environment. After the adolescent had been placed in residential care, the mother and boyfriend then asked to continue with the therapist to work on their own issues.

It is of interest to note that the family therapy student was an experienced mental health professional. At the beginning of her work with this family, she was able to help with matters of parent guidance and to give advice about limit setting and the provision of optimal conditions for the child. The mother, however, was not able to make progress in managing the child and her own life until the analytic therapy was added. This enabled the mother to understand why she was unable to follow the therapist's recommendations and to move to a new level of personal organization.

The examples so far have presented adolescents most usefully seen together with their families. We will see another such example in this chapter, and there are several others presented elsewhere in the book. There are also examples of the integration of individual and family treatment concurrently, as discussed in Chapter 12. However, we need to examine the situations in which it does not seem wise to propose conjoint family treatment.

Generally, there are two situations that seem to militate against seeing the whole family together as a primary mode of therapy, especially in an outpatient setting. The first involves the adolescent's refusal to be seen with the parents, a fairly frequent occurrence. It is considered to be developmentally appropriate by many child therapists and psychoanalysts. We think a broader view would be that, while it is one kind of age-appropriate expression of the push for autonomy, the insistence of being seen alone is neither good nor bad in itself. It may be the most useful arrangement, or it may not. But if it is an insistent stance, we simply "meet the patient where he or she is at."

A recent example was provided by Tamara, age 16, who was referred as her mother approached death from cancer. As one of her last acts of care for this child, the mother arranged the referral and brought the child to the evaluation. From Tamara and from her mother's therapist, I learned that the family was appropriately dominated by the illness. I suggested a family meeting. Tamara acted deeply offended, and it was clear that I was on the verge of joining the large group of adults whom she felt fundamentally mistook her situation.

She said, "I'm fed up with having to be submerged in Mom's illness. Anyway, Mom is doing OK, and I have other things I want to deal with. And I'm getting no time and no place to do it."

Just after she said this, her mother knocked on my door to say she had had some blood in her urine when she used the waiting-room bathroom. Could she use my phone to call her doctor? Even this did not shift Tamara's position. There was no point in suggesting a family meeting again. Tamara felt overrun by events and in danger of being pulled into the family's fused denial and preoccupation with Mother's impending death. The denial, I learned, seemed to be reinforced by the oncologist. In this case there was no choice: Tamara needed to be seen individually.

In the next example, a second contraindication to family work is illustrated. This one is more subtle and comes as a warning to family therapists who are too enthusiastic about the almost universal use of family therapy. In this case, the motivation of the adolescent is greater than that of at least one of the parents. Furthermore, the dynamics of the parental couple are such that the resistance of one parent cannot effectively be challenged in the conjoint setting, if at all. If the family therapist insists on gathering such a family in the room, the adolescent will often be accused of being the perpetrator of this challenge to the parent and will feel under attack from the threatened parent. Although this resistance may be manageable in the family therapy setting, there are many times it is not. In these families, it is better, again, to "meet them where they are at," inasmuch as there are other ways of dealing with the individual and family issues.

The Jansen family, described in Chapter 12, illustrates an example of this kind of resistance that yielded over time, leading to effective family work. The Taylor family, also described in Chapter 12, presented the example of a father whose marginal motivation was far less than that of the 12-year-old boy, Adam. There, the same therapist could see the boy and the parents, but the father's reluctance was not shared by the boy, who was extremely motivated. Ultimately, the father's reluctance could be understood to be closely allied to issues that resulted in the breakup of his marriage. In contrast, for Adam, those areas formed the transference issues that were susceptible to analytic understanding and were central to his growth.

The example described next presents the case of the family that could not work in a conjoint manner, and where the therapist did not think it wise even for the same therapist to work with both child and parents.

A FAMILY THAT UNDERMINED TREATMENT

Mrs. Cornell called about her 14-year-old daughter, Lisa, who was doing poorly in school and getting into constant battles with her father. She and her father had always had a battling relationship, which the mother described as equally provoked from both sides. They had already sought a referral for therapy from the staff psychiatrist at the Pentagon where Sgt. Cornell worked and had been referred for family therapy. In the first meeting, the therapist had said he would work with the Cornells only if all members of the family were present for every meeting. That had been "it" for Sgt. Cornell. He traveled on his job as a Senior Master Sergeant with extensive expertise in weapons systems, and he was not about to be told he had to be there for Lisa, who, from his perspective, was ungrateful and surly in any case. Mrs. Cornell told me she was sure that plan would never work. She did think that she could get her husband in for couple meetings but that, if she insisted, Lisa would come alone.

Lisa, herself, was resistant at first. She had learned her lesson and was never going to provoke her father again. It was all his fault anyway. As for school, it was a piece of cake; all she had to do was work. But she did say that she recognized some of the things she hated about her father in her own worst behavior, and if she did not have things so well in hand now, that could have been a crippling problem in her life and any marriage she would have.

I arranged to meet a few times with Lisa's mother, with Father, and with the couple. They were willing to support work for Lisa, and Mother was willing to insist that Lisa come. Father was marginally willing to meet as a couple with one of my colleagues to discuss ways of living with and managing Lisa, and this was arranged. I felt that Father's rivalry with Lisa, and her own way of managing her phase of adolescence, meant that if I also worked with them, Lisa could only be suspicious of me.

I met with Lisa for what I called an extended evaluation. Without pushing her concerning her motivation, I offered the idea that we would see how Lisa managed with school and family before making a definitive treatment plan. She agreed, and we met weekly for about six weeks while she maintained the self-imposed control. Then Father came back from one of his trips roaring mad, and in a shot, she crumpled back into the tumultuous battling with him and the spiraling school difficulties.

She said, "You know, I thought I could do this on my own. But it's too much for me. And I'm most afraid that I'm going to end up being just like him, especially the part of him I hate. He's not all bad, but I sure can hate him. Then I get just the same. Can you help me with all this?"

We were then able to set up a plan for analysis, which went on for a year with considerable hard work and much improvement internally and symptomatically. Lisa developed stronger motivation as time went on and toward the end worked with considerable insight and interest.

At the end of this time her father, congratulating her on her gains, pushed her to get out of analysis and take an after-school job. This occurred when he had just retired from the army and had a new job with no traveling. The result was a new challenge to family equilibrium. The parents were under stress again and felt that bringing her to analytic hours could be too much of a strain on their marriage. Mother's part in the family's earlier resistance to treatment became clearer as she now joined forces with her husband. They did this despite my colleague's continued work to overcome their resistance. Even at this point, Lisa was able to maintain weekly psychotherapy as a way of consolidating her gains and to work incrementally on her growth.

The family's resistance, as spoken for by the father but with considerable support from mother, meant that conjoint family work would have been under constant attack from the parents. Even if we could have arranged intermittent family meetings, Lisa would have been challenged in every meeting about any positive motivation she had for therapy. The parent worker took up these issues vigorously and regularly during the course of his work with the Cornells. Despite his support, Lisa's progress and a degree of parental stress combined to make Father push on her again a year later to leave treatment. Meanwhile, however, both she and the parents had made considerable gains.

The Process of Work with Families of Adolescents

The process of working with families of adolescents is much more akin to the process of psychoanalytic psychotherapy with adults and adolescents than is the working phase with families of younger children. It is conducted with words, and most of what the therapist comes to understand can be derived from what is said and from the accompanying nonverbal gestures. A number of examples of work with families who have one or more adolescents have already been described in this book. The next example gives a more complete description of "working through" in a series of family sessions.

Virginia Malone's parents came to see me because she fought them on many things, but chiefly on their attempts to help her with her homework. She was 13, and she still fought and bickered endlessly with her 10-year-old brother, Jay. Both parents felt that they had come from loving families where there was an ease about schoolwork, although Father had not done much of it until he "got turned on late in high school." At that point, he had burned up the traces, but he had still preferred sports, in which he was talented. He had done well in college, however, and had been able to get into engineering school with a scholarship. He was still accelerating through his engineering career, in which he was known as "a man of action." Mrs. Malone never had any academic difficulty and grew up in a large family that emphasized academics. Her parents had helped each of the children with schoolwork, and it was important to her to be able to continue this tradition, as a sign of being a good parent. She was the one in the family who was in favor of talking things out, which made it all the more frustrating for her that Virginia refused to talk to her about what was wrong. That did not bother Mr. Malone much, because he was not much of a man for words.

THE EVALUATION

In the evaluation, Virginia had little to say to me. She denied that she had any difficulty getting along with her parents and downplayed any significant anger at them. She avoided emotional topics and dodged any confrontation with me. She did not seem very sick, but neither did she seem insightful. In the interview she agreed to draw pictures of a person, presumably herself, and of her family. The picture of a girl (Fig. 15.1) showed a stereotyped girl, with little sign of sexual differentiation or individuality, and who was missing one hand. There was, however, some red outlining the lips and on her cheeks, and she looked fairly optimistic. It looked as though she were retreating from the developmental push toward sexual differentiation. In the picture of her family, she was more expressive. She drew them playing tennis, true to the family's sports orientation (Fig. 15.2). She was playing on Father's side and was a bit more differentiated than her mother, who was playing with her little brother, Jay. In this picture, she and everyone else had hands. Playing with Father meant winning, she told me. This and other material, including extensive psychological testing, supported the picture of Virginia as "an oedipal winner."

One striking feature of the individual interviews was the sparsity

Fig. 15.1 Virginia's picture of a girl.

of her answers. I felt, as any adolescent therapist does with some adolescents, as if I were pulling teeth. After the first diagnostic interview, I dreaded the second. Although we survived it, I did not look forward to the prospect of working with her individually.

The family session, however, was much easier on me. The parents, whose motivation seemed to be sustained, took the lead in "grilling" Virginia. When she resisted, Father closed in. I could see it was excruciating, but at the same time, I experienced relief that I was not the one having to try to get her to talk. Once I registered that feeling, I realized that Father was indeed honing in on her ferociously. Both Mother and Father had a pattern of turning to ask Virginia questions, and when she said "I don't know," they followed with "Is that true? Do you really mean that?" I began to feel sorry for

Fig. 15.2 Virginia's family picture.

her and have some appreciation for where her "clamming up" came
from. The family said that Father was also uncommunicative about
feelings and that Mother complained about this. He had gotten
better in recent years, but it was still hard for him. Mother still
wished he could loosen up more. During most of the session, Jay hid
behind the focus on Virginia. The family agreed that that was a
telltale position for him and that he was far from perfect. At the end
of the session, we agreed that we would work together in family
therapy.

THE EARLY PHASE OF TREATMENT

In the first treatment session, Mother outlined the difficulty with
homework, while Virginia glowered and Jay looked sleepy. Mrs. Malone said that Virginia would call to her to ask for help with some-

thing like a math problem. When Mother almost eagerly went to help, the situation would deteriorate in a matter of a few moments. Virginia would begin to scream at Mother, who would try to calm Virginia while getting her to pay attention to the problem.

At this point, Father intervened to say, "I wish you would say you're sorry to your mother."

"I'm sorry," intoned Virginia.

"Are you really?" asked Father.

"Yes!" she spat out.

"I don't think you mean it," he said, and he began to lecture her. The fight was on.

At the end of the hour, Mother had realized that her insistence on helping Virginia was not helping. She wanted me to tell her what to do about the situation. "Are you telling me that I shouldn't help her?" she asked. "Or should I leave when she begins to get nasty? Tell me, because I want to do the right thing."

I felt the pressure to help Mother with her "homework"—that is, with her work at home of trying to do better. I recognized that this pressure for me to give her the answer must be a replay of pressure between her and Virginia, although I could not be sure in exactly what way. My general guidelines to not give parents advice were getting me through this moment, but I felt I was hanging on to them for my own guidance, such was the pressure I felt to "be helpful" to Mrs. Malone. I could feel the longing in her voice to be a good mother, when she was feeling so defeated.

I was able to say to Mrs. Malone that it was important that she do this homework herself, and I pointed out the analogy of the wish for me to help her with Virginia's wish that Mrs. Malone help her.

She said, "I guess I have to leave the room when she gets abusive, huh? When can I go back?"

Again, I deflected her. Because I felt it was part of the difficulty that Mother was carrying the whole task, I made a point of speaking to both parents in saying, "Here again, I think you have to try to figure out what you both should do as best you can. And then we can look at it in here and see what that has meant to you."

They were rather unclear as to whether I had been helpful as they left the hour. Mrs. Malone gave me a friendly but dubious raised eyebrow as she passed me on the way to the door. Virginia was about as unexpansive as when she came in, whereas Father was formal and polite, and unconvinced.

In the next session, Mr. Malone started off by saying he was angry. There had been another fight with Virginia over homework.

But Mrs. Malone said that she felt proud, because when Virginia got nasty at the homework, she was able to leave the room. The first time, she had shouted at Virginia, it was true. But then she got the hang of it and left for the evening. Virginia had begged for her to come back, but she had decided that one evening's homework was far from crucial.

Virginia was sneering as they discussed this. I asked if Virginia were the only one who was upset and was surprised when Jay volunteered that he had been upset by something the other day. He told his father that he had scored his first point in basketball for the year, and his father had yelled, "Leave me alone!" Mr. Malone responded to this not by apologizing but by saying, "Haven't I told you that I was in a bad mood?" Jay agreed and sighed. I felt he was unable to get the hurt across to his father. So I intervened to ask Father if he had been able to hear what Jay seemed to mean, and as I did so, Mother was shaking her head, answering me that Father could not hear.

I felt that since this was the first time Jay had volunteered something, it was important to let him get it out, and also that he was trying to say something about how he agreed with Virginia's position. So I stuck with him and urged him once again to try to tell his father what he had been upset about. Reluctantly, he told Father that he had felt hurt. He denied, however, that Father overlooked him at times, but Mrs. Malone said that Father *did* do just that—not all the time by any means, but more than her husband would like to admit.

I now turned to ask Virginia if she understood all this. She said "No!" at first. I kept at it with her because I had now come to feel that denial of feeling was a shared style in the family and that, in this regard, she had learned a great deal from her father. I brought up the way her father habitually spoke to her. I noted that in our sessions he had asked questions like, "Do you really mean it?" Now she said that she felt Father's questions would get her in trouble somehow. Over the next minutes we got it worked out that if she said that she "*did* mean it," he did not believe her. And she could not say she *did not* mean it unless she wanted to "start a fight," so it seemed to be a no-win situation. I said that I thought we were in the territory of feeling that her father did not believe her answer, no matter what it was. She agreed. He was not going to believe her, so what was the point? I now turned to Mr. Malone and asked if he believed Virginia's answers.

He looked a bit taken aback and said, "No. I guess not. When I ask the question, I don't really think she's sorry."

I now said to Father that I thought he was presenting a "no-win" situation to Virginia. I was not denying that she was mad. She was. But his questions were primarily rhetorical. They were posed as questions, but they constituted an attempt to wring an admission or an apology out of her because he was angry with her. They were an expression of his disapproval and his anger at her, which he was not expressing any more directly than Virginia was. Virginia began to nod at her father, and Mrs. Malone smiled at me knowingly, in a "we're-partners-over-my-husband's-head" kind of way.

I had the sensation of liking Mrs. Malone but of not quite trusting either her or myself because she was so winning at this moment in appreciating my "triumph" in getting to her husband. But I felt too triumphant at getting some positive acknowledgment from Virginia at her father's expense. And I felt a bit set up for a partnership with Mother, which I realized I had been aware of without acknowledging it. So I felt quite wary at a sudden power tilt in the family, and I began to wonder what Mrs. Malone's role in all this was.

I now worked with Virginia about what she felt in these situations with her family. She was able to say that she often felt "not believed." As I talked with her about this, I felt that her trust in me was growing, that is "I would listen to her when they would not," and I felt identified with her adolescent sense of triumph or vindication over her family. In retrospect, I think this represented Mother's projective identification with Virginia—the hope of winning a battle over Father, despite Mother's history of having a loving and supportive father herself.

But in the session, I now wanted to get back to Jay and to link his feeling hurt by Father to what Virginia had elaborated. So I said that Jay seemed to feel some of the same sense of not being heard when he felt hurt. He denied it, shaking his head, and began to defend Father. I realized I had transgressed onto defended territory, and the protection of Dad was the sign of it. This gave me a sense of one pattern of alliance in the family: mother and daughter, unconsciously paired in an attack on Dad, who was paired with his staunch defender, Jay.

This immediately took the form of sibling bickering, which was one of the things the parents had complained about originally. When Jay denied my suggestion that he felt misunderstood, Virginia said, snidely, "Uh huh, you do!" And Jay returned, "No, I do not!" And they were off at the level of cutting each other down with disbelief in their responses.

Mrs. Malone turned to me and said, "You see, this is what we face at home."

Momentarily following the distraction, I asked, "What do you do about this when it happens?"

She said that they punished both children because they usually could not tell who began the interaction. I asked Jay who usually began the fights, not quite realizing I was still following the detour that the children had arranged in order to lead me away from the "attack" on Father.

Jay now admitted, with a sheepish grin, that he set up Virginia by giving her something like an elbow in the ribs, just as often as she turned on him without provocation.

Mrs. Malone said, "Well, I do know about this. But we punish you equally, don't we, Virginia?"

Virginia at first agreed. There was a moment of compliance. Then she hesitated. "No. I think you often punish both of us, but if it's only going to be one of us, then it's almost always me."

I felt confirmation was required because I also felt doubtful they could be so even handed, given what we were hearing. So I asked Jay for his opinion, having learned already today that, at bottom, he seemed to be in the category of the shamelessly honest youngest child, despite his wish to keep his parents looking good. Jay agreed that when one of them was punished, it was rarely him. He had to agree with Virginia.

At this point, I had recovered some perspective on the meaning of the sibling bickering as a distraction. I said, "The fighting between Jay and Virginia ends up with a draw or with Virginia taking the rap for the fight. But it began when I was taking on Dad. And I've noticed that the family is very edgy about taking on Dad. I think Jay just doesn't like it, so he started to defend him. Then Virginia and Jay agreed to take the fight on themselves to protect Dad from attack. This may well be something that happens at home, say if Mom is taking Dad on about something?"

Mrs. Malone made a face, considering what I said, and then slowly nodded. Mr. Malone gave a gesture of "Well, maybe so."

I continued. "You see, I think that in a way, Mom backs Virginia in her general attempt to get something out of Dad, who is so hard to get through to. In that sense, I think that you, Virginia, are doing some of the taking on of Dad for other people. Then you feel pretty let down if your Mom doesn't defend you."

"Maybe," said Virginia. But she smirked as she said it.

I felt some of the unpleasantness they complained about. Here I was supporting her and getting a grudging tolerance in return. But I continued. "Another important thing, which sets all this up, is the agreement Virginia and her Dad have about when they are going to fight. If Dad says, 'Apologize!' and Virginia is grudging about it, then they know they have just agreed to fight. How is it that this doesn't happen with Jay? Doesn't anyone make him apologize?"

They said that in fact they did ask him to say he was sorry, and he was almost always conciliatory. Whereas, when they said "Apologize!" to Virginia, she would say, "Sorry!!!" in her offensive manner.

I said, "And then, Dad can't resist the challenge, and he says, "Say it again with the right feeling." And everyone knows Virginia is going to have to refuse, to save face. That is what I mean about the fight they have agreed to have. Because when Dad asks her to say it again with feeling, and when she refuses to back down, he and she both know they are going to escalate the battle. It's no one's fault. It's just an agreement between the two of you."

Mr. and Mrs. Malone both nodded in agreement. I thought that at least they understood what I was saying. Virginia looked relieved.

I went on, summing up and wanting to lead to the future "because clause," which I could not yet supply in detail. "Now what we need to know as we continue to work on this is what in the family makes it important that the two of you go through this over and over. Because it must do something for everyone. For the moment, I think I can guess that Dad thinks he is supposed to take Virginia down a peg for sassing Mom, and Virginia thinks she is supposed to stand up to Dad because Mom can't and needs her to take the lead. And Jay hopes Virginia can do it so Dad will understand how he can hurt people without Jay having to tell him. For the moment, what is important is that you are all caught up in this without knowing how to do it any differently, because you don't know why you have to do it. Hopefully, we will find out why, and then you can each try new things."

As they went out, Virginia still eyed me with suspicion—perhaps a bit less than before. Mrs. Malone smiled as always. But Mr. Malone also smiled at me and, raising his eyebrows, said, "I wouldn't have believed it. Thanks!"

The family dealt with its initial reluctance to work, as expressed primarily through the adolescent. In this session it emerged that her nastiness, which was the referring symptom, was rooted in the interplay between father and daughter. This could now be put in the context of a difficulty between her parents in which she, in a paradoxical way, was trying to play a helpful role. She was actually trying to be a spokeswoman for her mother in trying to get her father to be more open, a complaint about the father that the mother would make directly but about which she felt helpless. On the other hand, the father felt he was acting on the mother's behalf, too. He was trying to get his daughter to behave for her mother and to take her help in the homework situation, where Mother desperately wanted to be helpful in order to be valued as she had valued her own parents, and especially her father. I thought that feelings about her father's death twelve years earlier had led to her attempt to replace him by helping Virginia with the homework whether it was useful or not. But it was too early to say this, because the material had not taken us there.

Many other matters were far from being elucidated, including the role of oedipal issues in Virginia's having such a heated interaction with Father and with both parents. I speculated that because of her early-adolescent developmental stage, it was a way of trying to distance herself from a wish to continue to depend on her mother that led to a renewed oedipal interest in her father, which also called up a defensive distancing. The development of a surly attitude in mid-adolescence often represents the attempt to become separate when the adolescent is defending against the pull to stay dependently attached. Many adolescents feel they can leave home only in a counterdependent stampede over their parents' dead bodies.

Virginia had a reputation in her family for having this kind of personality from early on. It was far too soon to know, but it seemed to stem from a mix of factors. Partly she seemed temperamentally difficult (Thomas, Chess, and Birch 1968), a "negative reactor" who backed away from new situations before she could begin to approach them. But I thought already that there was evidence that Mrs. Malone had been invested in staying too close to Virginia, hovering over her, unable to set limits, and then trying to get her husband to solve the situation. This was happening because of Mother's anxiety that she could not provide the same warmth she had gotten from her own family, and perhaps also out of oedipal guilt that she had bested her mother in getting so much from her father. In her history, she had said that her father did all the talking at the endless, treasured dinners that were at the center of the family's emotional life, and that she had taken her mother for granted until her father's death, just after Virginia's birth. But this had not yet come up in the family work, although it needed to in the near future.

Father's history was also relevant to the understanding of the family but had not as yet been interwoven into the therapy. Father had grown up in a family with very little talk. He was extremely close to his father, but they related through sports almost exclusively. He still felt that his father's death ten years before was the biggest blow of his life. He had also taken his mother for granted, as apparently had his father, although they had had a loving marriage. Thus, the model for an active and assertive wife was missing for both Mr. and Mrs. Malone, although they both consciously valued Mrs. Malone's being active in the family and in her own part-time job. We can see that the legacy of this struggle was also being lived out by Virginia, whereas Jay benefited from the shared assumption of a more comfortable role for boys, especially ones who enjoy athletics as Jay did.

In regard to the handling of this session, it is interesting to see the swings of partiality during the session. It was possible for the therapist to be more aware and more relaxed about these shifts because the overall family transference to his holding capacity was sound. At one point, for instance, the focus was squarely on something the father was doing, and clearly he was squirming under the scrutiny. Even with Mother's and Virginia's triumph, this moment did not sour things. It seemed to be a sign of the health of the family's holding capacity that this momentary focus on Father could be tolerated by him and by the whole family without being turned against him. Families mold a more solid alliance with the therapist by drawing on a stronger, more flexible contextual transference. This means that the therapist can allow more deviations in being momentarily partial to one or another family member without the family holding it against either the therapist or that family member.

This family was, on the whole, quite trusting, despite the misgivings of individual members or the momentary misgivings about what the therapist was saying. Mr. Malone's resistance did not present the therapist with a gruesome struggle. His cooperation in suspending his disbelief came partly from the fact that he valued his wife's confidence in talking as a form of communication and of intimacy; he probably married her partly to fill out this missing bit of himself. Although that had been a point of conflict earlier in their marriage, it was now a source of comfort and complementarity in their partnership. Their shared transference to the containment of the family therapy benefited from this agreement. In turn, Virginia, despite her conscious reluctance, could actually trust them in trusting the therapist. It took relatively little work to get her actively involved in saying the things she had to say to her father. Once that got under way, she was more invested in the therapy, and true to the adolescent pattern with signs of cooperation, she was "less unwilling to come." What we mean by this is that with Virginia, as with many adolescents, the only sign of cooperation we ask is that their objection to coming to therapy is not too vociferous.

THE MIDPHASE AND WORKING THROUGH

Over the next months in therapy, the Malone family was able to stay with the tasks of talking to each other and of using the discussions to increase their understanding of themselves and each other. The family histories began to come into the sessions at relevant moments, and the resistance to talking and sharing could be explored. For instance, in one session, Mother was puzzled because Jay had burst into tears on two occasions that week with no apparent explanation. He had done it after asking what his two supposedly wonderful grandfathers had been like (both had died before he was born). The crying was unusual for Jay, who was a hearty, optimistic boy. In the previous weeks we had been discussing the way they had handled the discovery of Mrs. Malone's sister's cancer. Until our sessions, Mother had not mentioned it, so the family had no way of understanding why she was so upset. In the beginning of the session, this lesson in the need to talk was mentioned. In the course of the session, it emerged that Mrs. Malone was about to leave town for a business trip.

When I suggested that Jay might be expecting to feel low while she was gone, she said, "Well, the last two times I left town, it was because people we love were very sick!" She reminded us that not only had her sister discovered cancer but, three weeks earlier, her mother had been deathly ill.

I said that this began to give us a good explanation, indeed, for Jay's "unexplained tears." The family had, of course, been bombarded with illness and threats of loss, and his tears were the only outward sign. In the countertransference, I had managed to forget all about the illnesses—just as they had, emotionally. Only Jay's tears served as a disembodied reminder of the threats surrounding them.

They accepted my remarks about this, and as they went out the door, Father said, "By the way . . . Jay has a big week coming up. He is going into the hospital for a tonsillectomy."

I felt so hit by this that I pulled them back from the door and said, "No wonder he's been crying. After all the family illnesses, and with his mother away for two days, he is also facing something which would be frightening anytime. These things and Jay's upset are all related but, in your family, connecting them is painful and difficult."

The next week, they came in saying it had been a good week. Mrs. Malone said she wished they could bottle weeks like that and save them for the hard times. They did not mention the illnesses nor the operation, which apparently had gone well enough. The flaw in the week concerned Virginia's tennis match. They thought she had started poorly but dug in and played well in the second half. The match ended with a narrow loss for Virginia. They told her how well she had done and were puzzled to have her say, "I don't care." Why, when they had complimented her, had she shrugged it off hurtfully?

By this stage of the work, Virginia could speak more directly for herself. She explained that what *really* happened was that as soon as she got in the car after losing her match, her mother had said to her, "I don't want to hurt you but . . ." and then had given a list of things she could have done better.

Mr. and Mrs. Malone said that they were clear they were supposed to provide instruction for their children, or else they felt they would not be doing a good job, and when either child rejected what they said, they felt quite dejected. I said that I now understood that the parents expected Virginia to provide validation of their parenting role. When she rejected their judgment and advice, they felt defeated in trying to be good parents and actually felt as if they were bad parents (i.e., "bad objects" to her).

Through the session, I was able to clarify that Mrs. Malone knew perfectly well that Virginia did not want to hear what she had to say in such situations. Virginia, again feeling understood, added her voice to mine. Mrs. Malone returned to asking me what to do and whether it was true that giving Virginia a critique of her playing was not right.

I said, "That would be doing for you what you feel you should do for Virginia. I'd be the parent to your parenting."

"I think I see what you're saying," she said. "You are saying I should get off her case. We should get off her case!"

I could now elaborate on the parallel between Virginia's feeling that they were giving her a bad grade on tennis or schoolwork, and their feeling that Virginia was giving them a bad grade on their parenting. Then they felt she was like one of their parents being critical of them. That is when they would look to me to tell them how to do better. Earlier in the work, they had the relatively easy task of learning to set limits for Virginia without feeling consumed with guilt. Now they had the more ambitious task of trying to discover how and why she got put into the role of being a judgmental parent for the two of them. Although this was more difficult work, Mr. and Mrs. Malone acknowledged that it was easier to keep going because things were so much better at home.

The sequence of these sessions demonstrates the uneven quality of progressive work in the analytic family therapy setting. There is no straight line of progress, any more than there is in the working through of individual psychotherapy or psychoanalysis. One week's progress is obscured by the next week's surge of resistance, and even progress in one area acts partly to obscure the other gains of a previous phase. This is the stuff of psychotherapy, and it is equally true of family therapy as of any other form. Progress is not linear; it is spiral. The same ground is covered many times as the core areas of difficulty emerge. Once these are focused on, differing aspects need to be taken up until, after some time, enough of the multiplicity of determinants have been explored that the overall pattern begins to shift fundamentally. If this is the basic truth concerning individuals and the tortuous process of individual working through, how much more true it is of the family, where each of the individuals has his or her own complex internal makeup, each of which is likely to require expression before the family can move to new and higher ground or explore the threatening depths.

With adolescents, improvements in the family's capacity for holding mean an increased ability simultaneously to hold the adolescent and to promote the adolescent's "second separation-individuation" (Blos 1967). Holding, in this sense, does not mean binding the adolescent or child close to the parents but providing a context for the process of helping all family members tolerate the anxiety of the developmental process. Working through then includes increasing the family's understanding of the ways in which the flaws in their holding capacity have made it threatening for the family to tolerate the phase-appropriate individuation. The bind between Virginia and her parents had centered on this issue: Her need to function in unconscious family avenues impinged on her freedom to individuate and to deal with her age-appropriate ambivalence about her parents' and her own identity.

What keeps the family working is the experience of its members refinding each other as the family shifts to being a more containing family, one with less imposition from the projective identifications that have kept its members bound together while still isolated from each other emotionally. As each of them begins to refind lost parts, and as they discover lost or denied parts of each other, the fabric of the family begins to shift fundamentally. Their shared holding capacity enlarges and becomes more flexible and more tolerant. And the ways they use each other become more differentiated, more respectful, and usually more loving.

CHAPTER 16

Families of Divorce and Remarriage

The family facing separation, the divorcing family, the single-parent family, and the stepfamily are all variations on family living. They represent points of transition, at any one of which the family may halt temporarily or permanently on its journey from the original nuclear family to a different family organization. At each point, the family has the task of developing a design that fosters the family's holding capacity within the reality of the circumstances. In each case the task is made difficult by the intense feelings engendered in children and parents during the separation-divorce-reconstruction process. Feelings of loss and guilt, poor self-esteem, anxiety about security in relationships, extreme anger, and feelings of helplessness are to be expected. But the single most upsetting problem such families face is the parents' diminished capacity to parent while attempting to cope with the enormously preoccupying personal challenge of getting through the pain of divorce.

Children suffer from the relative withdrawal of each parent and from the disruption in their ability to work together to provide a shared holding capacity for the children. Any of these family formats has the potential to provide a holding context that feels adequate, but not while the format is simply seen as a *forme fruste* of the "ideal nuclear family." In other words, if the reality of the difference is addressed, an effective family can form, supporting its members to express their sense of loss, anxiety, and helplessness. This task is hard enough for any adult to manage alone, but the parent finds it especially difficult to be creative and supportive when self-esteem and energy are at a low ebb at the same time that the children's distress is at its peak.

The Couple Facing Separation

Despite loving intentions, biological–social ties, and sincere effort in therapy, some marriages cannot be maintained. When the couple in treatment reaches this point, we can still be helpful by recognizing courage in facing reality and encouraging expression of feelings of loss, guilt, and ambivalence without suggesting that these feelings imply a need to undo the decision. The therapist treads a fine line here between promoting working through and preventing resolution. A conclusion is reached when the partners understand the valency each of them has for inciting troublesome object relations, or when at least one of the partners has given up the marriage. The separating couple can continue to work after resolution by each seeing the therapist individually for a limited period. The separating couple rarely reaches its decision in a mutually agreed time frame, and because one of the partners may be less ready than the other, the need for individual therapy is often a practical issue that can create problems.

The Darwins had a troubled marriage. They had a marvelous sex life but little other communication. Mrs. Darwin was trying to live within the limits of Mr. Darwin's limited income, but she found the anxiety quite unbearable. Mr. Darwin was becoming quite remote, spending more and more time on tennis. He found Mrs. Darwin's outbursts of anger and entitlement to more money and time outrageous, while his withdrawal aggravated her rage. Finally, Mr. Darwin agreed to separation and division of the proceeds of the house. Each continued to see the therapist separately, Mrs. Darwin doing so for a year after Mr. Darwin stopped. Then Mrs. Darwin lost her job and could not afford to see the therapist anymore. Some months later, she became very upset when Mr. Darwin met another woman who looked just like her. He began to take this woman to social clubs and gatherings where formerly she had gone with him. She felt totally replaceable, too humiliated and hurt to go out, eventually becoming agoraphobic. Nevertheless, she got a job and contacted her former therapist, who refused to see her because now he was her husband's therapist, and he felt it was important to recognize the boundary between them. This was an additional loss that cruelly reinforced her feeling of being replaceable.

In some cases, one member of the couple will need further individual therapy, and if the other member does not object, it is quite possible to move into that. But where there is any sense of competition to keep the therapist, it is better to end when the couple work ends and to refer the individuals to colleagues. More often than not, the decision to separate is not mutually agreed upon after achieving a sense of resolution of the object relations. Our therapeutic work is hardly ever so neat. More usually, one partner has finally had it and leaves, ready or not. Then the task shifts to helping the abandoned other with feelings of grief, guilt, and sometimes envy of the one that got away. And many couples have children, which only complicates the process.

The Separating Family

When the separating couple has children, the loss is magnified, for then there is loss not just of a pairing and of the couple's ideal of forming a family but also of the reality of that ideal family. Sometimes this is so painful that the couple overlooks it. The therapist should keep the children in mind, although the couple may not. The children's lives are deeply affected by the parents' decision, for better and for worse. We are often asked by parents, "When is the best time to divorce—how old should the children be?" We have to admit that there is never a good time, nor a perfect age. The reactions will always be profound, different only in quality, depending on the child's developmental stage. These differences have been described anecdotally in great detail and variety by Tessman (1978) and Wallerstein and Kelly (1980).

In brief, we may note that younger preschool children may suffer acute regression and separation anxiety, turning to transitional objects for support, whereas slightly older preschoolers may be more capable of recognizing sadness and feeling the blow to self-esteem, using play to integrate their experiences. Younger latency-age children may become intensely distressed, fearful, or depressed and preoccupied with fantasy, and cling to or reject their parents. The older latency-age child reacts in a more openly angry way, outraged at parents who have broken the rules, and may become rebellious or perform poorly in school. Often such a child fails to observe socially appropriate conduct with friends, who may then shun the upset child. Adolescents, who are best able to comprehend the meaning of their parents' decision, experience a profound sense of loss and worry about the realities of financial support. The phase-appropriate mourning of the loss of the ideal parents of childhood and the dependency and playfulness of earlier years is compounded for them by the additional trauma of the actual loss of

the parents' relationship and the childhood home. This complicates the adolescents' imminent task of separation from the family
and introduces a worry about the adolescents' capacities to form
stable sexual relationships.

Giving the couple such information about cognitive ability
and expectable reactions at different developmental stages can be
helpful to them as separating parents. The therapist's expectation
that they will communicate with and plan for their children en-
hances the couple's holding capacity. Wallerstein and Kelly (1980),
who followed a small cohort of divorcing families, reported that
one-third of mothers and one-half of fathers were unaware of their
children's distress. They found that children's adjustment to divorce was optimal when parents anticipated and planned for their
needs and were able to explain to them what was happening and
why, in language appropriate to the child's age.

All children want to have two parents who love each other. To
preserve this fantasy, they may repress knowledge of marital dishar-
mony. In their study, Wallerstein and Kelly found that one-third of
the children had no awareness of marital strife, while the one-third
of the children who were chronically aware of it and anxious about
it were nonetheless totally unprepared for the dissolution of the
marriage. As Dicks (1967) said, "I feel that mankind despite the
cynical surface deeply values because it needs the full marital
relationship as one of its major goals, and that such a relationship
answers the need of children for a stable parental dyad united in
love as an optimal condition for their personality growth" (p. 229).
It is well worth encouraging parents to work on their marriage in
couple therapy even if the shared pathology presents an awesome
task. But sometimes there is no motivation for or possibility of
achieving compatibility with that partner. Although they will always be upset by divorce now and through the years ahead, the
children can feel relief when the parents decide to terminate an
unhappy marriage, and they can benefit from seeing their parents
make a courageous decision, especially if each later recovers from
the loss and rebuilds a life.

When Families Divorce

In the United States in 1984, 1,155,000 divorces were recorded. The
figure of the number of children affected by these divorces is not yet
available, but an estimate made in 1983 suggests that 1,091,000

children suffered the breakup of their families in one year (National Center for Health Statistics 1983, 1984). When Wallerstein and Kelly (1980) followed their cohort of divorcing families for a five-year period, they found that although improvement in the postdivorce symptoms had been recorded by the end of the first year following the divorce, by the end of five years the children were still experiencing difficulties in adjusting to the situation, leading the authors to conclude that the divorcing process has an extended timetable. No wonder parents feel such guilt over the failure of their marriages. No wonder they postpone the decision, sometimes tolerating "an astonishing degree of long-standing sexual deprivation and loneliness" (p. 14).

Under the stress of the loss of the original family, which may include loss of the home, the neighborhood, and the standard of living as well as the more fundamental relative or absolute loss of contact with one parent, the family may regress to more primitive methods of dealing with its experience. Tessman (1978) describes how the children tend to identify with some parts of the absent parent, while at the same time repudiating other parts. We have noticed that when children feel bad and rejected, they deal with their feelings by experiencing them as due to the actions of one parent. Sometimes, the absent parent is held responsible: children, and often the parents, too, project onto the parent who left all their negative feelings about the failed marriage, the loss of two married parents, and the loss of the family holding capacity. Other times, the absent parent is idealized, and all the sadness and anger is leveled at the remaining parent who could not prevent the separation.

The internal bad object finds its external locus in one parent, who is experienced as rejecting. This happens to preserve the sense of goodness and trust in the good object and to protect it from the destructive forces of the children's anger and the parents' helpless attack on their marriage. Sometimes, the good object has to be seen to reside in the at-home parent because the child feels that that is the parent who is to be depended upon. The defensive polarization is liable to switch suddenly and rapidly. Then the absent parent is longed for as an exciting object, while the at-home parent suffers a relentless attack for not being able to keep the excitement in the marriage and the spouse at home to meet the children's needs.

It is not just that the children miss Mom or Dad, although they do, even when they enjoy frequent visitation; they also miss the parents' pairing, their grown-up, caring sexual relationship that holds the family together in an atmosphere of vitality and of future security. Children feel this loss most acutely at times of transition from the household of one parent to another. At this time, the holding context of the original family is most obviously absent, and the substituting holding capacities of the single parents are seen as clearly separate. The child depending on one parent for support has the anxiety of being transferred to the care of the other at a moment when both parents are maximally anxious. Coming into proximity, each parent is then vulnerable to the resurgence of feelings of loss and resentment and lingering attraction to the spouse, as he or she is kissing their shared child goodbye or hello.

The Single-Parent Family

Single-parent families have different origins: Some arise from loss of a parent after divorce or death, while others have never had two parents; some expect to be permanent, while others are seen as temporary institutions. Those that expect to be permanent are more often part of a culture of single-head-of-household families. In that case, a positive identity and real extended family support may allow such a family to manage well. As more women decide to have a baby by a certain age whether married or not, this pattern may become more prevalent. Such families ought not to be expected to feel incomplete, but because the children always want a father and a mother united in love as parents, they will experience the family with a sense of loss anyway.

A 16-year-old girl, Susannah, living alone with her mother since the death of her father two years before, had a brief relationship with an older married man, during which she became pregnant. Mother and daughter consulted me for abortion counseling. Attempts to focus on their grief at losing the father of the family were not fruitful. Susannah agreed that the baby might be a replacement for her lost loved one, but she nonetheless insisted that if her Dad were alive he would want her to keep the baby. At first adamant that Susannah should have an abortion, her mother finally accepted Susannah's preference to keep her child. The school system was able to accommodate Susannah's needs for flexibility, and Mother decided to rearrange her work schedule to help with baby-sitting. I did not hear from Susannah again, but three years later I met with Mother, who sought help. She told me that Susannah had graduated and was working, and that the baby, Paul, had been a joy. The reason she was in tears now was that she had met a man she wanted to marry, and she felt unbearably sad and guilty at leaving her grandchild to go on with her own life. Susannah, however, encouraged her to do so, feeling able to manage by herself now.

This single-parent family was unusual in that Mother supported her daughter but did not take over as mother of her grandchild too. So often the teenage mother is not competent to mother her child unless given a lot of support, which tends to undercut her confidence. For any toddler, the loss of his grandmother as a support for his single mother, direct playmate for him, and substitute for his missing father is immense. More often, future progression to life in a married family is made by the young mother and her child. Leaving the grandparent's home and interrupting the close living relationship is then also a circumstance of loss for the child, even though developmental progress is being made.

Dr. C. consulted us about the Donaldson family. Mrs. Donaldson, a schizophrenic woman just discharged from the hospital, was referred to him for individual psychiatric aftercare. Social service workers were supervising her home in order to protect her 10-year-old son, against whom she had had murderous wishes when she was psychotic. Dr. C. had elected to combine family therapy with individual therapy, focusing on medication adjustment and anxiety about getting a job. Mrs. Donaldson, who resented her psychiatrist's interest in her family, forgot to bring the family to sessions or used the family treatment situation to discuss her own concerns. When this envy was interpreted to her, she became able to allow the family members to express themselves.

Life was hard for all of them. When Mr. Donaldson had left the family six years before, he had taken two older children to live with him in another part of town. The two families had had no contact since. Mrs. Donaldson had not been able to work for two and a half years, and her welfare check did not go far enough to maintain her car or buy her clothes. Lizzie, the 16-year-old, was furious at her mother's passivity and poverty, angrily complaining about never getting a new dress for a prom. Micky, the 10-year-old, was hyperactive and unable to concentrate at school. Dr. C. described how Micky flew around the office like a dingbat, quite beyond his mother's control or tolerance. Once on Ritalin, however, he settled down and became more of a contributor to family meetings. Lizzie stopped pestering her mother to get work and got a job herself. She bought her own clothes and car but did not contribute to the family expenses.

The therapist experienced enormous feelings of helplessness and rejection in his dealings with the Donaldsons. In attempting to contain these, he might become rather passive himself; or when he roused himself to activity, he might become impatient and judgmental, trying to get the family to shape up, like a father who comes in as the "heavy." Sometimes he would collude with Mrs. Donaldson's wish to capture him for herself by agreeing to lengthy telephone calls. He was aware of Mrs. Donaldson's erotic feelings toward him, but she was so contemptuous of him that he felt unsure of his evidence.

Instead of commenting on Mrs. Donaldson's wishes toward him, he observed how much they all wanted someone like him to fill in for the missing father by being Mother's companion and the children's disciplinarian, because they could not bear to feel how much they missed the father and husband. Much scoffing greeted this interpretation, but there then followed a period of work in which Mrs. Donaldson began to speak sadly about her dependence on her former husband and on her Dad who had recently died, grieving for both of them.

Then Lizzie, displacing the transference and also moving beyond it, got herself a boyfriend with money, whom the family sheltered and welcomed as a savior—until he threatened to establish a sexual relationship in the house with Lizzie. At the same time Mrs. Donaldson got a boyfriend, but he was sexually rather timid, and Mrs. Donaldson felt jealous of Lizzie. Micky, the 10-year-old, was jealous of Mother's boyfriend. On a pleasant outing with him, Micky threw up all over the bus and said he had been poisoned. He reverted to crawling into Mother's bed again, or perhaps this habit was being noticed now that Mother had more reason to confront him than before, when she was glad of his warm body beside her. Micky wanted not only to occupy a position that would prevent Mother from taking her man into her bed but to chaperone Mother's individual sessions with her psychiatrist.

Mrs. Donaldson had trouble insisting on Micky managing by himself at night and could not assert any authority over Lizzie's comings and goings either. Her longing not to be a single parent led her to accept her daughter and her boyfriend as substitute parents for the family, until she realized how inappropriate that was for Lizzie. Then Mother threw him out of the house with all the disgust of a child who has just learned that her parents have sex. This opened up the barely concealed rivalry between mother and daughter and the pain each felt about the other, Mother unable to share her daughter's success and daughter unable to bear her mother's depression.

This family illustrates a number of features of the single-parent family that forms after divorce. In this case the loss of the previous family and of the husband/father was added to by the loss of the grandfather, upon whom the abandoned family had leaned. Mrs. Donaldson, receiving little gratification from any adult social, sexual, or work relationship, turned to her children, as many single parents do. The generational boundaries are unclear and cannot be drawn by simple directives for restructuring. Oedipal-level dynamics were present in the Donaldson family, but the basic anxiety about supplies of food and money interfered with the family's working through at the oedipal developmental level. In many single-parent families, the members worry about being taken care of or being able to take care of themselves. The therapist may be viewed as a nurturing figure who has everything the family wants to have. Whether male or female, the therapist is liable to be related to as the mate of the single parent. This is useful in two ways: It establishes support for the parent's authority by recreating an adult coalition, and it draws into consciousness the longing for such a pairing that has not been achieved in family life outside of treatment. Mourning may then be allowed to happen. The therapist has the task of containing rather than rescuing such a family until it can reorganize to meet the developmental needs of its members within its present reality as a single-parent family.

Single-parent families are often poor, which complicates their disadvantage, but many well-off families are in the single-parent situation, too. When basic supplies are met, anxieties about differentiation and satisfaction of needs can still be seen, now in pure interpersonal form.

Mrs. LaBrie and her daughter, Natalie, came to see me together. Indeed, Natalie refused to come alone, telling her mother that she hated to talk to people like counselors. "Together or not at all," she said. Mr. LaBrie had separated from them in the course of a mid-life crisis in which he became preoccupied with finding himself. As yet, he had not resolved his ambivalence about his future plans, but he provided generously for his family. Both parents were bright, hardworking academics, but Natalie was failing in school despite good intellect.

From my meeting with them, I could not have assessed Natalie's cognitive skills. Mother spoke anxiously about Natalie's school performance, whereas Natalie seemed unconcerned. Mother would raise all the questions, and when Natalie looked dumb, Mother would answer them herself. Natalie would say, "No, that's not right," but instead of explaining her point of view she would then listen as Mother tried another approach. Natalie projected all her verbal competence and her anxiety into her mother, while Mother asked all the questions that applied equally well to herself as if they were only about Natalie. They got into tussles that had to do with separating from each other and struggling against the mutual projections. This situation was aggravated by the loss of the father, whose presence tended to interrupt this symbiosis. But the basis for the problem predated the separation, when Father was too preoccupied with work and left Mother and daughter to meet each other's needs.

Mother at times would police the child's bedroom, acting as a motivating parent and alarm clock. At other times, when Mother felt Natalie had to be responsible for her own life as a teenager, she would warn Natalie she had to get herself up in the morning. But when Mother would sleep late, so would Natalie. Mother reported (while Natalie nodded) that Natalie complained that Mother said she was her roommate when it suited her and at other times would claim to be her mother.

In this case, the generational boundary was inconsistently maintained not because of lack of understanding of the roles but because of unresolved separation and individuation issues between mother and daughter.

The Family after Remarriage

The divorced single-parent family and the remarried family are built upon loss. Their existence depends on previous destruction to the parental relationship. This makes for grief and guilt. If these emotions can be recognized as such and worked with, the family will be able to function. But it is more usual to find the grief and guilt expressed in clinging to the memory of the absent parent, defensive rejection of the stepparent, and self-destructive or annoying behavior that seeks punishment. The new family differs from the old family not just in composition but in its history. It may also differ in neighborhood, financial circumstances, and everyday living experience.

Working with families of remarriage calls for a model appropriate to their unique circumstances and characteristics. Unless these are considered in making the treatment plan, therapy will not address reality. There is no point in treating a family as if it were a nuclear family when it is actually a part of a wider family. Yet there is considerable pressure from many stepfamilies to disregard their situation. They prefer their stepfamily status to be ignored because of their shame about their identity and the life history it implies.

Stepfamily Invisibility

Stepfamilies prefer to remain undetected, blending in with the other "regular" families. This is referred to by the Vishers in their book *Stepfamilies* (1979) as "the invisibility of the stepfamily." As the Vishers point out, there has been a lag between the statistical facts of divorce and remarriage and the acceptance of their occurrence in the lives of families. They note that currently in the United States one in three marriages is a remarriage, and that one in seven children can expect to have a stepparent. Yet, until the mid-1970s, there was little written about stepfamilies; stepfamilies and professionals colluded to support the invisibility of the stepfamily. We think that this happened to avoid painful knowledge of the destruction of a previous family.

Some stepfamilies pretend to be original families so as not to excite comment at school or elsewhere outside the family. Some stepfamilies deny their difference even to themselves, so that the stepparent takes the place of the original parent not as a substitute but in such a way as to obliterate the original.

Nancy was 8 when her mother died of breast cancer. Her attractive middle-aged father soon met and began to live with a girlfriend fifteen years younger than he was, who was very kind to Nancy. Nancy had suffered through a very difficult relationship with her mother, who had been chronically psychotic and, among other feelings, was somewhat relieved at her death. She said, "Life goes on." She eagerly connected with her father's girlfriend, Elizabeth, and prayed that her father and Elizabeth would marry.

After they did marry, they all decided that Nancy would call

Elizabeth "Mom." Some months later, Elizabeth adopted Nancy, now 11. They moved to a new city where no one knew the story. When Nancy started at a new school, she did not mention her adoption and preferred to let her friends think that her Mom was her biological mother. They did indeed look quite alike, but friends would ask, "How come your Mom looks so young?" At supermarkets, checkout girls would remark at the youthful likeness, and Elizabeth and Nancy would rather enjoy the secret.

I saw them some years later when Elizabeth was pregnant and Nancy seemed withdrawn and irritable. Nancy was ostensibly thrilled about the expected baby but focused her fears on her classmates' questions. They might say, "How come your Mom is having a baby after all these years?" Nancy's unconscious fear was that the biological baby would displace her, the adopted stepchild. In my office, Nancy and Mother faced the facts of the different status between a natural child and an adopted stepchild. Nancy was reassured of Elizabeth's continuing love and brightened up. As soon as they all felt reassured, they elected to maintain the illusion that Elizabeth was simply Nancy's mother, and they rejected further treatment.

Unresolved Mourning

After divorce, the new family is composed of two families, one clustered around the father and one around the mother. These families differ from each other by as much as the irreconcilable differences between the parents. One family may have parents and children living together, whereas the other family may be a single parent with occasionally visiting children. Obviously, the lifestyles afforded the two families may be worlds apart. Whether or not there is shared custody, the child is a member of two households, each of which tends to prefer to obliterate the other. Therapy needs to address this denial and to help the families exist as part of a wider family in order to confirm the child's reality. This can be done by seeing both families and by paying attention to the transitions between homes. Because mourning is perceived as a threat to the new family, it is often blocked. Therapy helps the family to develop a capacity for mourning, which is essential to the new family's growth.

The Cordoza family consisted of father, Fred, mother, Marge, and their two boys, Bruce, who was Fred's child, and Larry, who was

Marge's child, each from former marriages. Larry's father did not support him, lived out of state, and rarely saw him. Bruce's mother, who lived with a farming family in the same state, took Bruce every other weekend. I had not yet discovered the importance of seeing both families, and my sessions were only with the Cordozas, including Bruce and Larry.

One Sunday night, Marge got mad at Bruce for making Larry move away from the computer so that he could have a turn. He would not listen to her and instead began bashing all the keys at once. Marge finally pulled him off the chair. Then Fred arrived and accused her of being violent. Bruce said, "Well, you let Larry use the computer, so why not me?"

At first, they talked about Bruce not doing what his stepmother said, and about Bruce not being trusted with machines because, unlike Larry, he would not treat them carefully. I registered the fact that this event had occurred on Sunday night and was wondering if Bruce had been away at his mother's. So I asked what had been going on before this. Marge was already mad at Bruce for coming home late from his mother's, for being grumpy as if he had not had enough sleep, and for dirtying the living room with straw and mud from his boots. She and Fred were both mad at Bruce's mother for failing to supervise him adequately, whereas Bruce was delighted with the visit to his mother, feeling that he had had a great time doing farm work with her and playing until he felt like going to bed without worrying about being a mess. Marge was concerned that Bruce go to school with matching clothes and clean shoes, which was not the way his mother had raised him.

Although it was quite reasonable for Marge to prefer Bruce to shed his gear in the basement and behave in ways appropriate to their townhouse life-style, Bruce could not keep separate the two kinds of existence when unconsciously he longed to merge them. At the moment of returning home, he was still longing for his mother and holding on to her through bits of mud and hay. His "bad" behavior provoked Marge to be a "bad" mother, which emphasized the image of the "good" mother he was missing. The child was in the midst of two cultures in collision, for which the bashing keys was an apt metaphor. His comment, "But you let Larry do it" pointed to the fantasy that everything will be easy for the natural child.

Therapy was aimed at helping the family acknowledge, despite their criticisms of her, the validity of Bruce's attachment to the other parent and her living situation. It helped Larry to empathize with Bruce's conflict. This would otherwise have been difficult for Larry, who did not experience loyalty conflict because his own father was so negligent. He was able to acknowledge that what seemed like having it easy was actually a situation of loss. Both boys were able to help each other mourn, and the parents were helped to tolerate it without feeling their new life was thereby diminished.

Ambiguity and Permeability of Boundaries

Another feature of the stepfamily that requires attention is the ambiguity and permeability of boundaries.

Mary Beth's divorced parents were worried about her sudden drop in grades and felt it related to difficulties they were having in adjusting to their divorce. Although usually charming, lately she had been forgetful and crabby. She seemed not to listen. Any disagreement between her parents seemed to upset her. Her parents were aware of their bitterness and dislike for each other and were not ready to give up doing things to goad one another. But both sincerely wanted to avoid upsetting Mary Beth with this. Although both wanted a consultation on how to manage the situation, they had to be seen separately because one parent feared the entire consultation was a manipulation to force them to be together.

Mary Beth (aged 13) lived primarily with her mother, and yet the parents shared custody. She had her own room, television, and toys at her father's. His house was close by, permitting easy access. The time Mary Beth could spend at her father's was spelled out in an agreement, which, however, was open to misinterpretation. The parents argued over the definition of a weekend and a holiday, particularly a holiday weekend. This happened because Mother felt Father was always trying to establish an equal rather than a secondary home for Mary Beth and because Father felt Mary Beth was being tied to a smothering mother. Mary Beth was her mother's confidante and stayed up late at her house. Father and his wife alternated between including Mary Beth in grown-up dates to fancy places and expecting her to go to bed at a reasonably early hour. This illustrates the ambiguity of the boundary between parent and child, where at times Mary Beth seemed to be of the same generation as the parent.

Transition times and practical arrangements were very difficult, both because Mother got anxious and because Father was often late. So the time boundary was ambiguous. Then Father might walk in the house, claiming his right to do so because he was still part-owner. So the space boundary was not honored either. Furthermore, if Mother confronted Father about not sending his support check, Mary Beth left with an image of her parents divorced but still connected in angry exchanges. On a weekend at Father's, Mother might call with an urgent request that Mary Beth be returned for an evening to meet some important relatives. If Father agreed, he felt imposed upon, and when he did not agree, his plans got spoiled anyway because Mary Beth would be unable to relax. It worked the other way, too. Although he had agreed to have Mary Beth on certain dates, Father might have to go on a business trip. He then assumed that Mary Beth should return home to her mother without respect for Mother's right to make plans for herself.

Consultation focused on developing clearer boundaries and giving Mary Beth more support and responsibility for the transitions, allowing her to bicycle over to her father's sometimes. The parents agreed not to pass the check or discuss money in front of Mary Beth. They agreed to remain responsible for alternative care of Mary Beth in sudden absence if the other parent could not help out. They agreed to a rather rigid guarding of the weekend time, which they found necessary at this stage. Mary Beth's school performance improved within a month—without therapy.

Financial Strain

Many families of divorce or remarriage are under financial strain. This gives an edge to much of the resentment. At the same time, the children often appear greedy for material things, complaining to one parent that the other does not provide. For instance, Mary Beth's mother gave her an adequate allowance, but her father would buy expensive gifts that made a mockery of it. Children often show material acquisitiveness when insecure about the love of the parents, as if things to hold on to can make up for the security they do not have.

Apart from its effects on the family, the financial situation must be dealt with realistically when consultation or therapy is proposed, so that it is clear which parent should receive the bill. It is not wise to start work on the promise that the absent parent will pay for it. Quite apart from the problem of not getting paid for work done, it can engender hope and interest in the work that is then dashed. Moreover, it is best to assess what the family can afford, bearing in mind that a conjoint family session for each family and an individual session for the index patient may be indicated but may be impractical financially. Because we feel this format is crucial, however, we may reduce the fee or refer to a clinic or a therapist who can offer a lower fee that permits the correct frequency of visits.

The Couple's Relationship

The couple's relationship is under stress from many sources. Neighbors and friends are usually unable to remain friendly to both divorced parents and choose one to side with, most usually the mother. The father is often cut adrift from former friends of the couple and from his neighborhood. If he remarries, he probably depends on his new wife's circle of friends, some of whom will be suspicious of his divorced status. Others will compare him to her former husband or previous men friends. If the mother remarries and moves, she faces a similar situation of loss of community support. If her new husband moves into the old house, neighbors may feel uncomfortable about that. When relating to the children's schools, stepparents may feel awkward about the legitimacy of their authority.

Financial strain is an issue, too, in the remarried family. Most arguments among remarried couples are over money and children's behavior. The money issue is closely tied to threat from the former spouse. The couple fears retaliation in the form of withdrawal of child support or pestering for a share of the remarried family's emotional riches in financial terms.

In a call-in radio program on remarriage, it was my job to discuss the comments made by three remarried couples. Halfway through, I found I had to say, "This show is on remarriage. But what we've been discussing is the management of children." The couples laughed and admitted that this consumed their energy. They felt they did not have enough private time to enjoy each other because they had to work to earn money to support the family (often more than one) and because there was a tremendous amount of organization, management of comings and goings, and simply getting used to the behavior of children raised by different standards. Also, they had not had the year or so of time alone as a couple before the gradual arrival of children as in first marriages. Instead, they were thrown into a ready-made family with preexisting attachments. One man stated that he had had to make a statement to his children that he loved them as much as ever but they had better understand that his remarriage was primary and his overall family was secondary to this. He meant that his remarriage was at the center of his life, and so it had to be at the center of his family, to whom he wished to offer the experience of being a loving family with him and his new wife. But his daughter had been outraged, and it had taken considerable time to work things out. Audience response was on the side of the displaced daughter, with whom irate listeners had clearly identified.

The couple experiences attacks from the children, who are jealous of the new relationship. This may take the form of a child's inability to sleep, so that the couple's envied intimacy will be interrupted by their concern for the awake, nervous child. The insecurity of the parental relationship in the predivorce years often leaves the child with a need to test the new bond. The new couple is often perceived as a new edition of the parental couple of the oedipal-age child. In addition, because the stepparent joins an existing group much as a new baby does, the remarried couple may be perceived as a nursing couple. Like the mother and infant, the newly remarried parents are preoccupied with each other and with the formation of their own bond. The new stepparent is seen as a child who is getting the ultimate gratification and is, therefore, the object of wonder, envy, and hate. Just as the older child who is insecure about its parents' love when a baby arrives hates the rival newcomer rather than the parents for having the new baby, so the child may hate the stepparent rather than risk expressing hate, disappointment, and loss to the parent.

The marital partners are also threatened from within by their guilt about what they have, compared to the previous or other parent's family. Because of this, they are ready targets for a guilt-provoking assault from an unhappy, deprived child. Their reparative wishes are often strong but can be frustratingly spoiled by an ungrateful child. The couple needs help in therapy not to feel compelled to make it up to the child of divorce to fulfill their own needs for guilt reduction but, rather, to help the child face reality.

Role Stress for the Child

During the period after divorce or death, there is sometimes a pulling together of parent and child for warmth and comfort, each to some extent replacing the lost spouse or parent for the other and recreating a facsimile of the missed marital relationship. There may be an excited, guilty aspect to this, echoing oedipal triumph and displacement of the powerful mother or father. When the parent remarries, the child often feels dreadfully let down and experiences this loss and the original loss all over again. The child may look like the absent parent, more so as he or she matures in adolescence. This may be threatening to the couple, facing them with a constant physical representative of the ex-spouse. It is also hard for the child, who is conflicted over his or her emerging identity anyway but especially so when it threatens the parental couple. On the one hand, the child may enjoy the power and deliberately emphasize similarities; on the other hand, the child may hide them under self-disguising clothes or hair.

Many children maintain a fantasy of the reunion of their original parents for years. Remarriage confronts them with the unlikelihood of that fantasy, which may yet persist as a comforting secret that denies the importance of the remarried parents' lives. All children want two parents who love each other, but they mean the original two, not two pairs of remarried parents. If they accept reality, they then face the loss of their attachment to the original parental couple and an enormous ambivalence about their need for relationship to a loving, sexually bonded pair. They usually experience an aggravation of sexual curiosity, jealousy, and destructive attacks on the bonding.

Jerry's mother had raised him by herself, unsupported by his father, who had killed himself during an LSD trip. She was a compulsive person who dealt with her loss and anger at being abandoned by working very hard and devoting herself to her son, spending every evening at home doing homework and playing with him. Consciously, he longed for a father. After many years alone, Mother met a man she liked and developed a relationship with him. Jerry was apparently thrilled and enjoyed playing sports with him. When the man began to sleep over, Jerry became unable to sleep at night, obsessed by whether "they were doing it." He felt displaced from his mother by her boyfriend, but he also felt displaced from mother by his own intense longing for and new relationship to her boyfriend.

Role Stress for the Stepparent

Although some stepparents have had stepparents themselves, the majority are without role models. They do not know how to do the stepparenting work and have to learn on the job. Their interpretations of the role vary from that of friend to substitute parent. If the role suits the family, then all is well. In the families that seek treatment, the stepparent is usually the most uncomfortable in the area of discipline. What works best is for the stepparent to be a secondary or backup parent, one step removed from the child, following through on discipline set by the parent and sharing in discussion but leaving the major decisions to the parent and the ex-spouse. This can leave the child protesting at not getting a direct relationship with the stepparent as parent, but it is better than exposing the stepparent to becoming a transference object for projected ambivalence that derives from the difficult aspects of the relationship with the original parents. The stepparent does not have the alliance with the child nor the history of early attachment with which to work all that through. Some brave families do suffer but manage nevertheless to finally get through this.

The negative projection onto the stepparent is the hardest thing to bear. The community's relation to the stepparent continues to be influenced by the Cinderella myth. That myth, however, arose from experience in our culture. Aggression that the child feels toward his or her parents for not loving each other and keeping the family together cannot be expressed to the remaining real parent, who, it is feared, may also leave. Instead, the child hates the stepparent. For the stepparent, provocative, angry behavior is hard to absorb without responding in kind. Even a well-adjusted adult with good intentions toward the child may feel increasingly nasty and behave in punitive ways that soon lead to the feeling that the Cinderella myth is true. The stepparent feels alienated from him or herself, functioning with a part of the personality that is experienced as "not me." In this case, self-esteem is understandably low. Understanding this painful experience helps stepparents bear the emotional states of mind evoked in them through projective identification. Discussing the experience helps them to avoid identifying with the projections so that they do not become trapped in a hateful "not-me" experience.

Stepparenting is particularly hard on people who have not had their own children. Not only do they have the stress of being the outsider in a ready-made family, seen as the rival and the unauthorized disciplinarian, but they have no experience of living with children at all.

Arthur Newsome was 40 and lived alone in an orderly apartment. Then he married Molly, a woman with two children, Helen

(13) and Billy (14). Their father did not support them and Arthur was ready to step in and share their support with Molly. His income helped to improve the house. But soon he grew irritated with the children's noise and mess, and they got mad at him for being picky. Feeling like a stranger in the house, he would retreat to the bedroom to recapture the peace of his old existence. Molly was exhausted mediating between him and the children, trying to prove that they were not all that awful while pleading with the children to do as Arthur wanted.

We talked about this endless dispute in family sessions. I asked what kind of child Arthur had been. He had been an obedient child, accepting work and hardship as his father had insisted. Now he was a tightly controlled adult. After this session, Arthur got so angry at Bill's disobedience that he was overcome with a terrifying anger and hit him, much to everyone's surprise. In the next family meeting, Arthur remembered that he had had a similar feeling of wanting to strike out only once and that was in relation to his father. It happened when his father told him he was going to be punished for failing to carry in wood. Arthur had evidently suppressed his rage at his father's power over him, instead becoming like him—a rigidly controlled, successful person. It is likely that Arthur would have had difficulty dealing with a natural child when this repressed object relation returned. But in the stepfamily, it emerged suddenly full-blown in relation to a provocative adolescent without the tempering love between father and son built up over the childhood years.

Despite Arthur's genuine remorse, which was so great that he promptly began his own individual therapy, Bill was furious that he had been hit. He said that he had felt like killing Arthur. He wished he could live with his real father, who had never hit him. Molly said that, in truth, his father had often hit him. Then we were able to understand how Bill had provoked Arthur to behave more like his father, at the same time finding an excuse to reject Arthur in favor of his falsely idealized memory of his absent father.

A Treatment Model as a Denial of Reality

It was when I was working with the Newsomes that I learned the importance of keeping the wider family in mind.

We had been working together for almost a year, making progress on defining the nature of Arthur's authority. Molly had become more assertive as a parent, and together, they were able to support the growth of the children according to their values. Then the children began lying and staying up late again. As we spoke, the children sat very close together, excitedly poking, elbows bumping, and playing footsie with each other. Bill was drawing and covering his page with the words "Bill" and "Home." Summer was approaching, and the parents were anxious about unsupervised days, except for one week when the children would be going to California for a week. The children were reluctant to go and complained that they would have to share a room. To my surprise, I learned that they were going with their father, as they did for a week every year. I had accepted the family's identity as a stepfamily with a totally absent natural father. I said that they must long to exclude him because of their anger at his nonsupport of the children. The children talked of the ordeal of spending the week with him, because he would be drunk most of the time, and yet they enjoyed the beach. I was looking at Bill's drawing with "Bill" and "Home" written on it, thinking how frightened he must be about leaving home, but fortunately, I did not say so. I asked him about the words and what he made of them.

In astonishment, he replied, "It's my name, of course, Bill Home!" I felt quite stunned. I had never thought of him as having his own last name at all.

Obviously, this was not merely oversight on my part: I had gone along with the denial of the wider reality of the stepfamily. At the moment of revelation of his name, I realized that Bill's and Helen's identities had not been validated in treatment. This must have been contributing to the children's resistance to family treatment. How could it be helpful to discuss issues of everyday living when their reality was fundamentally not understood?

In Search of a Treatment Model Designed for Stepfamilies

This was the case that led to the development of the treatment model we now prefer. If possible, we meet with both families separately and with the child alone. Now, in the Newsomes' case, presumably Mr. Home would not accept treatment with his children. But the fact that he had been asked and turned it down would establish the importance of the children's identity and the nature of their relationship to their father as crucial issues requiring work. If there is no index child patient, we may see the children alone anyway to discuss their situation of moving between the two families and their independent areas of concern, such as school, peer and social relations, and sports life. Or we may simply see each family alternately, the children being seen with each family. The model offers the therapist as a vehicle with which the children can move between two often disparate areas of family experience and suggests hope for integrating these complex relationships at the centers of the children's personalities.

The example that follows is an account of this model of family treatment, showing the importance of seeing both parents and stepparents.

THE WILSON-HALL STEPFAMILY

Annie Wilson's mother, Mrs. Hall, was worried about Annie, age 14, who was failing in school, drinking to excess, and smoking dope. Her stepfather was concerned that she could not say "No" to anyone. When angry, she would stay silent and had on two occasions scratched her wrists. Her father, Mr. Wilson, felt she was quite open with him, but he was concerned about her school performance. Father, mother, and stepfather were all quite successful government lawyers who valued hard work toward professional goals and lived in a fashionable integrated downtown neighborhood. As blacks, they were upset that Annie rejected black boys and dated only whites or Orientals. Annie's attitude was a puzzle.

Annie experienced difficulty at school in literature and history but not mathematics. Psychological testing by a black psychologist revealed substantial intellectual potential, but the depression of her verbal scores indicated that Annie might have difficulty in articulating her thoughts and feelings. The Rorschach revealed a pattern of acting out conflict. The test results also suggested that her limited ability for abstract thinking would limit the usefulness of individual insight-oriented psychotherapy and that she might make more progress in family therapy, where the discussion of relationships and feelings would be more tangible.

Yet in her individual psychiatric diagnostic meeting, Annie was hungry to talk to me. She was preoccupied with themes of separation, rejection, and reunion. She had a tendency to use aggressive impulses to organize herself, as she did when she scratched her wrists. She viewed herself as needing admiration and caretaking. As part of the diagnostic process, I saw Annie with her sister, Cheryl, 16, her mother, and her stepfather. Then I saw her with her sister and father. In both families, Annie tended to be silent while the others tried "to get inside her head," until Cheryl would take over and speak angrily and provocatively. The family's only way to control this phenomenon (of which Cheryl was aware) was to let Cheryl leave.

Both families accepted a conjoint treatment plan. They preferred to work with me rather than be referred to a black therapist. (Racial differences and attitudes would be addressed during treatment, but because they are not central to the stepfamily issues, they are not focused on in this vignette.) Annie would see me once a week in individual psychotherapy. Once every two weeks, I would meet with the Hall family—Mother, Stepfather Bob, Annie, and Cheryl: and every other week, at the same time, I would work with the Wilson family—Father, Annie, and Cheryl. All the parents were enthusiastic; Cheryl seemed antagonistic to the plan, as she already had a therapist, but Annie agreed to try it. The parents, who were unusual in having little conflict over financial matters, agreed that the father would pay me directly, that both would file for insurance, and then the mother would pay him half the coinsurance amount.

The Wilson Family Meetings. At the first meeting with Father and the girls, Cheryl did not attend. Annie reported that Cheryl was too upset to come because she had gotten into a fight with her stepfather. At the next meeting with Father, Cheryl complained about my style, both finding me too silent and not liking what I said, namely that she might have provoked the fight with Stepfather that led to her missing the chance to talk with her father at the previous meeting.

At the next meeting with Father, Annie came dressed in white and Cheryl in black. Annie began cosily talking to her Dad about her first session with him, the meeting from which Cheryl had been absent. Cheryl was curled low on the sofa. But when Father began to talk to her, Cheryl in black uncurled and sat up, and Annie in white lay down and curled up. I said that Father had to talk with one girl at a time, perhaps because each longed to have a pairing relationship with him so she would not have to bother with the jealousies and competition of a threesome. Cheryl said she would happily drop out, but her stepfather kept making her come. She said she was not comfortable, there was not enough feedback, she was not learning, and it was a waste of time. That was why she was so mad at her stepfather for making her come, and when she complained about it, he hit her. She went on to describe her annoyance at her stepfather.

I said, "The family is letting Cheryl talk about her family life with Stepfather and Mother, because of a fear that . . ."

But I got no further. Cheryl interrupted to say, "You a psychiatrist? Where did you train? Do you know Letitia? Letitia, my therapist? She knows you."

I felt Cheryl was struggling to link me as a colleague of her black therapist so she would not see us as being at odds. I now engaged with Cheryl quite directly, as I felt it was necessary to build trust with her and I felt that my individual alliance with Annie was strong enough to permit it. I also felt she might be replaying her loyalty conflict between Father and Stepfather in the transference to me and her own therapist.

Father interrupted us: "To get back to where you were, Cheryl, you find your stepfather too controlling of you, right?"

I intervened: "You speak as if Cheryl has a problem being told what to do by her stepfather and not by you. But is that what you've noticed?"

Father replied, "Well, yes, her stepfather has more responsibility for her than I do. I'm not the adult male on the spot, except when they're on vacation with me in Florida."

I said, "You've committed yourself and your girls to this treatment contract, and one of them isn't necessarily going to be showing up."

"Gotcha there!" said Annie.

Father said, "Well, I expected that Cheryl wouldn't always come. There are things I'd like to discuss with Annie, but the more I come here, the more I see there are things I want to work out with you, too, Cheryl. I guess I'm contradicting myself, but I want you here. For instance, you don't return my phone calls, and you often sound condescending."

Cheryl rebutted, but Father stuck to his point. When he seemed to be getting irritated with her, Cheryl got mad—again at her stepfather. I confronted Cheryl about getting mad at her stepfather when she was here talking with and being pressed by her father. I said, "Perhaps you are afraid to get mad at your Dad." She said, "No, I'm mad at my stepfather for telling me what to do." I said, "It could be that you are really mad at your Dad, whose absence has led to your having to deal with a stepfather. And that's why your stepfather is the one telling you what to do now." Cheryl, a very bright girl, could not understand. Father paraphrased it for her, "You are pissed at me for leaving and causing a stepfather to come into your life." Cheryl began to cry. She said, "Dad, I'll tell you what I'm mad at. I asked you for $300 toward my computer and you said you couldn't afford the last $100, but right after that, you bought yourself a new camera. And you go, 'How do you like this?' and I go, 'Great, how much did it cost?' and you go '$500,' and I go 'OK.' I'll tell you: I *never* want anything from you."

They worked together on these feelings, Annie joining in now. They came to some understanding of Father's need to balance his own needs with providing extras for the children. And Father talked of his regret that he could not have been there daily during their growing up. He said that he loved them and he wanted to keep in touch, to know what mattered to them, and that's why it was important to spend time together every week. He was earnest and concerned, I thought, but the girls said they knew it was superficial. They kept criticizing his notion of "just spending time." They said, "You know nothing about us. You're not involved." He said, "That's why you have to come and talk to me." "No," they said, "You have to come and watch us play lacrosse and come to school parent meetings; then you'll know us." He said, "But you never invite me. You could call and say, 'Hey, Dad, come over on Tuesday for the game.'" The girls thought their father should be involved and know what was going on as their mother did. They resented having to educate him in his parent role. He felt excluded by their mother's management of their lives. Having given up so much authority to their stepfather, he found it difficult to feel he had a right to be there. His necessary participation in family therapy supported his parental authority and emphasized the existence of the girls' family with him as a current reality.

The Hall Family Meetings. Meantime, the Halls were also meeting. Although it did at first appear that Bob, the stepfather, was the one who told the girls what to do, later it became apparent that his disciplinary ideas were not followed. The couple had a rather liberal curfew system and were always willing to rescue Annie from late night drunken crises. They did not clamp down on Annie as she feared. Cheryl spoke loudly and angrily against Bob's right to control her life, and yet the only control I could be sure of was that he got Annie to family therapy. Cheryl criticized me, too. I felt she had to spoil Annie's therapist and Mother's husband. Annie was quiet in the family meetings, although she listened. But she talked nonstop in individual sessions, recreating a dyad that was gratifying for herself and for the family. The family tended to operate in a series of dyads, perhaps replacing the original broken marriage and the parent–child dyads from the predivorce years.

Annie came to life the day the family talked about Grandma. I had not realized the Hall family meeting was incomplete. Grandma, an 84-year-old alcoholic, lived in the basement and came upstairs to cook or eat and talk. Annie hated her. She had never wanted Grandma to live with them and was mad that her mother had taken her in anyway. She felt her mother did more for Grandma than for her, now and going back to third grade.

Bob felt it was the family's responsibility to shelter the woman who had raised Mrs. Hall. Mother wished she had not taken her in but could not find a satisfactory solution. I suggested Grandma should also come to sessions, but they rejected the idea, saying that their family therapy should be something just for them, not something dominated, as was their life, by drunken Grandma. Annie's drunkenness was seen as her being just like Grandma, and Mother and Stepfather worried that Annie, too, might become alcoholic.

In further sessions, Cheryl again expressed resistance to coming. I interpreted that she might be speaking for others who could have mixed feelings they were not owning up to. Mother then spoke very directly and assertively about her feelings toward me. She knew that I was an analytic family therapist and, therefore, thought that I was too cold and silent. Yet when she thought over sessions, I had not been so. She expected me to be remote, but when she called me on the telephone, she reached me and found me helpful. She had worried that because I was white I would not understand their culture, and yet she had not found me ignorant or unsympathetic. She felt my payment arrangements were very rigid, and yet, when she had discussed a delay in their insurance reimbursement, I had not pressed for money on time. She felt confused and thought that she should say so. I chose not to explore this transference as an individual focused transference. Instead, I took up the family's shared contextual transference. I thanked her for taking responsibility for these feelings, so we now knew Cheryl was not alone. Cheryl, agreeing with her mother's findings, was quite reassuring to her about me as a therapist and complained less about attending further sessions. Shortly after this, Mother was assertive enough to confront her mother, and arrange for her detoxification and admission to inpatient treatment.

Annie eventually stopped drinking but continued to work in

individual therapy on her problems relating to friends, most of whom drank. In family meetings with her mother and stepfather, she spoke openly of her wish to have Grandmother placed in a home. When this finally did occur, she became much more assertive, challenging her mother and stepfather about their policies, which they found a welcome relief from her previous passivity and noncompliance.

An Alternating Combined and Conjoint Family Therapy Model

Children of divorce and remarriage benefit particularly from a combined and conjoint family therapy model: The children are seen with Mother and her family and then with Father and his family. The index patient may be seen in individual therapy as well. This model maximizes the child's opportunity to integrate and yet differentiate the separate family experiences. The families work in therapy with full recognition of the importance to the child of the other family, which they otherwise prefer to ignore. The model places the children at the center of their experience and gives them responsibility for and help in dealing with their complex reality.

CHAPTER 17

The Family with Adult Children

The Variability of Family Patterns in Later Life

The family that has traversed its course as a reproductive unit faces the process of dwindling. Marital partners whose children graduate through adolescence have completed their reproductive biological task and now face each other once again. It is likely that for the last several years their family life has been dominated by the problems of adolescence and by the launching of one or more children. Some of these issues have been evident in the cases presented in previous chapters, as the growth of adolescent children pries open long-dormant adolescent issues of separation and individuation in the parents, and the family often experiences a storm of internal and external activity.

Then, usually, the children begin to leave. There is a kind of cultural myth that the leave-taking is a smooth and cleanly demarcated event. This is not a fast rule and may even be the exception. One mother remarked that her college-age daughter came home every summer "determined to get a year's worth of mothering in a month." This is the "pit-stop" phenomenon, in which the grown child feels he or she must get refueling quickly to survive the next leg of the journey. One such "child" in her midtwenties brought her husband across town to her parents' home one Sunday. In the middle of the afternoon, she said, "When we eat here, I'm your little girl. But when we go out, we can be adults together." She seemed to be rejecting her need for refueling. But then she continued, "So you have to take us out for dinner."

So this leave-taking is an uneven event, with more or less

involvement of the grown children with the middle-aged or aging parents, and with more or less returning to the nest for various kinds of supplies. Life patterns are variable and complex now, so that the model of the adult couple in their fifties with their married children and grandchildren is but one variant of the aging family. There are also the remarried couples in their fifties with their adult single children, or with their second families still in elementary school. And the families in this phase increasingly have the task of care or oversight of their own aging parents, now in their seventies or eighties.

The variability of family patterns in later life has increased with the destandardization of the nuclear family in earlier life. Accordingly, once we realize that the nuclear family with its one-to-four children is no longer a clearly predominant pattern during the child-rearing phase, then we have to recognize the variety of family constellations in later life. Remarried couples with two sets of grown children, divorced men and women with their own aging parents, or a couple with a widow or widower parent living with them or nearby in an apartment or nursing home are common patterns of the later life family.

It is not necessary to catalog each of the common or possible patterns here. What is necessary is to think of the dynamic ramifications of the pattern facing the clinician who confronts one of these situations. We want to educate the therapist, social worker, and physician so that they realize there is a family that forms the context of the clinical situations that arise. With the increase of interest and knowledge about treating the geriatric population, the relevance of dynamic family therapy to this group is now appreciated. This extends the application of psychoanalytic family therapy methods to every phase of the life cycle, where they belong just as surely as does dynamic psychotherapy (Butler and Lewis 1976, Clayton and Barnstein 1976, Scharff 1982).

FAMILY INTERVENTION FOR A COUPLE WITH LATE-LIFE DEPRESSION

Mrs. Winn, aged 83, was brought to the clinic by her 60-year-old son because she had recently been developing mild confusional signs and seemed agitated. Her husband, aged 85, came only because that clinic routinely requests that the spouse accompany adult referrals whenever possible, and because the intake worker had sensed a specific marital issue in the problem during a prereferral telephone conversation. Mr. Winn himself had no sense of participating in his wife's difficulty.

The clinical situation made it clear that there was a family dynamic powerfully at work. Mr. and Mrs. Winn had been happily married for fifty-two years, but recently Mr. Winn had been unable to move from his chair at home without extraordinary effort. His wife had been devoting herself to catering to him and caring for him since his retirement fifteen years earlier, but a marginal decline in her own capacities, including clouded eyesight from early cataracts, had made this more and more difficult. The son had intervened a few months earlier to urge them to move to a retirement community. Mrs. Winn would have been relieved to do so, but Mr. Winn refused. He insisted that this was his home and he was going to stay put. The sense of conflict between the couple had been urgent enough that the son had backed off, and his wife had stopped her daily visits to her aging in-laws because of the unpleasantness.

In this setting, Mrs. Winn began to feel helplessly lost, without a plan for being able to manage, with less support from her grown children, and without the full use of her bodily senses. She developed a reactive depression with the common symptom of agitation. Her confusional states, which came and went, could be seen to come on in the clinical interview when she tried to discuss the difficulty with her husband. Mr. Winn had became more sedentary, stubborn, and passive as part of his own increasing depression and isolation, which developed in reaction both to losing his home and to his wife's depression.

Here the intervention involved examining the difficulty with loss and mourning that often becomes such a prominent process in the continued development of the late-life family. Although many issues had been more than adequately handled during the long productive span of family activity and reproductivity, the context of dwindling resources and capacities reactivated old internal issues, long dormant. Thus the sadness of their loss of a son in World War II had returned to preoccupy Mrs. Winn, along with the loss of her mother at age 12. The reactivation of these earlier life events provided the substrate for her late-life depression.

For Mr. Winn, the threat of the loss of his home of forty-five years seemed to signify his personal decline, which he could not mourn. He insisted instead that his wife "manage" the situation for him, apparently a reliving of his early life situation when his parents could do that for him and had often been able to spare him considerable loss. There was an element of entitled self-centeredness here that had been only a minor feature of the couple's dynamics in health and maturity but was exaggerated during their shared difficulty mourning the losses of old age.

While couple therapy helped the Winns to mourn and to accept their new reality, their son and his wife met to discuss their reasons for withdrawal. They had had a loving and admiring relationship to the parents and could not bear the shift to a feeling of being burdened by them. They realized that their unwitting withdrawal represented a mixture of guilt, exasperation, and sadness that they had not been able to name and in the face of which they became helpless. With this recognition, they were able to mobilize to help their regalvanized parents make appropriate plans to move to a well-run retirement community where they could get the help they needed.

Loss and Mourning in the Adult Family

Loss and mourning are features of the family's passage through each stage of its development and through every life crisis. Parkes (1971) introduced the term *psycho-social transitions* to describe "those major changes in life space which are *lasting in their effects,* which *take place over a relatively short period of time,* and which *affect large areas of the assumptive world"* (p. 103). Some come with specific rituals and are clearly marked: birth, graduation, marriage, the birth of one's children, death. Others are more subtle, involving changes due to the process of aging. In every psychosocial transition, mourning the old situation and tolerating anxiety about meeting something new are required to negotiate the changed life situation.

Mourning and the management of the anxiety about a diminished life space are not so obviously a feature of the adjustment to each stage of the life cycle unless there is a situation of actual loss, such as the death or disability of a child or spouse, until the later phases of the family's life cycle. In the phases of the adult family after child rearing is more or less completed, the ability to mourn and to move on are most tested, as are aspects of the couple's capacity to be all-in-all to each other in a way they may never have had to face, or have not had to face since the very beginning of their marriage. In that earlier time, they had all their shared prospects for the future in the rosy glow of a predominantly positive tie to each other. The waning situation is likely to become a culture medium for any unresolved object relations difficulty.

Here a sense of disappointment in what might have been, and the loss of vicarious satisfaction from living through the children, can contribute to a sense of progressive depletion within the couple. Worse yet is the resurgence of a tendency to blame each other (which had been neutralized by the presence of children as mollifying objects) for this leads to a sense of being locked together in a situation that is both depleted and actually poisonous. As Erikson (1950) described, questions of personal integrity now become paramount, because the individual is facing the loss of himself and his own opportunity to be and to have been what his ego ideal would have called for. The individual struggle with this situation is apt to spill over into the life of the couple, because it no longer has the wider family field in which to be lived out.

The Family with Young Adult Children

Problems related to loss and mourning first become apparent when the family has young adult children who are in one or another phase of leaving the nest or of attenuated emotional and financial independence. The older parents may be having difficulty with the letting go of the child and the reinvesting in each other, or they may be "champing at the bit" to reestablish their own private intimacy. There will be variations along a continuum from those parents who miss their children enormously to those who cannot wait to get them off their hands. Each attitude and experience has its own potential trials and tribulations, relating to the capacity of the couple to mourn the change and to move on. The following examples illustrate a few of the endless variations that are possible. They will not be given in the same detail as the final example in the chapter, where some aspects of the treatment process with the elderly couple will be explored.

A RECENTLY SEPARATED COUPLE WITH YOUNG ADULT CHILDREN

Mick and Liz Williams had been separated for a year and a half when they called requesting conjoint therapy to see if they might work toward a reconciliation. Both in their late forties, they had been married for almost twenty-five years when they separated. Before the separation Mick had had an affair. Liz had felt taken for granted during the years since he had graduated from medical school and had become a hard-charging surgeon. Liz's breast cancer was discovered and treated, apparently successfully, two years before their separation.

During the first year of the separation, their bitterness focused on negotiations over a property settlement, although there was enough money to go around. In the last few months, however, a spirit of reconciliation had set in. The goal in couple therapy was unclear to them. They were not determined to end up together, but in some way each of them wished to. After a short while, it became clear that Mick was actually singleminded in his wish to reconcile, while Liz was wary, fearing the reestablishment of the same trap from which she felt she had barely extricated herself. Slowly, however, they moved together, exploring the ways they had changed over the years, including the year apart. When they again began to date each other exclusively, there were painful losses of other partnerships they each had developed in the year of separation.

Part of the work involved understanding and mourning the loss of Liz's breast. The cancer had been a blow to both of them. It meant the loss of a shared sexual part and had been felt by both as a sign of a failure of nurturing. Liz had felt spurned by Mick's difficulty with this loss, whereas he had felt she would be unable to care for him in her diminished physical state.

And as they became more of a unit, they again had to deal with their adult son and daughter. The son had gone to school in Germany, taking up the serious study of beer brewing in Munich. When he came home from vacations, he tended to develop a demanding, dependent relationship with his mother, which she found a difficult reinfringement on her autonomy and which she wished Mick would share. Mick did so but found he was no longer used to the daily demands of fathering. This feeling pointed out to him that perhaps he never had been.

Their daughter was in California in graduate school and would come home to continue an adolescent battle with both parents, adding her resentment that they had separated while she was in college. This child was easier for them, because they felt together in being under assault.

Finally, they had difficulties with their own parents. Liz's mother died during their work on reconciliation, and their first shared trip was to her funeral. This brought to awareness Liz's sense of loss in leaving a small midwest hometown to marry Mick during her own late adolescence. The death also meant increased responsibility for her aging father, who was lost without his wife. Liz's ambivalent relationship with her father could now be seen to have shaped her resentment of Mick because Mick and her father shared the attitude of taking their wives and families for granted.

Through all of this, their capacity to be more tolerant and respectful of each other's needs continued to grow. It looked as though they might manage a reconciliation. But, tragically, at this point Liz had a recurrence of the breast cancer in the other breast and was faced with the full challenge of making another earthshaking adjustment. This time, Mick managed to stand by her through the surgery and chemotherapy. The resulting strengthening of their love and respect was a source of support to both of them. They decided, however, out of deference to Liz's difficulty with the idea of living together again, to continue their relationship with the arrangement of remaining close without actually moving in together until she could regain her personal equilibrium.

This couple had to face many of the difficult passages of adult mid-life but did so in the unusual situation of trying to repair their rift from earlier adult life. As they did so, many of the more expectable complexities of dealing with their young adult children, with their parents, and finally with a tragic illness of one of them provided a string of almost constant challenges. But these challenges, coming usually at a less rapid pace, are the challenges of mid- and late-life for couples. Confronting these potentially destructive crises can provide opportunities for reworking old hurts. In this couple, the challenge did not destroy the couple's work on reconciling until, finally, the illness made it impossible for Liz to continue to move forward in the way she had hoped.

Refocusing on the Couple

There are many variations of the events that mark the adult couple's refocusing on their coupleship. As had been true for the years of child rearing, the children and the events around them determine a large part of the input into this psychosocial transition. For some parents, it is difficult to get beyond the events that initiate the transition. For others, their determination to reinvest in their own relationship carries them past much disappointment.

AFTER LOSS BY SUDDEN DEATH OF A CHILD

Mr. and Mrs. Greenson came to see me for help with their grief about the death of their son, Abe, who had been killed when the car he was driving hit a lamppost in the median strip of a highway. I had been treating Abe for anxiety as he faced the developmental challenges of adolescence. With his death, their life stage changed abruptly and tragically. They went from seeing themselves as parents of an anxious but lively adolescent son on whom they pinned their hopes for the future to being lonely survivors. This sense of tragedy and isolation was increased by their sense of failure in their other son, a semidelinquent boy who had been difficult and hyperactive while growing up and had gotten married at age 19 when his girl-friend got pregnant. In reaction to Abe's death, they renewed their investment in the young family of the older son but were neverthe-less thrown prematurely into painfully facing the limitations they felt about each other and their own relationship.

AFTER LOSS OF EXPECTATIONS OF A CHILD

Mr. and Mrs. Wagner, discussed in Chapter 12, came with their lesbian daughter Robin over their difficulty in accepting her homo-sexuality and in getting along with her generally. A brief series of six sessions was enough to establish a renewed basis for a relationship between Robin and her parents, and to discuss the need of each of the individuals for an independent therapeutic plan. Fundamentally, Mr. and Mrs. Wagner were invested in reworking their own rela-tionship rather than continuing to act as though their future were with Robin. Their stand helped Robin to let go of trying to please them or get them to "approve of her homosexuality," and to make her own plans, both therapeutically and personally. Nevertheless, she and her parents were much closer after the series of family sessions. It looked as though ongoing individual work might further facilitate their future relationship.

Failure of the Holding Context

Samuel and Prudence Nadelson were referred to me [D.E.S.] for Mr. Nadelson's impotence. Samuel was 62, Prudence 61. His impo-tence had come on six years after successful treatment of Mrs. Na-delson's sexual nonarousal and nonorgasmic status. They had seen a number of other psychiatrists, some of whom they had managed to work well with and had idealized, but most of whom they criticized roundly as too authoritarian, intrusive, or uncaring.

They were referred by a colleague who warned me they found most therapists lacking, and although they had tolerated him, it was "with a certain indulgence that he was not up to some of the great ones."

In the first interview with the Nadelsons, they described Sam's late-life crisis. He had retired a year earlier from a successful architectural practice and had been increasingly depressed since then. Both of them had mothers they felt to be dominating and fathers who had seemed critical and unavailable. As we dated the onset of the impotence from about the time of Sam's retirement and his fear of insecurity in his old age, the two of them gave me to understand that I seemed to be reading them exactly. They idealized me, saying they felt I understood things even famous physicians had failed to comprehend.

By the second interview, their idealization of me began to crack. My wanting to know about them individually challenged Mrs. Nadelson's tolerance. Nevertheless, in an individual interview with her, she described her resentment of her mother's domination and open disparagement of her father, which she held directly responsible for keeping her from access to him. When she began later to long for him, she had turned bitterly against her mother.

Mr. Nadelson's father was also overshadowed at home by a dominating mother. He had a black-and-white image of his father. He could be critical, scathing, and uncaring, or he was an ideal model whose approval Mr. Nadelson constantly sought.

Following these individual interviews, Mrs. Nadelson decided that I was expecting too much of her. She said she could not afford to dig up painful memories, and she stopped coming to see me. I seemed to have become her dominating and critical mother. Mr. Nadelson, on the other hand, decided to see me. He proceeded to tell me a much fuller story of the decline of his integrity. He had had multiple affairs throughout his life, which included almost every one of his wife's friends. He was at first hopeful that his integrity could be mended, and as he began to work with me, there was a kind of longing for a good father, which had the curious result that he continued to flatter me despite his wife's withdrawal and "rejection" of me. I began to feel some hope. Soon, however, the other side of his feelings for me surfaced. He felt a sense of failure in my capacity to provide hope for his damaged integrity, and he stopped coming.

In the failure, the main transference seemed to be to lost hope. It occurred after a dream in which he went to a man named David Mender, who was the only craftsman who could restore woodwinds (Mr. Nadelson was an accomplished jazz musician). He trusted this man to restore his clarinet to true pitch.

In my countertransference to Mr. Nadelson I felt a kind of excitement about this dream, and at the hope and magic he seemed to be investing in me. And then I felt distrustful. My suspicion that this was a seduction was confirmed when he suddenly stopped coming, saying that he and his wife would work things out together. The amplitude of the inflating of my powers, the smoothness with which he was able to do it, and the deftness of the puncture of my hopes for work with him were transference versions of ways in which he must have treated his wife before inevitably disappointing her.

This couple began their work with me with an idealizing transference that I already knew to be one-half of a split tendency to idealize and to denigrate. They seemed to be in lockstep in their idealization of me in the first hour, and my countertransference reflected it. I felt warm and responsive, and despite my better judgment, almost magically hopeful about working with them. But when I saw each of them individually (which I often do, usually with better results), the shared contextual transference dissolved into individual patterns: Mr. Nadelson continued to idealize me and infuse our relationship with a hope that seemed irresistible; Mrs. Nadelson quickly experienced me as her intrusive and threatening mother who would deprive her of her father, now in the form of her imperfect husband. Although this led to the dissolution of the shared contextual transference into these individual ones, in the end they joined ranks again as he also began to feel that continuing therapy would threaten his marriage. Additionally, he felt too exposed in front of me to continue to explore his failed integrity.

The two of them solved the assault on their capacity to hold together by merging the aspects of their individual reactions to me to flip the contextual transference to its opposite side. I now became a representative of the part of the object world they feared, resented, and denigrated. They closed ranks against me as a solution to the way their individual transferences threatened their own shared holding capacity. Clearly, any holding I had to offer the two of them together seemed inadequate.

In this example, the couple's alternation between contextual and individual transferences could be seen, all the more clearly in a

sense because their individual transference difficulties each constituted such an assault on their capacity to maintain a shared holding environment. In the end, they managed to maintain one by
turning to a shared vision of me and the external world as dangerous. They used this view to maintain a barrier against the assault
they felt to be coming from me, but which derived from their
internal objects. The assault of paired longing and disappointment
that they felt when we began to talk made it difficult to keep their
shaky holding environment together. My capacity to hold them
through this storm was inadequate to the task. In the process, I felt
my investment in being able to do such work alternately idealized
and severely attacked. Our encounter gave me a good sense of what
their life together must have been like.

The Nadelsons' difficulty and treatment failure relates to their
life stage. As their capacity to look forward to productive external
lives diminished, they were forced to turn more to each other. Here
their sense of despair, of loss of integrity, and of an accumulation
of difficulties in relationships all echoed in their own relationship.
The sum of these failures was present in their initial inability to
sustain a transference to my holding function that would let them
work. In the end, it increased their isolation from each other and
magnified their shared despair.

The Relationship to Children and Grandchildren

Many adult couples are intensely invested in their children and
grandchildren. If this investment, which gives a life to their own
past investment in reproductivity, is to be a continued source of
self-esteem, it now has to be carried out through their grown
children. For some couples, active grandparenting meets this need.
Others invest in volunteer work and activities outside the family,
many of which echo the activities of their reproductive years. An
interesting variant of this pattern can be seen in the next example.

THE SEARCH FOR A SUBSTITUTE

Pete and Sarah Masters, described in Chapter 4, had been married fifteen years and were without children of their own. Sarah,
however, had raised her younger brother, and his daughter was "like
a daughter" to her. She felt that in many ways she was too close to
this niece. On the surface she felt it was better she did not have any

children of her own because of her bitterness from feeling neglected as a child, when she was constantly sent to live with other people during her mother's many illnesses. But her wish to have an invest-ment in reproductivity was apparent in this vicarious parenting. Pete was able to support Sarah's investment in this niece, although his interest in his own grandchildren, the children of his daughters from his first marriage, was lukewarm. He had invested heavily in his engineering career throughout that marriage and showed no signs of slackening interest in the later part of mid-life.

THE SENSE OF LOSS OF PURPOSE

For some couples, the loss of the centering effects of the years concerned with productivity and reproductivity cause a kind of confused disorganization. An opportunity to invest in each other and in new activities is welcomed by healthy couples. Less mature couples may appear to welcome their freedom but actually have a panicky feeling that their purpose in life is gone.

Thus, Roy and Mable Underwood, he 60 and she 56, began to experiment with an open marriage after the last of their children left home. Mabel's conscious initiative in seeking lovers was aimed at finding someone to make her feel lovable when her husband did not. This stemmed partly from Roy's difficulty in investing fully in a relationship with her, and partly from her internalization of her parents' painful relationship. When she was a girl, her mother had frequently sent her to her father to ask him not to go out evenings, when the family knew he was seeing other women. While Mabel had her own two sons at home, the oedipal investment in the sons covered up the sense of the void in the marriage. When the sons left, the identification with her father led her to suggest the open mar-riage as a salve to her feeling of emptiness caused by her husband's lack of sexual fervor. Treatment for this couple involved both sex and marital therapy and eventually restored the capacity to invest in each other and in the marriage.

The Return of the Repressed

For all adult couples, there is a problem about the preservation of the loving feelings against the ravages of time and the repeated "return of the repressed bad object" (Fairbairn 1952). The need that everyone has for the repressed object and ego to be seen and heard means that these aspects of painful repressed object relations life must be tolerated within any marriage. An enlarged family offers more relationships in which these may emerge, thus protecting the couple's relationship. But when this emergence is restricted to the object relation system of the couple, it can take a toll on the capacity to idealize each other and can dampen the glow that sustains the marriage.

The problem for marriages, as they go on over extended—or even exhaustive—periods is the problem of the need for the couple to refind each other. It is the central problem for marriages that endure. Refinding is a matter of moment-to-moment rediscovery just as much as it is of coming back together after a difficult day with its wear and tear, or of making up following a fight. Refinding is the process of taking small, microscopic losses, allowing a small piece of mourning to occur, and then renewing attachment. This occurs with daily partings. Small increments of mourning also allow adjustment to the losses of aging that the couple must make. And this process of multiple small losses and refindings prepares the couple for the larger losses that they fear and that they can anticipate having to endure from time to time. The relationship of the couple's adjustment to their mourning of final losses is described beautifully in Lily Pincus's *Death and the Family* (1976).

The Need for Refinding

The next example describes work with a couple who had a lifelong difficulty with refinding, managing it only as they entered old age. Their work was also marked with concerns for their adult children and for their grandchildren, as well as with continued investment in their life together. This example is given in detail in order to illustrate treatment with a couple in this developmental phase.

OLDER PARTNERS WHO REFOUND EACH OTHER

Gene and Rose Holt had been married for forty-five years when Gene came to see me. He was 67 and came because of his impotence, which had become regular over the last year. (The frequent presence of impotence as an index referral symptom in several of the families is not to be taken as a characteristic of older couples; it represents an artifact due to D.E.S.'s specialization in problems of sexuality.) It felt different from the occasional impotence he had previously experienced since the year of his father's death, when Gene was 53. That transient impotence had occurred in the setting of a second honeymoon with Rose. They had married after being childhood sweethearts, and Gene had never had intercourse with another woman. Sometimes he wondered what it would be like with other women. Lately his acute interest in women who passed by, while he was unable to have an erection even in masturbation or on first awakening in the morning, had struck him as particularly contradictory. All in all, Gene described his marriage as a good one with the usual ups and downs.

When I saw Rose, who was 65, she presented a different picture of the marriage. She was a feisty and somewhat complaining woman, who said that Gene had not been easy to live with for all those years. They had two children, a boy and a girl, and she was left to raise them with little help from Gene. She had never had an orgasm and had difficulty allowing penetration when they were first married. She described their sexual experiences before Gene's current difficulty as being generally unsatisfactory, with his being unable to satisfy her, often having his ejaculation when she wanted more stimulation. In addition, he was interested in doing and making things, and tended to denigrate her interests and her mild infirmities. She had been in therapy for many years. He scoffed at her dependence on it, even though he had finally had an analysis himself, which she felt had made him much more available.

It was more than sex that kept them apart, Rose felt. There were differences over the management of the children. Rose had a difficult time with her daughter, who she felt had hated her and idealized Gene during her adolescence, and Gene had done nothing to interrupt this. Their duo had been part of what had driven her to long to have an affair. Although she never had, she had spent several years of their marriage finding things outside the family to make life worthwhile, and feeling bitter all the time. It was difficult to tell if Rose had actually felt as bitter as she described, or if the bitterness was a rereading of their history in the light of current disappointments.

In any event, the discrepancy in the picture that Gene and Rose gave was striking. He described a marriage that was basically good with some periods of strain, and she described one that sounded like a lifelong compromise. When I confronted them with this discrepancy, they laughed and acknowledged that this was their usual difference in attitude. Rose gave an ambiguous smile and said that she guessed things had not been as bad as they seemed right now, but that one of her repeated complaints about Gene was his inability to hear her negative comments and criticisms.

Their family histories supplied more than information. Reviewing these provided an initial burst of energy that enabled them to suddenly refind each other.

In an individual evaluation session, Gene told me about his fears of growing old like his father. His father was an immigrant who had been a blacksmith in his youth and then had gone into business. His mother's family had denigrated his father but had all come to depend on him. He had a zest for life, which had been apparent even at 80, but in Gene's youth, his mother kept him from his father, so that he did not get to know him as a friend until they seemed to find each other when Gene was 26. Gene described his mother as having "almost a sexual relationship with me. She would kiss me all over when I was little and would lay me across her bare breast. I think she wanted something from me, and she got it, but when I was older, I would manipulate her and tease her." With Father, however, Gene thought she was forbidding sexually, as captured in the story of his parents' fiftieth wedding anniversary. Father had run his hand across his mother's buttocks, and she had said, "Oh, Ralph, go away!" Gene had been struck at his father's zestiness and had thought, "I'll bet they have intercourse tonight." His father was dead a month later, and Gene had missed him terribly since then. He had followed his father's advice, "Don't let your mother come live with you if I die," and his mother had been bitter about it until her death.

When Gene told me these facts about his father and followed the recounting of his father's sexual zest with the facts of his death, I expected they were closely linked. *I had found myself liking and admiring Gene a good deal during the interview, and the account of his father's death left me feeling suddenly saddened.* I asked him about the links between his father's death and his own recent impotence, and in the next few minutes he was able to tell me about his recent fears concerning going to sleep at night. "I don't really fear dying. What I hate is the thought of being dead for eons and eons."

I said that I thought his fear of death and his identification with his father as an old man had been brought home to him lately by his retirement and his own age. Being potent seemed to mean that he would die, especially if he and Rose made love at night, a fact that was coupled with his view of women as seductive and entrapping. I told him, however, that it was likely there was also an organic component to his impotence.

The physical and urological examination had already indicated that Gene had an idiopathic form of impotence with a large component of nonspecific physical cause. His nocturnal penile tumescence test, used to tell the difference between physical and psychological causes of impotence, had suggested that he was suffering from a considerable physical difficulty and should consider a penile implant.

Gene's reaction to my interpretation, however, was striking. He and Rose were able to have successful intercourse three times over the next week, after six months of complete impotence. Gene came back, telling me that what I had said to him had hit home. He had felt freed to reconnect to Rose and to see if he could not get something out of his old age as his father had.

Rose was thrilled with Gene's renewed availability. However, she was still unhappy with aspects of their life together, some of which related to her early history. Her father was beloved by everyone, but he preferred her older sister. Rose identified more with her mother and thought that her father belittled and ridiculed her. She incorporated her mother's sense of deprivation from this. Her mother was 3 when her own mother died. "It was a typical cruel stepmother story," Rose said. "My mother always felt mistreated and deprived." That sense of deprivation had marked Rose's relationships, too. "So although I worshipped my father, I felt that, like my mother, I never got very much of him." This sense of being shut out and ignored had haunted her life with Gene. She identified with their son, who she felt was like her, and blamed Gene for her battles with the daughter, whom she saw as like him. Rose's sense of deprivation and of an unavailable father had been consistent with Gene's habit of distancing himself emotionally from her. The degradation she felt her mother withstood from her father was echoed in her surrender to Gene's controlling attitude about their marriage.

After the evaluation, the Holts began couple therapy. They found that they were more able to become empathic than either would have dreamed. Rose agreed to concurrent referral for group treatment for nonorgasmic women and, in the aftermath of learning how to have an orgasm, began to feel much more cared for by Gene. I treated them at first with a form of sex therapy I have modified from the techniques of Masters and Johnson (1970) and Kaplan (1974) and which is described in Appendix II of *The Sexual Relationship* (Scharff 1982). This model uses the behavioral format of graduated exercises (which the couple does privately) to bring the psychodynamic issues to the surface. In one exercise, Gene remembered the feeling of being inside the vagina as one of entrapment and restriction, as if something crucial had been taken away from him. It reminded him of the time he was briefly imprisoned five years earlier.

He now told a story of being mistakenly jailed in a degrading and frightening way. At first his family did not know where he was, and it was only through their intensive efforts that the mistake was cleared up. After he described the days of incarceration, Rose said, "The difficulty with erections really began then. He just wanted to be held when he got out of jail, but he couldn't get an erection. I didn't mind, but he was terribly upset."

Gene suddenly thought that the experience of having to inhibit anger was the link. In jail, he had quickly learned he could not express anger at the jailers without danger of being hit, or at least of losing privileges. He thought that things he stored up in anger at Rose felt similar: that he could not get angry without running a risk. And the risk seemed also linked to his seductive and overwhelming mother.

Much of the shared transference to me involved rivalry over a father. To Gene, I was the guiding and idealized father whom Mother wanted to keep for herself, leading to envy of Rose's feeling for me. For Rose, I was the sought-after father who preferred the older sister and belittled Rose. Thus, rivalry for me and my favor marked the difficulty in the contextual transference, which could be understood in terms of the failures in feeling loved by each other. In the process of working on these issues, the Holts found each other in ways they had not experienced in many years. After the sex was functioning for them in new ways, they continued to work on other burdens on their relationship. These were sapping the renewal of their relationship at a time when they felt they were having more fun than they had ever had together in the previous forty-five years.

One aspect they looked at was their shared relationship to their daughter, who was recently divorced. They had helped to buy her a house, which produced some minor difficulty economically for them. They had the usual debate over how to manage the money but noted that they worked together on monetary things far better than they had in the past. Still, the issue seemed basically to involve their attitude toward their daughter herself. They were both sorry her marriage had ended, but Gene was harder on her than Rose thought he should be about it. She was sympathetic, whereas he was the limit setter when their daughter wanted them to give her more money.

It turned out, however, that Rose had asked Gene to be the one to turn down the excessive request from the daughter. I pointed out that Rose was glad to "use" Gene to set limits, while he was glad to "use" her to feel warmly. They had polarized and divided these functions between them. If Rose would set limits with her daughter more instead of making Gene do it for her, then she would not have to feel he were cruel. And if he could insist that Rose do it for herself, then he might be able to have more spontaneous sympathy for his daughter. I said that if they could absorb some of the functions they assigned to each other, their ways of operating and feeling might be more balanced, and there might be less resentment of each other and of the daughter for coming between them. In the wake of this work, they volunteered to help their daughter by taking her son off her hands for school vacations, and both of them found they began to enjoy grandparenting. Their only complaint was the interference to their newfound sexual life of having a young adolescent in the house.

The work with this couple illustrates that work with an older couple brings up the same range and depth of issues as with a younger one. The work was catalyzed by examination of their interaction and of the transference and countertransference, and by using their original and current family histories to understand as much as possible about their internal object system and its influence on their current relationship. The further the work progressed, the more prominent was their focus on being a helpful part of the life of their grown children and their grandchildren. Work with this aspect never eclipsed the work on their own relationship and on the small reversions to vulnerable areas that momentarily deprived them of the gains they treasured. But the work on their relationship to their daughter and their grandson added to the depth of their satisfaction with their renewed capacity to be who they were by being important to their younger family members. This capacity to "be through others" is a crucial aspect of continued growth in later life.

Adult Couples and Their Aging Parents

The adult family often has to make provision for the care of aging parents. The "children," now in their fifties or sixties, face difficult decisions as to whether the parent is able to live alone, within a retirement community or nursing home, or whether the parent will live with "the children." When the aged parent does actually come to live with the adult couple, the infringement on their relationship may be absorbed and become comfortable; or it may be a welcome relief to a couple who were strained by living alone together; or it may constitute an acute disruption. The following example illustrates one of many possible situations.

A FAMILY WITH AN AGING ALCOHOLIC MOTHER

Mr. and Mrs. Hall, the remarried couple living with Mrs. Hall's adolescent daughters, Annie and Cheryl, described in Chapter 16, consulted me about Annie, who, among other symptoms, had been drinking excessively. I learned that they were worried Annie could become alcoholic like her grandmother. Not until we had worked together for some months did I learn that Grandma actually lived in their basement. Annie felt displaced by Grandma, who needed to be babied. The grandmother, however, also did some cooking and housework while Mrs. Hall worked, so Annie resented her partly as a parent substitute. I asked how long Mrs. Hall's mother had been living with them and was told that it had been ten years. Mr. and Mrs. Hall had been married just six months when she moved in with them. Mrs. Hall had gone to Georgia to help her mother find a suitable nursing home placement. But when she saw her deteriorated condition, she felt she would be putting her somewhere to die, so she brought her home instead. Her husband fully supported her sense of duty and compassion, although, like Annie, he resented Mrs. Hall's attention to her mother.

Hearing of the grandmother's drinking and Annie's hatred of her and resentment of her mother's preoccupation with her, I suggested they insist the grandmother attend. I hoped with the entire Hall household present to work with the destructive identification between Annie and her grandmother. The family refused, however, saying that family therapy was required for their own needs as a family without Grandma. At home, so much of their time was taken up caring for her and worrying about her that the parents did not have enough time for themselves or for Annie or Cheryl. When they said this, I felt it was a defensive position that would keep the grandmother drunk in the basement, but I respected it. I later learned to view it in a more positive vein.

A few weeks after this, the family confronted the grandmother, arranged for detoxification, and followed by insisting she be admitted for inpatient alcohol treatment. They faithfully attended the hospital program, which included family therapy, and were disappointed when she insisted on her right to drink. In a family meeting at the hospital, the family and Grandmother agreed she would be better living in a place of her own if she continued to drink as she intended. Throughout this intensive treatment for the grandmother, the Halls maintained both their commitment to try to be helpful to her, and their commitment to family therapy for themselves with me. The boundary they drew around family therapy was preliminary to drawing a boundary around their nuclear family so that the needs of the adolescent and of the couple's relationship could be attended to more closely. Without the stress of the hopelessness of their simultaneous unrealistic attempt to cure Mrs. Hall's mother, and without the stress of their unconscious facilitation of the problem, they were finally able to get on with the tasks of parenting their adolescent children and of renewing their own relationship.

For all adult families, the problems of mourning, of continuing to develop during the phases of life that follow the reproductive period, and of dealing with the diminishing time or circumstances left to the parents before death constitute considerable threats. The analytic family therapist has a great deal to offer families in this phase of life.

CHAPTER 18

Families Suffering Loss, Damage, or Death

Loss and mourning play a central role in family development, even in the family that is not hit with unusual or extraordinary losses. Each major transition for an individual family member and for the family as a whole requires mourning the loss of what has come before and the tolerance and testing of anxiety concerning the unknown worlds to come. We have previously referred to this developmental aspect of the processes of loss and mourning in each psychosocial transition as a fundamental building block of the capacity to grow (Parkes 1971, Viorst 1986).

The Phases of Grief

John Bowlby (1969, 1973a, 1980) is the major explorer of the processes of mourning losses during the psychological growth of human attachments, examining them in the light of knowledge about other species. Coming from the general psychoanalytic orientation of Fairbairn, Bowlby applied the principles of animal ethology to the study of human attachment. He was able to derive species-specific meanings for the processes deriving from the young animal's primary need for an attachment in order to survive. The model of grieving that Bowlby developed is based on that proposed by Lindemann (1944). It is a model in which the phases do not follow each other cleanly but have an approximate sequencing, as shown here:

1. Numbness and disbelief
2. Protest and anger
3. Despair and sadness
4. Resolution and acceptance
5. Capacity to reattach

The model can be seen to have heuristic value in the wild. Thus, a young animal, lost for a few minutes, has no need to panic, but as time passes, cries of protest will alert the mother to its whereabouts. The anger is also useful in scolding the mother for leaving the young animal so as to dissuade her from doing so again. If the animal is still lost after some time, however, it will go into a low-keyed attitude in order not to attract predators.

The importance of the processes of loss can be seen when they are juxtaposed with the process of attachment, as Bowlby (1980) has done. Citing attachment as the fundamental physical and psychological requirement for survival and for life, he notes that falling in love is the process that accompanies the making of a primary attachment; the feeling of security is the emotion that accompanies the maintenance of the attachment; and the process of grieving is the process that accompanies the severing of a primary attachment. In this regard, grieving is like the painful process of wound healing, which is necessary before the organism can be whole again. And like wound healing, it implies that there has been injury to, and loss of, a part of the self. In object relations terms, the loss of the external person brings a loss of the part of the self that represents the relationship to that person. Following Freud's formulation (1917a), we can say that this also involves transferring the image of the lost person into oneself, or into a part of the ego.

Loss and Failed Mourning

Bowlby's model of loss and mourning can be applied to any of the major losses of life, as it has been by Kubler-Ross (1969) to the phases of acceptance of death, the ultimate loss of oneself. The individual and the family are prepared for such major experiences of loss by the manner in which the family provides a container for the more ordinary processes of loss as growth proceeds for its individual members. In this process, each loss is also an opportunity for new development, and the family's balance between optimism and pessimism in each stage provides a context for the individual's negotiation of the losses at hand. Thus, in some families, the departure of the last child for school at the age of 5 or 6 is felt to be a tragedy for the mother, who is left feeling bereft and useless, and each subsequent stage of the child's growth is felt as a progressive loss. When there is an aura of depression and unrequited longing in such a family, we could describe the difficulty as a pathological grief reaction that occupies the space of the family as a whole.

In more adaptive families, the loss when the child leaves for school will provide a developmental crisis for the family in which the mother and the family explore new ways of being in the world and being together, and they move on to new opportunities. Many of these developmental "losses" or transitions are obligatory to the family as it grows and changes through time. Thus, the family with an adolescent child must undergo some change and loss as the child ages and either graduates from high school or drops out (Scharff 1975, 1976, 1980). Nonacademic children who leave school before graduating, and their families, struggle with a sense of loss of opportunity and of hope that the child will provide a fantasied solution to chronic loss and despair. Here the school can often be seen to react to the individual and family loss by closing ranks to prevent their disappointment from leading to the disillusionment of the staff. The child and his family then feel isolated and neglected in negotiating the transition into a wider world, usually perceived as threatening and unfriendly.

Other losses cannot be considered to be routine or inevitable, and it is the experience of families who endure these losses that we want to illustrate in this chapter. They constitute a large portion of our clinical population. Some of these families come with good constitutions and have weathered previous losses with resilience and optimism. This prepares them for the tragedies that befall them. Others are ill-prepared, with a previous history of difficult relationships and anxious attachments.

We have described many families that have experienced losses in the course of the clinical material thus far presented. The chapter on separation and divorce is about that particular category of loss and rebuilding. And there are the families where the "loss" is the chronic experience of early neglect or of actual threats of abandonment, which can have almost as powerful an effect on the child as the actual experience of loss of a parent (Bowlby 1973a).

In the rest of this chapter, however, we will deal with four clinical examples of definitive loss. The first is that of a family with good previous experience that had a first child who was retarded. This example recalls the work of Solnit and Stark (1961) on the need for mourning at such a birth. The second and third families were faced with the loss of a father and with compromised experiences leading up to those losses. The fourth family lost an adolescent son who had been their more highly valued child.

A FAMILY WITH A DAMAGED BABY

An obstetrician colleague asked me to see a family in consultation. Art and Ruth Bluestone had a 2½-year-old girl, Megan, who was born with "swallowed meconium," a low Apgar (the standard assessment scale for newborns), and weighing only four and one-half pounds, although she was full term. The placenta was about half normal size. So there was concern from the beginning about how Megan would do. The low birth weight and initial concerns had been followed by continued failure to thrive and slowed development. No definitive diagnosis had ever been made, but slowly it had dawned on the couple that the child was not normal, and that the best they could do was to invest in her development and give her every chance.

They had been told that in the absence of a definitive diagnosis, their chances for a normal child in a next pregnancy were quite good. With this gradual realization, they had become involved in the appropriate educational and developmental programs for Megan, and more recently in the county associations for retardation and handicapped children.

In recent months, Ruth had begun to realize that she was making every excuse for not getting pregnant at a time when they would have liked to have more children. She was afraid of a repetition of the outcome of the last pregnancy. She had no events to blame the outcome on. She did not smoke, had only one drink the entire pregnancy, and had only a single chest X-ray. Nevertheless, she was haunted by the fear of the second pregnancy. It was not that she resented Megan. She felt attached and caring of her. She gladly took her to the remedial programs and infant stimulation programs four mornings a week. Although Megan had remained small, weighing twenty-two pounds at 2½ years, she seemed to be catching up cognitively. She was only six months behind at the moment, but her cognitive growth was accelerating rapidly. So it was conceivable she could catch up completely. Art said that he thought Ruth was being optimistic, but that this difference of optimism and pessimism was characteristic of the difference between them. She agreed but said that she was uncomfortable with something else Art did. He would lash out at people, as he had done recently. Art had been carrying Megan in an elevator when someone commented, "Gee, she's small!" Art made the retort, "That's better than being fat like you!" and Ruth felt humiliated. Art said that he was uncomfortable with his own response, but his only option was to leave with his head hanging. In a comparable situation, Ruth said that she would say nothing but feel deflated and defeated.

I had been feeling quite sympathetic to the couple and rather on the side of Ruth's fear. I was admiring her adjustment and her dedication to Megan. The gains in development, which I linked to her dedication, had seemed to make her optimism pay off. On the other hand, she dreaded a repetition. I thought that Art's more defensive response in the elevator, and his warding off of the humiliation that Ruth could speak for, represented his own difficulty accepting what had happened and the loss it meant. So I said that the split of optimism and pessimism between the couple had its liabilities. Ruth seemed to show a kind of optimism, but maintaining it meant denying her worry about the repetition of this outcome of pregnancy. On the other hand, Art's pessimism pushed her further into maintaining the optimism for both of them, or else they would both feel hopeless. This left her unable to discuss her worry with Art, lest he magnify it, and the cost was her suppression of the worry, which then nagged at her from inside. On the other hand, Art was overprotective not only of Megan but of the two of them about the reality of their situation, as though admitting it would lead to despair. Art thought he had inherited a tendency to be overprotective of his child, as he was of his clients as an insurance salesman. I thought Art and Ruth were struggling to relate to Megan as an ideal object, but this involved both of them in repression of their disappointment in her.

I said that both of them were having trouble mourning the loss that Megan was less than fully normal, and without that, it was hard to tolerate the fear that events could recur. It was not possible for them to share the uncertainty when part of Ruth was still denying the current reality, and Art was still angry and caught in despair. When Ruth was presented with her own fears, their shared inability to talk and cry meant that Art abandoned Ruth with her worries, and she left him alone with his anger. I thought that if they could face each other with their fears and loss, they might be able to tolerate the anxiety and uncertainty they would need to face together to tolerate a second pregnancy. I noted that if things did go well, a second pregnancy could be enormously reassuring to both of them, but that first they would have to tolerate the period of uncertainty.

They came in again six weeks later, saying that everything was a great deal better between them. Ruth had been able to tell Art what she was upset about and to share a couple of nightmares. They felt their sharing was making them much stronger, as evidenced by Art recently being able to tell Ruth of having a client "come on" to him. She understood that he would never have been able to tell her about it before. She had finally been able to stop taking birth control pills in the attempt to become pregnant. When she had thought she might be pregnant but had bled during the month, Art provided support by accompanying her to the obstetrician.

They left feeling reassured about their capacity for mutual support. About a year later, I heard from the obstetrician that he had delivered their eight-pound four-ounce healthy boy.

The mourning in this case was blocked by the combined difficulty of husband and wife, each stuck in a different place of the mourning cycle. They were distanced from each other by having to reject each other's solution to the defensive isolation of the painful loss. Bowlby (1973a) has made the point that for the young child, naturally fear-inducing situations are made worse by certain conditions: unfamiliar circumstances, sudden movement, loud noise, the dark, and being alone. Of course, much of the same applies to us as supposedly mature adults, who never fully shed our childhoods or our fears. And as with children, unfamiliar circumstances, the dark of the unknown future, and isolation increase fear. In addition, the sense of being abandoned at a time of fear or anxiety magnifies the power of the rejecting internal objects, and the spouse who is felt to be abandoning, even if it is understood to be for defensive reasons, is experienced unconsciously as a rejecting object.

In contrast, the spouse who shares fears and exchanges defensiveness for companionship is felt to be more like an ideal and loving object, dealing with fears and providing holding and containing. In this case, each spouse was able to catalyze mourning for the other with the help of only a single session, which provided enough containment and permission for this basically healthy couple to get their mourning unstuck and to move on. Although they were not basically changed as people, the momentum of the successfully resolved crisis did give them an increment of growth toward more sharing and openness, which may have lasted beyond the time of the crisis itself.

A FAMILY WITH A DYING FATHER

Terri Lowe was a 5-year-old girl referred by her pediatrician. I saw her with her mother, aged 27, and her 6-year-old sister, Heather. Father had refused to come and had denigrated the whole idea of the referral.

The two girls looked very like each other, slight, blond, and attractive. At the beginning of the interview, they moved to a small play table and began to color silently with crayons while I spoke to Mrs. Lowe. She told me that Terri had had somatic symptoms, including headaches and stomachaches, almost every day over the last year. At preschool during the last year, she was said to have moderate behavior problems but had been found to have a high IQ. Terri also had a history of asthma and ear infections from birth, but these had subsided during her second year. Mrs. Lowe was clear, however, that Terri's somatic symptoms had been adopted in identification with her father, whose leukemia had been diagnosed three years earlier.

The history that Mother told me had a slowly building impact, giving me a sense of her accumulated grudge against her husband. He had moved out of the family when Terri was a year old, seeing the children infrequently and unreliably. But he had come back when Terri was almost 2 years old, although he had remained difficult and self-centered.

At this moment, Heather spoke. She said they knew a dog who was having a birthday. I used her spontaneous contribution to get them to talk. Heather said the dog, who was 4, was really therefore 28, which was the same age as her Daddy, and that she and Terri had two guinea pigs.

"Yeah!" burst in Terri for the first time, revealing her lisp. "When they have a baby, we'll have a boy."

Mrs. Lowe corrected her humorously: "She means that if we get a boy guinea pig, then they could have babies."

The girls went on to discuss the guinea pigs with a kind of excited, pressured enthusiasm. They each had a guinea pig, but Terri's was fat and it might have babies. She had had one before that was sick, so they had had to give it back. It's name was Roary, and the way she said this clued me in that her speech was quite immature and she could not pronounce r's.

The sick guinea pig led back to their sick father. Terri told me, "He's got cancer." Heather acknowledged that "sometimes he seems sick," while Terri chimed in, "He gets headaches a lot, just like me."

I asked what the children knew about their father's being sick.

Terri said, "When we grow up, he'll die!" She said that would be a long time from now.

I turned to Mrs. Lowe and asked what the children knew. She told the story that last Christmas, Father had been quite depressed as usual. He sat the kids down to talk, and Terri had opened with the statement, "Daddy, when I grow up, I'm going to marry you." He had answered, "No, when you grow up, I'll be dead." When the children pressed him to explain what that meant and what being dead was, he withdrew and refused to speak. Mrs. Lowe then said that Terri's saying this to her father had followed a few weeks of romantic discussions about an uncle. This had been the first declaration of her love for her father. There had been none since.

As we discussed this incident, Heather gave Mother the picture she had been drawing, which she said was their house, with the sun overhead (Fig. 18.1). I had interrupted the discussion to get her to describe the picture and then returned to finish the oedipal story with Mother. I felt the girls were warming up and that it made sense that Terri was symptomatic. And I felt already that her immature speech was likely to have something to do with retreating from growing up in the face of Father's extremely threatening pronouncement in answer to her oedipal proposal.

Mother now went on to discuss Father's behavior since returning to the house three years before. Over the first two years, he had been able to work part-time but elected to spend the rest of this time socializing. He had been adamant that he was going to make the most of his shortened life. He ran around with women and on one occasion had a girlfriend to a party in the house without telling Mrs. Lowe. She was infuriated and humiliated when she found out, but she felt that she had to stay with him for the financial support that his medical disability provided, so that she could get through college and "be able to have a better life in the future." *When she said this, my reaction to her shifted from being annoyed at her passivity to admiring something spunky about her.*

Mother went on to say that Father was sensitive and strict. He alienated people regularly. Terri was actually the only person who got along with him. It was only in the last year that he had realized that he even had a family. Lately, he had seemed to be trying to get

Fig. 18.1 Heather's "house."

to know the children, and he had given up the running around. They had been married for nine years, and the first three years had been pretty good. His personality had changed around the time he moved out. He had said to her, "I'm tired of being married, so I'm leaving. I'll pay the rent, but you'll have to support yourself." She was unsure if he had been feeling the premonitions of the illness at the time, but she thought the illness had magnified his personality difficulties.

As Mother described her struggles with Father, Terri walked across the room and gave her mother a picture (Fig. 18.2). I asked to see it and used it to explore both emotional and cognitive issues. It was a picture with several hearts hanging from the sky around a single flower growing in the grass. She was able to name the colors of

Fig. 18.2 Terri's "hearts and flower."

the hearts and to describe the picture, without relating it to anything specific. She seemed to be at least at age level cognitively, as best I could tell in this rough screening, but I was again impressed with the immaturity of her speech. I commented on the hearts and the grass, and she went back to drawing again as I picked up the conversation with Mother.

Heather was leaning back on her chair looking at her mother and listening as Mother described her husband calling from the hospital nine months later to tell her of his illness. He wept, "I love you. We ought to get back together." Despite her reluctance, she said, "he wore me down, and I let him come back. And the children begged me to take him back."

Looking at Heather, I asked how she had taken this. Mrs. Lowe said that she had been a model child until he came back, when she was 3. (As Mother said this, the children rocked the table they were drawing on, calling my attention to them.) Mrs. Lowe continued that Heather had become confused and had frequently awakened crying over the next year. She seemed depressed, could not form friendships in preschool, and isolated herself. This led Mother to seek treatment for her. She had seen a psychologist for a year with much benefit. (Heather had been between 4½ and 5½.) During the same period, Mother sought a referral for herself and was in therapy for six months, again feeling significantly helped. Her husband had insisted throughout there was nothing wrong and had refused to participate. He also objected to her bringing Terri today.

Now Heather gave me another picture (Fig. 18.3), which she said

Fig. 18.3 Heather's picture of Terri planting flowers.

was a picture of Terri playing under her pine tree and planting flowers. "She is putting flower seeds inside it and watering it," she said.

I asked if Terri liked making things grow, and Heather answered, "Yes . . . Do you?" As she said this, she pushed the picture aggressively into Terri's nose. It looked pretty unpleasant to me, so I asked them how they got along together. They began to tickle and pinch each other. Terri said that Heather pinched her nose so that she could not breathe, while Heather denied that she picked on Terri. Mrs. Lowe said that actually Terri was more likely to grab something from Heather. Until recently, Heather had not defended herself, but she had become more assertive after therapy.

I began to get the picture of Mother identifying Terri with Father as the aggressor, and Heather with herself. I thought the "grabbing" was a trait that had to do with Father. My observation in the interview was that Heather seemed more aggressively intimidating of Terri, but I did not want to dismiss Mother's observations.

Terri now showed me her picture (Fig. 18.4). She told me that it was a tree with flowers and a rainbow. A black broad line on the right side, she said, was either nothing or a stick. I thought this picture was more immature and I could make little out of it. Mrs. Lowe said that the children usually drew their house, and that she was surprised they had not done so.

Terri now began to draw her house, telling me that she had a red door and that the windows were white (Fig. 18.5). I used the picture to interview the children about their life at home, their rooms, and the sleeping arrangements. A vivid night portrait emerged: both children wanted to sleep with the light on. Terri was jealous of Heather for being closer to the bathroom light, so she frequently went into her parents' bedroom, down a flight of stairs, when she was frightened. Father expressed outspoken objection to the inconvenience, but she got in on her mother's side of the bed.

Both girls now began to tell me energetically what they were frightened about: monsters, ghosts, and "Grumblins" who lived in their closets and could come out and eat them. They brightened up considerably as they enlightened me about the Grumblins, who were a free transliteration of the creatures from the movie Gremlins. They had not seen it but had heard about it, and Heather now showed me the stickers of Grumblins she carried in her little purse.

I said, "If you have them in your purse, then they aren't scary because you're in charge." But they ignored my comment to tell me excitedly about the spiders and Grumblins in their house, even under their rug.

Fig. 18.4 Terri's "tree, flowers, and rainbow."

"Your house is a dangerous place," I said, changing the level of intervention.

Heather said, "But we walk on the rug and kill them. Anyhow, only Grumblins eat people."

Terri said, "The wind blows my door open and makes my curtains wave!"

I now wondered how long these fears had been present. The most clearly symptomatic fears had come on when Terri changed day-care centers ten months earlier, before the current fear of monsters. She had been fine in school until then, but with this change she became terrified of taking a nap. Now Mother had to read to her, or even lie down with her, to get her to nap or to sleep at night. As she said this, Terri pulled Heather's hair, and when I intervened, she said

Fig. 18.5 Terri's "house."

it wasn't fair, because Heather's room was closer to the light, but Heather retorted that Terri's room was closer to her parents. I commented that it seemed to be important to both of them. I asked Mother about the squabbles again, now being more convinced of Terri's difficulty under stress. Mother said that in one conflict two months earlier, Terri had run into the kitchen and made scratches on her arm with a knife.

"What were you mad about that time, Terri?" I asked.

"Daddy!" she said. "I wanted him to leave. I want to stay with Mommy. Sometimes he hurts me when I play with him. Once I wanted to give him love, and he knocked me off the couch." And as she said this, she stuttered fearfully.

"Do you feel he doesn't care about you?" I asked. She nodded. "Who does then?" I continued. She pointed to her mother. "Does Heather care about you?"

"I don't know," she said.

Heather said, "I do."

Now Terri gave me a picture that almost made me weep (Fig. 18.6). It was a picture of a baby, chubby and bouncy, drawn in black with a bright red mouth. In an excited, almost trembling stutter, she said, "The mouth is red because the mommy put lipstick on *him*. The baby is 1 . . . 1 ye . . . year old, and it's a girl, but *his* mother works, so the da . . . daddy takes care of him. They have a good time. They go to the museum and then they go to see one

Fig. 18.6 Terri's "baby."

animal at Wild World. They like . . . they like elephants. *She* climbs on the elephant at the zoo, and (calming down) then they go back to Wild World. That's her bathing suit. Her name is Tila."

Heather said, "Oh, I know who Tila is. She's on *He-Man* on TV!"

I said, "*This* baby and *her* daddy have a very good time."

As the interview was nearing an end, I said that I wanted to get a little information about Mrs. Lowe's family background. Her parents were divorced, and her father had been away at sea most of her childhood. Her mother was diagnosed as schizophrenic and had been unable to look after her children, so Mrs. Lowe's grandmother, with many protestations, had taken in yet another grandchild.

As Mother told me this, Heather gave her a picture (Fig. 18.7). Mrs. Lowe said, "It says 'I love you, Daddy.'"

Fig. 18.7 Heather's "I Love You, Daddy."

"That's right," said Heather. "It's two Care-Bears with hearts."

"I got on fine with my Grandma," continued Mrs. Lowe. "She had raised all her grandkids because her daughters were all weak. Maybe because they were from the South. But she was tired of raising kids, and she said, "This is the last grandchild I'll take." But we got along fine. She's 85 now, but healthy. I see her at least once a year. My mother lives in Arkansas. She isn't capable of a good relationship. When the phone rings, she thinks someone is after her."

Heather was now whispering to her mother that she wanted to go to the cafeteria because she was hungry, but Terri had another picture for me (Fig. 18.8). "That's the baby girl's mother. She has red lips, too, because she put the mother's lipstick on, too. I'll draw a

Fig. 18.8 Terri's "The Baby Girl's Mother."

picture of the daddy. He's out working." She went back to work, drawing.

I felt that Terri was responding quite directly to her mother's story of losing her mother, and that this had seemed to help her identification with her mother in a small way within the hour. I thought this held out promise for a shift in her identification that might support the oedipal development seemingly blockaded by her father's brutal treatment of her developmental initiatives toward him.

Before making a summary statement and recommendation, I wanted a bit of Father's family background. Mrs. Lowe said that his father was a "bad alcoholic who was always drunk." He had apparently abused the children, once breaking her husband's arm when he was small. In addition, her mother-in-law was so upset about Mr. Lowe's leukemia that she insisted that he would have to "beat the leukemia" before she could bear to see him. This had resulted in a break with the grandparents, and the children missed them.

Terri now pulled my arm to show me the picture of the baby's daddy (Fig. 18.9). This picture was much simpler and did not seem so hysterical. She showed me that she had rejected a version in which she had "messed up" by putting eyelashes on him. He did not have eyelashes. I could not tell if this was a mark of sexual differentiation, or a side effect of chemotherapy that she was chronicling.

"Is this a happy family?" I asked.

"Yes," Terri said. "They go to King's Dominion [a local amusement park], and they go swimming together in the pool."

It was now time for me to close the interview and sum up my thoughts. I felt filled up with the tragedy and hardship through the generations of this family, but I was also impressed with the tenacious efforts Mrs. Lowe made on behalf of her children and herself. I felt my job was to provide some additional understanding of their experience to the girls so that the interview would make sense, before discussing my thoughts with the mother.

I turned to the two girls and said that I thought their being frightened at night came from their worries about their father's being ill and dying. They were scared about their Daddy, and then for themselves, too.

Terri said, "No! I'm scared about the Grumblins."

I said, "I know you are. But I don't think you'd worry about the Grumblins if you weren't upset about your Daddy—when he's mad at you, and when he's going to die. I think you *feel* you're scared of monsters, but I think it *comes from* worrying about your family. And

Fig. 18.9 Terri's "The Baby's Daddy."

I think you worry for your Mommy, too. Like will she do OK, and can she take care of you. But that's something that has to be talked about."

To Mrs. Lowe, I said that I appreciated her being willing to talk in front of the children, and I thought it certainly was right to pursue help for Terri. We made arrangements for the further diagnostic meetings.

Because this was only the first interview of the diagnostic study, there was no need to make a recommendation. We needed to assess the degree to which Terri was able to work individually, and to hear from her mother if there were further things she could not say in front of the children. But I was clear that family therapy, with or without Father, ought to be a part of the therapeutic plan, given the pervasive nature of what they were all up against, and given that it looked as though they would be facing Father's death in the foreseeable future. With that, we ended the interview.

In this family, the capacity to mourn was compromised from many sides—foremost among them being the children's age. Children of this age do have an innate grieving process, which can be demonstrated by observation (Robertson and Bowlby 1952, Robertson and Robertson 1971). Nevertheless, as has also been demonstrated, their grieving process cannot really get them over the loss of a parent, so that the incidence of serious psychopathology is high following the loss of a parent anytime before late adolescence. Treatment can be crucially helpful in staving off the worst of these effects (Furman 1974, Tessman 1978).

In addition, the capacity of everyone in this family to mourn is compromised by their relationship to the dying father. In the discussion that follows, we will assume (for purposes of discussion) that he is much as he was presented. We recognize that if I had had the opportunity to meet him, he might have appeared differently. I tried to persuade him to represent himself in sessions, but he was unwilling to come. He certainly came across as a difficult, defensive, and abrasive man, about whom the girls could be expected to be ambivalent at best. Ambivalently held objects are the most difficult to mourn at any age. The rage and disappointment at the antilibidinal object, and adhesiveness of the antilibidinal ego for its object, make it difficult to free up enough of the problematical relationship to move on. There is a tendency to a "manic restoration" of an idealized exciting object, one that is split widely apart from the threatening one. By manic restoration, we refer to the Kleinian concept of the false solution to the depressive position, in which ambivalence toward the object cannot actually be tolerated, and in its stead there is a triumph over the object and the situation that is unrealistic and often contemptuous of the object (Klein 1935). We see this in the triumphant reinstatement of a happy family by Terri at the end of the painful interview—a family that will go off to a promised land, a King's Dominion, and essentially be happy ever after. This does not constitute worked-through mourning and will break down as the monsters emerge from the closet at nightfall.

In the face of the massive failure of the holding context of this family, Terri's immaturity and difficulties are not unexpected. It is not the single incident of her father's rebuff as she makes an oedipal advance that stymies her progress; it is the ongoing sense of the futility of relating to her father and the difficulty of growing up. Although the specific incidents the family tells us about enable us to reconstruct a narrative history of their difficulty in a way that begins to make sense, both to them and to us, we do not conclude that the fault lies with a small number of discrete traumatic episodes. There is an accumulation of multiple, daily traumatic events (Khan 1963). These take place in the core holding relationships and in the faulty holding of the contextual relationships. The effect is the broad immaturity that Terri shows. Another effect is the constellation of specific behavioral difficulties and neurotic fears from which Terri and Heather both suffer.

But in another sense, we can see that Terri, as the most vulnerable of the family members developmentally, is the spokesperson for the difficulties they all face. Indeed, Mother's recognition of the environment in which she lives makes the holding situation a great deal better than it might have been, although her decision to stay with her husband was also a decision to expose the children to the difficulties he presents.

In this case, Mother's decision to get help with each of the children is part of her provision of a transforming container to them. During the interview, it became clear that the contextual transference of the three family members to the holding aspect of the consultant was extremely good. It looked as though the girls felt entirely trusting in the situation arranged by their mother, a contextual transference that presents a good prognosis for family treatment.

This example, then, presents some of the difficulty of the impending death of a parent in the family with young children, and in a family where the prior separation of that parent is part of the prior establishment of vulnerability. The parents' own histories of early parental loss are a significant part of the backdrop, which sensitizes this family to loss and to difficulty in grieving. This is most marked for the father, who seems to be so disabled that he cannot tolerate facing his own death or the consequences to his family. Mother, on the other hand, seems to have managed to obtain enough caring parenting that, in spite of her own difficulty in choice of partners and in arranging her life, she is determined to provide holding and containing to her children and to herself. Her model for this is her grandmother. She has taken in her husband as her grandmother took her in. To refuse would have been to be like her schizophrenic mother.

The next example is one in which a father died when the children were adolescent. Again, the family's reaction to loss is significantly compromised, but not as much by the children's immaturity as by the previous family history of damaged relationships and parental separation.

A FAMILY OF FATHERLESS ADOLESCENTS WHO TEMPORARILY LOST THEIR MOTHER

Maria Hodges was a 14-year-old girl who lived with her mother, aged 42, and her brothers, Antonio, aged 16, and Paolo, aged 19. Maria had been evaluated by a psychiatrist a year previously for depression and poor school performance, and it had been agreed she could return to spend the rest of the school year with her grandparents in Italy, where she had been living before her father's death. Mrs. Hodges called now because of Maria's depression, but on the phone she said, "Maria says that as a family we do not talk to each other, so I think it's better if you see us all together at first."

The family arrived for their interview and sat with Maria next to her mother on one end of a line of chairs, with her brothers closest to me (D.E.S.). There was an air of sadness about the family, but they were able to talk easily, except for Paolo, the 19-year-old, who said little through the first part of the interview. The family said that they had come because Maria was depressed and weepy. But she then helped them to realize that none of them was doing well. Antonio was perhaps doing the best. Having donned a single earring and styled his hair to look punk, he had found acceptance in a small peer group. But Paolo, in his first semester at a local community college, was listless and apathetic. He drank a good deal and studied little.

The story that emerged during the hour was a painful one. Mr. Hodges had died three years ago, while serving out the last days of his assignment at the American Embassy in Rome. Since then, the family had been at odds. They were already back in the United States when he died, living in Boston where Mrs. Hodges was working, having just completed a paralegal degree. She had left the children and her husband when they were in Italy because she had felt the marriage was not going to survive and she had to get a degree to be able to take care of herself. So when Maria was 9, she left, telling the children it was only for a few months. She stayed in Boston for eighteen months getting her degree, returning to the family in Italy only once in the middle of that time. At the end of that visit, Maria remembered clinging desperately to her mother, crying, "Don't go. Don't go!" The boys, too, remembered missing Mother terribly.

Paradoxically, when Mother was gone, Father became available to them for the first time. He had always been distant and uninvolved. But all three children, feeling abandoned by their mother, said they had discovered a relationship with their father, who had become the primary parent to them.

Mrs. Hodges returned to Italy the next December, and she and her husband planned for the family's relocation. Their tour of duty with the embassy was to be over in two months, so they planned to move to Boston. The parents brought the family to the United States, and then Mr. Hodges returned to Rome to finish his contract. But two weeks before he was due to return home, Mrs. Hodges got a telephone message that he had died of a heart attack.

When Mrs. Hodges described this in the interview, she wept bitterly and seemed to be consumed with guilt. She wondered if there were things she might have done to have gotten him to medical care, particularly because she had noticed his swollen ankles and shortness of breath. He had passed off her concern and refused to keep doctors' appointments she made for him. After his death, she learned that an American physician had done a thorough workup and recommended cardiac bypass surgery but that her husband had refused. Curiously, as she told this story, the children did not cry but seemed impatient or angry. *For me, the experience was a confusing one affectively, in that I found myself feeling upset by Mrs. Hodges still being so caught up with the death three years later, while the children seemed impassive.*

Only later in the hour did this confusion make sense to me, when Mrs. Hodges told me that she had told her husband shortly before his death that she had decided to ask him for a divorce. At this the children came to life and looked angry. They seemed to be siding with their dead father, and I noticed that I felt a bit betrayed by her previous show of grief, only to discover now that she had already been planning to leave him. The story did not seem understandable without the history of the marriage, so I asked about it.

Mr. Hodges had been working with the State Department in Italy, where they had met. Mrs. Hodges was Italian and had always lived with her parents in Rome. In retrospect, she saw her precipitous marriage as an escape from her mother. The couple moved to Mexico, where her first child, Paolo, was born. Mr. Hodges was drinking a great deal, and she contemplated leaving him then. But when his father died and they journeyed to Texas for the funeral, something happened to Mr. Hodges. He gave up drinking altogether and became emotionally more available. They had Antonio as a way of renewing their marriage, and partly, on Mrs. Hodges' side, so that in case she got divorced she would have a second child. But things went a bit better, and he was able to get sent to the embassy in Paris, where they were at least closer to her family in Italy. After a brief Washington tour they were transferred to Rome. Maria was born before they went to Paris. All three children went to the American School there, but when they got to Italy, they went to a small school for embassy children, where they felt very much at home. This, together with being close to their grandparents (and Mrs. Hodges having her parents) meant this was the closest family experience they had ever had.

While Mrs. Hodges told of her experience with her husband's period of alcoholism, the children listened attentively and seemed surprised. And I felt again more sympathetic to her situation, which I understood to be that of a young woman who had grown up being very close to, and somewhat oppressed by, her parents, and especially her mother. The experience with her husband seemed to represent a rude awakening and an enormous distance from her cultural and family ties. Even when they were back in Italy, she felt abandoned by her husband's emotional distance.

The emotional difficulty in the interview turned first on Maria's feeling of abandonment by Mother when she left Italy, promising to come back. When Maria said that Mother had lied to her, Mrs. Hodges said, "Did I say that I would come back soon? . . . Yes, I did. I didn't know what to say. I just felt I had to get away to survive."

Maria said, "When my mother came home, I stayed with her all the time. And when she left again, I just kept telling myself, 'She isn't here any more.' I was so lonely!" And she began to weep.

Mrs. Hodges began to cry, too, and said, "She clung to me all day long during those two weeks. It was very difficult for me to get on the plane to return to school."

When Mrs. Hodges said that, I could feel myself being angry at her for leaving Maria, but at the same time I was feeling more sympathetic to her life story. So I was beginning to have a feeling of her passing on to her children her own tragic internal struggle, and I felt less like blaming her.

After Mother's eighteen months away, the events of the family's planning to move and Father's death had occurred. Mrs. Hodges' immediate reaction to the news was guilt: "I knew he couldn't live without me. I thought, 'I took away his will to live. That's why he died.'"

Once the family reached Boston, Mother began working long hours, and the children were left to make an adjustment on their own. She said, "I never had time to do any grieving. There were days I felt I couldn't go on. The children were having a difficult time, and I didn't know what to do. I cried on the way to and from work because I didn't think I should let them see me cry at home. Now I know I made a mistake. Because we never really showed our grief to each other. I felt everything had fallen on my shoulders. I knew that by being away the year and a half I had pushed the children onto their father, and now he was gone. And the kids were faced with me to be their parent. And they really didn't know me any more!"

The children were upset now. Maria was crying, Antonio was staring into his lap. Paolo, the 19-year-old, gave his mother a stony stare, pointed his finger at her, and said, "After my father died, she made us go to Boston. Everything had been taken from us. It was unfair! We didn't know a soul. The only person I knew was her!" He was able to say that when she had left them in Italy, he also felt lonely but that, with difficulty, he felt they had reconnected with their father. By default, Father and the children had gotten over Mother's absence, at least as far as Paolo was concerned. They had ended up feeling close in a rough sort of way. For instance, Father had been able to learn some tolerance for Paolo's trying to look punk for a year, without overreaction. This was the same persona that Antonio had been trying on since they had moved to Washington.

The last year in Washington now made sense as the aftermath of the family's distance and hostility. They had moved to Washington from Boston because the children were so lonely there that they pressured Mother to move elsewhere. They had some friends in the Italian community in Washington, and the family had briefly been assigned there several years before, so Mother looked for work there. When they got to Washington, Paolo had found a few friends in high school and did average work while drinking increasingly; Antonio retreated from the family to his small idiosyncratic peer group; and Maria began to argue with and badger her mother, and to look more homesick. It was because of this that she had been sent to Italy for the rest of the last academic year to live with her grandparents and to attend the small school where they had all felt at home. At the end of six months there, she had felt strong enough to come home. She did well at first, but when she made no friends, she became increasingly depressed.

Mrs. Hodges had been in group treatment for depression and "a blocked grief reaction" since the consultation that had supported Maria's move back to Italy, but she had not managed to find peace with herself or a way of being more supportive to the children. This view of Mother as a bad object was shared by Mrs. Hodges herself. This meant that there was no effective containment for the family, although in bringing the family for help, Maria was trying to substitute for Mother in providing the direction and containment. Therefore, at the end of the family and individual interviews, the recommendation was made for an initial phase of family therapy to help the family understand their shared experience as a context for the profound difficulty of each member.

It turned out, however, that the family could brook no delay in a more massive treatment approach. Maria was more depressed than could be seen in the initial assessment, when her brave front had seemed to carry her through the worst of the hardship. She said that as the others worked in the family sessions, she felt shut out. When she felt her own troubles were being overlooked, she felt once again abandoned. Within a few weeks, she took an overdose of her mother's sleeping pills, "hoping to sleep forever," and was admitted to the hospital. At that point she was sent to an inpatient unit where both individual and family therapy were provided with the added resources of the hospital. This gave an intensive beginning to the work with her and provided firmer holding for her and the whole family.

I felt critical of myself for having failed to see Maria's more pressing need amidst the turmoil of the family as a whole. In retrospect, I can see that in the aspect of the countertransference that played on my judgment, I joined the family hope that Maria would be the new and loving mother to answer to the "bad object mother" they felt Mrs. Hodges was. I realized that when Maria could no longer sustain this role, her profound depression broke through.

In this family, the capacity to mourn was invaded by many things. From the mother's side, the ambivalence about her marriage and her husband, her anger at him, and her guilt about leaving the family were all still acute at the time of the family assessment. When she felt guilty, the children were then living accusations of her as a bad and unloving mother, and in this way they came to stand for harshly critical internal objects of her own, accusing her of the things she feared.

From the children's side, the early deprivation of living in a family damaged by parental hostility set the stage from infancy for anxiety and concern about the parental couple, long before Mrs. Hodges left for the prolonged separation. For all of the children, there was the sense during their early childhood of Father as an absent parent, followed by Mother's desertion. This was especially hard for Maria. There was also the itinerant history, which meant they had no geographical roots, no home.

There must have been something as well in Mother's internal object relations system that left her hampered in her capacity to mother, which was exacerbated by her experience of a compromised marriage. While I do not have any direct information about Mother's experience of her own parents, there is the information about her difficulty separating from them as a young woman, and the suggestion that part of what she fled when she left her husband and children for Boston may have been not just her marriage but a feeling of being swallowed up by the renewed closeness to her parents, who lived in Rome.

The children's experience of being lost led them to a depressed, stuck, isolated feeling, with a great deal of shared hopelessness and a longing for an illusory warmth they felt they had had in Rome. In fact, their mother had left them, and it seems likely they were depressed even then. Thus, the longing for the good and caring parent had been traded in for a fantasy the children shared, in which loving and rescuing were seen as attributes of the dead father and of the grandparents, while the anger was focused on Mother as an abandoning figure. Because mother's own anger and guilt pointed at herself as well, there was family fantasy agreement that she was the culprit, responsible for the children's effectively being orphaned and for Father's death.

The totality of the family's experience can also be described as a shared pathological grief reaction, in which parts in the tragedy are doled out so that anger and blame are safely focused on Mother and the children are the victims, depressed and helpless. In this version, which is a fantasy that Mother shares, Maria is the mistreated daughter who represents the wish to love and contain that Mrs. Hodges can no longer find in herself. Paolo and Antonio have identified with aspects of the dead, and also putatively victimized, father—his drinking, his anger, and his distance. Between them they reenact the relationship in which Paolo rebelled against Father with his punk dress and Father lovingly tolerated it. Now Antonio is punk and Paolo tolerates, but their need to do this for each other is another angry reproach at Mother.

This was an angry and depressed family. No single formulation can do justice to the shared difficulty they had providing holding for each other or to their inability to use the original provision of family therapy to develop more mutual understanding and support. Nevertheless, a clearly crucial aspect of their difficulty can be seen to lie in, and to impinge on, their difficulty mourning their losses, sharing their sadness, and moving on to better provide for each other. They were each entrenched as rejecting objects for each other, and this was the major obstacle to their finding other, more loving aspects in each other or anywhere.

A FAMILY THAT LOST ITS SON

A brief vignette of another family fills out our picture of family loss. In many ways, this family was like the Hodges in being compromised long before the loss occurred.

The Greensons (see Chapter 17) came to see me after the death of their 16-year-old son, Abe. I had seen him twice just before his death when he had asked for help for what he called "his trouble with sex." He had described extreme sexual anxiety over beginning to date, although the underlying difficulty was a profound fear of relationships. Then he had been killed when drinking beer and driving. He was killed instantly when the car he was driving hit a post in the middle of a divided highway. I wrote his parents a note of condolence and offered to be of help. They called me about six weeks later and asked to come to see me.

The picture was pathetic. Mr. Greenson was an immature man who managed a shoe store belonging to his extended family. There was a certain tenuous tolerance on the part of the family in allowing him to continue in his job. Mrs. Greenson put up with him with desperation, feeling he was difficult and often outrageous, and that she resented the efforts she had to make with his family in order to keep them happy with his stewardship of the business, which provided income for a number of families.

They had a 20-year-old son, Stan, who was a severe disappointment to them. He had been dyslexic and hyperactive, and on the verge of being delinquent as a teenager. Ten months earlier, he had had to get married when a girl he was dating casually got pregnant and refused to get an abortion. This event probably contributed to Abe's anxiety about sex and girls. That family, now with a newborn, was already experiencing trouble and had, as Stan had frequently done before, turned repeatedly to Mr. and Mrs. Greenson. Stan and his father had always had a difficult relationship, which Mrs. Greenson often buffered.

It became clear that Abe had been the family's hope. They had seen him as their "normal boy," and the one who might join Father in the business. Father's relationship to Abe was, however, quite critical and forbidding of pleasure. Abe's kindness and tolerance for people (including his father) made him a favorite in the family. Although his academic performance had been mediocre, he had been able to work at outside jobs in a way that made his parents proud and seemed to justify the hopes they vested in him.

His death devastated them. They understood the role of the drinking, but they felt "he had been a good kid." It seemed especially unfair that they were left with the burden of the older brother, who had flirted with death so often and who was an endless source of difficulty. Even now, he could not hold a job. Mr. Greenson dreaded the thought that he might have to let him work in the shoe store.

I met with the couple over a period of eight months to help them mourn Abe's loss and move on with their lives. The bitterness and anger between them constituted the main difficulty, for it would resurface whenever they felt on the verge of the despair that his death meant to them. About six weeks after we began meeting, Mr. Greenson began to act inappropriately around his business. He was apt to begin to rail at customers about the risks they were letting their children take, or to turn on them angrily if they were unappreciative. With his extended family, he would lecture them on the unfairness of Abe's death. In the sessions, Mrs. Greenson warned him that she felt they were beginning to question letting him continue to run the store, but he had difficulty hearing her.

Through the period of several months, however, the couple was able to begin to mourn and to pull together. Mrs. Greenson forgave her husband for what she felt had been punitive treatment of Abe since the onset of adolescence, and the couple began to invest in Stan and his wife, and especially in their infant granddaughter. With a new capacity to get past the accumulated resentments and disappointments with each other, they began to work together in ways that had not been possible for them. Over time, Mr. Greenson began to calm down, and Mrs. Greenson worked both to support him and to renew the relationship with the extended family. Both of them felt more invested in Stan and his family, and they made the extraordinary move, with a small group of other bereaved parents, to set up a branch of an organization that offered support to parents who have lost a child.

They left treatment, still a couple with years of accumulated difficulty, but reinvested in their remaining family, in their productive lives, and in each other.

Two of these families were seen only for evaluation, so that we were not able to follow their treatment. The other examples, and many examples elsewhere in the book, document the treatment experience of those families who come to us with their losses lodged as immovable foreign bodies in their internal worlds. Although the families described in this chapter have suffered from open and obvious loss, the treatment of loss and the facilitation of mourning are relevant to every case of family therapy, for loss, separation, and the pain that accompany them are at the heart of every impediment to family and individual growth.

PART V

Endings

CHAPTER 19

Termination of
Family Treatment

In the individual psychotherapeutic and psychoanalytic literature, the criteria for a correct termination have been discussed at great length (Nacht 1965, Ticho 1972). In practice, however, terminations may occur in one or another compromised fashion. Perhaps the therapist is a trainee who moves on, or the patient decides he or she has had enough when the therapist does not agree, or the patient's family is transferred geographically, or insurance runs out, and so on. Because in family therapy a number of people are involved, the likelihood of such external factors leading to termination is increased. In addition, the progress of individual members will hardly ever be in synchrony. The standards for what constitutes a process of termination need to be considered relative to the goals and the realities of the family being treated.

When the Goals of Family Therapy Have Been Met

In considering when the goals of family therapy have been met, we have found it helpful to think of the family as a horticultural enterprise, an analogy used by John Hill in discussing family research project design. We draw on Hill's metaphor to say that the needs of the family can be viewed metaphorically as the needs for the growth and maintenance of a garden. The environmental needs for clean air and water are comparable to the social provisions for family health; the fences around the garden protecting it from invasion compare to the family boundaries; the fertilization and care of the ground are comparable to the family's shared holding capacity; and the customized care of different individual plants is analogous to care of the individual family members. All these factors have a role in the growing of a garden, and each kind of activity is called for at some time.

It is the family-as-a-whole, however, that tends the garden, not ourselves. We come in when there has been a failure or temporary crisis, not to take over the enterprise. And we need to do what is required to best get the gardeners going again, not simply to harvest one plant or one crop. In this endeavor, family therapy as we have been working with it is an intervention that aims to focus somewhere beneath the social level and above the level of the individual. It is compatible with both social and individuals levels of intervention, and specifically, it is entirely compatible with individual psychotherapy. But the goals appropriate to the family level of intervention are those of getting the gardeners to gardening again in a reasonably effective way. When we have done that, it is time to stop. This is not to say that the family will always see things the way we do. Probably more often they will not. But having this kind of framework will at least give us an idea of when we think we have done our job, and wherein we have fallen short.

The general goals of object relations family therapy include the following:

1. The recognition and reworking of the defensive projective identifications that have previously been required in the family.

2. The treatment of the family's capacity to provide contextual holding for its members so that their attachment needs and conditions for growth can be met.

3. The overall reinstatement or construction of the series of centered holding relationships between each of its members to support their needs for attachment, individuation, and growth sufficient to allow each individual to "take it from there."

4. The return of the family to the overall developmental level appropriate to its tasks as set by its own preferences and by the needs of the family members.

5. The clarification of remaining individual needs in family members so that they can get them met with as much support as they need from the family. By this, we specifically include individual needs for psychotherapy, as well as more general needs for other growth endeavors.

Criteria for Termination

In a general case that is not subject to external constraints, meeting the goals of treatment constitutes the criterion for the consideration of termination, both by the family and the therapist. It is important to treat the initiative by the family with seriousness even if the therapist does not agree, especially because of the absence of clear guidelines. Of course, if an arbitrary number of sessions is imposed on the situation from the beginning, this more complex and subjective consideration is avoided. But as we noted at the outset (Chapter 2), that is not generally a useful approach, inasmuch as the multiple factors relevant to how long to work and when to stop constitute just the kind of complexity we prefer to consider and work with rather than to simply manage by formula.

WHEN ARE FAMILIES READY?

Families feel ready to take things onto themselves at different times and in different ways. A family whose adolescent is being discharged from an inpatient unit may feel that it has had enough exposure to our way of working and so uses the discharge to discontinue work, whether that is the recommendation or not. Or the end of the school year and the adolescent's summer plans may be used to impose an ending that has little to do with the internal needs of the family. At other times, these calendar events form a frame that bounds a piece of work, and we may feel there is synchrony with the substantive progress. A few brief examples will demonstrate the range of possibilities.

The Dickie family, described in Chapter 14, used a long summer break to test their capacity to be a family. By the fall, they found they had gotten enough of what they needed to feel they could now manage. The therapist's feeling that they had more internal work to do no longer coincided with their feeling of need.

In contrast, the Wolff family, also described in Chapter 14, met in family therapy over a period of several months while the parents worked out their marital reunion and until the children's relationship to their parents reached a more solid footing. At this point, family and therapist decided that individual therapy for three family members—Mother, Father, and Wilson—made sense. Subsequently, the older sister also came back and was referred for individual and group work. The family as a container was able to support the individual therapies in a way it previously could not.

Another family group consisting of three adult children—two sisters and a brother—and their mother had met for a period of six months to work on the relationship of the children with their mother. Although there was some sense of increased communication, the children continued to feel that the mother remained fixed in her need to deny negative feelings, and therefore still in the position of their childhood of being unable to hear anything realistic from them. The mother had been able to share some of her memories of strain and loneliness while the children were growing up, but to a considerable extent she still felt misunderstood and maligned. When she retired to New Mexico's warmer climate, there was an acknowledgment that this meant the end of the attempt to get her to understand the children's complaints, and that they would have to proceed with their adult tasks by themselves.

The vantage of analytic family therapy is useful to therapists in formulating their understanding of the family and of their task, whether the task itself is long-term or short-term, by circumstance or default. The training of the therapist in the analytic view of the family and its members offers a long-term, life-cycle perspective, but this by no means dictates that the choice be to conduct long-term therapy on every occasion. If therapists find themselves working in a setting or with a family where long-term work would be the ideal but is not possible, there is no reason to limit their conceptualization of the context in which they carry out a shorter piece of work. We hope that their training or experience with this point of view will enrich whatever work can be done and give a way of viewing the place of the limited piece of work that can be offered. This would be true, for instance, if a family was seen during the hospitalization of one of its members and could not continue after discharge, or if a military family was transferred after a few weeks. In these cases, we hope therapists will formulate the role of their limited interventions and share with the families their views of the work that remains. In doing this, their brief encounters with the families should be enriched by their larger understanding of the processes, even if they are not able to offer all they might under other circumstances.

Varieties of Termination

We will review the gamut of termination situations: those that represent failures in treatment, termination in constrained situations (such as the departure of the therapist or a geographic move by the family), and satisfactory completion of treatment.

A SATISFACTORY TERMINATION WITH AN OLDER COUPLE

Gene and Rose Holt, described in Chapter 17, were approaching 70 when we finished our work, which included both sex therapy and marital therapy. They had refound each other just as when they were high school sweethearts.

As we neared the end, I [D.E.S.] began to have feelings of sweet sadness. I thought of Gene's father, still energetic and loving in his eighties, just before his death. I ruminated pleasantly ahead to what my own life might be like in its later years. I thought of what I had been able to help them achieve.

This fit with what Gene was feeling, but Rose had other, more difficult reactions that were a "rude" invasion of my quiet idylls. Gene noted that she was angry at him because he had said he was ready to stop, even though she agreed that they were ready. "We're having a great time being so close. But something is in the way right now. I feel uneasy, and I want to get through it."

Gene had had a dream the night before, set in his New England childhood town. "I was on the trolley in Boston, wishing for a father to talk to. That is what you've been to me, and I'll miss it . . . like losing my father again, and I only found him when I grew up. In the dream I thought, 'There are no trolleys in Washington.'"

This fit with my fond countertransference for him and for them, and I felt the fondness and flattery in what he said, and the ease with his sadness about our parting with good feelings.

But Rose said that she had more difficult feelings—that there was a child in her that did not exist any more. She had grown up, and the child was dead. That was frightening. It was not just herself, it was both of them and their children who were grown. "My father is also dead. I share some of this longing with Gene, for a father, like a Catholic father confessor. But I'm feeling angry at you, I know it. In spite of all the good that has come, feeling closer to Gene and to my children, I feel it's been such a waste all these years." She then said that she had had a dream the night before, too.

"I was in a big hall at a party with some people we were friendly with but no longer see. Then it was as if I were in a hospital and going to see a psychiatrist I did not particularly want to see. He was not very friendly as we shook hands. I said to him, 'Would you like to go into the other room?' and he answered, 'No. I don't think this is going to work.' I agreed and thought, 'If this hasn't worked after all this time, how can it work now?' The psychiatrist said, 'What are you going to do about it?' I thought, still in the dream, 'It's like with alcohol. I have to take it as my own responsibility to get well.' "

We all understood this dream as speaking for her experience of rejection by me, and the hopelessness and anger she kept at bay about it. At the end of the dream was the resolve to take responsibility for her own difficulty, which she saw as "having been sick and now being well." But she felt frightened by becoming old, at the same time that she felt, in a way, separate for the first time.

She said, "I felt real love for my mother recently, which I have hidden away. To my knowledge, I've never felt it before. I also have a feeling of being alone, which is great . . . you know, separate. A lot is positive."

"Except being mad at me," I said, able to address this because I was getting over being angry at her for not appreciating me, and was seeing the chronic anger and longing she had and would have to live with.

"Yes," she said. "I've changed, but I feel toward you right this minute as I did about my old psychiatrist. He said, 'You'll figure out how to have an orgasm, and then you'll be a woman.' But he also said, 'Perhaps you'll never have an orgasm.' Well, now I can, thanks to you. And I'm terribly grateful, really I am. Don't think I'm not, please. But I have to let you know that I will be angry about the things I have to go on living with. Just so you know about that."

"I know about it," I said.

I was feeling grateful to her for letting me know about the disappointment, and for not letting me go off with my false idyll intact. And I thought perhaps I had been reinstated as a mother who could hear her disappointment and anger without insisting on whitewashing and denying her inner experience.

"Do you think Rose's talking about the disappointment and anger along with the good things helps the two of you?" I asked.

Gene said, "I do think so. It's so hard for me to tune in on her reservations, and on this side of the feelings. But when I can't, I know it's harder for her, and then something comes between us. And she's the one who brings more feeling into our relationship anyway, so it's important. I do think we're ready to stop, but it's true that it's not all easy."

I now understood his need, too, to have the darker side of the termination spoken for. The loss of the Boston trolleys to hold him, the anger at his mother for denying his father to him in childhood, and the impossibility of being angry at his father were difficulties he put into Rose, thereby getting help from her about them. And I felt a renewed fondness and sadness. The work this couple had always been willing to do was not a kind many families faced so doggedly and persistently, and I would miss them, too.

This couple presented some of the pleasures and sadness that make termination work rewarding in its own right, especially when it is accompanied by a consciousness in the therapist of comparable mourning in the countertransference.

TERMINATION WHEN THE WORK STOPS BEING HELPFUL

The next case is one of a mixture of success and failure. The family members felt they were not ready, but the therapist felt that there were not likely to be further gains in the foreseeable future. At termination, there remained a quality of the family being stuck.

The Roberts family had come to see me [D.E.S.] originally because of a sexual problem. Mr. Roberts had lost interest in sex soon after marriage, and Mrs. Roberts, who had an active sexual life before marriage, had unconsciously chosen him because she felt his sexual timidity ensured he would never abandon her. We worked first in sex therapy, with a moderate restoration of the couple's capacity to be more regularly intimate. At that point, it became clear that the difficulties lay more in the overall design of their partnership and their family. Mrs. Roberts wished to remake her husband, just as she had chosen someone she would have to teach about sexuality. She had a dream during couple therapy. While she was having a picnic with someone else, Mr. Roberts roared up, riding on the largest motorcycle imaginable. Both of them were able to laugh at the unmasking of the wish contained in the dream that she be carried off by him as a secret convert to a supermasculine, wild cult.

Even while they were struggling with the areas of disappointment and lack of fit in their marriage, it became apparent that their two children were involved in many of the areas of conflict. I began to meet alternately with the family as well as the couple, dealing with the projective delineation of the 12-year-old girl as the reincarnation of Mrs. Roberts's own impulsive, immature, and self-centered mother. (See Chapter 9 for a session with this family.) Over the year of work, the intensity of the projection onto the girl, with a complementary idealization of the 10-year-old son, diminished, and both children emerged as more individuated and more flexibly viewed within the family.

The parents' marriage, however, did not change much. Mrs. Roberts extended her decision-making period indefinitely, while Mr. Roberts seemed to reach a stage in which he could not become more flexible. Neither individual nor couple sessions changed either of these positions over the next few months.

I began to feel that the family had managed quite a lot of progress but that therapy was beginning to be used as a reason for not taking responsibility for their decisions. It seemed to me it was becoming part of a mildly disintegrative pattern, unmodified by my efforts to understand. So, with a painful sense of resignation, I suggested termination. I felt they knew what I had to offer and could judge their capacity to use it, and they were free to return at some point in the future. I also shared with them my fears that it was becoming counterproductive.

They were reluctant to sever the ties with the work, especially Mr. Roberts, who said he liked "to be taught." Nevertheless, because I could see no realistic chance of offering more to them, and because the sense of hanging on seemed to be part of avoiding facing pieces of their reality, there was no realistic alternative.

Through the last several sessions, the mourning of the treatment focused on the compromised quality of the family members' relationships to each other and their difficulty with making use of therapy. This work focused their attention on how they shortchanged themselves in a way they previously could not see. As often happens, the mourning of lost opportunity in the termination phase was able to highlight the work to be done with a new intensity, but the family left, still uncertain about their capacity to do better.

The compromise in this family is of the sort we sometimes have to accept, usually quite painfully. Not every family will be able to follow the lead of the therapist in constructing a better containing environment, and not every family therapy will lead to a better functioning family. We have to be able to terminate when we have outlived our usefulness and to accept the limits of what can be achieved, leaving the door open for future contact.

TERMINATION DUE TO ABSENT CONTEXTUAL HOLDING

Sometimes the family's holding capacity is so impaired that the focused transference to the core issues shows up at the very beginning of treatment, seeming to preclude the contextual transference. Although the treatment seems to be dominated by this difficult focused or core transference, it is actually the absence of any contextual relationship that causes therapy to fail. In the following case, the difficulty was partly one of parental abdication of holding functions, and partly the insufficiency of those efforts they could offer.

The Marions were referred after the discovery of sibling and step-sibling incest in a remarried family. The previous marriages of both parents had been difficult. Mr. Marion's first wife killed herself during a psychotic episode and was discovered by the youngest boy, then 3 years old. Mrs. Marion's first husband was alcoholic and had been jailed briefly for rape.

Mr. and Mrs. Marion had every conscious wish for treatment for their combined six children but were hardly able to maintain their efforts against the many destructive attacks against therapy. The derisiveness of the oldest teenage boy, who had been the leader in the sibling incest, was copied in the sessions by the two other boys, aged 11 and 5. The oldest boy took the lead in transforming play activities such as drawing into spitball fights, and would mock our interventions with verbal abuse. On many occasions, the three boys ended up dismantling toys and tearing up the girls' drawings.

In the same way, the other children had followed his lead in extending the sexual activities during the previous year. The family was so difficult to work with that one of us could not manage and asked the other to collaborate in cotherapy, but with only slight improvement in the therapeutic holding capacity. We shared the feeling, after several months of work, that institutional care and massive intervention were required for the two older boys before anything could change, despite the parents' overt cooperation. Although the second boy did receive long-term hospitalization for his congenital hyperactivity and combined learning and behavior disorder, the parents were unable to accept our recommendation for the older boy, who continued with another therapist in weekly psychotherapy, which was inadequate for his mounting characterological difficulty and delinquency.

The work with them continued to be dominated by accumulated destructive attacks, so that those who did want help could not get it in family therapy. Accordingly, we recommended the dissolution of the family work and the continuation of individual therapy with the 5-year-old boy and the preadolescent girl who had been the principal object of the sexual activity. One of us would also work regularly with the parents. It turned out that this approach was not altogether successful either, but it did seem to allow the best leverage on the most workable aspects of the situation.

ABRUPT TERMINATION AFTER CONSULTATION

During my residency, I [D.F.S.] had the experience of having Nathan Ackerman conduct a demonstration interview with the first family I had in treatment. I had been dealing with their feelings about the presenting problem: school phobia in their 17-year-old boy. The phobia was rooted in the mother's dependency and her guilty reaction to the death of her brother in his adolescence. The father was a passive man who was as phobic of the treatment as the boy was of school. Father did not show up for the interview with Ackerman, and Ackerman made hay of this. During the interview he asked the boy if he had ever thought of asking his mother to one of the school dances, exploring fully and dramatically the oedipal ramifications of his staying home with his mother. The audience loved it and so did I. It was also the last I saw of the family.

It is entirely possible that this family would have balked at treatment without the provocative interview conducted by "The Master." Any of us could make a similar mistake in our approach with a family, perhaps especially in a teaching consultation, when we are being dramatic or entertaining. This lesson in humility is important to us as therapists as well as teachers. It is more important to demonstrate careful work with resistance in the initial interview and attention to the contextual transference than to delve for defended material for our own aggrandisement as spectacular therapists.

PREMATURE TERMINATION WHEN THERAPIST OR FAMILY MOVES

Some treatments are limited by the calendar, by moves or changes of assignment that are imposed on the natural course of the work from the outside. This includes the time that a therapist will be employed at an agency, or the job reassignment of one of the adults in the family. A child going off to college may impose the same constraint, if the difficulty is not seen by the family as sufficient to require keeping the child at home. In some of these changes, the therapist may feel the family is being shortsighted in allowing the external events to govern the duration of the work, as in the case of insisting that a child go to college when the therapist doubts the child's capacity to operate independently. Careful interpretation and working through can extend the treatment until its natural ending. When there is a degree of volition in the planning, the question must be asked about the defensive use by the family of the external constraints. Nevertheless, even the conclusion by the therapist that the external plans are motivated by a wish to escape from therapy will not necessarily enable him or her to demonstrate this to the family and persuade them to continue.

Other external circumstances are beyond the control of either the family or the therapist, such as the duration of training assignments for the therapist, or the cycle of military reassignment. The time limit may be used to encapsulate a mourning process and to demonstrate the effect of loss in the family. This work with time-limited family therapy derives from the formulation of brief psychotherapy, which plans a set number of sessions and focuses on the process of loss and mourning in that work to illuminate the patient's difficulty.

Short-term therapy has a specific place in the dynamic and psychoanalytic psychotherapies. Balint and colleagues (1972) demonstrated the application of interpretation derived from psychoanalysis to brief psychotherapy. Since then, methods of short-term dynamic psychotherapy have been outlined by Mann (1973), Sifneos (1972), Malan (1975), and Davanloo (1978). Mann has conceptualized short-term therapy as a bounded process organized around mourning the inevitable end of the therapy itself, which is a paradigm of other losses in the patient's life. This is close to Norman Paul's early work (1967, Paul and Grosser 1965) on the central role of mourning in family therapy. Sifneos has described the use of short-term therapy for an intensive, goal-focused piece of work, in which the therapist either purposefully provokes anxiety or uses the anxiety that accompanies a crisis. Our conceptualization of short-term family therapy draws on these ideas.

If family therapy has to be shortened because of external constraints set either by the institution or by family considerations, we would use the time available to examine the problem and its parameters, to address the current crisis, and to help the family plan for the future. If the constraint derives from the members' ideas of what they need, then we tread the fine line between interpreting the restriction of their vision and accepting their right to set their own goals. If it is imposed by factors external to the family, then part of our work will be to help the family members understand the impact on their lives of this external reality and to make plans keeping this in mind while indicating what longer-term therapy could offer if they became able to control their life circumstances to accommodate it. In either case, however, we would rather do a bounded piece of work that gives the family members an understanding of what they need but are lacking than make a bold intervention and saddle them with the idea that that should be enough when it probably is not.

This use of the termination to highlight the family's reaction to loss is intrinsic to the process of any termination work. As in any psychoanalytic process, the loss of the therapist and the therapeutic context is dealt with in the parting from the therapy. This is demonstrated in the next two vignettes, which illustrate the reemergence of issues during the separation from a therapist when the family was being relocated for occupational reasons beyond their control.

The Grieving Process in Incomplete Therapy

A supervisee, himself a faculty-level clinician at a training institution, discussed the Dunstan case in consultation. Mr. and Mrs. Dunstan brought her three children from a former marriage to treatment because the 15-year-old daughter, Rachel, had refused to visit her father as ordered by the court, claiming he had made sexual advances during her last visit. Her younger brothers, however, were attached to the father, and one of them, Louis, 8 years old, was bitterly identified with the absent father and railed at his mother and stepfather for taking him away from him by moving. The family had moved temporarily to Washington while the stepfather was enrolled in a graduate degree program.

In the family treatment, which was carried out with parallel couple therapy and individual therapy for the girl, the sexual attempt by the father was confirmed. This could be related to the mother's own experience of rejection by her family and her use of sexualized approaches to men during childhood as a way of getting herself taken care of. She was able, both in the couple therapy and in the family work, to share her own previous plight and to mourn the absence of effective parenting for her that had led to this. It could then be seen to link to the choice of her first husband. This was not easy work, because Mrs. Dunstan had the drama and flair that went along with her borderline personality. The capacity to lose control and feel empty, and the swings of rage that can accompany this diagnosis, were demonstrated. In the process, however, the relationship between the couple was strengthened, and both Rachel and Louis improved their relationships within the family and outside. Louis, for instance, was able to use his stepfather's newfound support to mourn the loss of the relationship with his father, since it turned out that the father was actually on the verge of being sexually exploitative of the boys as well.

At the end of a year of treatment, Mr. Dunstan finished his graduate degree, and so the family was ready to return to Oregon, which was where the children's father also lived. This time, however, it was the relationship to the therapist that had to be mourned. The family members felt they had grown a great deal but were frightened about having to leave treatment before the work was done. In the face of this threat, fear and panic could be felt to pervade the sessions, as Mrs. Dunstan turned first on her husband and then on the therapist to blame them for not caring or helping. The children seemed more depressed, and Mr. Dunstan seemed more helpless. In her individual sessions, Rachel again turned angrily on her mother and then seemed to be trying to seduce her therapist in the same way that she had presumably used with her father.

In the countertransference, the therapist began to doubt the efficacy of the work done with them, which had until now seemed satisfactory. He wondered if they would manage and felt hurt by the sudden and seemingly relentless attack on his ability to be helpful. In supervision, he was able to understand this as the renewal of the initial difficulties and to see that it provided new information about the difficulties with object loss, which were the underlying presenting difficulties.

With this understanding, the new difficulty could be interpreted as family and individual regression in response to loss of the therapist, both as an individual who was important to each of them and as the representative of the holding capacity of the therapy, which meant so much to their new ability to help each other. This work went on for the three months before they had to leave, with the good result that by the end they felt calmer and had worked through the losses of therapy and therapist so that they were able to regain the highest level of mutual support and relatedness they had managed during the therapy. They felt strongly that they would need more therapy in Oregon but were grateful for the work they had thus far done and optimistic about the use they could make of additional work.

In this termination, the family was not ready to stop therapy and recognized that from the outset. Nevertheless, the termination of this phase of their work with the therapist they had come to value and trust proved to be a valuable spur to their growth. This kind of work can be expected to pave the way for a successful transfer to a new therapeutic situation.

In the next example, a similar situation had a different but equally satisfying result.

Mr. and Mrs. Pearson and their 9-year-old daughter, Julie, were difficult to treat. Mr. Pearson was a schizoid, borderline man who externalized blame and found it impossible to discuss feelings. Mrs. Pearson was a histrionic woman from a deprived background. She had locked herself in a closet several times to avoid harming Julie. Both Mr. and Mrs. Pearson had been hospitalized in rapid succession in a dramatic folie à deux with psychotic and suicidal content. A fairly junior family therapy student took on this family that had been labeled as "untreatable." With the dedication and persistence of the therapist, they calmed down and came to family therapy regularly over the next two years, eventually requesting an increase to twice a week. Initially, there was the threat of psychotic decompensation, especially on Mr. Pearson's side, while Mrs. Pearson would leave the family habitually for periods of a week at a time to avoid raging at them or feeling trapped by them. The child attended every session and drew pictures of monsters and animals with large teeth. With the progress of the therapy, she put braces on the teeth and the mouths altered so that they became mouths for being able to get nourishment and for speaking, rather than the original mouths, which were mainly for biting.

When the father received the reassignment that was a required part of his job, the family began to work on the loss six months before the expected termination. They regressed to the issues that had faced them at the beginning of the therapy. But with persistent interpretation that this reaction was in response to the loss, they were slowly able to articulate their sense of loss and their feeling of dependence on the therapist.

Then Mrs. Pearson did something entirely unexpected. She took a job that would bring her back to the area weekly and asked to continue working with the therapist. This was agreeable to the therapist, but no sooner had this been agreed on than Mr. Pearson suggested that they travel back to the area together every three or four weeks so that they could all continue. This was agreed on, and the work resumed the quality of midphase working through, much enriched by the mourning and resolution that had been followed by a renewed commitment.

In this case, the therapist wondered if she had agreed to an arrangement motivated by a collusive process to avoid the grief of termination. Because the ending of the work had not grown organically out of finishing the work the family actually needed, the supervisor felt there was no reason to refuse the family's renewed dedication to therapy. The mother's request for individual therapy represented her newfound ability to turn to someone in a trusting way to attempt work she found threatening. The father's offer to make the effort to do that much traveling represented an open commitment to the work, which he had been unable to demonstrate previously. In this instance, it was important not to get caught in the notion that the process of the termination itself was the sacred item but to attend to the family's persisting need.

The next example demonstrates the countertransference experience of a therapist who did not feel too much had been accomplished, and who had to stop with the family because his own training rotation was over.

Countertransference to Loss of a Therapist Leaving

The family consisted of a somewhat paranoid, defensive father who was a university professor, a chronically psychotic mother with a simplified personality, and two children. The older girl, a freshman in college, had had a brief psychotic breakdown and now appeared to share many of the characteristics of the mother and to become less functional over time. The younger child, a boy, was alert and energetic intellectually, and the family vested him with a great deal of the hope for a better future and continued growth.

The continued difficulty of the girl left the family with a sense of overinvestment in this boy, and the hopelessness about the mother made them fearful for the girl. During a year's work, the father became a bit more trusting and was able to share some of his disappointment in his marriage. This helped the mother to become more directly responsive to him and to become, in general, partially rehabilitated. She began managing social activities at their church, for instance. In turn, the girl became less crippled by her identification with her. The boy was able to speak more directly of his fears for his own mental health and about the constraints the family's previously guarded and overprotective stance about him had imposed.

When the therapist, a young man, was leaving because of the completion of his psychiatry fellowship, he felt a sense of disappointment for this family with their limited capacity. Their improved ability to express gratitude, however, and the improvement in the mother were sources of satisfaction. At this point, the boy asked the father for some individual therapy for the issues that had just been uncovered for him, and this was arranged.

The therapist felt a particular loss at not being able to work with this boy, with whom he realized he was identified. It was this that enabled him to speak to the family's investment in the boy. Throughout this process, the countertransference feeling of loss was a mixture of his own lost opportunity and his experience of the family's sadness and lost opportunity. He then realized that what had been helpful to the family was its experience of having been able to trust and work with him, and then experience the loss in a new way.

This family presented a complex experience of loss. The loss of the therapy brought up their years of empty longing but enabled them to experience it in a modified way. Nevertheless, the therapist's carrying away the sense of failed opportunity represented the family's sustained attitude of tragedy and failure, and his losing them included his having to recognize the limits of what he could offer them, both because of the brevity of his availability and because of their inherent limitations.

Termination When Family Therapy Leads to Other Work

The termination picture is attenuated when family therapy is only one phase of the work a couple or family is engaged in, and the ending of family work leads to a continuation of work for most or all of the members of a family. If, of course, some of the family members are *not* going to continue, then they need to be given the chance to carry out their piece of the grieving.

Jordan and Penny Fogg consulted me about their marital issues for six months. Part of the work involved their relationship to her daughter by a first marriage, a girl who as an older adolescent was a burden to this couple, refusing to do much in school and unmotivated for treatment. Another part of the work focused on the question of whether their marriage would survive. Penny found Jordan unresponsive and remote, whereas he found her demanding and controlling.

The work in the couple therapy helped them to understand these characterizations as projections based on their internal object worlds, and they began to own their own projections. As they did so, the daughter began to do a bit better at school, although it was clear she would never do well. After this period, I referred each of them for intensive individual therapy. Jordan had difficulty establishing a relationship with his therapist at first, because many of the same issues that had disabled him in the marriage interfered there as well. Penny found the establishment of intensive therapy easier, and by the end of a year after I had first seen them, both were working well in their individual therapies. By this time, their fights were quickly ended when they could each identify the issues projected into the fight, and each continued to feel they had their own work to do, although Penny could voice this with more commitment than Jordan.

We now agreed that the couple therapy had run its course. We stopped with the proviso that they could come back if either of them felt it would be useful. We met a few more times over the next three months to confirm their sense that they could manage things themselves and to allow for ending our work together. During this time, they both expressed a worry that they would not do so well without the couple therapy setting, and they talked of missing me. But the anxiety about having to manage on their own was not marked, because they each felt they had plenty of resources. Over the next two years, each of them thrived individually, and the marriage grew stronger. When I last saw Penny, she said that their individual growth had brought the family a closeness that now seemed permanent.

In this case, the mourning was not intense, as the loss of the contextual aspect of the therapy was only a relative loss. It was tempered by the continuing presence of a therapist for each of them, which let them feel they would continue to be supported in their provision of mutual holding. The loss was centered on the loss of the person of the therapist as someone they felt was a friendly and helpful support, and on their mild anxiety that this specific therapeutic setting was the crucial element in their well-being.

Transfer Following Termination

The process of termination will also be different if the family is going to continue in treatment by being transferred to a new therapist or a new cotherapy team. In this case, the mourning and processing must focus on the aspects of the loss that are felt to go with the *person* of the therapist or therapists. This can be a useful exploration in itself. The family that has benefited from the therapy will have an investment in the therapist. Often, especially if the work has gone well, they are also fond of the therapist, and there is the real loss of a helpful person. Unlike life outside therapy, however, the process of scrutinizing losses here makes that loss available as a growing and learning experience.

Many therapists who are fond of their patients do not want to face the anger that the family may feel toward them for leaving. It is especially important to pay attention to this phase of the mourning process in the case of termination, and to clarify the way in which it belongs to the departing therapists. The anger is directed at them in the contextual transference for abandoning the family, and not at the new therapist as an interloper. If the departing therapist does not do this work of clarifying and accepting the anger, there is a substantial danger that the family will pin it on the contextual transference to the new therapist and will be unable to make a new connection.

TRANSFERRING FAMILIES IN CLINICS AND PRIVATE PRACTICE

In any event, this kind of danger is a major reason that transfers of families often fall through. (This is equally true of the transfer of individual patients in the clinic setting.) One way of handling this problem is to suggest that some time be allowed to pass for mourning to proceed after the therapist has gone, before reassignment is made. After a period of a few weeks or months, the family can be reevaluated, perhaps by a senior clinician at the clinic, who can assess the need and current goals of continued work. At this point, the family that can articulate its continuing need is less likely to hold it against the new therapist for not being the old one.

In the private practice setting, the need for transfer is a less frequent occurrence. It is less common for the therapist to move, so that the need for transfer is more apt to come from something initiated by the patient (e.g., the kind of geographical move we discussed earlier). The changes initiated by the patients and families themselves are less likely to lead to an open, angry assault on the contextual transference, but they often lead, nevertheless, to unconscious anger toward the therapist, as though it were the therapist abandoning the family, instead of the family leaving the therapist. Family members may feel it is the therapist's fault for allowing them to leave and sever their connection, just as an adolescent departing for college or leaving home will often turn angrily on the parents who allow this risky step. This projection has its roots in the way the young child takes it for granted that parents are responsible for their child's well-being. Any anxiety about this is felt to be the fault of their holding context, inasmuch as all that is beyond his or her capacity to endure. Age, however, does not erase the transference to us that holds us responsible for patients' safety and well-being.

With all these vicissitudes of the termination process, the question arises whether to transfer a given family or whether to recommend that the family take some time to consolidate before returning. With some families, it will have been possible to anticipate the therapist's or family's availability for only a limited period of time and to plan for the therapy as a time-limited piece of work with its own rhythm and integrity. If this goes well, then the final part of the work is an assessment of where the family is and of their continuing needs.

In other cases, the therapy will have been open-ended in the ordinary way family therapy should usually be, and the imposed ending will seem more as though it happens in the middle of things. In this case, the therapist and family should carefully consider together whether the balance lies with encouraging the family to "take a breather" or whether they are in need of and ready for direct continuation. This consideration will, as we have said, involve the shared work of mourning.

WHEN THE THERAPIST ACCEPTS A FAMILY IN TRANSFER

When we are referred families that have been in treatment with a previous therapist, we must deal with this part of their history at every level. First of all, seeing a new therapist will bring up the feelings of loss of the former therapist. The thing to do is to ask about the therapist, what he or she was like, not in a suspicious way but simply to indicate understanding and tolerance of their continuing attachment and ambivalence. The transference to the former therapist affects the development of the contextual transference to us and needs to be worked on in the first interview. Second, the focused transference to the previous therapist is now part of the family's history and should be dealt with as such. It is of equal importance to other matters of their history. Put another way, the previous therapist is part of the family's internal object relations system. We can grow weary of hearing about some other therapist when we are ready and willing to work, so it helps to remember that this *is* the work of transfer. At a certain point, the family will be able to accept an interpretation based on our understanding of their defensive clinging to the former therapist out of fear of engaging with us and being left again. Without this work, a transfer often will not take.

The Object Relations of Termination

We have reviewed many of the major processes and kinds of work required during the termination process. Although one setting for termination will emphasize some aspects more than others, the general outlines follow the phases of the grieving process described by Lindemann (1944) and Bowlby (1960) and elaborated by Parkes (1972).

DENIAL

This begins with attention to each possible way the family and its members may treat the loss of termination. We understand that some family members will feel differently from others. Some will consciously be glad to get away, whereas others will be worried and lost. Each of these components should be highlighted and acknowledged as contributing to work on the experience of loss that many families express.

ANGRY PROTEST

Frequently, one or more members of the family will speak for the anger, denigrating the therapist or the clinic. Or anger may be voiced only indirectly, with its verbalization assigned by the family to someone who is allowed to express anger without the acknowledgment that others also own the same feeling. For instance, a frequently outrageous teenager may rail about his treatment by a coach in a way that expresses an important feeling about the "family coach," that is, the therapist. Here, exploration of the sharing of the anger by others is important in revealing its ownership, then reaching the underlying disappointment and discovering the consequences the family fears.

SADNESS, DEPRESSION, AND DESPAIR

Acceptance and tolerance of the affects of depression and sadness are hallmarks of the mature capacity to manage loss and to rework the ambivalence concerning an attachment figure in each instance of loss (Zetzel 1965). In Melanie Klein's formulation (1935), this means a reworking of the depressive position, the achievement of a relationship to an object about which angry and loving feelings are felt.

The expression of sadness about the loss of the therapist and about the family's position is an important component of the process of mourning in the termination, although the sadness may not always be about the loss of the therapist. For a more narcissistic family, or for a family who has felt disappointed with the work, the loss will be of opportunity, of a thing rather than a person. The processing of this disappointment is harder for the therapist, but for that reason, all the more important.

For the families whose situation is less hopeful, or where clinical depression is a more significant part of the picture, the feeling of hopelessness and despair may be prominent. This has to be understood as the representation of the schizoid problem that Fairbairn (1940) and Guntrip (1969) have helped us to understand. Being left has the internal meaning of confirmation of the family's badness or worthlessness. In therapeutic terms, this often means to them that they are bad patients, incapable of being helped. If the object is felt to neglect or punish the self because the object is bad, then the self has no hope because there is nothing the person can do to improve the object. The internal maneuver that makes the situation feel more hopeful is to turn the accusation of badness onto the self, thereby preserving the image of the object as good. Then there is more hope that the object will become kinder if the person can improve a situation, which Fairbairn (1943) noted made the badness seem "conditional"—that is, capable of amelioration.

This explains a frequent reaction of patients to loss. They become self-accusatory and self-denigrating, rather than focusing anger on the therapist and allowing themselves to feel the sadness of the loss. A family may turn the anger inward by blaming one of their own members for the "badness" that explains the loss of the therapist. The close relationship between the internalization of anger and the feeling of hopeless despair is important whenever repeated loss is on the table, and especially in termination.

ACCEPTANCE AND READINESS FOR REATTACHMENT

Whether the family members are preparing to go off on their own or planning to "reattach" to another therapist, the phase of acceptance is important. Much of this will come after the full impact of the loss sinks in, after we actually stop meeting. Usually there are premonitions of this aspect of mourning, however, as when the family begins to envision the things they might be able to go on to, or to imagine what the therapist might think of them if he or she saw them at some point in the future. The inability to do any of this is often a sign either of undisclosed anger at the therapist or of being stuck in the depressed and hopeless aspect of the previous phase, and is a matter of concern. This does not mean the termination will not ultimately go well, but the stuck quality has to be understood and interpreted wherever possible.

The major importance of the emerging capacity for reattachment has to do with the family members giving up their attachment to the therapy's holding, which has allowed them to rework their own holding capacity for each other. Mourning this aspect of the therapy and of the therapist facilitates the family's reattachment to one another, and particularly the taking in of those aspects of a benign attachment and shared holding capacity that had been delegated to the therapist. It is particularly these that have to be returned, and if the therapy has gone well, they will be reabsorbed in a much modified and matured form.

Transference and Countertransference in Termination

Much of what we have been saying will be seen to describe the contents of the transference the family brings to the therapist during the termination phase. Once again, it is the contextual transference that is most in focus in the work with the whole family. In couple therapy the loss may have a larger component of focused transference. Even in individual therapy, however, a good deal of the sense of loss is directed at the loss of the therapist's holding capacity. Herein the transference returns to the situation of the beginning of therapy. In all forms of therapy, the early transference is predominantly to the capacity of the therapist to form a container. The loss of the therapy, thus, completes the cycle, and in a way, brings the end back to the beginning.

The countertransference process of termination is a crucial component in letting the family go in a positive way. As we first contemplate that the family will leave, and then as the end draws near, we will have feelings about the loss that are comparable and complementary to the ones the family members express. If the family has been a disappointment to treat, or a difficult one to manage, we may feel principally relief and good riddance—as may the family feel about us. We may be angry at them for leaving us, as though our services are being thereby denigrated, and this will be an especially important feeling in the case of a family that quits therapy in anger. Or we may be fond of them and feel a sense of deep and personal loss, or the mixture of loss and pride felt upon launching children who are growing up and separating healthily on their own.

The range of feelings and fantasies is endless, as complex and varied as the feelings and fantasies that the families bring to us. Harold Searles (1979) has taught us that the exploration of the therapist's countertransference to the patient's growth and to loss of the patient is a crucial part of the therapist's work in deciding when termination is appropriate, and what the meaning of the termination is to the patient or family.

The last example of termination involves the first patient and the first sustained family treatment by one of us [D.E.S.]. This case was commented upon in his first psychiatric publication and is presented at the end of the book with the sense that it also brings to completion, for the moment at least, a cycle in the study of the family, an odyssey begun with this family (Scharff 1969).

Termination of Simultaneous Individual and Family Therapy

I first saw Judy Green a few days after beginning my residency, when she was 14. She was admitted for an overdose of one hundred aspirin, taken after two brief hospitalizations elsewhere. Her history included growing up with a depressed, borderline mother who once forced her to nurse at the breast long after weaning her, when she was 4; a compensatory oedipal sexualized closeness to her father, who died when she was 5; incest between the ages of 9 and 10 with her brother, who was a year older; and sexual promiscuity during the year before admission. On admission, she was diagnosed as a borderline adolescent, and I saw her in intensive psychotherapy while the ward social worker saw her parents.

Judy continued to act out on the ward and after six months had to be discharged to another hospital because we could no longer stop her from being self-destructive. This precipitous discharge worked to her therapeutic advantage, since it provided a reliving in the treatment of the loss of her father through the transference loss of me. This time the loss was not permanent, because she came back into treatment with me when she returned to outpatient status. Her acting out stopped. She became an inhibited mid-phase adolescent and soon began to do well.

As her parents developed more perspective in therapy, they were able to heed Judy's initiative in suggesting her brother also needed treatment. She noticed that Bob, aged 11, seemed to take punishment for others in the family. Bob had been conceived as his father was dying and was born after he died. His mother was certainly depressed during his infancy. He was adopted at 3½ by Mr. Green, as the other children had been. When Bob also needed to be evaluated, family therapy seemed to make sense. At first this recommendation hit Judy hard. She felt family therapy conducted by myself and her parents' social worker would mean I would abandon her. After a few weeks she accepted the arrangement and became a most helpful adjunct therapist in the meetings, taking the lead in dealing with difficult subjects and providing support for family members while probing difficult topics.

The family was made up of Judy, now 17, occasionally her 18-year-old brother Tom, when he was home from college, her 12-year-old sister Deb, Bob, age 11, and 6-year-old Sam, the only child of the remarriage. The family as a whole brought an intense dedication to the work. They attended faithfully although they had to drive for over an hour to get to each session. They worked on several levels of issues.

In one session they took up a "family dream." Mrs. Green said she had a dream that she thought related to her guilt that the family had picked on Bob in the car after the last session. In her dream Bob faced a friendly lion with a purple necktie. She wondered if she should protect Bob, who was a baby in the dream, or even if she needed to evaluate the situation. Was the lion really friendly?

She associated the dream to her neglect of Bob when he was little. Mr. Green thought it had to do with her not trusting men, as she often did not trust him. Perhaps "lion" meant "lying." Mrs. Green said she felt that in the dream Bob was saved, whereas perhaps she would not be. Bob deflected the focus on him by saying that perhaps the lion was after his little brother, Sam. Meanwhile, Sam was having a ball. He went to work drawing a picture (Fig. 19.1). He asked if anyone had noticed his father's purple tie, which he had on in the session, and he drew a picture of "Andy, the Purple Lion."

My own countertransference was to think the words, "David in the lions' den" with complete conviction for the moment that "David" was the correct name of the Biblical hero so endangered. It took me several minutes to realize my slip in thinking and that it meant that I felt attacked by the family and identified with Bob.

During the session, the family worked with the projections onto Bob and Mr. Green, with the result that I felt less as if I was in a lions' den. With the passage of time, and further experience, I now realize that part of the dream spoke to the family's transference fear that my cotherapist and I could not provide an adequate holding environment, and this may have already presaged the approaching termination.

As we reached a period close to termination, the family did

Fig. 19.1 Sam's "Andy, the Purple Lion."

regress in their fright about how they would do without us. Judy was going off to college, with the feeling that she was ready, but others did not feel ready. We were terminating because I was finishing my training and leaving the city, not because the family had decided to stop. For Judy individually, there seemed to be a natural stopping point since she was going to college in the fall and seemed to be largely on track, but there was no reason for the family to stop. The family worked with their fear that the termination was premature while continuing to consider other topics.

For instance, in a session about eight weeks before the end, Judy said she thought Bob and Deb had feelings for each other that were not too unlike feelings she and her older brother had had when the incest had occurred. At this, Bob began to hum and Deb sang the Beatles' "Hey, Jude," which says that tolerance and restraint can transform a song, healing sadness, making a sore heart better. It seemed understood between us that the song was about the healing experience in therapy and the internalization of change. Meanwhile, Sam was busy drawing again. He drew a picture of a tulip with a dragonfly and a butterfly buzzing around it, the sun overhead (Fig. 19.2). When we asked him what this was, he said that the insects were him and his brother, Bob, flitting around their sister, Deb. Or perhaps it was his mother. And the sun was his father smiling over the family. We were able to agree that feelings that had formerly been toxic in the family were now handled by redirection and humor, all quite creatively.

My own response to the loss of the family now emerged consciously, as I felt that I was parting from a family with whom I had grown up professionally. To a lesser degree, my cotherapist felt the same, inasmuch as she had also begun doing family therapy with them. This feeling was marked both in the termination of my individual work with Judy and with the family.

With Judy, I weathered her feeling regressively pulled toward impulsivity during the final weeks, only to see her steady and gain perspective on her fear about going on without me. As we worked one day, the words to a tune from the musical "Carousel" echoed in my head. In "Soliloquy," the hero sings, "My boy, Bill," while expecting his first child, convinced it will be a boy. He is killed before the birth of a daughter, but he is allowed a day's visit from heaven fifteen years later. He comes back to see his daughter, now a sturdy and beautiful girl, looking like his wife on the day they married. This fantasy led to my countertransference.

The sense of loss and of missing the beauty of my first patient's

Fig. 19.2 Sam's "tulip, with dragonfly and butterfly."

continued growth brought tears to my eyes with the rush of aware-
ness that our termination was a mutual loss. As we discussed her
sense of loss, of her losing a father she felt she had refound, I did not
discuss the details of my countertransference, but my work on ana-
lyzing them was part of the mourning process, freeing me to let
her go.

In the family meetings, the mourning also proceeded. In the last
session, 6-year-old Sam again took the emotional lead. As his parents, brothers, and sisters discussed their sense of loss and plans for

continued therapy, he drew two pictures. One he gave to me (Fig. 19.3) and the other to the cotherapist (Fig. 19.4). Mine was a friendly and cheerful goodbye. Hers was a masterpiece of ambiguity and meaning. It resembled a cradle, a bed, a grave, an ocean, and a sunset with sketchy birds resembling submerged hearts all around. Not until I was reviewing it for this book did I realize how much this picture, with all its innuendo, was his age-appropriate oedipal trans-ference gift to his female therapist.

I heard from Judy once shortly after I moved, and recently I have received a letter detailing her family's progress in the fifteen years since I last saw them.

She wrote, "I believe that I was not ready for therapy with you to end when it did; that I would have made a stronger transition into college life, and the accomplishments so important to me there, if I had been able to work through with you my week-to-week new challenges." I thought that her description of trying new things and of considerable ups and downs in her twenties bore out this conten-tion. After a precipitous marriage and divorce, and a moderate

Fig. 19.3 Sam's termination present to D.E.S.

Fig. 19.4 Sam's other termination picture.

amount of young-adult turmoil, her recent second marriage is to a man who resembles her stepfather and who gets along well with her parents.

The family has remained close and has done extraordinarily well, especially considering our early assessment of them as quite damaged. Judy described a continued quality of growth and working through in the family relationships. For instance, her older brother, who has been steadily married to his college girlfriend, has recently undertaken therapy to deal with his guilt for childhood incest. In the course of this work, he asked Judy to accompany him to see the grave of their natural father.

She also reported that her other brothers and sister were doing well in various endeavors, including Sam, the family therapy artist, who was currently enrolled in art school. The description of the progress of each of the family members made a convincing case that each child had grown in individuated ways and was productively developing in adulthood. Judy wrote that her parents had continued to cultivate their relationship as the children grew and left. They had mellowed together and seemed satisfied at this stage in a way that would have been hard to imagine at the beginning of our encounter.

Judy wanted me to know that she was now doing well. In advance notice to her long letter, she sent a postcard in which I saw an uncanny echo of Sam's farewell picture (Fig. 19.5). Family and therapist had carried away movingly similar motifs from our experience together.

Fig. 19.5 Judy's postcard fifteen years later.

Epilogue

In this book we have described the object relations family therapy that we practice and teach, our theoretical framework, and our thinking processes. But writing or teaching is not the same as doing. We write of engaging with the family while being experienced as an external version of its shared internal object relations. We do not talk like that with families; we do not want to impose theory or artificial technique on the situation. We want to behave naturally and spontaneously, speaking simply and not doing too much. Putting words to what we do changes it inevitably; for so much of our work is intuitive, unconscious, and sometimes preverbal. Retrospectively analyzing everything that has happened, while necessary for reporting, is actually the opposite of how we work. We cannot make every response conscious. Process-and-review becomes integrated as an automatic, largely unconscious piloting mechanism. So although we have said what we do, we are not always aware of doing as we say.

To establish confidence in the unconscious, we have to let go of certainty. Writing a book implies that there is a right way of doing things, but we do not want to work entirely by the book. Having formulated ideas, we have to let go of them so as to refind the spontaneity of ordinary personal response and interaction. We want to be open to learning from each new family, which means not knowing where we are and what we are doing much of the time. Therapy is always work in progress. So, too, in this book; at times our concepts failed to come out neatly, consistently, or permanently. We hope these areas of ambiguity will lead to avenues for further exploration. Uncertainty and incompleteness are painful to bear but fruitful for inquiry and growth.

Because our approach is based on an internal openness to engaging with the family's object relations system, family therapy often resonates uncomfortably with our own family experiences. The ability to allow unknown parts of ourselves to emerge in interaction with families is often rewarded by enlargement of the capacity for accepting and understanding. In this way, the work offers the opportunity for continued growth for family and therapist. This is the appeal of object relations family therapy.

References

Abelin, E. L. (1971). The role of the father in the separation–individuation process. In *Separation–Individuation*, ed. J. B. McDevitt and C. F. Settlage, pp. 229–252. New York: International Universities Press.

—— (1975). Some further observations and comments on the earliest role of the father. *International Journal of Psycho-Analysis* 56:293–302.

Ackerman, N. W. (1958). *The Psychodynamics of Family Life: Diagnosis and Treatment of Family Relationships.* New York: Basic Books. Reissued Harper Torch Books, 1972.

—— (1966). *Treating the Troubled Family.* New York: Basic Books.

—— (1970). Child participation in family therapy. *Family Process* 9:403–410.

—— (1982). *The Strength of Family Therapy: Selected Papers of Nathan W. Ackerman,* ed. D. Bloch and R. Simon. New York: Brunner/Mazel.

Andolfi, M. (1985). Master videotape presented at the annual meeting of the American Association of Marriage and Family Therapy, New York, October.

Andolfi, M., Angelo, C., Menghi, P., and Nicolo-Corigliano, A. M. (1983). *Behind the Family Mask: Therapeutic Change in Rigid Family Systems.* Trans. C. Chodorkoff. New York: Brunner/Mazel.

Aponte, H. J., and VanDeusen, J. M. (1981). Structural family therapy. In *Handbook of Family Therapy,* ed. A. Gurman and D. Kniskern. New York: Brunner/Mazel.

Arnold, L. E. ed. (1978). *Helping Parents Help Their Children.* New York: Brunner/Mazel.

Balint, M. (1952). *Primary Love and Psycho-analytic Technique.* London: Tavistock. New and enlarged edition, 1965.

—— (1968). *The Basic Fault: Therapeutic Aspects of Regression.* London: Tavistock.

Balint, M., Ornstein, P., and Balint, E. (1972). *Focal Psychotherapy: An Example of Applied Psychoanalysis.* Philadelphia: J B Lippincott.

Bannister, K., and Pincus, L. (1971). *Shared Fantasy in Marital Problems: Therapy in a Four-Person Relationship.* London: Tavistock Institute of Human Relations.

Bateson, G., Jackson, D. D., Haley, J., and Weakland, J. (1956). Toward a theory of schizophrenia. *Behavioral Science* 1:251–264.

Beels, C. C., and Ferber, A. (1969). Family therapy: a view. *Family Process* 9:280–318.

Beiser, H. (1976). Play equipment. In *The Therapeutic Use of Child's Play*, ed. C. Schaefer, pp. 423–434. New York: Jason Aronson.

Benedek, T. (1959). Parenthood as a developmental phase: a contribution to libido theory. *Journal of the American Psychoanalytic Association* 7:389–417.

—— (1960). The organization of the reproductive drive. *International Journal of Psycho-Analysis* 41:1–15.

—— (1970a). Fatherhood and providing. In *Parenthood: Its Psychology and Pathology*, ed. E. J. Anthony and T. Benedek. Boston: Little, Brown.

—— (1970b). The family as a psychologic field. In *Parenthood, Its Psychology and Psychopathology*, ed. E. J. Anthony and T. Benedek, pp. 109–136. Boston: Little, Brown.

Berkowitz, D., Shapiro, R., Zinner, J., and Shapiro, E. (1974). Concurrent family treatment in narcissistic disorders in adolescence. *International Journal of Psychoanalytic Psychotherapy* 3:379–396.

Bibring, E. (1954). Psychoanalysis and the dynamic therapies. *Journal of the American Psychoanalytic Association* 2:745–770.

Bibring, G. L., Dwyer, T. F., Huntington, D. S., and Valenstein, A. F. (1961). A study of the psychological processes in pregnancy and of the earliest mother–child relationship. *Psychoanalytic Study of the Child* 16:9–72.

Bion, W. R. (1961). *Experiences in Groups and Other Papers.* London: Tavistock.

—— (1967). *Second Thoughts.* London: Heinemann.

Bird, B. (1972). Notes on transference: universal phenomenon and hardest part of analysis. *Journal of the American Psychoanalytic Association* 20:267–301.

Blos, P. (1967). The second individuation process of adolescence. *Psychoanalytic Study of the Child* 22:162–186.

Bodin, A. M. (1981). The interactional view: family therapy approaches of the Mental Research Institute. In *Handbook of Family Therapy*, ed. A. Gurman and D. Kniskern. New York: Brunner/Mazel.

Boszormenyi-Nagy, I. (1972). Loyalty implications of the transference model in psychotherapy. *Archives of General Psychiatry* 27:374–380.

Boszormenyi-Nagy, I., and Framo, J. L. (1965). *Intensive Family Therapy.* New York: Hoeber Medical Div. Harper & Row. Reprinted New York: Brunner/Mazel, 1985.

Boszormenyi-Nagy, I., and Spark, G. M. (1973). *Invisible Loyalties: Reciprocity in Intergenerational Family Therapy.* Hagerstown, Md.: Harper & Row.

Bowen, M. (1978). *Family Theory in Clinical Practice.* New York: Jason Aronson.

Bowlby, J. (1960). Grief and mourning in infancy and early childhood. *The Psychoanalytic Study of the Child* 15:9–52.

—— (1969). *Attachment and Loss.* Vol. 1: *Attachment.* London: Hogarth Press. New York: Basic Books.

—— (1973a). *Attachment and Loss.* Vol. 2: *Separation: Anxiety and Anger.* London: Hogarth Press. New York: Basic Books.

—— (1973b). Registrars' Seminar, Tavistock Clinic, London.

—— (1980). *Attachment and Loss.* Vol. 3: *Loss: Sadness and Depression.* London: Hogarth Press. New York: Basic Books.

Box, S. (1981a). Introduction: space for thinking in families. In *Psychotherapy with Families: An Analytic Approach*, ed. S. Box et al. London: Routledge and Kegan Paul.

—— (1981b). Working with the dynamics of the session. In *Psychotherapy with Families: An Analytic Approach*, ed. S. Box et al. London: Routledge and Kegan Paul.

—— (1984). Containment and countertransference. Paper presented at the Washington School of Psychiatry, Fifth Annual Symposium on Psychoanalytic Family Therapy, Bethesda, Md., April.

Box, S., Copley, B., Magagna, J., and Moustaki, E., eds. (1981). *Psychotherapy with Families: An Analytic Approach.* London: Routledge and Kegan Paul.

Brazelton, T. B., Koslowski, B., and Main, M. (1974). The origins of reciprocity: the early mother–infant interaction. In *The Effect of the Infant on Its Caregiver*, ed. M. Lewis and L. Rosenblum. New York: Wiley-Interscience.

Brenner, P., and Greenberg, M. (1977). The impact of pregnancy in marriage. *Medical Aspects of Human Sexuality* 11(7):15–21.

Britten, R. (1981). Reenactment as an unwitting professional response to family dynamics. In *Psychotherapy with Families: An Analytic Approach*, ed. S. Box et al. London: Routledge and Kegan Paul.

Bruggen, P., Byng-Hall, J., and Pitt-Aitkens, T. (1973). The reason for admission as a focus of work for an adolescent unit. *British Journal of Psychiatry* 122:319–329.

Butler, R. N., and Lewis, M. (1976). *Sex After Sixty.* New York: Harper & Row.

Byng-Hall, J. (1973). Family myths used as a defense in conjoint family therapy. *British Journal of Medical Psychology* 46:239–250.

Call, J. (1984). Early patterns of communication. In *Frontiers of Infant Psychiatry*, Vol. 2, ed. J. Call, E. Galenson, and R. Tyson. New York: Basic Books.

Clayton, P. J., and Barnstein, P. E. (1976). Widows and widowers. *Medical Aspects of Human Sexuality* 10(9):27–48.

Cooklin, A. (1979). A psychoanalytic framework for a systemic approach to family therapy. *Journal of Family Therapy* 1:153–165.

Davanloo, H. (1978). *Basic Principles and Techniques in Short-Term Dynamic Psychotherapy.* New York: Spectrum.

Deutsch, F. (1957). A footnote to Freud's 'Fragment of an analysis of a case of hysteria.' *Psychoanalytic Quarterly* 25:159–167.

Dicks, H. V. (1967). *Marital Tensions: Clinical Studies Towards a Psychoanalytic Theory of Interaction.* London: Routledge and Kegan Paul.

Duhl, B. S., and Duhl, F. J. (1981). Integrative family therapy. In *Handbook of Family Therapy,* ed. A. Gurman and D. Kniskern. New York: Brunner/Mazel.

Edgcumbe, R., and Burgner, M. (1975). The phallic-narcissistic phase: a differentiation between preoedipal and oedipal aspects of phallic development. *Psychoanalytic Study of the Child* 30:160–180.

Eissler, K. (1953). The effect of the structure of the ego on psychoanalytic technique. *Journal of the American Psychoanalytic Association* 1:104–143.

Erikson, E. H. (1950). *Childhood and Society.* New York: Norton. Revised paperback edition, 1963.

—— (1958). *Young Man Luther.* New York: Norton.

—— (1962). Reality and actuality. *Journal of the American Psychoanalytic Association* 10:451–473.

Ezriel, H. (1950). A psychoanalytic approach to group treatment. *British Journal of Medical Psychology* 23:59–74.

—— (1952). Notes on psychoanalytic group therapy II: interpretation and research. *Psychiatry* 15:119–126.

Fairbairn, W. R. D. (1940). Schizoid factors in the personality. In *Psychoanalytic Studies of the Personality,* pp. 3–27. London: Routledge and Kegan Paul, 1952.

—— (1941). A revised psychopathology of the psychoses and psychoneuroses. In *Psychoanalytic Studies of the Personality,* pp. 28–58. London: Routledge and Kegan Paul, 1952.

—— (1943). The repression and the return of bad objects (with special reference to the war neuroses). In *Psychoanalytic Studies of the Personality,* pp. 59–81. London: Routledge and Kegan Paul, 1952.

—— (1944). Endopsychic structure considered in terms of object relationship. In *Psychoanalytic Studies of the Personality,* pp. 82–136. London: Routledge and Kegan Paul, 1952.

—— (1952). *Psychoanalytic Studies of the Personality.* London: Routledge and Kegan Paul. Also published as *An Object Relations Theory of the Personality.* New York: Basic Books, 1954.

—— (1954). Observations on the nature of hysterical states. *British Journal of Medical Psychology* 27(3):105–125.

—— (1963). Synopsis of an object-relations theory of the personality. *International Journal of Psycho-Analysis* 44:224–225.

Flügel, J. C. (1921). *The Psychoanalytic Study of the Family*. In the International Psycho-analytical Library, No. 3, ed. E. Jones. London: International Psycho-Analytical Press.

Foulkes, S. H. (1948). *Introduction to Group-Analytic Psychotherapy: Studies in the Social Integration of Individuals and Groups*. London: Heinemann. Reprinted London: Maresfield Reprints, 1983.

—— (1964). *Therapeutic Group Analysis*. London: Allen & Unwin.

Foulkes, S. H., and Anthony, E. J. (1965). *Group Psychotherapy: The Psychoanalytic Approach*, 2nd ed. Harmondsworth: Penguin.

Fraiberg, S., Adelson, E., and Shapiro, V. (1975). Ghosts in the nursery: a psychoanalytic approach to the problem of impaired mother–infant relationships. *Journal of the American Academy of Child Psychiatry* 14:387–421. Also published in *Clinical Studies in Infant Mental Health*, ed. S. Fraiberg. New York: Basic Books, 1980.

Fraiberg, S., ed., and Fraiberg, L., collaborator (1980). *Clinical Studies in Infant Mental Health*. New York: Basic Books.

Framo, J. L. (1970). Symptoms from a family transactional viewpoint. In *Family Therapy in Transition*, ed. N. Ackerman, pp. 125–171. Boston: Little, Brown.

—— (1976). Family of origin as a therapeutic resource for adults in marital and family therapy: you can and should go home again. *Family Process* 15:193–210.

—— (1981). The integration of marital therapy with sessions with family of origin. In *Handbook of Family Therapy*, ed. A. Gurman and D. Kniskern. New York: Brunner/Mazel.

—— (1982). *Explorations in Marital and Family Therapy: Selected Papers of James L. Framo, Ph.D.* New York: Springer.

Freud, A. (1958). Adolescence. *Psychoanalytic Study of the Child* 13:255–278.

Freud, S. (1895). The psychotherapy of hysteria. *Standard Edition* 2:255–305.

—— (1905a). Three essays on the theory of sexuality. *Standard Edition* 7:135–243.

—— (1905b). Fragment of an analysis of a case of hysteria. *Standard Edition* 7:7–122.

—— (1909). Analysis of phobia in a five-year-old boy. *Standard Edition* 10:1–149.

—— (1910). Future prospects of psycho-analytic therapy. *Standard Edition* 11:141–151.

—— (1912a). Recommendations to physicians practicing psychoanalysis. *Standard Edition* 12:111–120.

—— (1912b). The dynamics of transference. *Standard Edition* 12:99–108.

—— (1914). Remembering, repeating, and working through. *Standard Edition* 12:147–156.

—— (1915). Observations on transference love. *Standard Edition* 12:159–171.

—— (1917a). Mourning and melancholia. *Standard Edition* 14:243–258.

—— (1917b). Transference. *Standard Edition* 16:431–447.

—— (1917c). Analytic therapy. *Standard Edition* 16:448–463.

—— (1921). Group psychology and the analysis of the ego. *Standard Edition* 18:69–134.

—— (1923). The ego and the id. *Standard Edition* 19:3–63.

—— (1926). Inhibitions, symptoms and anxiety. *Standard Edition* 20:87–174.

—— (1937). Analysis terminable and interminable. *Standard Edition* 23:216–253.

Friedman, L. (1962). *Virgin Wives: A Study of Unconsummated Marriages.* London: Tavistock. Springfield, Ill.: Charles C Thomas.

Frost, R. (1969). "The Oven Bird" and "Nothing Gold Can Stay." In *The Poetry of Robert Frost,* ed. E. C. Latham. New York: Holt, Rinehart & Winston.

Furman, E. (1974). *A Child's Parent Dies: Studies in Childhood Bereavement.* New Haven: Yale University Press.

Gill, M., and Muslin, H. (1976). Early interpretation of transference. *Journal of American Psychoanalytic Association* 24:779–794.

Graller, J. (1981). Adjunctive marital therapy. *The Annual of Psychoanalysis* 9:175–187. New York: International Universities Press.

Greenberg, M., and Brenner, P. (1977). The newborn's impact on parents' marital and sexual relationship. *Medical Aspects of Human Sexuality* 11(8):16–28.

Greenson, R. (1965). The problem of working through. In *Drives, Affects and Behavior.* Vol. 2, ed. M. Schur, pp. 217–314. New York: International Universities Press.

—— (1967). *The Technique and Practice of Psychoanalysis.* Vol. 1. New York: International Universities Press.

Greenspan, S. (1981). *Psychopathology and Adaptation in Infancy and Early Childhood.* New York: International Universities Press.

—— (1982). The second other: the role of the father in early personality formation and the dyadic phallic phase of development. In *Father and Child: Developmental and Clinical Perspectives,* ed. S. H. Cath, A. R. Gurwitt, and J. M. Ross. Boston: Little, Brown.

Gross, A. (1951). The secret. *Bulletin of the Menninger Clinic* 15:37–44.

Grotjahn, M. (1960). *Psychoanalysis and Family Neurosis.* New York: Norton.

Grunebaum, H., and Chasin, R. (1982). Thinking like a family therapist: a model for integrating the theories and methods of family therapy. *Journal of Marital and Family Therapy* 8(4):403–416.

Guntrip, H. (1961). *Personality Structure and Human Interaction: The Developing Synthesis of Psychodynamic Theory.* London: Hogarth Press and the Institute of Psycho-Analysis.

—— (1969). *Schizoid Phenomena, Object Relations and the Self.* New York: International Universities Press.

Gurman, A. S., and Kniskern, D. P., eds. (1981). *Handbook of Family Therapy.* New York: Brunner/Mazel.

Guttman, H. (1975). The child's participation in conjoint family therapy. *Journal of the American Academy of Child Psychiatry* 14(3):490–499.

Haley, J. (1971). *Changing Families.* New York: Grune & Stratton.

—— (1980). *Leaving Home: The Therapy of Disturbed Young People.* New York: McGraw-Hill.

Hartmann, H. (1939). *Ego Psychology and the Problem of Adaptation.* New York: International Universities Press, 1958.

Henderson, E., and Williams, A. H. (1980). An essay in transference. Paper presented at the Washington School of Psychiatry, Fifth Annual Symposium on Psychoanalytic Family Therapy, Bethesda, Md., April 1984.

Hopper, E. (1977). Correspondence. *Group Analysis* 10(3):9–11. April.

Jackson, D. (1965). The study of the family. *Family Process* 4:1–20.

Jackson, D., and Weakland, J. (1961). Conjoint family therapy: some considerations on theory, technique, and results. *Psychiatry* 24:30–45.

Jacobsen, E. (1954). The self and the object world: vicissitudes of their infantile cathexes and their influence on ideational and affective development. *Psychoanalytic Study of the Child* 9:75–127.

Jacques, E. (1955). Social systems as a defence against persecutory and depressive anxiety. *New Directions in Psycho-Analysis*, ed. M. Klein, P. Heimann, and R. Money-Kyrle. London: Tavistock. New York: Basic Books.

—— (1965). Death and the mid-life crisis. *International Journal of Psycho-Analysis* 46(4):502–514.

Jessner, L. (1966). On becoming a mother. In *Conditio Humana*, ed. R. Griffith. Berlin: Springer.

Jessner, L., Jessner, N., and Abse, D. W. (1964). Pregnancy as a stress in marriage. In *Marriage Counselling in Medical Practice*, ed. E. M. Nash, L. Jessner, and D. W. Abse. Chapel Hill, N.C.: University of North Carolina Press.

Jessner, L., Weigert, E., and Foy, J. (1970). The development of parental attitudes during pregnancy. In *Parenthood: Its Psychology and Psychopathology*, ed. E. J. Anthony and T. Benedek, pp. 209–244, Boston: Little, Brown.

Johnson, A. M., and Szurek, S. A. (1952). The genesis of anti-social acting out in children and adults. *Psychoanalytic Quarterly* 21:313–343.

Kahn, M. (1986). The self and the system: integrating Kohut and Milan. In *The Interface of Individual and Family Therapy*, ed. S. Sugarman. Rockville, Md.: Aspen Systems.

Kaplan, H. S. (1974). *The New Sex Therapy: Active Treatment of Sexual Dysfunctions.* New York: Brunner/Mazel.

Kernberg, O. (1975). *Borderline Conditions and Pathological Narcissism.* New York: Jason Aronson.

Kerr, M. E. (1981). Family systems theory and therapy. In *Handbook of Family Therapy*, ed. A. Gurman and D. Kniskern. New York: Brunner/Mazel.

Khan, M. M. R. (1963). The concept of cumulative trauma. *The Psychoanalytic Study of the Child* 18:286–306. Reprinted in *The Privacy of the Self.* London: Hogarth Press and the Institute of Psycho-Analysis, 1974.

Klein, M. (1928). Early stages of the Oedipus conflict. In *Love, Guilt and Reparation & Other Works: 1921–1945.* London: Hogarth Press. Reissued 1975.

—— (1932). *The Psycho-Analysis of Children.* Trans. A. Strachey. Rev. A. Strachey and H. A. Thorner. London: Hogarth Press and the Institute of Psycho-Analysis, 1975.

—— (1935). A contribution to the psychogenesis of manic-depressive states. *International Journal of Psycho-Analysis* 16 and in *Love, Guilt and Reparation & Other Works: 1921–1945.* London: Hogarth Press and the Institute of Psycho-Analysis, 1975.

—— (1936). Weaning. In *On Bringing Up of Children*, ed. J. Rickman London: Kegan Paul.

—— (1946). Notes on some schizoid mechanisms. *International Journal of Psycho-Analysis* 27:99–110. And in *Envy and Gratitude & Other Works, 1946–1963.* London: Hogarth Press and the Institute of Psycho-Analysis, 1975.

—— (1948). *Contributions to Psychoanalysis, 1921–1945.* London: Hogarth Press. Also published as *Love, Guilt and Reparation & Other Works: 1921–1945.* London: Hogarth Press and the Institute of Psycho-Analysis, 1975.

—— (1957). *Envy and Gratitude.* London: Tavistock. New York: Basic Books.

—— (1961). *Narrative of a Child Psycho-Analysis.* London: Hogarth Press and the Institute of Psycho-Analysis, 1975.

Kohut, H. (1971). *The Analysis of the Self.* New York: International Universities Press.

—— (1977). *The Restoration of the Self.* New York: International Universities Press.

Kraft, I., Marcus, I., et al. (1959). Group therapy as a means of studying family diagnosis and dynamics. Presented at the annual meeting of the American Group Psychotherapy Association. Cited in Grotjahn (1960).

Kramer, C. (1968). *The Relationship Between Child and Family Pathology: A Suggested Extension of Psychoanalytic Theory and Technique.* Chicago: The Kramer Foundation.

Kubler-Ross, E. (1969). *On Death and Dying.* New York: Macmillan.

Kwiatkowska, H. Y. (1971). Family art therapy and family art evaluation. In *Conscious and Unconscious Expressive Art, Psychiatry and Art,* ed. I. Jakab. Vol. 3, pp. 138–151. Basel: Karger.

Laing, R. D., and Esterson, A. (1964). *Sanity, Madness and the Family.* Vol. 1: *Families of Schizophrenics.* London: Tavistock.

Langs, R. (1976). *The Therapeutic Interaction.* Vol. 2: *A Critical Overview and Synthesis.* New York: Jason Aronson.

Levay, A. N., Kagle, A., Weissberg, J. (1979). Issues of transference in sex therapy. *Journal of Sex and Marital Therapy* 5(1):15–21.

Levi, L. D., Stierlin, H., Savard, R. J. (1972). Father and sons: the interlocking crises of integrity and identity. *Psychiatry* 35:48–56.

Lichtenstein, H. (1961). Identity and sexuality: a study of their interrelationship in man. *Journal of the American Psychoanalytic Association* 9:179–260.

Lidz, T. (1963). *The Family and Human Adaptation.* New York: International Universities Press.

Lidz, T., Cornelison, A. R., Fleck, S., and Terry, D. (1957). Schism and skew in the families of schizophrenics. In *A Modern Introduction to the Family,* ed. N. Bell and F. Vogel. Glencoe, Ill. Free Press, 1960.

Liley, A. W. (1972). The foetus as a personality. *Australian/New Zealand Journal of Psychiatry* 6:99–105.

Lindemann, E. (1944). Symptomatology and management of acute grief. *American Journal of Psychiatry* 101:141–148.

Loewald, H. (1960). On the therapeutic action of psychoanalysis. *International Journal of Psycho-Analysis* 41:16–33.

MacGregor, R. M., Ritchie, A. M., Serrano, A. C., and Schuster, F. P. (1964). *Multiple Impact Therapy.* New York: McGraw-Hill.

Madanes, C., and Haley, J. (1977). Dimensions of family therapy. *Journal of Nervous and Mental Disease* 165:88–98.

Mahler, M., Pine, F., and Bergman, A. (1975). *The Psychological Birth of the Human Infant: Symbiosis and Individuation.* New York: Basic Books.

Main, T. F. (1966). Mutual projection in a marriage. *Comprehensive Psychiatry* 7(5):432–449.

Malan, D. H. (1975). *A Study of Brief Psychotherapy.* New York: Plenum.

Malone, C. (1974). Observations on the role of family therapy in child psychiatry training. *Journal of the American Academy of Child Psychiatry* 13:437–458.

Mann, J. (1973). *Time-Limited Psychotherapy.* Cambridge, Mass.: Harvard University Press.

Masters, W. H., and Johnson, V. E. (1970). *Human Sexual Inadequacy.* Boston: Little, Brown.

Masterson, J. F., Jr. (1967). *The Psychiatric Dilemma of Adolescence.* Boston: Little, Brown.

McGoldrick, M., Pearce, J. K., and Giordano, J., eds. (1982). *Ethnicity and Family Therapy.* New York: Guilford.

Meissner, W. M. (1978). The conceptualization of marriage and family dynamics from a psychoanalytic perspective. *Marriage and Marriage Therapy,* ed. T. J. Paolino, Jr., and B. S. McCrady, pp. 25–88. New York: Brunner/Mazel.

Menzies, I. E. P. (1960). A case study of the functioning of social systems as a defence against anxiety. *Human Relations* 13:95–121.

Miller, E. J., and Rice, A. K. (1967). *Systems of Organization: The Control of Task and Sentient Boundaries.* London: Tavistock.

Minuchin, S. (1974). *Families and Family Therapy,* Cambridge, Mass.: Harvard University Press.

Minuchin, S., Montalvo, B., Guerney, Jr., B. G., Rosman, B. L., et al. (1967). *Families of the Slums: An Exploration of Their Structure and Treatment.* New York: Basic Books.

Murray, J. M. (1955). *Keats.* New York: Noonday Press.

Nacht, S. (1965). Criteria and technique for the termination of analysis. *International Journal of Psycho-Analysis* 46:107–116.

Nadelson, C. C. (1978). Marital therapy from a psychoanalytic perspective. In *Marriage and Marriage Therapy,* ed. T. J. Paolino, Jr., and B. S. McCrady, pp. 101–164. New York: Brunner/Mazel.

Nagera, H. (1975). *Female Sexuality and the Oedipus Complex.* New York: Jason Aronson.

National Center for Health Statistics (1983). Advance report on final divorce statistics. *Monthly Vital Statistics Report* 34:9, Supplement. Washington, D.C.

—— (1984). *Annual Summary of Births, Marriages, Divorces, and Deaths, U.S.* Vol. 33, no. 13. Washington, D.C.

Paolino, Jr., T. J., and McCrady, B. S., eds. (1978). *Marriage and Marital Therapy: Psychoanalytic, Behavioral and Systems Theory Perspectives.* New York: Brunner/Mazel.

Parkes, C. M. (1971). Psycho-social transitions: a field for study. *Social Science and Medicine* 5:101–115.

—— (1972). *Bereavement: Studies of Grief in Adult Life.* London: Tavistock. New York: International Universities Press.

Paul, N. (1967). The role of mourning and empathy in conjoint marital therapy. In *Family Therapy and Disturbed Families,* ed. G. Zuk and I. Boszormenyi-Nagy. Palo Alto, Calif.: Science and Behavior Books.

Paul, N., and Grosser, G. (1965). Operational mourning and its role in conjoint family therapy. *Community Mental Health Journal* 1:339–345.

Pearce, J. K., and Friedman, L. J., eds. (1980). *Family Therapy: Combining Psychodynamic and Family Systems Approaches.* New York: Grune & Stratton.

Peller, L. E. (1954). Libidinal phases, ego development and play. *Psychoanalytic Study of the Child* 9:178–198.

Piaget, J. (1962). The stages of the intellectual development of the child. *Bulletin of the Menninger Clinic* 26:120-128.

Pincus, L., ed. (1960). *Marriage: Studies in Emotional Conflict and Growth*. London: Methuen.

——— (1976). *Death and the Family: The Importance of Mourning*. London: Faber & Faber.

Pincus, L., and Dare, C. (1978). *Secrets in the Family*. New York: Pantheon.

Pines, M. (1982). Mirroring and group analysis: an illustration with reference to the group treatment of borderline and narcissistic disorders. Paper presented at Washington School of Psychiatry Symposium on the British Group-Analytic Approach to Group and Family Treatment. Washington, D.C.

——— (1985). Mirroring and child development. *Psychoanalytic Inquiry* 5(2):211-231.

Racker, H. (1957). The meanings and uses of countertransference. *Psychoanalytic Quarterly*. Vol. 26. Reprinted in *Transference and Counter-Transference*. New York: International Universities Press, 1968.

——— (1968). *Transference and Counter-Transference*. New York: International Universities Press.

Reiss, D. (1981). *The Family's Construction of Reality*. Cambridge, Mass.: Harvard University Press.

Rice, A. K. (1965). *Learning for Leadership*. London: Tavistock.

Rioch, M. (1970a). Group relations: rationale and technique. In *Group Relations Reader I*, ed. A. Colman and W. H. Bexton. A. K. Rice Series, Sausalito, Calif.: Grex, 1975.

——— (1970b). The work of Wilfred Bion on groups. *Psychiatry* 33(1):56-66. Reprinted in *Progress in Group and Family Therapy*, ed. C. Sager and H. Kaplan, pp. 18-32. New York: Brunner/Mazel, 1972.

Robertson, J., and Bowlby, J. (1952). Responses of young children to separation from their mothers. *Courier du Centre International de l'Enfant* 2:132-142.

Robertson, J., and Robertson, J. (1971). Young children in brief separation: a fresh look. *Psychoanalytic Study of the Child* 26:264-315.

Sander, F. (1979). *Individual and Family Therapy: Toward an Integration*. New York: Jason Aronson.

——— (1985). Family or individual therapy: the determinants of modality choice. *Hillside Hospital Journal of Psychiatry* 7(1):37-41.

———, ed. (1987). *Report of the Task Force on the Integration of Individual and Family Therapy*. Washington, D.C.: The American Family Therapy Association. Draft in Preparation.

Satir, V. (1967). *Conjoint Family Therapy: A Guide to Theory and Technique*. Rev. ed. Palo Alto, Calif.: Science & Behavior Books.

Savege, J. (1973). Psychodynamic understanding in community psychiatry. Proceedings of the Ninth International Congress of Psychotherapy, Oslo. Reprinted in *Psychotherapy and Psychosomatics* 25:272–278, 1975.

Scharff, D. E. (1969). The inpatient treatment of a borderline personality disorder. *Psychiatric Opinion* 6:37–43.

—— (1975). The transition from school to work: groups in London high schools. In *When Schools Care*, ed. I. Berkovitz. New York: Brunner/Mazel.

—— (1976). Aspects of the transition from school to work. In *Between Two Worlds: Aspects of the Transition from School to Work*, D. E. Scharff and J. M. M. Hill. London: Careers Consultants.

—— (1978). Truth and consequences in sex and marital therapy: the revelation of secrets in the therapeutic setting. *Journal of Sex and Marital Therapy* 4(1):35–49.

—— (1980). Between two worlds: emotional needs of adolescents facing the transition from school to work. In *Responding to Adolescent Needs*, ed. M. Sugar. New York and London: SP Medical and Scientific Books.

—— (1982). *The Sexual Relationship: An Object Relations View of Sex and the Family*. London: Routledge and Kegan Paul.

Scharff, D. E., and Hill, J. M. M. (1976). *Between Two Worlds: Aspects of the Transition from School to Work*. London: Careers Consultants.

Scharff, D. E., and Scharff, J. S. (1979). Teaching and learning: an experiential conference. *Journal of Personality and Social Systems* 2(1): 53–78.

Schwarzbeck, C. (1978). Identification of infants at risk for child neglect: observations and inferences in the examination of the mother–infant dyad. In *Traumatic Abuse and Neglect of Children at Home*, ed. G. Williams and J. Money, pp. 240–246. Baltimore: Johns Hopkins University Press.

Searles, H. (1979). *Countertransference and Related Subjects: Selected Papers*. New York: International Universities Press.

—— (1986). *My Work with Borderline Patients*. New York: Jason Aronson.

Segal, H. (1964). *Introduction to the Work of Melanie Klein*. London: Heinemann.

—— (1973). *Introduction to the Work of Melanie Klein*. New, enlarged edition. London: Hogarth Press.

Selvini Palazzoli, M. (1974). *Self-Starvation: From the Intrapsychic to the Transpersonal Approach to Anorexia Nervosa*. Milan: Feltrinelli. Trans. A. Pomerans. London: Human Context Books, Chaucer Publishing.

—— (1985). Towards a general model of psychotic family games. Paper presented at the annual meeting of the American Association of Marriage and Family Therapy, New York, October.

Selvini Palazzoli, M., Boscolo, L., Cecchin, G., and Prata, G. (1975).

Paradox and Counterparadox. Milan: Feltrinelli. Trans. E. V. Burt. New York: Jason Aronson, 1978.

Shapiro, E., Zinner, J., Shapiro, R., and Berkowitz, D. (1975). The influence of family experience on borderline personality development. *International Review of Psycho-Analysis* 2(4):399–411.

Shapiro, R. L. (1966). Identity and ego autonomy in adolescence. In *Science and Psychoanalysis,* ed. J. H. Masserman. New York: Grune & Stratton.

—— (1979). Family dynamics and object-relations theory: an analytic, group-interpretive approach to family therapy. In *Adolescent Psychiatry: Developmental and Clinical Studies,* ed. S. C. Feinstein and P. L. Giovacchini. Chicago: University of Chicago Press.

Shapiro, R. L., and Zinner, J. (1971). Family organization and adolescent development. In *Task and Organization,* ed. E. Miller. London: Wiley, 1976.

—— (1979). The adolescent, the family, and the group: boundary considerations. In *Exploring Individual and Organizational Boundaries,* ed. G. Lawrence. London: Wiley.

Sifneos, P. (1972). *Short Term Psychotherapy and Emotional Crisis.* Cambridge, Mass.: Harvard University Press.

Skynner, A. C. R. (1976). *Systems of Family and Marital Psychotherapy.* New York: Brunner/Mazel. Also published as *One Flesh, Separate Person: Principles of Family and Marital Psychotherapy.* London: Constable.

—— (1981). An open-systems, group-analytic approach to family therapy. In *Handbook of Family Therapy,* ed. A. Gurman and D. Kniskern. New York: Brunner/Mazel.

Slipp, S. (1984). *Object Relations: A Dynamic Bridge Between Individual and Family Treatment.* New York: Jason Aronson.

Solnit, A., and Stark, M. (1961). Mourning and the birth of a defective child. *Psychoanalytic Study of the Child* 16:523–537.

Springmann, R. (1976). Fragmentation in large groups. *Group Analysis* 9(3):185–188.

Stanton, M. D. (1981). Strategic approaches to family therapy. In *Handbook of Family Therapy,* A. Gurman and D. Kniskern. New York: Brunner/Mazel.

Stern, D. N. (1977). *The First Relationship: Infant and Mother.* Cambridge, Mass.: Harvard University Press.

—— (1985). *The Interpersonal World of the Infant: A View from Psychoanalysis and Developmental Psychology.* New York: Basic Books.

Stierlin, H. (1971). Adolescents who run away. Presented at NIMH Residency Program. St. Elizabeth's Hospital, Washington, D.C.

—— (1974). *Separating Parents and Adolescents: Individuation in the Family.* New York: Jason Aronson.

—— (1977). *Psychoanalysis and Family Therapy.* New York: Jason Aronson.

—— (1985). Results of a catamnestic study of family therapy with anorexics. Presented at Psychosomatissche Klinik, Heidelberg, February.

—— (1986). Therapy of anorexia in a family therapy context. Presented at Leonard Morse Hospital, Natick, Mass., October.

Stierlin, H., and Ravenscroft, K. (1972). Varieties of adolescent separation conflicts. *British Journal of Medical Psychology* 45:299-313.

Strachey, J. (1958). Editor's introduction to papers on technique. In *The Standard Edition of the Complete Psychological Works of Sigmund Freud*, ed. J. Strachey, 12:85-88.

Sullivan, H. S. (1953). *The Collected Works of Harry Stack Sullivan*. New York: Norton.

Sutherland, J. (1963). Object relations theory and the conceptual model of psychoanalysis. *British Journal of Medical Psychology* 36:109-124.

—— (1980). The British object relations theorists: Balint, Winnicott, Fairbairn, Guntrip. *Journal of the American Psychoanalytic Association* 28(4):829-860.

—— (1985). The object relations approach. Paper presented at the Washington School of Psychiatry, Sixth Annual Symposium on Psychoanalytic Family Therapy, Bethesda, Md., April.

Szurek, S. A. (1974). Concerning the sexual disorders of parents and their children. *Journal of Nervous and Mental Disease* 120:369-378.

Tessman, L. H. (1978). *Children of Parting Parents*. New York: Jason Aronson.

Thomas, A., Chess, S., and Birch, H. G. (1968). *Temperament and Behavior Disorders in Children*. New York: New York University Press.

Ticho, E. (1972). Termination of psychoanalysis: treatment goals, life goals. *Psychoanalytic Quarterly* 41:315-333.

Tower, L. (1956). Countertransference. *Journal of the American Psychoanalytic Association* 4:224-255.

Tronick, E., Als, H., Adamson, L., Wise, S., and Brazelton, T. B. (1978). The infant's response to entrapment between contradictory messages in face-to-face interaction. *Journal of the American Academy of Child Psychiatry* 17(1):1-13.

Turquet, P. (1975). Threats to identity in the large group. In *The Large Group: Dynamics and Therapy*, ed. L. Kreeger. London: Constable.

Van Trommel, M. J. (1984). A consultation method addressing the therapist-family system. *Family Process* 23(4):469-480.

—— (1985). Institute presented at the annual meeting of the American Association of Marriage and Family Therapy, New York, October.

Viorst, J. (1986). *Necessary Losses: The Loves, Illusions, Dependencies and Impossible Expectations That All of Us Have to Give Up in Order to Grow*. New York: Simon and Schuster.

Visher, E. B., and Visher, J. S. (1979). *Stepfamilies: A Guide to Working with Stepparents and Stepchildren*. New York: Brunner/Mazel.

Wallerstein, J., and Kelly, J. (1980). *Surviving the Break-Up: How Children and Parents Cope with Divorce.* New York: Basic Books.

Wenner, N. K. (1966). Dependency patterns in pregnancy. In *Science and Psychoanalysis* Vol. 10, ed. J. Masserman, pp. 94–104. New York: Grune & Stratton.

Williams, A. H. (1981). The micro-environment. In *Psychotherapy with Families: An Analytic Approach,* ed. S. Box et al. London: Routledge and Kegan Paul.

Williamson, D. S. (1981). Personal authority via termination of the intergenerational hierarchical boundary: Part I, a 'new' stage in the family life cycle. *Journal of Marital and Family Therapy* 7:441–452.

—— (1982). Personal authority via termination of the intergenerational hierarchical boundary: Part II, the consultation process and the therapeutic method. *Journal of Marital and Family Therapy* 8:23–37.

Winer, R. (1985). The recreation of the family in the mind of the individual therapist and the recreation of the individual in the mind of the family therapist. Paper presented at the Washington School of Psychiatry, Sixth Annual Symposium on Psychoanalytic Family Therapy, Bethesda, Md., April.

Winnicott, D. W. (1947). Hate in the countertransference. In *Collected Papers: Through Paediatrics to Psycho-Analysis.* London: Tavistock, 1958, and Hogarth Press, 1975.

—— (1951). Transitional objects and transitional phenomena. In *Collected Papers: Through Paediatrics to Psycho-Analysis.* London: Tavistock, 1958, and Hogarth Press, 1975.

—— (1956). Primary maternal preoccupation. In *The Maturational Processes and the Facilitating Environment.* London: Hogarth Press, 1965.

—— (1958). *Collected Papers: Through Paediatrics to Psycho-Analysis.* London: Tavistock, 1958, and Hogarth Press, 1975.

—— (1960a). The theory of the parent–infant relationship. *International Journal of Psycho-Analysis* 41:585–595. Reprinted in *The Maturational Processes and the Facilitating Environment.* London: Hogarth Press, 1965.

—— (1960b). True and false self. In *The Maturational Processes and the Facilitating Environment.* London: Hogarth Press, 1965.

—— (1964). *The Child, the Family, and the Outside World.* London: Penguin Books. Reprinted 1965, 1967.

—— (1965a). Ego distortion in terms of true and false self. In *The Maturational Processes and the Facilitating Environment.* London: Hogarth Press, 1965.

—— (1965b). *The Maturational Processes and the Facilitating Environment.* London: Hogarth Press.

—— (1971a). The location of cultural experience. In *Playing and Reality.* London: Tavistock, pp. 95–103.

—— (1971b). *Playing and Reality*. London: Tavistock.

Wynne, L. C. (1965). Some indications and contradindications for exploratory family therapy. In *Intensive Family Therapy*, ed. I. Boszormenyi-Nagy and J. Framo. New York: Hoeber.

Wynne, L. C., Ryckoff, I. M., Day, J., and Hirsch, S. I. (1958). Pseudomutuality in the family relations of schizophrenics. *Psychiatry* 21:205–220.

Yogman, M. (1982). Observations on the father–infant relationship. In *Father and Child: Developmental and Clinical Perspectives*, ed. S. H. Cath, A. R. Gurwitt, and J. M. Ross, pp. 101–122. Boston: Little, Brown.

Zawada, S. (1981). An outline of the history and current status of family therapy. In *Psychotherapy with Families: An Analytic Approach*, ed. S. Box et al. London: Routledge and Kegan Paul.

Zetzel, E. (1958). Therapeutic alliance in the analysis of hysteria. In *The Capacity for Emotional Growth*. New York: International Universities Press, 1970.

—— (1965). On the incapacity to bear depression. In *The Capacity for Emotional Growth*. New York: International Universities Press, 1970.

—— (1970). *The Capacity for Emotional Growth*. New York: International Universities Press.

Zilbach, J. (1974). The family in family therapy. *Journal of the American Academy of Child Psychiatry* 13:459–467.

—— (1986). *Young Children in Family Therapy*. New York: Brunner/Mazel.

Zilbach, J., Bergel, E., and Cass, C. (1972). The role of the young child in family therapy. In *Progress in Group and Family Therapy*, ed. C. Sager and H. S. Kaplan. New York: Brunner/Mazel.

Zinner, J. (1976). The implications of projective identification for marital interaction. In *Contemporary Marriage: Structure, Dynamics, and Therapy*, ed. H. Grunebaum and J. Christ, pp. 293–308. Boston: Little, Brown.

—— (1985). The use of concurrent therapies: therapeutic strategy or reenactment. Paper presented at the Washington School of Psychiatry, Sixth Annual Symposium on Psychoanalytic Family Therapy, Bethesda, Md., April.

Zinner, J., and Shapiro, E. (1975). Splitting in families of borderline adolescents. In *Borderline States in Psychiatry*, ed. J. Mack. New York: Grune & Stratton.

Zinner, J., and Shapiro, R. (1972). Projective identification as a mode of perception and behavior in families of adolescents. *International Journal of Psycho-Analysis* 53:523–530.

—— (1974). The family group as a single psychic entity: implications for acting out in adolescence. *International Review of Psycho-Analysis* 1(1):179–186.

Index

Credits

Unpublished early versions of the following chapters were previously presented by David E. Scharff: *Chapter 3*, at the Fourth Annual Symposium of the Psychoanalytic Family Therapy Training Program of the Washington School of Psychiatry in Bethesda, Maryland, April 1983; *Chapter 4*, at the annual meetings of the American Academy of Child Psychiatry in Toronto, August 1984, and the American Association of Marriage and Family Therapists in New York, October 1984; *Chapters 4, 10*, and *12*, at the Sixth Annual Symposium of the Psychoanalytic Family Therapy Training Program of the Washington School of Psychiatry in Bethesda, Maryland, April 1985; *Chapter 6*, at the Group Analytic Institute Workshop, London, September 1983, and at the Fifth Annual Symposium of the Psychoanalytic Family Therapy Training Program at the Washington School of Psychiatry in Bethesda, Maryland, March 1984.

Unpublished early versions of the following chapters were previously presented by Jill S. Scharff: *Chapter 2*, at the Sixth Annual Symposium of the Psychoanalytic Family Therapy Training Program of the Washington School of Psychiatry in Bethesda, Maryland, April 1985; *Chapter 3*, at the Family Therapy Network Annual Meeting in Washington, D.C., March 1981; *Chapter 7*, at the annual meetings of the American Psychological Association in Toronto, August 1984, and the American Association of Marriage and Family Therapists in New York, October 1984, and at the scientific meeting of the A. K. Rice Institute in Washington, D.C., April 1985; *Chapter 16*, at the Second Annual Symposium of the Psychoanalytic Family Therapy Training Program of the Washington School of Psychiatry in Washington, D.C., May 1981.